STRANGE TERRAIN

STRANGE TERRAIN

THE FAIRY WORLD IN NEWFOUNDLAND

BARBARA RIETI

MEMORIAL
UNIVERSITY
PRESS

© 2021 Barbara Rieti

All rights reserved. No part of this publication may be reproduced, stored in a retrieval system, or transmitted in any form or by any means, without the prior written consent of the publisher.

LIBRARY AND ARCHIVES CANADA CATALOGUING IN PUBLICATION
Title: Strange terrain : the fairy world in Newfoundland / Barbara Rieti.
Names: Rieti, Barbara, 1952- author.
Series: Social and economic studies (St. John's, N.L.) ; no. 88.
Description: Second edition. 30th anniversary edition. | Series statement: Social and economic studies ; no. 88 | Includes bibliographical references and index.
Identifiers: Canadiana (print) 20210248556 | Canadiana (ebook) 2021024867X | ISBN 9781894725804 (softcover) | ISBN 9781894725897 (EPUB)
Subjects: LCSH: Fairy tales—Newfoundland and Labrador—History and criticism. | LCSH: Fairies— Newfoundland and Labrador. | LCSH: Folklore—Newfoundland and Labrador.
Classification: LCC GR113.5.N5 R53 2021 | DDC 398.209718/01—dc23

Cover image: iStock.com/stereohype
Copy editing: Richard Tallman
Cover design, page design, and typesetting: Alison Carr

Published by Memorial University Press
Memorial University of Newfoundland
PO Box 4200
St. John's, NL A1C 5S7
www.memorialuniversitypress.ca

Printed in Canada
27 26 25 24 23 22   2 3 4 5 6 7 8

Funded by the Government of Canada | Canada

To the memory of my mother, Mary Angela Rieti Dilworth

The first edition of this book was published with the help of a grant from the Canadian Federation for the Humanities, using funds provided by the Social Sciences and Humanities Research Council of Canada.

Contents

Foreword *by Diane Tye* . . . . *ix*
Epigraph . . . . *xvi*
Preface to the Second Edition . . . . *xvii*
Preface to the First Edition . . . . *xxv*
Acknowledgements . . . . *xxvii*
A Note on the Documentation and Transcription of Sources . . . . . *xxxi*

1 Always Going and Never Gone? 1
2 Fairy Forms and Narrative Contexts: An Overview 17
3 Bread, Wind, Old Paths: The Texture and Planes of
 Everyday Life in Fairy Narrative 65
4 Tradition and the Interpretation of Experience 109
5 Fairies, Devils, and Other Impostors in Bishop's Cove:
 Tales of a Trickster 153
6 UFOs: Urban Fairy Oddities, and Some Modern Influences
 on the Genesis and Evolution of Fairy Tradition 189
7 Fairy Tradition as Discourse on Time and Change 227
8 Conclusion 265

Notes 271
Bibliography 309
Informant Index 337

Foreword | by Diane Tye

In her Preface to this special anniversary edition of *Strange Terrain: The Fairy World in Newfoundland*, Barbara Rieti claims she must have been in the fairies because there's no other accounting for where the last thirty years have gone. Clearly, I must have been with her.

In 1991, when this book was first published, Barbara and I were both recently minted PhDs from Memorial University's Department of Folklore; she had entered the program in 1982 and I came a year or two later. By the time we were doctoral students, the Folklore Department was well known and well respected within the province and had earned an international academic reputation. Founded in 1968 by Herbert Halpert, who arrived at Memorial to teach in the English Department, in the approximately twenty years of its existence it had grown to eight faculty members and housed the Memorial University Folklore and Language Archive (MUNFLA), Canada's largest archival collection of folklore materials. By the 1980s, important publications that drew on those archival holdings, including the *Dictionary of Newfoundland English* (Kirwin, Widdowson, and Story 1990) and *Folktales of Newfoundland* (Halpert and Widdowson 1996), were well underway.

The Department of Folklore also had an established relationship with the Institute of Social and Economic Research (ISER), founded at Memorial in 1961 to foster and undertake research into the many social and economic questions arising from the circumstances of Newfoundland and Labrador. Over the years, ISER and/or ISER Books (now Memorial University Press) funded and/or published folklore research on a wide range of subjects from mummering to material culture and folksong; Barbara held an ISER research grant and ISER post-doctoral fellowship.

Strange Terrain, based on Barbara's doctoral thesis, captures the very best of the Folklore Department in those years. Halpert, and the other faculty members who followed him, believed that folklorists should ground their work in extensive fieldwork, contextualize it by equally exhaustive archival research, and present their findings in a clear, straightforward writing style. Barbara brings together all of these elements in this wonderful study of fairy traditions in Newfoundland and Labrador.

Fairies are a challenging subject for a folklorist. For starters, people often believed it was bad luck to talk about fairies and that you should not refer to them directly. Add to that the understandable reluctance of folks to discuss such experiences, which outsiders could potentially interpret as old-fashioned, superstitious, or even delusional, with "someone from the university" who wants to record them, and you've got a daunting prospect for a student folklorist. But from the first page, when Barbara describes in 1983 running into a twenty-one-year-old who told her of being followed by the fairies, it's clear she rose to the challenges. Taking full advantage of being in Newfoundland and Labrador at a time when there were individuals with first-person accounts of fairies, and many others who had heard about them from grandparents and parents as children, she scoured the province for people with stories. She put them at ease and created a safe space in which they could share their experiences. Because of her persistent and fearless efforts as a fieldworker, she created a remarkable snapshot of a tradition that otherwise would have been lost.

Barbara's work celebrates MUNFLA's rich collection, which, as she explains, was founded by folklorists Herbert Halpert and John Widdowson in the mid-1960s as a repository for their work as well as that of their students, whom they sent off to collect in their home communities over the Christmas holiday. Although she cautions that the archive doesn't present a full picture of the province's fairy tradition, it does offer a good indication of variation and spread. Barbara draws on archival accounts in just the way Halpert envisioned, to contextualize her own collecting and illuminate the nature of fairy tradition. Combining the accounts she personally recorded with ones she discovered in MUNFLA, Barbara highlights the voices and experiences of the people of Newfoundland and Labrador. Never othering, and always respectful, *Strange Terrain* remains, thirty years after it was written, an exemplary ethnographic text.

These were ambitious intentions: to look at the nature of the fairies themselves, the forms in which ideas about them are expressed, and the meanings and uses of these ideas. But right from the start *Strange Terrain* hit the mark. It spent several weeks on the *Newfoundland Herald*'s best-seller list when first released and ever since it has been a best-seller for Memorial University Press. It continues to be used in university classrooms and sought out by readers curious about the fairy tradition. In fact, *Strange Terrain* has emerged as *the* resource on fairy tradition in Newfoundland and Labrador and for thirty years has shaped how we understand the province's fairy tradition. It is because of this book that we know how diverse earlier forms of fairy belief were, places where fairy belief was particularly fervent, and how thriving the fairy tradition was in urban St. John's as well as in rural communities.

At the same time, *Strange Terrain* has made a major contribution to international scholarship on fairy traditions. This is in part because Barbara embraces approaches and themes that were only emerging or anticipated at the time she was doing her work. For example, she reflexively positions herself in the study in a way that has become more common in the decades since. Encountering the Newfoundland fairy tradition at a transitional point when, as she says, the complete belief of the past was an overstatement and the complete lack of belief today an understatement, she shows how the fairy tradition was always open to interpretation, dispute, and manipulation. Stories were a medium of debate that she places herself in, claiming, fairies "probably don't exist but I wouldn't say they don't" (p. 17). She also explores significant interpretations of fairy tradition that were to run through the scholarship of the next three decades, including humans' relationship with nature; interpersonal relationships, specifically around knowing and not knowing, and being known; and fairies as ultimate strangers and a metaphor for all that is strange in nature and in other people.

Barbara reminds the reader that these are complex stories and beliefs that cannot be easily classified or interpreted, and she refuses to let them off the hook even when the going gets tough. For example, she argues that while evidence from Ireland proves stories can sometimes be actual accounts of violence, this is not the only answer. Certainly events did not happen as many times as there are stories. She also challenges familiar folkloristic explanations as inadequate, warning that it is not enough to say that changelings "explain" mental and physical conditions that would not have been diagnosed at an earlier time, because modern medical terms don't fully explain them either. This refusal to fall back on a single explanation, or to simplify any aspect of a complex tradition, is one of *Strange Terrain*'s lasting gifts.

Its careful consideration of all dimensions of Newfoundland and Labrador's fairy tradition, from form and genre to interpretation, earned *Strange Terrain* the Raymond Klibansky Book Prize in 1993 from the Canadian Federation for the Humanities as the best scholarly English-language work in the Canadian humanities for 1992–93. Barbara Rieti's work also has earned a wide international reputation. It has had far-reaching impacts on scholars of belief traditions in countries including England (Young 2016; Young and Houlbrook 2018), Ireland (Bourke 1996; NíCheallaigh 2012), Scotland (Purkiss 2001), Norway (Paine 2001), Cyprus (Kyriakides and Irvine 2019), and Thailand (Wattanagun 2016). Beyond folkloristics, it has influenced fields as diverse as landscape and sustainability (Benson and Roe 2007), globalization (Wylie 2011), and mental health (LaFrance and McKenzie-Mohr 2013).

An important study of vernacular belief traditions for thirty years, *Strange Terrain* will now reach a new generation of readers with this anniversary edition. As magical as the passing of time since its original publication, *Strange Terrain* shows no signs of growing old any time soon.

REFERENCES

Benson, John F., and Maggie Roe, eds. 2007. *Landscape and Sustainability*, 2nd edition. London: Taylor & Francis.

Bourke, Angela. 1996. "The Virtual Reality of Irish Fairy Legend." *Éire-Ireland* 31 (1):7–25.

Corrigan, Timothy Correll. 2005. "Believers, Sceptics, and Charlatans: Evidential Rhetoric, the Fairies, and Fairy Healers in Irish Oral Narrative and Belief." *Folklore* 116 (1):1–18.

Halpert, Herbert, and J.D.A. Widdowson. 1996. *Folktales of Newfoundland: The Resilience of the Oral Tradition*. St. John's: Breakwater Books.

Kirwin, W.J., J.D.A. Widdowson, and G.M. Story. 1990. *Dictionary of Newfoundland English*. Toronto: University of Toronto Press.

Kyriakides, Theodoros, and Richard D.G. Irvine. 2019. "Not-Knowing Magic: Magical Memory and Ineffability in Contemporary Cyprus and Orkney." *Ethnos*: 1–22. https://doi.org/10.1080/00141844.2019.1697336.

LaFrance, Michelle N., and Suzanne McKenzie-Mohr. 2013. "The DSM and Its Lure of Legitimacy." *Feminism and Psychology*. https://journals.sagepub.com/doi/10.1177/0959353512467974.

NíCheallaigh, Máirín. 2012. "Ringforts or Fairy Homes: Oral Understandings and the Practice of Archaeology in Nineteenth- and Early Twentieth-Century Ireland." *International Journal of Historical Archaeology* 16:367–84.

Paine, Robert. 2001. "A Note on Ethnography & Interpretation & Imagination." *Acta Borealia* 18 (2):86–94.

Purkiss, Diane. 2001. "Sounds of Silence: Fairies and Incest in Scottish Witchcraft Stories." In *Languages of Witchcraft: Narrative, Ideology and Meaning in Early Modern Culture*, edited by Stuart Clark. London: Macmillan, pp. 81–98.

Wattanagun, Kanya. 2016. "The Ravenous Spirit (phii pob) Belief Tradition in Contemporary Thailand: Pluralistic Practices versus Monolithic Representation." PhD diss., Indiana University.

Wylie, Herb. 2011. *Anne of Tim Hortons: Globalization and the Re-Shaping of Atlantic Canadian Literature*. Waterloo, ON: Wilfrid Laurier University Press.

Young, Simon. 2016. "Pixy-Led in Devon and the South-West." *Transactions of the Devonshire Association* 148:311-36.

—— and Ceri Houlbrook, eds. 2018. *Magical Folk: British and Irish Fairies 500 AD to the Present*. London: Gibson Square.

Strange Terrain

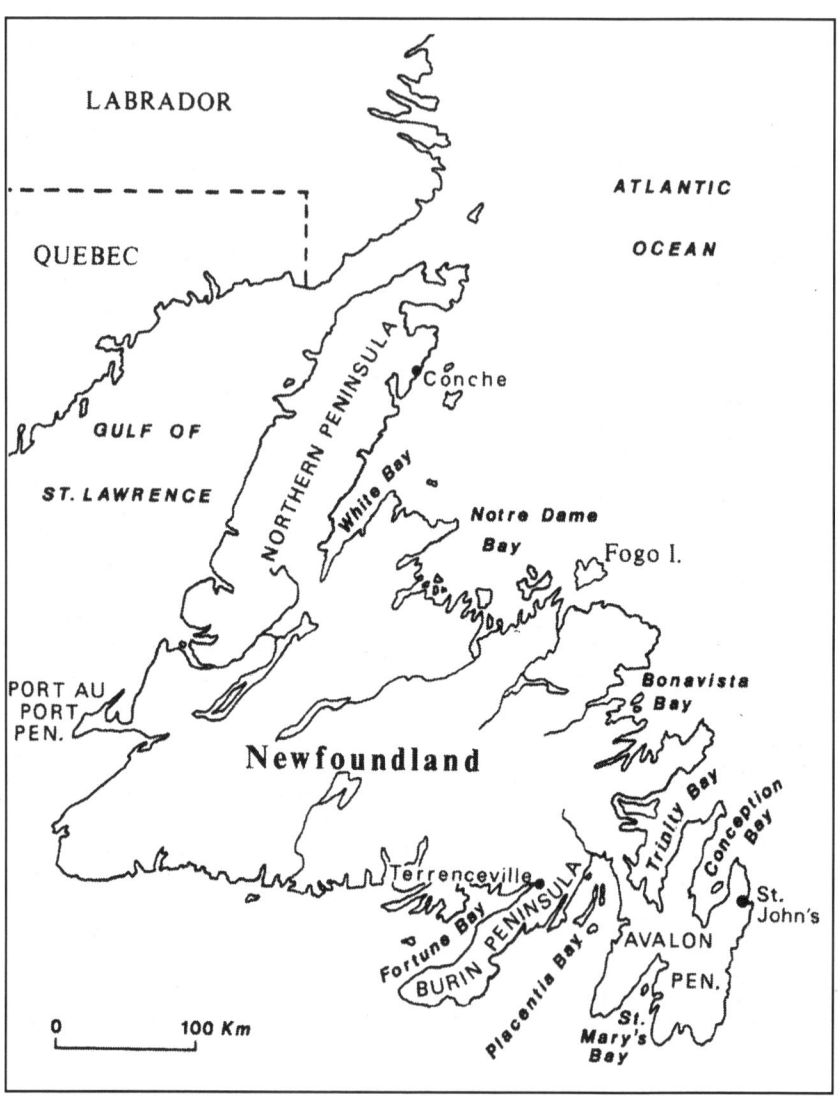

Map 1: Newfoundland
Credit: Austin Rodgers

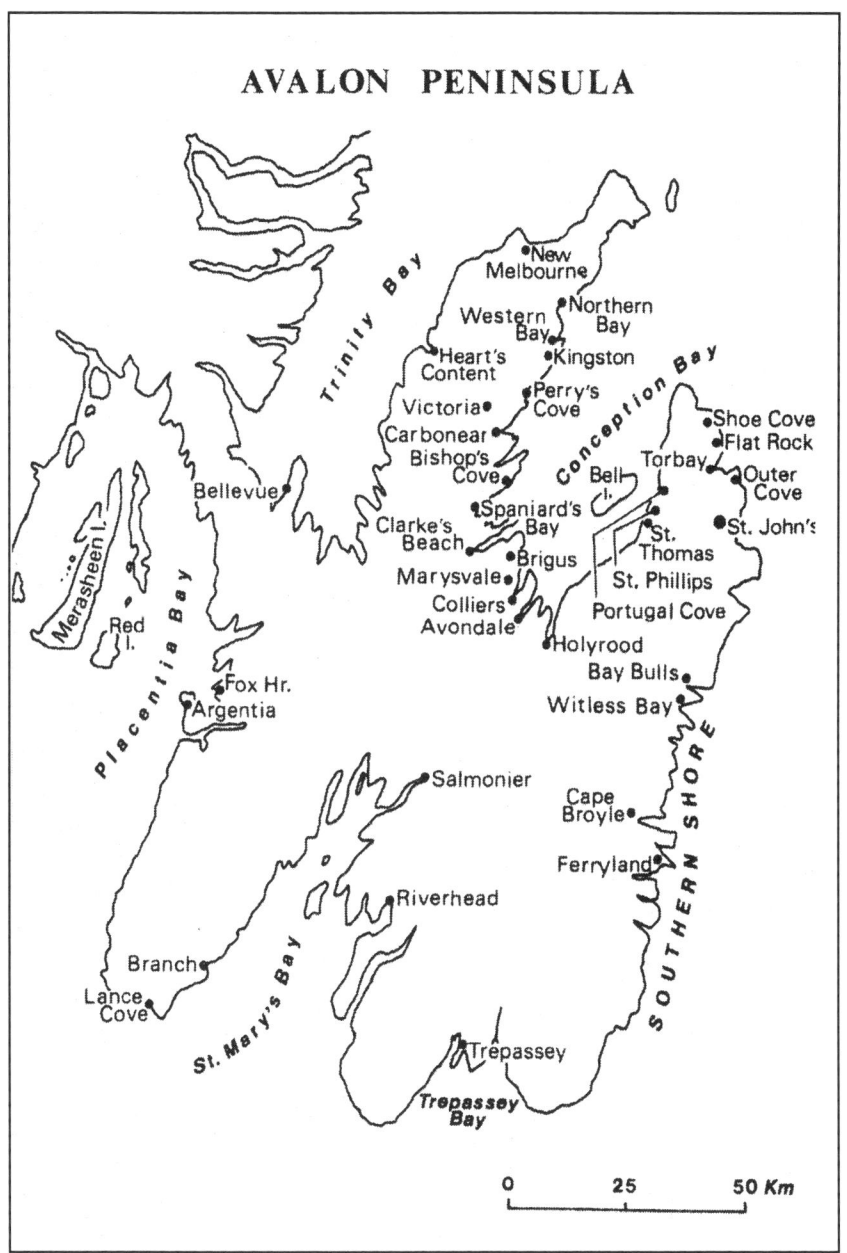

Map 2: Avalon Peninsula
Credit: Donald Battcock

Epigraph

In March of 1991, an eighty-two-year-old Spaniard's Bay man told a university student how he once found himself disoriented in a small thicket of woods, a five-minute walk from his house. "Never lost my cool at all," he said, "and I turned my cap inside out, and of course I said I must be in the fairies." He emerged from the trees onto the barrens, and saw a man several hundred feet away; so he sat down on a rock to contemplate the land, which "looked different" than any he had ever seen:

> I didn't recognize the ground I was on, so I said I must be astray. I went down to the gentleman, knowing he was a fairy that looked like any human being. I went down in a casual sort of way and said, "Good afternoon." He said, "Good evening." Not letting him know that I was astray, I said, "Can you tell me how far Mainline is, going through New Harbour?" "Oh, yes," he said, "just up there, up straight over the hill and you'll find the road." I said, "Thank you very much." Now I still had my cap turned inside out. As I was going up the hill, I figured like I could hear my father calling, which was only my imagination, to be straight about it. After five or ten minutes I finally came to myself, whatever did happen. But I says I was led astray and in the fairies. (91-221/9-10)

Preface to the Second Edition

Dear Readers,

I have been in the fairies! That is the only explanation for how, as the editors at Memorial University Press claim, thirty years could have passed since the publication of *Strange Terrain*. Surely it was only months ago, a few years at the most, that I was pulling draft pages out of a clattering dot matrix printer. And somehow even less that I was beating the roads 'round the bay, looking for people to tell me about the fairies. Yet records show that it was 1982 when I arrived at Memorial to do a PhD in the Folklore Department.

Newfoundland was strange terrain to me then — true *terra incognita*. I left California after finishing an MA in Folklore at UC Berkeley, more in search of adventure than the fairies — I didn't even know they existed! That is, I didn't know that the tradition existed in Newfoundland and Labrador, much less in living oral tradition. When I started reading the stories in the Memorial University Folklore and Language Archive, I was intrigued, and when I actually started hearing them myself, I was hooked. Since I hadn't crossed the continent to do something that could be done just anywhere, it seemed a perfect thesis subject; I also wanted to do something "classic," in contrast to my master's topic, folklore in the anti-nuclear movement. But the best thing about my thesis was the fieldwork, which let me go out and meet people and explore the fabulous land I had so fortuitously lit upon. Driving around in my 1976 Honda Civic with my little dog Solo is among my fondest memories of my early time in Newfoundland. My luck only got better when

I was joined by Martin Lovelace and later by our son, John Rieti-Lovelace. Yet further gifts from that time were fellow students and boon companions Drs. Diane Tye, Janet McNaughton, Elke Dettmer, and Julia Bishop.

I did have some reservations along the way. "What's a big girl like you doing going around asking about the fairies?" one man asked, and it's true that to some it might not seem quite dignified or practical — but then neither am I, so who better? Some people reasonably assumed that I would be making money from a book (if only!), and had I known it would take so long I might have paid more attention to financial concerns. Some people thought I was investigating the actual reality of fairies; others didn't see why I was so interested in stories about people or places that I didn't know and had no connection with. So I did sometimes ask myself just what I was up to, and the answer usually just came down to an affinity for the subject. I was drawn not just by the narratives themselves, but to the astonishing longevity of a tradition that lived almost entirely through words. Its immateriality was almost disturbing, when I thought that had the Folklore Department not been set up in the 1960s, we would have nothing but a few printed glimpses — we would know that it existed, but nothing of its depth and variation. And, of course, it is mutable over time; the stories are not just about fairies but reflect a whole way of life, so will inevitably change too. (A midwife, for instance, could not nowadays be called out to deliver a fairy baby [p. 9] or to diagnose an adult changeling and heave it into a pond [p. 160]). So my project did seem to be socially useful beyond my own purposes. I didn't want to be a cultural interloper or appropriator, but no one else was out there doing it. As a graduate student, I had the obligation and apparatus to deposit the stories safely in the archive, where they can remain portals to a numinous past.

I liked to think that I had joined an august company of fairy chroniclers. The wonderful QEII Library at Memorial gave access to the work of early folklorists, antiquarians, and other students of fairy lore, such as Robert Kirk, the minister in Aberfoyle, Scotland, who in 1692 compiled information from his parishioners in a manuscript, *The Secret Commonwealth*. It was left behind upon his sudden untimely death the same year while walking on a fairy hill, and was not published until 1815 by Walter Scott. Scott offers local legend to the effect that after his funeral, Kirk appeared to a cousin to tell him that he wasn't really dead but was captive among the fairies. He would appear again at the christening of his posthumous child, where another cousin could save him by throwing a knife at him. In the event, the cousin was too unnerved to do it, so Kirk was lost forever, apparently punished (Scott says) for having offended "the invisible people" by prying into their affairs "for the purposes of giving them to the public" (Letters on Demonology and Witchcraft V, Gutenberg.org). (The manuscript title page does suggest an element of promotion: "a subject not heretofore discoursed of by any of our writers, done for the satisfaction of his friends by a modest inquirer") (collections.ed.ac.uk/iconics/record/51414).

One might have thought this would be a cautionary tale, but I was more focused on parallels in Newfoundland tradition of missing or "dead" people who had been taken by the fairies and their attempted rescue — sometimes successful, sometimes not: Liz Fagan, for instance, whose brother (or mother) could not wrestle her away from a crowd (p. 38), or the woman pulled off on a sleigh drawn by a white horse (pp. 68–69). Just as Robert Kirk's grave was reputed to be empty, the disinterred coffin of a woman saved by her husband was found to contain only a broom (p. 42). (My notes to this story type in note 15, Chapter 2, pp. 279–80, show how many happy procrastinatory hours can be spent assembling comparative material.)

Between the archive and library and going out and about, I loved my research. The writing, not so much. To be nakedly confessional here, at one point I lay paralyzed on the floor of my study room in the library (the kind where people tape paper over the windows so no one can see their napping, coffee-drinking, or despair) because it all seemed impossible. I share this because I know that students sometimes read *Strange Terrain* for their courses, and I want them to know: you can do it! (Finish your thesis, that is, not lie on the library floor, because rules about covering the windows are now enforced.) Eventually I gained enough momentum to randomly experience the holy mystery of writing: how one can struggle fruitlessly over a paragraph or phrase, only to have it pop fully formed into the mind while doing something entirely different, like sleeping or swimming. It helped me put in the hard hours at the desk in hope that the subconscious mind would do its conjurations at leisure.

My only regret about *Strange Terrain* is that I didn't keep recording after it was done. I seldom gave a talk or guest lecture without someone afterward telling me a fairy experience of their own or from someone they knew or from their community. I did exert myself on occasion, if a situation practically fell into my lap, or if I got paid. In 1999, for instance, the filmmaker John Walker hired me to find participants and to scout locations for a film, *The Fairy Faith*. He was especially interested in a connection with music, which immediately brought to mind "The Fairy Tune" known in Branch and St. Bride's. According to a student in a class I taught in 1994, Dick English, a trapper who lived hermit-like in the woods, heard the fairies pass outside his cabin one night playing a melody, which he introduced on his next trip into town. (For that and a version in which the tune is played by a fairy named Peggy Birch, see Constance Foley's essay in the archive.) I enlisted the help of Delf Hohmann, former fellow folklore student and organizer of the Cape St. Mary's Performance series (now in its twenty-second year), and Tony Power, a native of Branch and naturalist who worked for many years at the Cape St. Mary's bird sanctuary, and on March 1 we set out through the woods to find the site of Dick English's cabin on the cliff above Wreck Cove. Starting near Spirit Knap (where a person could be immobilized by spirits) and overlooking the River Styx (where, unsurprisingly, mysterious deaths had occurred), we crossed Little Meadows (a known fairy spot, where Tony cautioned respectful silence) and a river into which Delf was dunked when *something* (he felt) pushed him off the bridging log. Recalling the hike in a recent conversation, Tony says that "something" was leading us in circles — which I don't think he happened to mention at the time. It is perhaps just as well that Walker never made it to Newfoundland but stopped in Cape Breton.

(I only found these notes after a days-long search, because as I said to Martin, I had vaguely named the Walker file "Hunting the Fairies" after a 1949 comic novel by Compton Mackenzie; Martin said that it sometimes seemed more like *they* hunted *me*. He reminded me of the time I was interviewed by Peter Gzowski for *Morningside* in the St. John's CBC studio. Not five minutes into the interview the nationwide broadcast cut out, apparently due to a glitch in the transmitter in Halifax or something like that. It had never happened before, according to Mr. Gzowksi.)

Bushwhacking fieldwork was not always required. In October 2008, I recorded a story in my own kitchen from Rudy Oliver, a painter working on a renovation, about his grandfather being fairy-led near the Three Pond Barrens outside St. John's. An accordion player, he and his partner, a fiddler, were taking a shortcut through the gully on Ridge Road after leaving a dance at the Airport Inn, when they were beset by a crowd of little people. The fiddler escaped, but they kept Rudy's grandfather playing all night while they danced.

A short time later (January 2009), in the bookstore in the Avalon Mall I noticed a man perusing *Strange Terrain*, so I recommended it to him highly. His interest became apparent as we talked, for Tom Fitzpatrick had vivid stories of his own from Bell Island. One concerned a group of five children who (*circa* 1965) encountered a group of little people making merry with games and music; they gave the children tea in little cups and wouldn't let them go until their parents found them, standing rigid in the marsh. Another time, Tom's brother Jim, at about the age of fifteen, was bringing cows back to the family farm in the evening but kept walking and walking but getting nowhere until they climbed a little hill. There he was transfixed by the sight of little people: some were playing "cobby" (making little houses with sticks), some danced, and others sat on rocks and stools while an old gentleman played mesmerizingly on a violin. It was no fleeting vision — he watched, "spellbound" as Tom said, for a long time until he came to himself and got home with the story he told for the rest of his life, until his death only the previous year. Their father said that Jim must have come upon a fairy hill, because those can manifest anywhere at any time. This pop-up world adds imaginative dimension to the mundane, even beyond established fairy haunts like Butler's Marsh. Tom regrets that "we don't hear about such things today" because "our minds are slammed shut" by overly scientific thinking, and our world is the poorer for it. Certainly his sharing these stories punched a hole in the bleak banality of a midwinter day at the mall.

(Luckily I was able to confirm with Philip Hiscock, the folklorist who knows just about everything about Newfoundland and everyone in it, that Tom Fitzpatrick is a real person. Otherwise I might have suspected he was a magical helper, because I had been invited by former fellow student Marie-Annick Desplanques to give a talk that very month at the University of Cork in Ireland. I was worried that I had been dining out on my original fieldwork for some time now, and it and I were both getting a little long in the tooth. Tom generously gave me permission to use his stories there, which was fitting since his forebears had come from Mothel near Waterford, not far away. Thanks to him and Rudy, I was able to speak with renewed enthusiasm, especially to the point that fairy lore is not all that hard to come by, at least not for the *cognoscenti*.)

For all their phantasmagorical aspects, fairy stories are not fantasy; they are not "fairy tales" of the "once upon a time, in a faraway land" type in which "she married the prince and all lived happily ever after" — both lines from a story called "Open! Open! Green House" told by Alice Lannon (1927–2013). Her tales and those of Pius Power (1912–1993) are presented in a new book, *Clever Maids, Fearless Jacks and a Cat: Fairy Tales from a Living Oral Tradition* (2019) by Anita Best, Martin Lovelace, and Pauline Greenhill. Also known to folklorists as "wonder tales," these usually have formulaic openings and closings, like Pius's: "There was one time/in olden times/in farmers' time/it wasn't in your time/or in my time/but in times ago," and his ending: "They had coffee for tea when I came away/and if they don't live happy, I hope we may." This kind of story is much rarer than fairy lore. Alice and Pius had that, too, but it is matter of fact in comparison: Pius's story of the broom in the coffin, for instance, or how the fairies threw something at Alice's Uncle Joe Strang when he applauded upon seeing them dance; a painful year later a thorn worked out of his knee. A certain few storytellers did cast their fairy narrative in a formal performance-oriented style (Marie Meaney of Chapter Two, for example, or John Smith of Chapter Five), but the stories were nevertheless set in the everyday world — no dragons, seven-league boots, or the like. The "other world" and its "others" were still treated as potential reality. Neither wonder tales nor fairy narratives were intended particularly for children; all ages were potential auditors, to take or leave them as they liked.

"My fairies — I did see them," Mary Flynn assured Martin and me. She was ninety-five when we interviewed her in 2013. The sighting happened one evening around 1960, when she and her husband were driving along the main road near Otterbury, Conception Bay, where she still lives. They passed what looked like a red bandana blowing across the road, and she looked back to see "two little ones" — about the size of two-year-olds — dressed in "beautiful little red windbreakers" and red peaked caps; they waved until they were out of sight. "I didn't think it was fairies at the time," she said, but when she got home she called a woman who lived nearby, who told her there were no children around that day, so "I knew what it was then." She had seen them once before, when she was ten, as she and some other children were walking home from school "between day and dark": two figures the size of small children, dressed in brown with brown caps, "dancing around circles" by a marsh.

Fairy experience seemed to run in the family. I heard about Mary from Peggy Wakeham, a student with whom I was working on a summer job with the East Coast Trail Association. Her grandmother, Mary's cousin, had been taken by the fairies as a child, after leaving a group of other children (including Mary), but was found unharmed asleep under a blanket of blue flowers on the beach. Her older sister Bride saw them once, when she was about twelve years old, while she was minding the child of a couple who had left her and the child with their horse and wagon while they went trouting. A dozen or more figures dressed in brown jackets and caps were kicking a ball, but "she didn't think [it was] the fairies." When the couple returned from the pond, she tried to show them what she still took to be small children: "Look, they're over there, don't you see them? My, aren't they cute." But Mrs. Dawe called her husband away urgently, because she "knew right away what it was," unlike Bride, who was ready to "go among them." I was struck by the likeness in some of these accounts to Tom Fitzpatrick's: the collective vision by children of other "children" at play in a kind of mirror world, and the adult participation in construing a fairy experience. Also, there was no sense of menace, although Mary did know of people who fared less well: "Fairy Jake," for instance, who was normal until he went missing with his horse and dray, and was

xxiii

found on a small island; or a young woman who became ancient overnight. But for herself, "nothing bad, I had good fairies."

In 2019, Mary told the folklorist Dale Jarvis the secret to living to a hundred: "salt beef, cabbage, and whisky" (ichblog.ca). I live in Victoria, BC, now (British Columbia, not Behind Carbonear), so no salt beef for me — but cabbage, yes, and if I can substitute wine for whisky, maybe I will live to see a sixtieth anniversary edition of *Strange Terrain*. Maybe I'll even add to it. I had thought Mary Flynn's would be the last stories I would record, but talking to Tony Power about our trip into the Wreck Cove woods twenty years ago, I felt a certain stirring. He lives in Trepassey now, and monitors the fossil site at Mistaken Point, with the massive Avalon Wilderness Reserve "at his back." Sometimes he leads hikes for visitors at the local hotel, telling them of fairies, ghosts, phantom ships, and miscellaneous mysterious phenomena and inexplicable events. Traversing the land and shores year-round, as he does, Tony says he hears the most marvellous tales. Was he writing them down? I asked. No, he just remembers. The big girl in me sat up. How fun would it be to jump in the truck with him and go visiting, and get it all down?

But probably I won't revisit *Strange Terrain*. Probably it's best to leave well enough alone, and I will leave it to others to follow the faint music over barren and bog. This new edition is thrill enough for me. The fairies have "many light toyish books," wrote Robert Kirk in *The Secret Commonwealth*, and I commend this to their collection. And to you, dear readers, with the greatest pleasure.

Preface to the First Edition

In the Memorial University of Newfoundland Folklore and Language Archive (MUNFLA) there are hundreds of accounts of the fairies and descriptions of associated custom and belief, recorded mostly by student collectors over the past twenty-five years. When I came to Memorial in 1982. I was astonished by this abundance; I was familiar with Reidar Christiansen's 1973 statement that "in most places the [Fairy] Faith is by now almost entirely extinct," and had not imagined that it was to be found at all in North America.[1] But in MUNFLA I read personal experience narratives of recent vintage, and despite a wide consensus among collectors and informants on the decline of fairy traditions, it was clear that an extensive body of these traditions still had never been examined in depth.

I heard my first fairy narrative in the winter of 1983, when an ethnography course took us into "the field" on Bell Island. It came from a twenty-one-year-old man, Andy Newsome (a pseudonym), who did not know that Richard MacKinnon, Elke Dettmer, and I were folklore students when we struck up a conversation in a restaurant. Richard was asking about older houses when Mr. Newsome mentioned that his own was built on the site of a former cemetery. "Plenty of ghosts there," I said jokingly. It was as if a hidden button had been pushed as Mr. Newsome, hitherto monosyllabic, launched into a series of supernatural tales, including the time he was picked up by the devil while hitchhiking and the night he was followed by fairies. The fairies were the size of children, had withered faces, wore gray suits and red caps, and marched single file ("military-like") behind him up a hill; they disappeared with a wave of their hands when he dropped to his knees and prayed. Hearing this was beginner's luck — I have not heard anything so spontaneously offered in so natural a context since, and subsequent attempts to record Mr. Newsome proved futile — but it was enough to set me off on the inquiries that became my doctoral thesis and then this book.

Aside from the intrinsic fascination of the narratives, I was motivated at first by simple curiosity as to whether fairy stories are still told or not. Was Mr. Newsome an isolated case? If nobody believed in or talked about the fairies anymore, why were there so many stories about them in MUNFLA? Some accounts were of relatively recent events, like this one from a twenty-year-old St. John's student:

> About six years ago [i.e., 1968] my cousin's mother disappeared into the hills one afternoon and she was never seen again. Many of the old people who believed in fairies said that the fairies took her away. Her red sweater was found and they said that they left this as a sign she was taken by them. We believed that she fell over the cliff and was taken out to sea because her body was never found. (FSC74-101/41)

Could there really be such a complete break in world view between the "old people" and contemporary culture? I felt that even if I could not answer such questions, posing them would reveal facets of change and continuity in oral tradition. And even if I were not able to "get" any fairy stories myself, the collation of MUNFLA material alone had never been undertaken and would in itself provide the first formal presentation of Newfoundland fairy lore. As it turned out, my field research became the first extended investigation of the subject, and my field recordings the first major verbatim collection of texts. I have tried to combine both sources — MUNFLA material and my own field research — to give as round a portrait as possible of a complex tradition.

Acknowledgements

Since this book would not exist without the help of my informants, my debt to them on that score alone is enormous. But I must also thank them for introducing me to the magic of Newfoundland and making a stranger feel at home here. My deepest thanks to everyone who told me about the fairies, especially Dan Costello, Joe Costello, H. Miles Furlong, Annie Hayes, Frances Kavanagh, Roy and Mildred Kelloway, Ellen Keough, Jim and Katharine Lynch, Ed MacDonald, Queen Maloney, Marie Meaney, Richard Murrin, and William Clive Tucker; thanks also to those not named in the book in order to protect their privacy (especially that trickster in Bishop's Cove). I am indebted as well to the many collectors who made their work available in MUNFLA, especially Anita Best, Virginia Dillon, Colleen Meaney, Tom Moore, Cavelle Penney, and Eleanor Penney.

I owe much to David Buchan, who made Herculean editorial efforts as thesis supervisor, and to Robert Paine, who did the same for its conversion to a book. Helpful comments came from thesis readers Diane Goldstein, Reimund Kvideland, Peter Narváez, Gerald Pocius, and Larry Small. Gerald Thomas, as Head of the Folklore Department, offered kind words — and better still, letters — of support. Herbert Halpert and John Widdowson generously allow less intrepid types to avail themselves of their pioneering field tapes and experience. Fellow students and folklorists who gave me references and ideas include Julia Bishop, John Cousins, Marie-Annick Desplanques, Elke Dettmer, Laurel Doucette, Philip Hiscock, Kathryn Kimiecik, Janet

McNaughton, and Clara Murphy. Sharon Cochrane and Karen O'Leary in the Folklore Department office helped untangle computer files and print out seemingly endless drafts.

I would like to thank my first Folklore teacher, Alan Dundes; although it is over a decade since I first sat in his seminar, I still sometimes imagine him, when I am bogged down in a passage, demanding that I come to the point and explain what it all means. During the long course of this project, it also helped to know that I could always count on two weird sisters, Nancy and Janet Rieti, as well as William Gross, to offer California comforts and counterpoint.

It was a treat to be able to put the manuscript into the hands of the publications staff at ISER (now Memorial University Press); Susan Nichol's eagle editorial eye and Jeanette Gleeson's swift efficiency inspired confidence in the face of improbable deadlines. A talk with Kevin Pittman helped hatch the title, and Dick Buehler's careful copy-editing caught things no one else had.

A fellowship from the Memorial University School of Graduate Studies helped support my graduate work. A research grant from ISER helped to cover some fieldwork expenses, and an ISER post-doctoral fellowship has allowed me to continue Folklore research.

It has been my great good luck to have had the help and companionship of Martin J. Lovelace throughout this project. John Rieti-Lovelace, ever since dismantling a tape at the age of two, has displayed an earnest concern for my work. I cannot imagine having done it without them.

Acknowledgements for the second edition

The only work I did for this edition is the new Preface, and I would like to thank the people mentioned there who weren't in the book's first round: Mary Flynn, Tom Fitzpatrick, Delf Hohmann, Tony Power, and Rudy Oliver.

For orchestrating the new production I thank Diane Tye in the Department of Folklore, ever generous and supportive of everyone's work; the editors at Memorial University Press, Fiona Polack and Alison Carr, and their copy editor, Richard Tallman.

Martin Lovelace's hair didn't turn white overnight, but it didn't take long after he and I became co-parents, co-habitors, and occasional co-researchers in a protracted *folie* à *deux* — with his teaching all the while. (My hair is still mostly brown.) And now I can renew my thanks to him under the grandfather clause.

A Note on the Documentation and Transcription of Sources

All material from the Memorial University of Newfoundland Folklore and Language Archive is identified by accession or reference numbers. The first number (before the dash) shows the year in which the item was recorded (unless noted otherwise); the last number(s) — after the slash — refers to the page(s) of the manuscript. The prefix "FSC" indicates a Folklore Survey Card rather than an essay, and the last number identifies an individual card in a collection (FSC80-322/1 and FSC80-322/2, for example, would be two different cards from the same collector); an asterisk is used instead of a final number when cards in a set have not yet been assigned individual numbers. A "C" number indicates a tape, and a number after a slash following a C number indicates the page(s) of a MUNFLA transcription of the tape. These archive-produced transcripts are not intended to be polished products but a rough guide to the material, so for most quotations I did the transcription myself; "my transcription" is abbreviated "m.t." The occasional "Q" indicates a questionnaire response.

The names of individuals figuring in reports are changed unless otherwise stated; some collectors' names have been changed as well, since they may not have envisioned publication of their efforts even though deposit in MUNFLA allows it (with permission of the director) unless specific restrictions were made at the time of deposit. Archive documents are reproduced exactly, with two exceptions: occasionally a collector tries to render dialectal or informal speech through non-standard spelling, such as the substitution of "d" for "th," or the dropping of "g" (de addin' o' d's an' de droppin' o' g's); I have put such efforts (as well as inadvertent misspellings) into standard orthography, for I think they do nothing to convey the spoken word, are potentially offensive to the speakers, and distract from what is being said. The only other change is modification of punctuation for readability. The use of square brackets in a quotation or archival text is always mine, and parentheses are the collector's.

Transcripts of my own field tapes are verbatim, with asterisks in places where I could not make out the exact words. (The number of asterisks indicates approximate length of the uncomprehended utterance; they are important because often the informants drop their voices, speak quickly, or trail off at crucial points, as when identifying the fairies or expressing doubt.) Ellipses usually indicate that I asked a clarifying or repetitious question, or made some remark; these were cut for the sake of space, but I left in any questions or comments of mine that influenced the direction of the speaker's thoughts. I left out "uhs," "ahems," and the like except when they were marked, that is, when I thought that they showed a significant pause or hesitation (as before naming the fairies, for example).

My field recordings and notes are in MUNFLA under the numbers 86-124, 88-055, and 90-421 (they are restricted). I have used the real names of my informants except where indicated, but changed the names of most individuals figuring in the narratives who were not directly connected to my informants.

1 | *Always Going and Never Gone?*

*F*airy manifestations often have the quality of mirage. An Avondale woman heard "a gay, soft music," and saw what looked like small children in white clothes; they were holding hands and "dancing on the top of the little hilltops, and when she approached they moved on to the next one further in the distance. She walked the shoes off her feet following them," and was found the next day deep in the woods (71-42/22). Fairy lore itself is like these fairies, ever receding into the distance before the eyes of the beholder (or ears of the hearer). Present-day traditions are but a shadow of their former selves, people say, shreds of a once robust folklore fast fading into oblivion. Or are they? Almost a hundred years ago, W.B. Yeats pondered the same question in *The Celtic Twilight*, in which he quotes Douglas Hyde's epigraph for *Beside the Fire* — "They are like a mist on the coming of night that is scattered away by a light breath of wind" — and continues:

> I know that this is the common belief of folk-lorists, but I do not feel certain that it is altogether true. Much, no doubt, will perish — perhaps the whole tribe of folk-tales proper; but the faery and ghost kingdom is more stubborn than men dream of. It will perhaps be always going and never gone. (208)

The folk view of the fairies' disappearance often includes the idea that they once did exist. "In th'olde dayes," said Chaucer's Wife of Bath, ". . . Al was this land fulfild of fayerye" (84). A Newfoundland informant was telling Herbert Halpert, the founder of Memorial's Folklore Department, about a man who got lost one night and "didn't even know his own community":

> ... he was led astray by something, back in the days of the fairies. That's like spirits, you know, plenty of spirits down north one time, no more now. In my father's time there was a few. (71-54: C986/15)

The Nolans, a couple in their seventies, told me that the fairies used to be seen on a bluff near their community:

> Mrs. N: They'd be all going around of a ring, you know, dancing around in a ring, dressed in red.
>
> Mr. N: But that wasn't our time; that wasn't in our time. That wasn't in our time, but it was in our fathers' time.

They went on to tell about Mrs. Nolan's mother being "towed away," their neighbour's baby being changed, and about a woman who explained her yearly disappearance in October by saying she was with the fairies. The Nolans are thus typical of informants who declare fairy traditions dead even as they recount fairy incidents involving themselves, relatives, friends, or community members. It may be that they deem certain aspects of fairy tradition more likely to still exist than others — being towed astray versus seeing the fairies dance, for example — but they also assure me that "there's no talk of them now." Their report of the fairies' demise, however, would seem to be (like Mark Twain's) greatly exaggerated.[1] There is no doubt that Newfoundland fairy narratives do not enjoy the currency they did when storytelling was a major pastime; the decline of narrative contexts (performance or transmission situations) has had, by all accounts, a corresponding decline in oral tradition. Fairy tradition has been weakened as well by changes in experiential contexts, or situations in which one might have a "fairy" experience, such as cutting wood, picking berries, or walking long distances on dark roads. But in the course of research over the past eight years I have come to regard the "complete belief" of the past as an overstatement, and the lack of belief today an underestimation. Even when contextual data is scant, it is possible to see that fairy tradition has always been open to interpretation, dispute, and manipulation, that a play between belief and disbelief is prominent, and that the exchange of stories is the medium of debate. This study will attest that there are still many people willing to consider that there is "something to it" (to use the common phrase), and many for whom "belief" is not a pressing issue in retailing tales of the fairies.

This study aims to examine the nature of the fairies themselves — who and what are they supposed to be? — and the forms (such as narrative and custom) in which ideas about them are expressed. It also considers the meanings and uses of these ideas: why do people conceive of, and tell stories about, such entities? The latter question is infinitely harder to address than the first, for there are perhaps as many answers as there are people; the more fieldwork I did, the more wary I became about asserting deep meaning or design, for fieldwork shows how narratives with essentially identical content may be understood and used in quite different ways. This is not to say that general theories cannot be made — I shall offer a few forthwith and many throughout — only that they are bound to be less certain than insights drawn from particular situations. And when the difficulties of assessing any single situation are taken into account, the tenuousness of grand interpretations becomes even clearer. Yet it could be argued that the very uniformity of fairy traditions belies contextual and individual variation and demands explanation. Why do the same outlines assert themselves (for it does seem that they have an almost independent life of their own) so insistently? Clearly there is something satisfying in them, but what? This is another basic question with which I began.

I found answers at two levels, in what I call explicit and implicit themes. By "explicit" I mean overt, inarguable content, such as the matter of fairies "taking" people or leading them astray. Implicit themes — they can also be called sub-themes or subtexts — are those that I think can be discerned underlying Newfoundland fairy lore as a whole; they reflect cultural concerns and help explain its functioning independent of genre and belief. One such theme is the human relationship with nature. In a harsh environment, under precarious economic and material conditions, one's niche is ever under siege;

fairy narratives reflect the struggles and hard-won survival of culture and human creation, and the tenuous imposition of order on the wilderness. It is nothing new to suggest that the fairies symbolize "nature": Robin Flower calls them "an image of man's unreconciled distrust of nature" (140), and Alan Bruford suggests that they "represent in anthropomorphic form the mysterious and numinous in wild nature, the part of the world which is beyond mankind's understanding — 'the raw' of Levi-Strauss, as against 'the cooked,' what man had mastered and put to his own use" (in MacDougall ix). Lauri Honko sees the Scandinavian nature spirits as part of "a map of man's conquest of the environment" ("Adaptation" 21), and Kvideland and Sehmsdorf suggest they are patterned on nature itself, which was experienced as "animate and possessed of will and thus capable of aiding humans but also of doing them harm" (9). There has been, perhaps understandably, little close analysis of such general propositions, but attention to a nature/culture dichotomy with reference to specific narratives and motifs offers considerable insight into the codes and symbols of fairy narrative.

A second implicit theme in Newfoundland fairy lore revolves around interpersonal relationships, specifically around knowing, not knowing, and being known. The fairies are the ultimate strangers, and serve as metaphor for all that is strange not only in nature but in other people. A concern with recognition can be seen in fairy traditions from simple sayings — "When his son acted any way strange, weird, or incomprehensible when he was young, Mr. Collins usually said to him, 'I believe you're in the fairies!'" (74-152/13) — to the most serious of personal experience narratives — "My mother said as far as she was concerned that was true, she said that girl never came back, there was someone in her place" (64-13: C73/20).

The plan in organizing this study was to set my field research in the context of related data, and to elucidate issues or lines of thought arising from that combination of material. In order to preserve the integrity of the field research by keeping narrators and narratives together, chapters are organized around informants or sets of informants rather than along tidy typological lines. This means that major types of narratives or fairy experiences appear in almost every chapter, but from a different perspective in each. One problem in working with material as rich as fairy tradition is that almost any text presents numerous points of interest, and the pursuit of any one is often at the expense of others. Thus there is an unavoidable labyrinthine quality in much of the discussion; scanning an early draft of one chapter, a bewildered reader remarked that it was like being fairy-led — you never knew quite where you were going or why — and indeed, while writing I felt sympathy with those persons who in fascination follow small figures or luscious berries until they suddenly "come to themselves" deep in the woods with no idea how they got there or how to get back. But the underlying principle of each chapter is to let my attempts to impose order on the wilderness of field, archive, scholarly and comparative material be guided by affinities inherent in the material as well as by theoretical considerations.

Centring chapters on informants also seemed the best way to take the reader along the course of my ventures. He or she may scrutinize my field methodology, gaffes and all, as I knock hopefully on kitchen doors, and tell the occupants that I heard they might know something about the fairies. The process of investigation is also mirrored in the weighting of chapters: Two and Three are the heaviest in archive and comparative data, since I started in the archive and library; the last four contain more of my own field research. I would like the material to unfold, as it did for me, until not only the general patterns but turns of phrase, elliptical references, and recurrent images resonate against all the narratives heard (or in this case, read) before. By the seventh chapter — if not much sooner — the reader will probably chafe at the "tedious consistency" that Barbara Allen Woods points out allows the folklorist to distinguish genuine from dubious sources (4), but the redundancy is an assurance of accuracy, so that the reader will, for example, readily recognize the artificiality of certain literary representations mentioned in Chapter Six. I have also preferred to demonstrate rather than simply to state that one thing or another is "common" or "widespread," and to avoid a generalized "profile" abstracted from individual accounts. Besides producing an unfortunate coy tone, this composite approach has serious shortcomings when applied to folk narrative or belief in general, for the voices and views of "the folk" as individuals are lost. I have tried to keep these voices foremost, and not drown them in comparative material or my own ideas, and to keep my interpretive suggestions separate enough to be taken or left while informants' contributions stand. At the same time I have described my own role as carefully as possible, since the researcher's approach is bound to influence what informants tell (or do not tell) her, even if she does not know what it is. That this is a particularly complicated matter in regard to the fairies will become clear in the following note.

SOME PRELIMINARY METHODOLOGICAL CONSIDERATIONS
Contrary to popular opinion among non-residents and even some livyers (people who live here), Newfoundland has never been an isolated place with a closed or homogeneous society; rather, there has always been travel both on and to and from the island, and a marked distinctiveness of communities. Seary, Story, and Kirwin discuss the "remarkable and continuous interchange and shift of population" throughout the recorded history of the Avalon Peninsula, and point out that migratory and seasonal work patterns "made Newfoundlanders one of the most mobile of people," which "helped to modify, though not to cancel out, that separateness of the people of different areas remarked long ago by Wix" (35–36). In 1836, the missionary Edward Wix had commented that inhabitants of the different bays differed from one another "as much as if they were of a distant nation" (Seary et al. 36). The special character of communities continues to be noted by student collectors and by observers like Melvin Firestone, who in the 1960s found it hard to account for the differences in communities he studied on the Northern Peninsula, when surface characteristics like economy and heritage were the same (*Brothers* vi–vii). Within villages or towns, neighbourhoods may form smaller informal communities with their own particular character. George Casey, for example, writes in an ethnography of his home community that although the younger generation see Conche as a whole (58), in the past there were distinct neighbourhoods that were noted for different narrative specialties (52). Casey himself had never heard fairy stories:

> However, Dr. Halpert insisted that since Conche was an Irish ethnic area there was every reason to expect fairy lore, so I even

> attempted to collect this narrative genre. To my amazement not only were fairy legends known in Conche but even my mother knew several of these stories. Neither my older brother nor I ever heard her tell any. (225)

There are plenty of Newfoundlanders like Casey, as surprised as I was to learn of fairy tradition. Others know of it, but not at first hand; an informant at Port Saunders directed Halpert and the English folklorist John Widdowson to the other side of the island to find out about it, "because they talk about fairies over there just the same as we do ghosts over here" (66-24: C272/m.t.).

MUNFLA data show that there are "good" and "bad" areas for fairy lore; that is, some places offer relatively little while others, like Upper Island Cove or Bell Island, can be seen from the number and detail of reports to be veritable hotbeds. Informants sometimes attribute the difference to "Irishness," and advised me to seek out "Irish" or Catholic enclaves for my research; and they are right that in heavily Irish areas like the Southern Shore and Cape Shore fairy traditions are found in profusion. Fairy lore is by no means limited to such areas, however, as there is abundant data from Protestants and Protestant areas. Upper Island Cove, for example, is mainly English/Protestant, as is neighbouring Bishop's Cove where I recorded some of my richest material; Bell Island is mixed. (I chose Conception Bay for most of my fieldwork not only because it is the oldest settled area, but because of its inextricable ethnic mixture.) Since Newfoundland settlers came mostly from southwest England and southeast Ireland (with smaller but significant elements from France, Scotland, Wales, the Channel Islands, and Brittany), it would seem evident that fairy lore came from these places as well, but because of the popular notion of "Irishness" I have devoted some attention to the matter at various points.

More important questions about antecedent sources concern adaptation. Is it possible, for example, in comparing Newfoundland material to its parent stock, to see selection and shaping according to the features of the "new" environment? What are the distinctive contours here? I have used comparative material mostly to consider such questions of continuity and change, as well as processes of oral tradition and the interpretation of experience. I have not been comprehensive in the provision of analogues — all the material in this study could be extensively annotated from the major collections and motif-indexes — but have used them mainly as they illuminate the material at hand. Occasionally the similarities in other cultures or eras that excited early students of fairy lore like Keightley, Wright, and Hartland have proved irresistible to me, too; there is a certain professional thrill in the sheer antiquity of fairy lore, as when someone, for example, tells the plot of the ballad "Tam Lin" as it happened in her community. Historical and literary reverberations, however, are not a feature for the tradition bearers, who have a different set of associations. Since this study is primarily an attempt to understand — or at least to present — fairy tradition from their point of view, I have limited historical material to as much as will demonstrate the extraordinary continuity that shows fairy tradition to contain powerful expressions of human interests and needs.

Comparison must be tempered, too, by consideration of the limitations of the data. The documentation of fairy tradition in Newfoundland is a relatively recent undertaking that has been neither systematic nor sustained. Except for a bit recorded by MacEdward Leach in his 1950 quest for ballads, there was no collection until the mid-1960s, when Halpert and Widdowson began their fieldwork on all folklore genres. Some of their students did superior "early" collections, and my reliance on them will be apparent. A list of MUNFLA materials on the fairies (compiled by myself and available in MUNFLA) shows that there has been little abatement of material since then, although some years were "better" than others. The quality and quantity of material from the early years were enhanced by courses taken on a year-long basis, in which students could use the Christmas break to collect in their home communities, and by Halpert's survey approach that explicitly included fairies as a subject for inquiry. The shortening of courses to semester length made them less conducive to the recording of long narratives, and students could not always turn to their home communities to do fieldwork. As more instructors taught more courses with special emphases, fairies would not inevitably be mentioned as a possible topic for collection. Reporting has thus been random, depending on there being a student from a community with fairy traditions, who had an interest in those traditions herself, and the mobility to get to informants within the required time. (Students have, of course, collected from each other at university, and are often excellent self-informants.) The element of chance makes it dangerous to conclude that any motif or narrative type is absent from Newfoundland just because it is not found in the archive. Sometimes a single text is all that bars such a conclusion; for example, the midwife-for-the-fairies legend, widespread elsewhere,[2] appears in MUNFLA in a single version (72-95/33-35:C1278/3-5). Told by someone who heard it from the midwife herself, it is so complete, and so clearly assimilated to local tradition, that it is impossible to believe that it could be the sole version in Newfoundland. The apparent absence or even "unusualness" of any particular item, then, must be treated with caution. On the other hand, it can be stated with confidence that some things are common or widespread, such as carrying bread for protection; and when there are a great many versions of an item, it can be seen that this or that variation is unusual by comparison. In general, however, "unusual" (in this study) means "unusual in the archival data."

Another reason why a full range of fairy traditions cannot be assumed to be represented in MUNFLA is that some people consider it dangerous to talk about the fairies. There is even a formula to circumvent the prohibition:

> [The informant's grandmother] believed in the fairies and their powers although she had never seen them. She had a good collection of stories concerning them which she and the other neighbors [on Bell Island] would gather together to discuss after tea when it was dark. However, the fairies did not like being discussed and would punish anyone who told stories about them. She would in opening the conversation say, "This is Sunday, Monday (whatever day it was) and the fairies won't hear us." This statement would prevent the fairies from hearing the ensuing conversation. (FSC67-3/33)

Failure to maintain a respectful attitude could have dire consequences, according to an Upper Island Cove collector:

> If one should talk about or mock the fairies, the old people will get really upset. The old people of this town, most of them, that

is, really believe in fairies. . . . The old people say that if you talk bad about them they will try to get you and punish you. It is said that people have been captured by fairies and brought back crippled up or blind or gone mad. (79-317/13-14)

Some students confessed to unease themselves. One composed a set of "rules" for dealing with the fairies, and concluded:

> Most of all, a mortal should never inquire too deeply into the fairies or their world for those who pry too much into fairy affairs may never live to write about them. If I were a believer in fairies I would not continue to write this paper, but I admit the idea is a bit frightening, because I have heard so many stories all my life about fairies and fairy encounterments. (79-378/5)

Another, attempting to record her family's store of supernatural lore, said:

> Now stories of fairies, ghosts or tokens are not easily obtained from these people because it is mostly a taboo subject, especially tokens — taboo because they are not told for the sake of telling stories or stories to be laughed at. The people who were the main characters in these happenings have a rigid belief in their truths and in their powers; and while listening to them, I found myself, if not exactly fearful, then certainly a bit apprehensive and a mite nervous at laughing at some of the seemingly humorous episodes. I found it interesting that neither my uncle, my mother, or my grandfather wanted to talk to me when there were others present. My aunt even left the house when Nash told her I was coming in to talk to him, or rather, to listen to him. (79-404/3)

Some people will talk only about what they themselves have experienced, while others will talk about anyone *but* themselves. Some will discuss certain aspects of fairy tradition but not others, usually those of a tragic nature. One collector knew about a girl who was "captured by fairies" when she left the informant's house one day and was found "in a poor condition" a week later.

When she asked the informant about it, he said, "We won't talk about that poor little thing. She ended up in the asylum" (74-210/11-12). For some students, stories they heard all their lives became elusive when pursued as a formal project. One wrote:

> My father is from Carbonear which many people claim was the land of the fairies. His grandparents and parents mentioned many stories of the fairies and the devil to him when he was young. Dad believes in them to the extent that they were told to him by his parents as true. During my childhood I heard such stories, therefore, became interested in this type of folklore. My original plan was to visit my older relatives in Carbonear. However, it turned out to be not as successful as I thought. I found that they were reluctant to talk about it, especially Aunt Ann. She apparently knows many fairy tales but since my uncle died last fall she refuses to talk about such tales and claimed to have forgotten them, and each time I mentioned stories that my father had told me she would just say, "Is that so," and start on a new topic.... I don't know if I used the wrong approach or not but few people were willing to sit down and talk about fairy tales and the devil, especially when I mentioned anything about an assignment in folklore or their names in the archives. (71-75/2-4)

A Cupids collector set herself up to record fairy narratives from her older relatives:

> They eye my tape recorder with a certain degree of mistrust and for a while I believe I will be unable to evoke any material from them on this occasion. My grandmother for one does not understand my true purpose in recording their conversation and believes they are being ridiculed by higher education. For some time she refuses to partake in the discussion. She is a woman who dislikes to have her picture taken, and similarly does not want her voice recorded on tape.... Fairy stories seem to figure prominently in this particular family. Stories of strange phenomena are slightly scoffed at ...

ghosts most likely do not exist. Fairies on the other hand most probably do. (83-39/3,6)

Sometimes university projects are mistrusted on other grounds. One student reported that her informant's brother would leave the house in disgust when she arrived with her recorder: "[He] said I would get no stories there because I was getting them too cheap. He did not like the idea of those 'big university fellas getting their information for nothing'" (76-82/33).

I encountered evasion early in my inquiries but was not discouraged by it because I did not know at the time that I was being put off. After meeting Andy Newsome, I began to ask everyone I met about the fairies. Richard Murrin of Shoe Cove and the late Alice (Picco) Hayes of St. Thomas (1911–1991) denied knowing anything about them; it was not until I got to know them better that I heard of the "blast" Mr. Murrin's father got in the leg, and the time Mrs. Hayes's father encountered fairies, a few feet tall, who leered at him and jeered, "Nyah, nyah, Tom b'ye" (see Chapter Seven for details). But meanwhile I had begun reading in the archive, and found potentially discouraging information in this vein. One informant told the collector that it would be a waste of time to look for fairy stories in Salmonier:

> He said that the people would be quite suspicious of an inquiring stranger and simply would not cooperate. He also mentioned that I would very likely run into persons who sincerely believed in fairies and who knew the stories that he had related to me but would not admit to either believing in fairies or to knowing any of the stories. (72-16/1)

Another student determined to record the supernatural stories that had terrified her during her childhood in Bonavista:

> I approached several people who used to be good storytellers but they insisted that they didn't know any stories. It was frustrating to be told by everyone that I talked to that if poor Alb or poor so and so were alive now, they could tell me stories.... So at this point I had to reassess the situation. I knew the stories I wanted

to hear, so I put away the tape recorder and my notebook and just went visiting. Since I was visiting older people and since these stories are generally woven into the conversation, I took my mother along with me. This turned out to be a good idea. Mom is sixty-one, old-fashioned, knows everybody's relatives and enjoys tracing back people and events.

She found that her informants did not understand her desire to hear a story for its own sake; for them, it was so crucial to know *who* the story was about that she sometimes resorted to a pretence of acquaintance or recollection because "there's always the danger that you might not get the story if you do not know the person involved" (79-708/4-7).

A Bell Island collector also noted the advantages of previous contact:

> I found that I had to know what my informant had in terms of fairy stories. Both men were very reluctant to talk about the fairies and I was constantly mentioning stories that they had told previously. My pre-interview research consisted of talking to the children of the men. In this way I was able to get the stories I needed and was able to use them in prodding the men to relate the experiences I later collected. (74-43/21-22)

Pondering the difficulties of being an ignorant outsider, I hit upon the plan of contacting some of the student collectors who had written on the fairies, or people who had already served as informants or been mentioned as potential informants. This is how, directly or indirectly, I got most of my informants. In place of knowing an individual's particular repertoire, I knew the general outline of the tradition and things to ask about, and in place of personal acquaintanceship with informants, I offered a wide-eyed interest in their experience and knowledge, a new audience who placed great value on their words. I have described my method in each case, which usually consisted of an informal conversation on the first meeting and a request for a second visit to make a tape-recorded interview. I recognize the potential indelicacy of importuning people to talk about something, then writing it all down for an audience outside their culture or control, and I was tempted to use pseudonyms on that account; however, most of my informants are self-assured and articulate people, and there seemed no need to disguise them on account of any wild ideas I might (and probably did) advance about them or their stories. I tried to record faithfully — indeed doggedly — what I was told; but a certain amount of imagination is essential (and inevitable) in any investigation of human thought, and so I have done a lot of guessing about my informants' ideas and motivations. If students of folk belief (or folk narrative, for that matter) were to stick only to demonstrable facts, many of its most interesting dimensions would go unexplored.

A NOTE ON ACADEMIC TERMINOLOGY

"Tradition" is a workhorse of a word because it covers a full range of genres and is neutral in terms of attitude and belief. "Narrative" is another usefully neutral word, but to avoid monotony I also use "tale," "account," and "story"; the latter is closer to folk usage than "legend," which in spite of professional definition suggests distance and doubtfulness more than "story" does. One non-emic (or non-native) term I use with reluctance is "supernatural," which is objectionable in the semantic sense that anything that is in the world cannot be considered "outside" or "above" nature; it carries an implicit judgement on objective reality that I wish to avoid because for many people the existence of the fairies is an empirically verified fact. The term can be misleading, too, in its popular sense of "strange" or "uncanny," because not everyone considers the fairies particularly extraordinary. One man calmly stepped off a road to allow a fairy funeral to pass: "This was told to my father by his grandfather Ross as a sort of night-time story," said the student, "it seemed that at this time the people were not alarmed by seeing the fairies and as far as my great-grandfather Ross was concerned it was just a natural thing" (71-75/12-13). While this may be a romantic projection onto the past, there are without a doubt people (including some of my informants) who take a matter-of-fact rather than awestruck view of the fairies.

There is also an ironic aspect in calling the fairies "supernatural" when an association with nature — in the general sense of uncultivated wilderness — is one of their most salient characteristics. John Lindow calls "the world of the nature-beings" of Swedish tradition "the other world," but points out that it is nevertheless "essentially the one in which the tradition-bearers live" (31–32); I have also used "other world" and "otherworlders" with the same reservation. In general I tried to use "supernatural" and "otherworlders" as shorthand at times when there is no simple way to refer to the range of traditions concerning the spiritual or extramundane world without distracting lexical convolutions.

A NOTE ON MY OWN "BELIEF"
It is well recognized, as David Hufford writes, that "a scholar approaching any interesting subject with human implications must do so with bias"; more debatable is Hufford's view that academic inquiries on "supernatural" folk belief start with the premise that the "beliefs" under investigation are "false" ("Supernatural" 24–25). This book is a study of the opinions of the tradition-bearers, not of my own; but as I have taken it upon myself to "interpret" their narratives, I should probably make my own views as clear as possible. I am basically of what Gillian Bennett calls the "'more things in heaven and earth, Horatio' school" (27), and although I have never seen anything worse than myself (as the saying goes), I would not rule it out entirely. On the other hand, I am of such an agnostic and materialist tendency in general that a relativistic view comes easily for some things: the fairies seem as reasonable to me as "God" as "he" is envisioned in formal religion. I am nevertheless irrational about some things, possibly more so than many people; for example, I am always amazed — quite aside from the question of morality — that able-bodied people would tempt fate by parking their cars in a spot designated for the disabled. I have no reason to believe, other than his word for it, that Mr. Tucker, the dowser of Chapter Six, can discern unseen essences in houses, but I would not buy one that he said had "bad energy" (the better-safe-than-sorry school). As to the fairies, I am like Mr. Smith of Chapter Five, who says, "From my point of view, probably they don't exist, but I wouldn't say they

don't." I feel there is a certain unwarranted arrogance on the part of those who dismiss them out of hand.

A NOTE ON TOPOGRAPHY

The landscape is so central to Newfoundland fairy tradition that its aspect will soon be apparent, but for the reader unfamiliar with it a brief description may be in order. Most communities cling to the coast, often near vertiginous cliffs by deep bays and inlets. Aaron Thomas's 1794 description is still good: "Newfoundland being in all parts intersected with Bogs, Barrens, Lakes, Morasses, Hills, Rivulets and Woods we find all places are plaster'd or thickly scatter'd with stones of all shapes and of all sizes" (63). He gives a good picture of the summer weather as well: "It often happens that one hour is hot, the next hour is cold, then a Fogge afterwards clear, then Rain — so that it commonly falls out that you get Four or Five kinds of weather in one day" (123). Winter is equally changeable, especially on the Avalon, where continual freeze-thaw cycles create hazardous and deceptive conditions, so that apparently solid surfaces are only skins of ice over water or chasms. Temperatures can drop many degrees in hours, and blinding storms whip up with little notice. Even more unpredictable are the drifts of fog, which, at any season, shift the landscape into new patterns and perspectives, when not obscuring it entirely. The seasonal work patterns that took people into this strange terrain — wood-cutting, berry-picking, hunting, trouting, travelling — will also become apparent in narrative, with the notable exception of fishing. "They don't agree with fishing," Ellen Keough of Chapter Seven says of the fairies. It was on the land that one carried bread in case of meeting them.

2 | *Fairy Forms and Narrative Contexts: An Overview*

The fairies are protean beings, appearing here in one form, there another, sometimes changing right before a person's eyes. They are also "skilled in comical tricks and delusions," able to "cast glamour, contrive hallucinations, cause apparitions so as to veil reality and produce a false and absurd appearance," as a fallen angel (fairy) of the twelfth century says (quoted in Hartland 1923, 176), and as a Boat Harbour man found when, lost in well-known woods, he climbed a tall tree to get his bearings and "lo and behold the tree he had climbed was not the big tree he thought he had seen, but a small tree. Uncle John came to his senses then and knew exactly where he was and how to get home, but he knew that the fairies had him for awhile" (79-404/7). In addition to their elasticity of form, there is great plasticity in the fundamental nature of the fairies, the most striking variation having to do with whether they are considered to be good or bad. Corresponding extremes are found in genre and narrative content, which range from ludicrous tales to hushed personal testimony, and in attitudes, which range from scornful dismissal to careful respect. The relationship between the human world and the fairy otherworld may be depicted as one of mutual accommodation or antagonism; the fairies are sometimes shown as amenable to human manipulation and thus controllable, other times as unpredictable and therefore feared.

Given the expansiveness of the rubric "fairies," and that people often avoid direct reference to "fairies," it is not always immediately apparent when someone is talking about "them"; one must be familiar with "their" ways, or a narrator's subtle cues, to know that something "fairy" is going on. Only the last sentence of the following, for example, spells it out for the uninitiated:

> I can't remember this fellow's name now, he used to live on that flat down there by Ned Welsh's. He was coming out from the Crossing Place one day, and all of a sudden the whole place was full of those glass alleys, and they dancing up and down. You know what those glass alleys are — big glass balls with colors going through them, like marbles. He had to pick his steps through them. When he got home he told the priest about it. "Did you touch any of them?" the priest said to him. "No," he said. "And 'tis a good thing you didn't," said the priest, "cause if you did, you wouldn't be here talking to me now." They were fairies of course. (67-4B/13-14)

This is one of ten "Tales of the Fairies" recorded from Angela Mason of Riverhead, St. Mary's Bay, by Michael Fagan in 1967, in which "they" appear as horses, bees the size of chickens, ordinary people, cats, and in assorted other guises. The texts are not verbatim (they were written from recollection after an interview), so it is uncertain whether "it was fairies of course" is the collector or informant's conclusion; it is clear, however, that Mrs. Mason used the word "fairies" sparingly, if at all. This collection was one of the first things I read in MUNFLA, and one of the first "field" trips I made, in July 1984, was an hour's casual drive to Riverhead to see where such extraordinary material had come from.

Riverhead is not in fact at the head of a river but at the mouth, and as one student describes it, "is basically a cluster of houses dotted along either side of the U-shaped valley" with "salt water" between (80-296/4). Most houses are strung along the main road, and it was in a small shop among them that I inquired about Michael Fagan. The proprietor informed me that he was dead,[1] but on hearing my interest, suggested that I see Marie Meaney. Fagan had mentioned her, saying that she and Mrs. Mason "consider themselves, or I should say are considered, specialists in the area of the supernatural, especially fairy legends" (67-4F/9). Angela Mason was in her eighties when he recorded her and is dead now, but Mrs. Meaney is in her nineties, and although somewhat deaf, in good health. At her house, I explained my errand to her daughter-in-law, who went back inside; then a tiny ancient woman appeared in the doorway and demanded, "Do you think I'm a fairy?"

I was invited into the kitchen where, without preamble, Mrs. Meaney began to tell stories. I did not tape-record them that day, but asked to come back another day; before the second visit I found in MUNFLA a paper by her granddaughter, Colleen Meaney, who said that Mrs. Meaney is "well-known throughout the community for her stories and songs" (79-374/3). On the second visit Mrs. Meaney was not well, but insisted on doing the interview anyway; she spoke into the recorder in a clear and authoritative manner that made it apparent that she was accustomed to public performance. A formality of style will be noted even in personal experience narratives like the first one she told on both occasions:

> One evening my girlfriend and I went on the north side of the village to visit another girlfriend. And when our visit was finished we left to come home. And in walking over along the road, a crossroad at the head of the harbour, when we came to the foot of a hill in the road, our way was blocked by a forest of trees, where there was never a tree known to be before. So we were frightened, my girlfriend and I, and we turned and we ran back to the house we had visited. And the old lady said to us, "Don't worry about it," she said, "alright." So she gave us pieces of bread, and she sprinkled holy water over us. She said, "Make the sign of the cross over yourselves and go on. And when you reaches over to where the trees are, throw some pieces of bread. Put a piece of bread in your left hand and throw it with your right hand all around everywhere, and you'll be alright." So while we were throwing the bread, the trees banished [*sic*] and we went on home. And we were frightened when we went home. My mother said to me, she said, "Don't go on the north side anymore," she said, "That's fairies. The fairies lives over there in the hollow of

> that road." And she said, "Ye were in their way, so they had to block your passage until they got through themselves."

This story is included in summarized form in the granddaughter's paper, in which neither she nor Mrs. Meaney mention fairies (79-374/16). But the first time Mrs. Meaney told it to me, she concluded, "Now, what was that but the fairies?" This question begets questions about methodology and the interpretation of archive data. Did the granddaughter know that "fairies" were involved? How important is such an identification, and does it affect the natural text? There is no doubt that some of my informants, kind and obliging people, used the term where it would normally be left unsaid. Such explicitness probably yields a text different in this respect from one that would be given to a native audience with a shared background. On the other hand, it does make clear the nature of an incident that might be missed by listeners unfamiliar with fairy tradition. The decision (or recognition) that "fairies" were involved often depends on familiarity with patterns, language, and motifs, rather than explicit identification. Illusory trees, for example, are almost invariably a fairy manifestation, as in this account from the Southern Shore:

> [The informant's father] had been walking along on the well beaten path and had even seen the lights of Fermeuse when he sensed he was walking on unfamiliar ground. All around him were high trees, the height of which he had never seen before. Then he began to curse and swear and in the madness at having lost his way took off his cap and flung it to the ground. Immediately he was on the correct path again. He picked up his cap and continued on his way. Aunt Eileen was certain he had encountered the fairies who had tried to lead him astray. Something strange had certainly happened to him because he was still cursing and swearing when he entered the house that evening — and he was never known to curse inside his own home. (72-73/9)

2 | *Fairy Forms and Narrative Contexts*

A Bell Island student wrote:

> I asked Uncle Steve [in his 80s] if he knew any fairy stories and he looked at me and said no. Aunt Lizzie, who was behind him, nodded her head to say that he did, and so I told Uncle Steve about a story that I had heard previously. When he saw that maybe I believed he told me that one time he had gone into the gardens and as he was crossing a path that he usually crossed he saw trees that were never there before. The trees were about fifty or sixty feet high. He went down the road a ways and then went back again. He did this three times and the third time he went back, everything was back to normal. He told me that the "Little Johns" must have been there.[2] (FSC71-22/29)

Although illusion, the trees might have a very physical presence: a St. Mary's woman and her son put bread in their pockets because they had to pass a fairy place, but even so they "came upon a forest of great trees which had never been there before and could not have grown up since she had last been there. She was seized with a sudden determination to go through the wood and so she took her son by the hand and found herself climbing over huge fallen tree trunks." When she came out and looked back, the trees were gone (78-274/9). Mrs. Meaney also had an experience in which they presented a tangible barrier:

> Another evening, it was Sunday evening, and there was a young man in the house, he was a cousin of ours, a friend used to come in Sunday afternoon, you know, and evening. And Mother had a cow, you know, and a lovely bell around her neck so you could hear her, know where she was. And she said to us, "Go in there," she says, "in a little ways in the road, and drive home the cow and we'll milk her." So we went. We went — we could hear her down by the river. So we went a little narrow pathway, we walked on a pathway down to the river, and we saw the cow and we sighted her now. We meant to walk down with her, see? So a few minutes after we sighted her the place was blocked with trees,

> we couldn't get to the cow. And there was no trees there any before that. But we couldn't reach her with trees ***. We were frightened. We didn't know what to do. So Henry said, "Better turn back." So we come back up the road and come home to Mother's. And Mother said, "[grumble], ye spent your time sitting around, girl, ye didn't go hunt for the cow at all." We said, "Yes, we hunted for her, we couldn't get to her." I commenced to cry. I was frightened, you know. And a few minutes after, Mother looked out through the window and said, "Here's the cow coming down the side of the river now, coming home." So the only thing she could arrive at, see, *they* wanted a little drop of milk for their supper. [pause] The fairies.

Here, "fairies" is so obviously an afterthought for my benefit that it does not distort the text, and it does not occur in the rest of her narratives at all.

The avoidance of naming has an ambiguous function in that it leaves interpretation open even as it implies fairy influence. In an essay on the fairy traditions of four Riverhead natives who moved to Stephenville (on the west coast) in the 1950s, Wayne Lee observed that:

> . . . the "fairies" are never mentioned by name in the stories. Indeed, no name is given to the supernatural beings at all. The tales are simply recounted and the listener is left to fill in what is left unsaid. This obviously requires experience in the tradition as the same tales told to a more cosmopolitan audience today would make little sense. (82-206/7)

The knowledgeable audience would suspect from the beginning what was involved in "a strange experience of Roland O'Connor" of Placentia as related by his grandson, for Mr. O'Connor and his brother set out hunting on the first of October in 1925 (October 1 is a well-known fairy day). When he left the camp alone, his dog's whining gave a second clue (dogs and horses being sensitive to supernatural presence). He shot two black ducks, and when he went into the tuck (i.e., underbrush) to get them, he could hear "someone talking

2 | *Fairy Forms and Narrative Contexts*

all around," although he could not make out the words even as the sound drew closer. Starting back to the camp:

> jeez, I was surrounded by rocks, cliffs, everything. Well, I traveled all night 'til it got dark and I got beat out and I fired thirteen shots. Ralph never heard them; Ralph fired ten or twelve and I never heard them.

He sat down to wait for morning, and at dawn found himself on the familiar path a mile from camp: "had no more trees, no more nothing":

> Now that is true as God is in Heaven, my son. Them people was there, I thought they was French but they had to be little elfs, that's what they used to be called. Then I never got hungry or never got tired or never got sleepy. There's something in the world other than me and you. (90-57/25-27)

Mr. O'Connor's crossing of some invisible line put him in a primeval landscape, inhabited by a foreign people with a foreign tongue. Respect is generally recommended toward these shadowy neighbours ("guid neighbours" in Scotland) at the untended edges of human space:

> My father said that [fairies] are little people who live mostly in the marsh who wear red stocking caps on their heads. My aunt Ann McCarter said that they have a language of their own, a sort of gibberish. She said nobody said harsh words about them but always called them the little people or the good people. (71-75/11)

Mr. O'Connor's account is the only good evidence I have seen that the fairies were called "elves" (or elfs), but "good people" is common. Mrs. Meaney mentioned it at the end of our second interview, after a story about a lost baby:

> And they couldn't find it. And they were a long time, searched everywhere for the baby. And after, oh, I don't know how many days, the parish priest took over. And he went with the searchers, you see. And they went over to the sort of the edge of the forest

> or something, and the baby was sat out on one of the big limbs of a tree, sat up like a ***. Not a single thing wrong with the baby.
>
> BR: So the fairies didn't always hurt people? The fairies weren't bad?
>
> MM: No. They were always called good people. That was the right name, not fairies, but good people.

A Terrenceville informant "recalls that her grandmother (born 1858) wouldn't even refer to the fairies as fairies because she was afraid she might anger them. She always referred to them as 'good people'" (73-103/38). Pius Power of Southeast Bight in Placentia Bay told Anita Best (in 1976, when she was about to become his daughter-in-law) about a man who was passing a schoolhouse one night; looking in, he saw:

> a little light on every desk, and little fellas sat down to the desk, little children sat down to the desks in school. I suppose that's what they was: all good people, we always called them, we weren't allowed to call them fairies, good people was all we was allowed to call them. (88-14:C7671/m.t.)

"Good people," however, is not always synonymous with the fairies, and fairies are not always "good people." One student's mother told her:

> ... one evening when she was a young girl her mother and her were returning from picking berries when all of a sudden two women dressed in black crossed the road in front of them carrying buckets of water. Mom said that their faces could not be seen — it was almost like they had none. Mom did not recognize the women and asked her mother who they were. Her mother told her to ask no questions, to make the sign of the cross and to walk on as fast as she could towards home without looking back. On reaching home Mom again questioned her mother about the identity of these women. Her mother replied that they were two women who had belonged to the community,

> but died some time ago. She said that God must have permitted them to do their purgatory on earth — this was why they were carrying buckets of water. Her mother referred to such people as "the good people".... Many people in my community also believe strongly in fairies. However, they do not really associate them with dead people. To them fairies represent supernatural elements of evil. There are stories of people who were apprehended by fairies in the not too distant past.[3] (73-169/25-28)

Another student wrote that in Branch, St. Mary's Bay:

> [The informant's grandmother] said that a long time ago, about forty or fifty years, it was believed that a herd of horses that roamed around the place every night was a group of good departed who were allowed back to their home for a period in the guise of horses. Some people believed that these were phantom horses but others believed that they were the horses of the farmers of the places. The ghosts took possession of these horses during the night. People referred to these horses as "the good people." (FSC71-26/53)

The term "good people" and related ideas of Purgatory on earth derive from Irish tradition, as would be expected in an area of heavy Irish settlement like Riverhead.[4] Another Irish importation — although once found in Britain as well — is the idea that the fairies are the angels who fell from heaven in the biblical battle between God and Lucifer.[5] A few examples show how the character of the fairies can range from diabolical to angelic — or include both — within this explanatory framework:

> At the time of the fall of the angels there was a group of angels that sided with neither Lucifer nor St. Michael; they remained neutral and since they didn't want to go to heaven or to hell they were sent to earth as spirits.... [A second informant says] The fairies were supposed to have *been* the fallen angels. They weren't ringleaders among the fallen angels, but merely followers. They

weren't bad enough to go to hell or good enough to go to heaven so they were put on earth as "little people." (73-103/10-11)

[The informant says the fairies or good people] are "people 'as thick as that' who'd tear the earth up if they thought they wouldn't get relieved on the last day. If these people weren't forgave they wouldn't leave a thing standing." But she says now there are too many prayers and masses said to have that happening. (72-95/38)

[The informant] believed the faries [*sic*] were fallen angels thrown out of heaven and they had disappeared when the priest blessed the woods near Flatrock. [She] especially feared the little people on All Souls' Night when they were found in greatest numbers and were up to their most tricks. (72-181/4)

Fairies are bad angels who were cast out of heaven along with the devil. However, they were not quite as bad as the really bad angels and were therefore sent to earth. Only their assurance from the Almighty that they will be the last to enter heaven on Judgement Day prevents them from wreaking havoc on earth. As it is, they only perform minor pranks; however, they are known to have led people astray to be never seen again, and are also known to capture the souls of human beings. (72-73/9)

[The informant] told me "fairies" for them were "outcast angels" who had turned evil and came to take others to join them in their evil ways. Her mother had told her that they would always try to take small children or teenagers, because they were at a more impressionable age and not strong enough to fight off the evil powers. (81-319/6-7)

[The informant referred to fairies as] the fallen angels who were not good enough to be saved, nor bad enough to be lost; she told me that the angels who fell to the sea were mermaids and those who fell to the earth were fairies. (79-340/12)

"All you have to do is look into your Bible and you'll see all that," one informant asserted (64-13:C55/m.t.); another referred both to Genesis and a popular radio show in explaining that the "good people" were "driven out of the Garden of Eden. They were real people once upon a time. And they were unsettled, you see. I would say something like we heard on the open line the other morning, something about discontented spirits" (74-209/n.p.). Michael Fagan asked Austin Breen of Riverhead who the fairies were:

> He replied, "Oh, they're the fallen angels. They rose up against God and He drove them out of Heaven." I asked him why there weren't any fairies today. He said, "I don't know, boy, I suppose they're all gone. Maybe they're after doing penance and got back into Heaven." (FSC67-4/58)

For all its explicitness — or perhaps because of it — the idea of the fallen angels must be treated cautiously as an "explanation" of the fairies. For one thing, it is not known to everyone, even in Catholic communities; for another, it is not usually embedded in narrative, as is the pervasive connection between the fairies and the dead. The exception is the legend type known to folklorists as "The Fairies' Prospect of Salvation";[6] it is rare in Newfoundland, but Angela Mason knew it:

> Down in St. Mary's one time to Mass there was this little foolish fellow. The priest was up on the altar and up he gets and asks the priest would the fallen angels ever be forgiven. The priest said, "Damnation itself chose those words." Right away there was an awful screeching outside the church. See, they were after getting the little boy to ask the question for them, and they were outside waiting for an answer. The priest must of said that without thinking when the little boy interrupted him or something.
>
> Now there was a strange priest in to St. Mary's one Sunday, and he was saying Mass, and this little boy asked the same question again. "God's mercy is worth waiting for," the priest said. There was no screeching that day. (67-4B/4-5)

A version from Carbonear reflects the distinct tendency in that area to equate the fairies with "devils":

> On Sunday afternoons people would go for walks, visiting their friends and maybe stay for supper. If they did they went home about ten P.M. One Sunday night Paul Cook, one of the local guys around home, on his way home tripped and fell. When he did he said, "God save us!" A man appeared and said, "When is he going to save us?" Paul was really scared and didn't know what to say. This man said he would be in the same place at the same time the next evening and Paul had better come with the answer. Paul went home and told his folks about what happened. It didn't take long for the word to get around and since no one had an answer they told Paul to go and see the Bishop. He did, and the Bishop told him to go back and take some holy water with him and sprinkle it around into a circle and stand in the circle. If it was a good devil it would come inside the circle, but if it was a bad devil it would stay outside the circle. The Bishop also told Paul to say, "When God is pleased." So he went back again, made a circle with holy water, got in and waited. When the man appeared he asked the same question, "When is He going to save us?" Paul answered, "When God is pleased." The man went off in a ball of fire. (71-75/7-8)

In a third version (from Western Bay), the disappointed stranger plummets into the sea in a ball of fire, his flaming exit the only clue to his infernal identity (76-137/10-12).

Some variations on the "fallen angels" shade into the association with the dead:

> The fairies were souls hanging between heaven and earth. They don't have a place to go. It wasn't decided, or they didn't know, if they would be going to heaven or hell. (71-121/7)

... the people of the community always felt that fairies were cast away souls from heaven. (FSC74-117/50)

[The informant] believed that fairies were little children who had died but were too good to go to hell and too bad to go to heaven. (72-181/13)

Such misleadingly neat statements belie the difficulty, if not impossibility, of getting a "definition" of the fairies from animated natural context. The following conversation among informants from Colinet, St. Mary's Bay (transcribed by the collector), illustrates this difficulty; it also shows how participants in the same discussion may have quite different ideas, and while one might be specific about the distinctions between supernatural figures, another will be unconcerned with niceties of nomenclature:

Mrs. S: There used to be fairies on the go, you know, one time. Little people they calls them.

Paddy: Yes, one time, the darbies, they used to call them. Darbies, mummers. They dress up, you know, go around and blacken you and everything. Torches on sticks.

Interviewer: This was during Christmas, wasn't it?

Paddy: Yeah, and they were in a house one night — no, it wasn't, they were out around in the cold, you know, watching for them. They didn't want to be caught, see, and 'twas no sign. It was so cold, so they said they'd go in to a — our uncle was telling me that. And he said, he said, "We'll go to some house now for a game of cards and keep watch." So they went into a house and there was a girl there and I don't know if she was a serving girl or one of the girls around the house, but they got her watching. They told her to go out a scattered time and have a look; if she see any sign of the mummers coming, come and tell them and they'd all get out and run. She got out. So by and by she hears them coming, they come down the back of the meadow. She hear the fences busting and cracking, and she ran to sing out to tell them that they were coming. And they were gaining on her so fast that she, see, she couldn't do it and when she got to the door they were nearly on top of her and she sung out, "Darbies." And as quick as that, they said, you could hear the big ruption. They trampled her in the door, flattened her out, and she was black as tar. And the whole house, our uncle said, full her up. Great big long white feathers was full from the floor right up to the ceiling, he said. And a cold breeze going through the house, frightening everyone to death, and about two seconds everyone was gone. And when they went out she was — and her face and eyes and that flattened right out. And she was all black in the face.

Chris: She was dead, was she?

Paddy: Yeah, they trampled on her, see...

Interviewer: Were they ghosts or were they real people? Were they ghosts?

Paddy: Oh, yeah, they were ghosts. They had darbies. They were dead, they were people, now, who used to be in the darbies years ago. And they were dead, see. Big long paws [?], he said. The great big long white feathers about that length, he said, and it was right from the floor, he said, right, right, right. And they'd be in the house busting and cracking, the walls cracking and everything. And he said about two seconds and all, everything was gone and when they went out she was dead on doorstep.

Mrs. S: I heard that too and I forgot about it. They used to be fairies.

Paddy: Yes, that's what they called them.

Mrs. S: And they calls them good people, you know. They were bad angels cast out of heaven. And our aunt said that one time someone she knew —

Paddy: The priest said that they're so plentiful that they'll destroy this world only for they want to get forgiveness.

Mrs. S: They're expecting to get forgiveness on the last day.

Paddy: Forgiveness on the last day, only for that they'd destroy everyone.

Interviewer: Oh, so they're actually good. They're in Purgatory, I suppose.

Mrs. S: But our aunt used to tell us all about them.

Paddy: And they say there's some good more than bad. There's some that'd harm you.

Chris: But them ones that killed the girl weren't good.

Mrs. S: No, they couldn't have been good, no.

Paddy: They didn't want her… [reiterates]

Mrs. S: I wouldn't call them fairies. I'd call them the real bad spirits, you know.

Chris: But these fairies are supposed to be angels, are they? That are looking to get forgiveness?

Mrs. S: Yeah, they're bad angels cast out of heaven but they're expecting to get forgiveness on the last day so they try not to affect anybody. [She finally gets to tell her story.] (81-207/89-95)

The linkage of mummers and fairies is significant for the thesis that the fairies are in essence strangers. In "Mummers and Strangers in Northern Newfoundland," Melvin Firestone suggests that mummers become temporary strangers, not only through disguise but by the uninhibited and unpredictable behaviour in which they indulge until their identity is revealed (72). The term "darbies" forms a conceptual bridge between mummers and fairies, for "darby" can denote a mummer — in Colliers one did not go mummering or janneying but "darbying" (67-31:C356) — or a supernatural figure: "If you go out tonight the boo-darby will carry you away" (FSC67-5F/19). "Janny," pronounced much like "Johnnie," is another mummer/fairy/bogey link, as in "Littlejohns" mentioned earlier and the Bishops' Cove jannies' query. "Any little jannies in tonight?" (70-25/78). One bedtime warning to children was "Johnny's coming," Johnny being "the sandman" (67-31:C370/10-11), and the threat that the mummers would carry away naughty children is widely reported. So Paddy's equations are logical, if uncommon. In any case, he clearly regards the register of frightening figures — mummers, fairies, ghosts, the dead — as interchangeable, while Mrs. S. is more discriminating about who is who.

In contrast to Paddy's wild inclusiveness is the distinction observed by a Branch student:

> I had heard many ghost stories from older people but I was unfamiliar with fairy stories. They are never told as ghost stories are — I never heard any fairy stories until I started collecting information for this course. (FSC71-26/45)

Wayne Lee, however, found just the opposite:

> The borderline between fairies and ghosts or other spirits is not well defined, as exemplified by the story of "Liz's Light," a phenomenon with similar characteristics to "Jackie the Lantern" [which is "generally ascribed to the fairies"] but with a very different explanation. "Liz's Light" supposedly presaged an easterly wind and was the spirit of "Liz" who was lost in an easterly storm at the mouth of the harbour.... One can cross the border from fairy tales completely and examine the story of the ghost ship that comes into Point le Haye harbour every Christmas Eve carrying the spirits of those who drowned in a storm as they were coming home for Christmas. When questioned about this tale people will respond that it has nothing to do with fairies although they are prone to jump from a "fairy" story to a "ghost" story without making any overt distinction. (82-206/11)

This narrative fluidity and the elasticity of the concept of "fairies" would be important tools for the innovative narrator, and Fagan and Lee noted elements of invention and competition in the telling of fairy stories in Riverhead. Lee's informants told him that:

> not everyone told them. At any gathering which constituted a public performance (as opposed to private culture) one person was generally acknowledged to be the teller of fairy tales and the telling of the tale was usually preceded by a period of prompting or "coaxing." Those rare instances when several tale tellers were present in the same context were to be relished as they invariably tried to outdo one another — much to the delight of the assembled audience. (82-206/13)

Fagan found people reluctant to talk of sea and fishing lore:

> In the area of the supernatural, however, if someone knows, or can invent a ghost or fairy story, or otherwise motivate an audience, he will get a host of such tales, one a little better than the other. This is by far the most popular topic of folktales, and some people rather specialize in the bearing of this body of tradition, for example, Angela Mason. (67-4F/4-5)

Mrs. Mason, he said, "takes a great pride in her knowledge of the old traditions" (67-4B/2); this pride is mirrored in her repertoire, in which knowledge and appropriate conduct are critical to the outcome of each narrative. The fairies in her "Ten Tales" manifest themselves so variously that recognizing them is usually the crux; sad fates await those who fail to do so, while those who realize with whom they are dealing and act accordingly escape harm. A couple, surrounded by a "flock of horses" that snapped at the baby and at the loaves of bread they were carrying, didn't have the sense to give "them" some of the bread, and the baby was dead when they got home; Bill Biggs knew better than to disturb the cats that filled a shack on the barrens where he was spending the night, even when "they'd look at each other and nod"; John Bruce complied with a strange man's request that he restore some land he was clearing to its original state, and was rewarded by the instant doubling of his stock of cattle.

John Bruce's gift is unusual, for fairy largesse is generally not to be trusted. Pius Power described a woman lured astray by a lovely kettle, "shining like gold" — "That's how they went astray, people did get astray, some foolish thing like that they went for, got off the path" (88-14:C7671/m.t.). The hero of Mrs. Mason's "Brass Castle" was tempted with much-needed household goods:

> This Dalton fellow up to the Beach, and a fine, real big man he was. This strange fellow came up to him one day and told him about the Brass Castle down on the Harbour Point. Now he heard tell of it before this you know. He told him they had one chance to get up out of the ground and escape, and that was if someone living would go down and take something from them. He told him they had everything, and he could take whatever he wanted. But if he decided he wouldn't take anything, he promised him nothing would happen to him.
>
> He went with this fellow anyway. They went down this long stairs and he showed him all through the castle. In one place there was big long tables all set out with all kinds of food, there where all the food used to be stored up, and clothes, and fishing gear, and in one place all those real lovely ladies were sittin' around with their sewing baskets. These weren't very good times, and he needed a lot of this stuff, but he didn't touch a thing. When he got back to the foot of the stairs and they saw he wasn't going to take anything, they all turned on him. But this fellow that made the bargain with him gave him a ram-rod to keep them off. They twisted the ram-rod right around and around his arm, but he got away.
>
> Some of the Daltons up to the Beach still have the ramrod, all bent up like it was. I saw it one time I was up there a nice bit ago.

> You know how big and strong the Daltons are, and sensible too. This was their mistake, picking a man like that. If they had of picked a foolish fellow he'd do what they wanted. (67-4B/19-22)

This is a widespread narrative type represented in North American oral tradition only in texts from Angela Mason and Mrs. Meaney.[7] The version Mrs. Meaney dictated to her granddaughter sounds as if it comes from a storybook, and indeed the singularity and elaborateness of the whole Riverhead repertoire could well owe something to a printed source.[8] "My grandmother told me that she knew another interesting story called 'The Twisted Ramrod,'" Colleen Meaney wrote. "She claims that it is true but I find it rather hard to believe. Anyway here it is as she told it to me":

> It was a crisp winter's day as a certain man began his daily walk to the home of a friend. The man had not gone far when he was brought to a stop by a stranger. The man who had appeared so suddenly, as if from nowhere, was about twenty years old and most fashionably dressed. The stranger spoke in a deep husky voice commanding the man to be on the Point the following day at a specific hour. There he would find a cluster of trees which he was to push open.
>
> On the next morning the man did as he had been asked and walked toward the appointed place. When he arrived he found a few young fir trees which he slowly separated. To his surprise there was the young stranger standing at the top of a staircase. The stranger silently opened a gigantic wooden door and led the startled man deep down into an underground chamber. The first room which they entered was illuminated with brightly coloured lights. This room had the appearance of a dining hall. It was decorated from side to side with long tables. Upon the delicate lace tablecloths stood elaborate candlesticks and silverware.
>
> While the two men were walking along a narrow corridor the stranger noticed that his companion was carrying a ramrod. But

of this the stranger said nothing. On and on the two men walked, along the dimly lit passage, until they reached a gigantic living room. Deep, soft carpets covered the floor and beautiful furniture of every form was to be found there. Again the stranger never mentioned the ramrod and here, as in the first room, the terrified man laid his hand upon nothing, but silently followed the stranger into another passageway.

The third room which the men entered was a little different from the others. For here, shiny counters lined the walls and behind these counters stood many silent young men, each displaying different merchandise. Everything from thimbles to rich silks were arranged before the men. The poor man was terrified by this time and refused to take anything but turned quickly and left.

Through the door he ran, down the passage to the living room, past that to the dining hall and up the stairs. When the man found himself again in the open air he paused to catch his breath. He felt a sharp pain in his arm. He was bewildered to find that the ramrod which he had been carrying was wound tightly around his arm and could be removed only by filing it off. It was later discovered that the men in the underground cave were enchanted. If the man had taken as much as a thimble, these men would have been freed. The ramrod had been wound around his arm as punishment for not freeing the enchanted people. (79-374/16-19)

Mrs. Meaney may have memorized this from a written text, or she may have been emulating literary style (she recites the history of the community in a similar manner). When I tried to ask her about "Twisted Ramrod," she said she did not know anything like it, but I do not know whether she had forgotten it or I was unable to make myself understood. Certainly Mrs. Meaney's songbooks attest to a remarkable memory, at least until quite recently. These are scrapbooks in which she has written the texts of about eighty songs, mostly broadside ballads and sentimental songs of many stanzas, which

Mrs. Meaney says represent only a fraction of those she used to sing; she could start at three in the afternoon and not be finished the next morning. The songbooks show the high degree of literacy Mrs. Meaney attained for one with little formal education, and the fondness and retentive memory for the formal and poetic language that characterizes her fairy narratives.[9]

For all their similarity, Mrs. Mason's and Mrs. Meaney's texts differ on one crucial point: in "Brass Castle," it was a good thing that the underground people were not freed, but in "Twisted Ramrod" the visitor is "punished" (it is not clear by whom) for not freeing them. The same variation is found in the European type: in some versions the hero is scorned for his failure to release the captives, but in others he did the right thing by not doing so.[10] The variation in "Brass Castle" and "Twisted Ramrod" also bears the narrator's personal stamp. Mrs. Mason's hero displays the nerve and perspicacity central to almost all her tales, including one about herself:

> When Annie's mother died . . . I went over and took Annie and reared her. A little spell after she died I used to hear this noise every night, 'twas her poor mother, you know. I used to hear the stairs squeaking, and like someone walked into the room. When I heard her coming in the room one night, I got up and took Annie out of the crib. I held her out in my arms and said, "Here she is now, if you want her, take her. If you don't, then don't come back here any more, 'cause if you do I'm going to take her back to the dirt and poverty I found her in over there on the other side." And I promise you she never came back either. (FSC67-4G/68)

In contrast to the stalwart Dalton (and the authoritative Mrs. Mason), Mrs. Meaney's hero is "frightened," like her other protagonists and herself in her own fairy encounters. He flees because he is terrified, not because he is pursued.

Tales of captivity and escape reveal the fundamentally dangerous nature of the human/fairy relationship. They often include a test or contest, as in a Riverhead story of a "servant girl" who was "surrounded by small little men" while hunting a cow one evening. One demands that she answer the question, "What is a woman's secret?" She answers, "something she don't know," and is released, but dies shortly afterwards (Q68-32/4-5).[11] Sometimes the test takes the form of a physical struggle, as in the story of "Liz's Point." According to Mrs. Mason:

> This girl Liz, Fagan I believe her last name was, I'm not sure about that. She's none of yere crowd, anyway. The fairies took her. She was gone about three months, I suppose. They were having a time in one of the houses down in St. Mary's this night. Her brother was there. You know how the houses used to be built in them days, with the big piece built on the back downstairs. This is where they were having the shindy. The brother looked out through the door and here she was. There were two doors in this place, one in each end. The brother went out through the other door and came up behind her and grabbed her. All of a sudden there was I suppose thirty or forty fairies all around her and grabbing at her, trying to pull her away. He was trying to get her inside; she'd be safe then. He got so mad that he cursed on them. With the same she slipped out of his arms and away she went. This was the last chance she got to get back, but he cursed them and that was the end of that. They used to see her after that, sitting on a rock over on Liz's Point. That's how it got the name. (67-4B/6-8)

The back section of the house was probably a linhay, a place where rough work was done and not a fully domesticated space; hence, perhaps, the appearance there of Liz and the fairies. In a version from Austin Breen, Liz appears in the kitchen door but comes no further into the human domain:

> Liz Fagan, who lived down at the Graven Bank (shown on maps as Graven Beach), was missing for two or three months. The fairies had her. One day she appeared in the kitchen door. "O now I have you," her mother said. "No you haven't, Mother," she said, "not now or ever." If she didn't speak she'd get her. She chased her out the landwash as far as Liz's Point, that's where she lost her. People used to see her there, sitting on a rock, late in the evening.[12] (FSC67-4/61)

2 | *Fairy Forms and Narrative Contexts*

Liz's lingering fate on the fringe of the community, untouchable as if behind glass, mirrors the everyday state between the neighbouring but separate worlds. The occasional breach of barrier and the incursions of the inhabitants into one another's worlds form the dramatic nucleus of fairy narratives. Some people cross the bounds with impunity; Mrs. Meaney tells about a man who fared well among the fairies, perhaps because the elegant tea party of which he partook was in his own territory. The "king and queen" were even there the first time Mrs. Meaney told it; this is her second version of what I shall call "Night Kitchen":

> This young man, he used to banish [*sic*] from home, you know, and they wouldn't know where he was gone. He'd be gone for a couple of days and nights, and they wouldn't know where he'd be gone, see? So, his brother and his parents used to hear some goings-on down in the kitchen at night, see? Table, light, table and dishes, and everything on the go. So he determined, the older brother determined to watch. So one night he heard a noise; he got out of his bed and he came down. And he only had an underpants on. And when he came down, his brother, who was with the company, his brother was so offended because he should appear among all those grand ladies they had in their crowd in his underpants, that he, he threw a cup belonged to his mother's china set which they were using; he threw it at him, and broke a piece out of the cup. And the piece that came out of the cup struck the brother in the leg. And the brother went away to bed, well, he went almost distracted with the pain. And the leg got bad, got sore and got bad, and he nearly lost his leg. And they wouldn't believe him, nobody believed him. So they went, he went over to the cupboard and took down the dishes. And there was one of his mother's cups broken with a piece out of the side of it. The piece was there, they could fit it into it. [They could fit the piece that came out of the brother's leg into the cup.] You don't believe that, do you?[13]

Marie Meaney

I did not know how to answer that! The truant brother's presence among the fairies, with whom he is literally quite at home, is extraordinary, for usually fairy revels are depicted as taking place in woods and bogs, far removed from the prosaic warmth of the domestic sphere. A Bell Island man claimed to have had a grand time in the woods with "a whole pile of little people" who had "food and beer, and danced and played the accordion" (81-55/4-6; also 72-97:C1286/16-17); another man was forced to play the accordion for them while they danced in the woods above Mt. Scio Road in St. John's (FSC74-1/13). "Night Kitchen" confounds the usual boundaries and expectations when the missing man's whereabouts are discovered at the very centre of the home. There he treats himself as a stranger, using the fine china normally reserved for guests or holidays ("Would you like a mug or a cup?" those offered tea in Newfoundland homes are asked). The nosy brother's uncouth intrusion is rewarded in kind by the shaft of a teacup, which in keeping with the reversals and twists of fairy metaphor has changed from a tool of gracious hospitality to one of aggressive injury.

Several accounts in MUNFLA describe nocturnal household arrangements for the fairies. An informant from Red Island, Placentia Bay, said:

> They believed in the fairies like anything. This old woman said that just between sunset and dark you'd hear the fairies chattering. She'd light a big fire to make a big smoke. This was old Mrs. Lizzie Norman, now, and she believed it with all her life. She'd light the big fire, put a cross on all the windows. She said the smoke used to banish them, because in the old days they used to use smoke as some kind of incense and she believed there was a blessedness in the smoke that would banish them. She often told me, "The fairies were here last night, girl, don't go out after dark," or, "Be sure and go home before dark, don't be here when the dark comes." I'd be foolish enough to believe her and kill myself getting home before the sun went down behind the hill. I'd watch that sun like anything, so I could judge how long I had left before taking off for home. [Another] old woman, an old Mrs. Mulrooney, used to live alone, and every night before she went to bed she'd make in a big fire, put all the chairs around the stove, leave the door unlocked, put bread, water, whatever she had on the table, and go to bed. This way, if the fairies came in, they could sit on the chair and warm themselves, get a bite to eat, and wouldn't bother her. She said if you're good to the fairies they won't bother you. (79-435/38-39)

Propitiation is mentioned in a report from another Placentia Bay island:

> Up to the time they left Merasheen about eight years ago, [the informant's] wife would put a saucer of milk outdoors for the fairies before going to bed every night without fail. The fairies supposedly fed on this and thus their friendship was ensured. (FSC69-8/43)

Strange Terrain

One student, comparing the fairy traditions of her childhood in Trinity Bay and on the Southern Shore with the Irish traditions described by Conrad Arensberg, remarked that she never saw food and water left out for the fairies — only water or milk (67-12D/8).[14]

"It is very difficult to draw a clear line of demarcation between the kingdom of the dead and the fairy world in Irish popular belief," Sean Ó'Suilleabhain writes, "stories of persons who reappear after death are inextricably confused with tales of the fairies" (*Handbook* 450). The same is true of Newfoundland, where fairy lore, death customs, concepts of the soul and spirits, and revenant (ghost) stories converge in a complex of ideas and motifs that have an underlying consonance rather than an explicit rationale. Food or water might be set out for the dead as well as the fairies, as by a Riverhead woman who would leave a glass of water in the kitchen for her deceased husband every night: "Every morning the water was gone and the glass turned upside down on the table" (FSC67-4/74). It might be suspected that some seemingly "dead" people had been taken by the fairies; one informant knew a Bell Island woman who "had a son who died, but everyone knew he had become a fairy because every night she left bread and tea for him and the next morning it was gone" (72-181/12). Pius Power told (in 1976) about a woman who "died" and was buried but who appeared in the kitchen several midnights afterwards getting water, bread, and molasses. On the third night her husband kept vigil, and she explained to him that she had been taken by the good people while bringing in clothes from the line. She had to eat, she said, but the next night would be her last; after that she would be "gone, and gone forever" unless he would wait at the gate, which she would be the "last to go through," and grab her. "You can't touch me now," she said, "because there's hundreds [hundreds of fairies around her]." The husband got her, although she "tore him up." Later the priest restored her to health, and when they dug up the grave they found a broom in the coffin (88-14:C7671/m.t.).[15]

The provision of food, furniture, or other amenities for the "normal" dead was usually associated with certain times, such as the period just after death, when the table might be laid in the event of their return (FSC67-4/72). A cup of water and bread were left out on All Souls' Night (variously identified by students as November 1 and 2), said a Bell Island informant, because "it was good to have something on the table for the dead person if he returned to the house that night" (FSC73-99/27). On the same night in King's Cove, Bonavista Bay, candles were placed in the windows "to guide the wandering souls that may pass by," and in neighbouring Keels "people would leave their doors unlocked and they would put knitted articles, such as socks and mittens, on the kitchen table for the souls to pick up if they happen to pass that way" (FSC73-98/27). A Branch collector wrote that the practice of putting chairs out "for the departed in your family" during November, the "month of the holy souls," had mostly died out by 1970, but:

> A friend of mine spent a night with her great-aunt and great-uncle just a few weeks ago. She said that when they were going to bed her aunt put out two chairs in front of the stove. When my friend asked her why she did this, she said that they were for her da and her ma — both dead over forty years. (FSC71-26/38)

Those bereaved by an unexpected death might extend such arrangements beyond the prescribed times, and adapt them to their particular circumstances. The mother of a man who fell over a cliff while hunting refused to disturb a chair he had knocked over when he left the house earlier that day. Finally she was persuaded to pick it up:

> Still she regarded it as her son's chair and would allow no other person to sit on it. When my brother taught in Point Lance, the chair was standing in a small alcove where the stove was situated. If anyone made as if to sit on this chair — usually a stranger like my brother, for the people of the community knew and understood — she would ask them to sit somewhere else.... This old woman is still alive but I don't know if she still expects her son to return and use his chair during the night as she did then. (FSC71-26/36)

When a Placentia man drowned while returning drunk from the christening of twins, his mother, "a psychic," put a curse on the twins (eventually fulfilled) that they too would drown. "In the meantime, every night when the clock struck twelve Mattie would fill up the kitchen stove, send everyone to bed and set a chair for Jim, who would come in soaking wet and get warm by the fire which Mattie had lit" (72-60/29).

These fond mothers cannot be considered typical; for one thing, most people devoutly wished *not* to entertain any spirits. Some people in Branch would overturn the chairs the night after a burial "so that if the spirit returned it couldn't sit on them; this would cause the spirit to leave and return no more" (FSC80-315/*); on All Souls' Night in Deer Lake, "it was unlucky to open the doors because wandering souls were trying to get in" (FSC84-283B/*). The offer of food, drink, or seating should probably be viewed less as a welcoming than an attempt to placate and confine by granting a specific time for the spirits' use. Still, most death custom — folk and official — is informed by the refusal to accept death as final. The otherworld of fairy tradition provides an alternative from which one might even return.

Material comforts proffered the dead (or fairies) match the almost tangible reality accorded a person's soul or spirit, envisioned especially graphically on its separation from the body at death. The interests of good and evil hovered about the deathbed awaiting the event. Fagan wrote:

> It is very important that a dying person have a blessed candle in his hand when death finally overcomes him. The blessed candle will protect the dying person from the devil, who will make a final bid for his soul during the last moments of existence. (FSC67-4/4)

The banshee sometimes heralded the event. One student, describing "the bangree" [*sic*], wrote, "as soon as the blessed candle was lit or the rosary started, a bunch of weird-looking spirits appeared outside the window and started screeching, moaning and groaning while the old man or old woman was dying. This as far as the old people were concerned years ago was expected to happen and no fear accompanied these spirits" (77-168/28). In Branch, some people sitting up with a sick woman heard "the banchee [*sic*] cry":

> They heard voices, too, saying, "Oh my, what'll we do? Oh my, what'll we do?" This was "the good people" (or ghosts of the good dead) coming for Mrs. Moon. (FSC71-26/35)

Mrs. Meaney tells about two men who are summoned to their sister's deathbed by "the bibe," persistent voices calling, "we are coming," and "hurry, hurry" (79-374/15-16).[16] In Mobile, on the Southern Shore, a child who was lost overnight on a reputed fairy marsh died a week later:

> While the child was dying cries and lights could be heard and seen all around the house. People said that these noises were the fairies waiting for him to die, so that they could take him back to the marsh with them. (FSC73-157/3)

Upon death, the soul required release from the room, although Fagan gives an account suggesting that this was not necessarily common knowledge:

> When a person dies, the spirit immediately departs. According to my informant, it is very important that the spirit be given an immediate means of escape from the sick-room. He (my informant) promised an elderly lady who lived with him that "as soon as the life went out of her" he would open the window to let her soul out. However, she became suddenly worse, and died while he was out fishing. The other members of the family didn't know anything about "letting out the soul," and it remained in the room for many months. Several months after her death, my informant acquired a serious infection in his knee. There was no apparent cause for the infection, but he later learned that his family had not opened the window to let the soul out. He then understood perfectly. He had broken his promise with the old lady, and she "had given him the nip."[17] (FSC67-4/3)

A St. Mary's student described not only the release of the soul from the house but its routine re-admittance:

> When Hannah's mother died [*c.* 1962] they immediately rushed to open the doors and windows of the house to allow the spirit an exit. In accordance with family tradition, when her mother was buried she would, and still does to this day, open the door every night at ten o'clock to allow her mother's spirit in to say prayers before retiring for the evening. (FSC73-95/10)

The safety of the soul was not exclusively a Catholic concern. A collector from (Protestant) Bishop's Cove said although it is now done as a "sign of respect," the blinds used to be drawn after a death to keep out "evil spirits" (FSC70-25/39). In nearby Bryant's Cove, a Protestant informant said that the person who washed and dressed a dead body had to sit with it "to guard against evil spirits entering the body thus preventing the ghost or soul ever reaching heaven" (75-5/n.p.). Precautions were necessary even at the gravesite. The late Michael Hayes of St. Thomas said that after a coffin was lowered into the grave, the ropes were cut so that the fairies or "bad people" could not get at the body.[18]

The repose of the dead was desired not only for the sake of the deceased but for the living, and given the great mobility of souls and spirits, measures to speed them on their way or keep them in the grave were crucial. Sometimes the dead retained a jealous interest in their earthly affairs. A man who promised his wife on her deathbed that he would not marry again was crossing an area between Branch and Point Lance known as "a haven for fairies and other unexplainable supernatural phenomena" on his way to his second wedding; he was found dead, his belt wound around his neck and the contents of his knapsack, including the dress for the bride, strewn about: "Some people believe that the look of horror [on his face] was because of the sight of his dead wife ... other people maintain that it was the fairies who attacked and killed the man because of his failure to keep the promise he made to his dead wife" (79-108/1-4). The latter opinion makes the fairies arbiters of human behaviour, although not in favour of the norms of the living — which would expect a widower to remarry — but in vindication of the "betrayed" dead wife. (Perhaps, having died young, she was among them.)

With all the things that might keep a person from "resting" — unfinished business, Purgatorial sentences on earth, interference by fairies or the devil at death, inadequate deathbed services — it is not surprising that there is a vast anonymous body of souls about, neither in the everyday world nor quite out of it. To their number can be added those taken by the fairies, like Liz of Liz's Point or Margaret Bursey:

> Mrs. Margaret Bursey, the fairies came and took her. They brought her back when she was dead. I often heard old Maurice talking about things she used to do. Old Margaret was a real fairy alright. She was sick in bed for a long time. She was paralyzed and everything. One day her brother was up in Riverhead. When he went back Margaret was on her mattress out in the yard dead. She looked right different — just like her real self. (FSC67-4G/64)

Infants and small children are especially vulnerable to theft. Mrs. Meaney said:

> They [fairies] used to take the babies, long ago you know, that babies would banish, banish [sic] out of the crib, or out of the bed or somewhere. And the mother would hear the baby screech, screech, and screech, and when she come in to check on the baby's crib, 'twas a real old ugly old effigy was in the crib, an ugly old baby, and her lovely baby was gone. So all she could do was mind the baby. She minded that baby for a long time. And after awhile, the baby got sick, the ugly old baby got sick or something and died. And when it died, they laid it out for burial, and it was the most beautiful baby that ever was looked on. You see, her own baby was brought back to her and they took the old effigy away. See? The baby died, the baby died and they brought it back to the mother. But it was beautiful. And the one in the cot changed as quick as that! [pause] I don't know if that ever happened or not, but it was told to me....

Mrs. Mason explained to Fagan that:

> If someone became suddenly ill, or suddenly began acting in a peculiar manner, it was often suspected that they had been taken by the fairies. (Nobody knows why the fairies might want to capture a human being.) The person was supposed to be stolen away, and a fairy, in the semblance of the individual, left in his place. To find out if such a transfer had actually occurred, a shovel was heated until it became red, and then brought near the body of the victim. If he were a fairy, he would show violent reaction or hastily retreat. The fairies, knowing then that their plot had been discovered, would soon return the person. (FSC67-4G/59)

Mrs. Mason also gave an example of the shovel test:

> My mother, you know, she was from the Goulds. The people who lived next door — that's in the Goulds — had a baby boy, and he was swapped. He was only just a little baby but he was starting to look just like an old man. The woman's brother used to live there with them too. He kept telling her the baby was swapped, and wanted to redden the shovel and throw him out, but she wouldn't hear of it. One day she was in town and there was nobody home only this brother and the baby. This was his chance. He reddened the shovel in the fireplace and brought it to the side of the crib. Just as he did the baby flew right up out of the crib and out through the door, and he chasing it with the shovel. When he came back the real baby was back in the crib. (67-4B/16-17)

Changeling narratives, with their themes of loss and potential violence, are among the most difficult of fairy traditions to assess for meaning and function. They abound in MUNFLA, but are almost invariably at a further remove from informants than other types; there are no first-hand accounts from someone who heated a shovel, for instance, as there are hundreds from people who saw the fairies or were led astray by them. However, the more distant the event, the more graphic it seems to become. Wayne Lee's Stephenville informants, away from Riverhead for over thirty years, had a changeling story beside which those of Mrs. Meaney and Mrs. Mason pale:

> Alice Ryan was born a "nice child" but at two or three weeks of age got "cross and ugly" and showed behavior inconsistent with a child of that age, for example, responding to adults.[19] Mrs. Cook was an old woman who lived in Mussel Pond [now O'Donnell's], a community some distance removed from Riverhead, and the acknowledged authority on supernatural events. Three people from the community of Riverhead set out on the considerable journey cross-country to eventually arrive at Mrs. Cook's house with the baby and find three cups of tea waiting for them. Mrs. Cook, when presented with the child, said, "Give me that!," threw the child in the bedroom, put a shovel in the stove to heat and invited her three visitors to sit down to tea. When tea was finished and the shovel was red hot, Mrs. Cook went into the bedroom from which emerged loud cries and shrieking and a noise "such as the side was coming out of the house." Then, after a short period of quiet, Mrs. Cook emerged with a "cute" baby to announce that all was well. (82-206/6-7)

Another vivid account comes from an informant who in the 1930s heard it from his parents, who said it happened around 1900:

> A St. Mary's Bay woman, Mrs. Morris from Mt. Carmel, had a thirteen-year-old son who had never walked. She had heard about a Mr. Kelly from Holyrood who was the seventh son of a seventh son. Now it is believed by the people of the communities of St. Mary's Bay that the seventh son of a seventh son is supposed to have special powers. Mr. Kelly was supposed to have special powers to cure. People claimed that Mr. Kelly was a fairy. When he was a young man he had disappeared into the wood for three months. Now, at this time, he was an old, humpbacked man.

However, Mrs. Morris sent for him. When Mr. Kelly arrived at Mrs. Morris's, he held up his hand and said, "Jump up, you little bugger, and walk." The boy, Mike, did so, and was immediately cured.

Now, a Mrs. Haynes from Mitchell's Brook many years before this, had a tragic experience (believed to be around the 1880s). She had gone to the clothesline to hang out her clothes, and upon returning found her baby missing and another one in its place. She knew it was not her child for it looked deformed and its facial features were like those of an old man.

Now twenty-seven or twenty-eight years later she heard of Mr. Kelly coming to Mt. Carmel so she sent for him. (This was after the time that Mr. Kelly had cured Mrs. Morris's son.) Mrs. Haynes wanted to get him to return her own son, or man he would be by now.

When Mr. Kelly entered the home of Mrs. Haynes, the boy, Teddy, crouched on the woodbox snarling at him. Mr. Kelly said, "Shut up, you king of the fairies." Mrs. Haynes couldn't believe this, she said, "My goodness, Mr. Kelly, don't tell me he is a fairy?" Then she begged him to get her own son back.

Mr. Kelly could not do this, for he said if he did return her son, his own army of fairies would come and kill him. However, there was one way she could get him back but for Mrs. Haynes's own sake she would have to get someone else to do this for her.

He said if you redden a shovel in fire and stand him (Teddy) on the shovel and throw him over the left shoulder, she would get her own son back. Mrs. Haynes didn't have the heart to put Teddy through this ordeal for she had grown attached to him.

Mrs. Haynes questioned how she was to know Teddy was a fairy for she somehow doubted Mr. Kelly's word for it. Mr. Kelly told her to dig Teddy up thirteen months after he was buried and there would be a broom in his coffin. No one ever did dig the body up but it wasn't very long after this incident that Teddy died. (74-114/51-54)

Time and distance, which might be expected to obscure narrative features such as detail and dialogue, seem to have aided rather than impaired these performances (which would probably contain even more detail if they were verbatim rather than summarized texts). Perhaps distance affords the narrator greater freedom on potentially discreditable matters; it is easier to impute questionable behaviour to people in other places and other times than to one's neighbours, the spatial equivalent to the temporal proposition that "everyone used to believe in fairies" being "everyone in x believes (or believed) in fairies." It seems paradoxical that generalization should lead to concreteness in narrative, and that the removal of the constraints of immediate reality should allow for the construction of a more "realistic" narrative, but the principle of increasing elaboration over time and space may be particularly applicable to supernatural material.[20] Distance likely lent enchantment to Mrs. Cook's and Mr. Kelly's powers as well (the same may be said of priests, who were often itinerant, not resident, figures in outport society).[21]

In Riverhead, Mrs. Meaney herself was "well known for her many old cures," according to her granddaughter, and even in 1979 people still went to her for "advice and cures" (79-374/13,22). She may well have known about reddened shovels and about Alice Ryan, but they are, after all, hardly edifying tales to offer an inquiring stranger. Reticence on sensitive subjects, together with the dynamics of distance and distancing, complicates the question of how changeling traditions functioned. Did people really think Margaret Bursey was a fairy, or was it a figure of speech? Did anyone really ever take a hot shovel to a child, thinking there was a fairy in its place? Or might the idea have the opposite effect, as suggested by a Bell Island student who wrote, "It was widely thought that mongoloids were children which the fairies had left in a home in place of the people's own child. Because all mongoloids look much alike, it was said they were the feeble work of the fairies and usually they were treated with respect" (73-171/12). Accounts involving abnormal children often suggest that they were patiently cared for. In one version of "Teddy Haynes," Teddy is replaced by a monkey; his mother calls Mr. Kelly, who tells her it is too late for his services, so "she raised the monkey who grew up to be very mischievous. He died when he was about twenty-five years old" (FSC74-102/40). In international tradition, kindness to the changeling is sometimes recommended (on the premise that the fairies will treat the stolen baby the same way), but I found only one example in MUNFLA:

> In a small settlement in Trinity Bay where fairies are well-known because it is a wooded area, the thing there to do was never leave a baby alone because the fairies were known to steal babies. One woman in the community, after putting her baby asleep figured he was okay for a couple of hours, so she went to the store which was a short distance away. She wasn't gone long but when she returned she found her baby sat up in the crib with a corncob pipe in his mouth, and he had all the features of a little old man. Of course she was very upset and called a priest. When the priest arrived he told her to wear a shawl and pet her baby. After she had to warm a blanket, put her baby on it, and put the baby out the door while she was turned backwards. She did this and when she turned around she found that the baby had changed back again.[22] (72-117/12-13)

In 1989 I mentioned the singularity of this recommendation to a Folklore class, and a Bell Island student subsequently discovered that as an infant her grandmother had been exchanged for an "old-faced, big-headed, monstrous-looking baby." Seeking advice, the mother found that:

> According to the older people, when something like this happened, you were to treat the creature as if it were your own baby. Great-grandmother did what she had heard. She fed the creature, rocked it, sang to it, but never kissed it. Within a week or so, the fairies brought Grandmother back home and took the ugly creature away. Great-grandmother then took her child to see the priest and to have her blessed. The priest said that no one should ever leave a young baby near an open window alone. (89-215/20-22)

2 | *Fairy Forms and Narrative Contexts*

A related feature in European tradition is the test that makes the fairy reveal its identity before drastic measures are taken. This is some ridiculous activity that causes the fairy to exclaim — usually a rhyme or formula — about its great age: "I am old, old, ever so old, but I never saw a soldier brewing beer in an egg shell before!"[23] I found only one Newfoundland example of the telltale remark. The informant said:

> I heard Pop talking about when he was up in Sydney [Nova Scotia]. He was boarding in this house when he was working there and she had a small child and the fairies took her. She couldn't figure out what was wrong with the child. She gave him something to eat this day and she went out, and he was in swearing the big oaths, he said, "I never tasted anything as hot as this since the Battle of Waterloo." So she got the priest to come and he banished them. (74-150/6-7)

Perhaps it is an unwarranted projection to read the fairy's unlikely utterance as comic, but it would be equally misguided to suppose that "the folk" took all fairy stories equally seriously. It is my guess that "Battle of Waterloo" is an entertaining yarn, a category into which I am tempted to put hot shovel narratives altogether. One hopes that hot shovels were not really brandished at suspected changelings in Newfoundland, though they were in Ireland,[24] and of course child abuse is excruciatingly well documented today. But even if the threat was actually used now and then, it could not possibly have been as many times as there are stories; moreover, the shovel is eminently successful in narrative, as it would not be in the case of a truly abnormal child. The appeal of the widespread motif, then, must be explained on other grounds. Perhaps it is symbolic, with the horrid "fairy" representing the obnoxious tyrant in all babies, and the shovel representing the repressed parental wish to be rid of it. Thus an "exchange" might be indicated by nothing more than ordinary behaviour:

> If a woman returned to her home after leaving her baby alone and unprotected (no breadcrumbs left in crib) and she found that the fairies had succeeded in possessing her child, then she would stand where the baby could hear her and remark that the

baby was behaving so badly (baby would be cranky and crying) that the only thing left to do was "hotten the coal shovel and put the baby on it." Then the fairy that was in the baby would leave because it was afraid of the pain and the baby would no longer be possessed. Mrs. Landon did not know of anyone who had used the cure; she had just heard her mother and grandmother talk about it. (73-103/22-23)

"The fairies would steal babies but sometimes instead of stealing babies they would switch them, that is, take the baby and put a fairy baby in its place. A sure sign that this had been done was a very cross baby" (FSC69-19/41). As applied to "normal" children — cranky, crying, wakeful, tiresome — changeling tales could express normal, but personally and socially unacceptable, parental feelings of anger and rejection. As a sublimating device, they are a model of structural economy: the "real" child (beautiful, happy, lovable) is safely removed, and abuse heaped upon the ugly, cantankerous substitute. Often the mother virtuously resists the diagnosis and remedy, which is done by someone else (sometimes with the sanction of a priest). Spleen thus vented, the real child is returned, its desirability affirmed by the retrieval efforts and by the fairies' theft of it in the first place.

There has been little analysis of possible symbolic aspects of changeling traditions, most commentary consisting of the identification of mental and physical conditions that would not have been diagnosed in an earlier time.[25] As an interpretation of changeling stories, however, the folkloristic commonplace that they "explain" such conditions is inadequate. For one thing, it ignores contextual data that they are often told by people with no need to "explain" anything, like the narrators of "Alice Ryan" or "Teddy Haynes." For another, in presupposing a literal acceptance on the part of the folk, it misses entirely their aptness as metaphor — that far from mistaking reality, they represent it rather well. Medical terms are, after all, only labels that do not necessarily "explain" any more than "changelings" do; they do not show why, for example, one child and not another is afflicted. Some changeling stories do this by showing the ailment as the consequence of a broken taboo, but in most cases the fairies' depredations are as capricious and unwarranted as the freakish gene that has replaced them. In recognizing this randomness they are a mirror, not a denial, of reality. They also accurately reflect the sad situation that occurs when, through mental or physical disease, a person is no longer "himself." Even the medical profession is slow to accept a biological basis for behaviour or personality; at present, for example, childhood autism (which usually manifests itself around age two) is treated as a psychiatric problem despite increasing evidence that it is caused by a physiological malfunction, probably of the immune system (Ross). Personality-disordering afflictions such as brain damage, schizophrenia, or Alzheimer's disease may well, like the fairies, take someone away — the "former" person *is*, in effect, gone, and an unknown person *is* in her place (Paul S. Dinham [53] gives "unknown" as an idiomatic outport reference to mental illness). As long as this "stranger" remains, the lost person cannot be officially mourned; perhaps this is why in fairy tradition, on the death of the body, the person may "come back to himself" — so that he can be properly bid farewell and buried at last.

There is no doubt that changeling traditions have their basis in pathology; indeed, it is the very obviousness that stops analysis short along other lines. There are good reasons for attributing abnormality to the fairies beyond the comfort of an "explanation." By fixing the blame on an external source, parents would be absolved to an extent of responsibility for a "changed" child's condition; they might be guilty of carelessness about precautions, but this censure is mild in comparison to other possibilities. Birth defects might be taken as retribution for parental misdeeds: "'Mocking is catching' is a common expression with special significance for pregnant women," wrote one collector, giving the example of a pregnant woman who made fun of a "retarded" boy and gave birth to a son who was "retarded in the same manner" (75-295/32); another said that a woman frightened by a cow might have a baby with a cow's head, or that such a malformation might be the suspected result of the mother having had intercourse with a cow (68-2D/2).[26]

Clearly, changeling stories are freighted with messages on proper behaviour — usually for women — before and after the arrival of a child. The didactic element is made explicit by one collector:

> A North Shore woman who wasn't a good mother or wife and was always off at night came home one morning to find her baby gone from its crib. In its place was a baby with a big head that spent its time "bawling" no matter what she did for it. She knew it was a fairy child so she called the priest and somehow he got her own baby back. After that she never left the house again. (72-181/11)

Cautionary value is countered, however, by security measures like the bread, coins, or Bible put in babies' cots or clothes to keep the fairies away.

While offering explanations, excuses, instruction, and perhaps even entertainment for parents and other community members, changeling stories would seem to be rather harder on the "changed" child. Clara Murphy (111) recalls that in her home community in Conception Bay, it was "normal" for anyone different in appearance or mental capacity (including a woman of her acquaintance said to have been taken by the fairies) to be shunned by children and adults. But eccentric individuals might have their own niche in the community or family. A priest who grew up in Placentia Bay described one family's "changeling" (in interesting contrast to other accounts, the priest had to resort to subterfuge in order to see him, and there is no suggestion that he might have done anything about him):

> On the lower end of Merasheen Island living alone are a family called Travis, there is the father and mother, three sons and a daughter.... They're rich as anything because they pay no doctor or no dues to the priest. They have all their own medicines. You go in the kitchen and you see all their cures, essence of ginger and liver pills and olive oil and all that.... Her son "dim Pat" is never there when we come around but you see him hiding behind the door or running off up to the woods. Once I told her I had to meet him, I said I was taking the census for the bishop so she brought him in. He's about thirty-two and he's ordinary but he always wears a skirt made out of canvas like you'd make sails with or you'd wear splitting fish. No pants underneath but the big boots and a shirt and this skirt. He's right odd but quite intelligent to

> speak to and he can fish and make little boats that his brothers sell for him. People say he's a changeling and the fairies took the real one away, they're always saying that about the odd ones. They dress the young ones up in dresses to fool the fairies. I wore one until I was six or seven till I had enough sense to get into pants. Mrs. Travis said that she bought medicine for her feet and he drank it and he's been odd ever since.[27] (FSC66-1D/15)

Chapter Six emphasizes that fairy traditions are not the exclusive property of old people or the outports, and that they are essentially the same when they are found in the city. An advance example of this comes from a teenager who said that "there are still many fairy and ghost stories that are commonly believed in the Mt. Scio Road area [of St. John's]," and that his aunt and uncle got a changeling around 1968. The collector wrote:

> They had a little baby, about four to five months old, and it was a very active, happy child. After a while, the parents began to notice one day that their baby was not very active and wasn't as happy as it had been. The child's father (my informant's uncle) then realized that the child that they had in the cradle was not their own. The fairies had changed their human baby for a full-grown adult fairy that looked like the human baby, but did not act exactly the same way. What we had called in class a "changeling." To get his own baby back the father had to threaten the fairies. He built a large fire and put the fairy baby on a shovel and held it over the fire. He spoke out and told the fairies that if they did not give him his baby back, then my informant's uncle would throw the fairy-baby into the fire to perish. When he said that, suddenly the fairy-baby disappeared from the shovel and the parents heard a baby crying in the house. When they went inside they found their own baby crying in the cradle. (FSC74-1/12)

The etiology of disease is not enough to account for such persistence into the era of modern medicine. Implicit cultural themes offer additional explanation: one changed child "never played with toys, as normal children do, but found great pleasure with leaves, insects, trees, or butterflies — all things that had to do with nature" (72-60/28). The psychological roots of changing and changeling stories, however, are not peculiar to Newfoundland. Contemporary oral legends of child abduction are widespread (Brunvand 78–92), and changeling stories find continuity in modern popular culture in the tabloid fascination with preternatural infants (space babies, infants born singing Elvis songs or speaking a foreign language), striking birth defects and strange diseases, and hospital mix-ups of babies. These analogues suggest that, for whatever reasons, such stories hold a powerful appeal for the human imagination.

Inversion is a key element of fairy tradition, personified in the old man in the crib (the arresting image itself may explain its narrative tenacity). Changeling stories have a comic counterpoint in pranks, in which humans might make trivial switches in imitation of the fairies; since it is a fairy characteristic to play tricks, the stories are doubly effective as pranks-within-pranks.

> Jack Bursey was up here one day on the horse and long car. While he was in, some of the young fellows unhitched the horse, pushed the shafts of the long car in between the longers, and hitched up the horse on the other side of the fence. Jack thought for sure it was the fairies. (FSC67-4/66)

Often young people play tricks on their supposedly gullible elders, perhaps turning the tables after a childhood full of fairy threats. Two "old ladies" in a Riverhead story propose to trick the fairies themselves, after some jokers switch the lids on their different-sized but otherwise identical teapots:

> Well, next morning anyhow, the two old ladies got up and went to get their cup of tea and Aunt Maggy went to have her cup of tea and then she said, "Gosh, what's happened to the cover of my teapot? I had it on the teapot last night, it was perfect, now it fell down in the teapot." She took the cover of the teapot and went up with her sad story to Aunt Peggy, that the little people were after getting in and making the cover of her teapot smaller. And Aunt Peggy said, "That is a funny thing, Maggy my dear,

because," she said, "they came here last night, too," she said, "and what do you think they did," she said, "only they made the cover of my teapot larger. When I went to put the cover on my teapot I couldn't get it on it. I'll tell you what we'll do now," she said, "I'll give you the cover that I have," she said, "and you give me the small one, sure," she said, "We'll be just as well off, and the little people will never know." (79-362/29-30)

The playful manipulation of fairy traditions in tricks and deceptions (and the stories about them) is an old genre, with examples dating from at least the fourteenth century.[28] The fairies might be used to cover a good turn: Wayne Lee wrote that "old people appear to have been aided in many cases as stories are told of gardens being weeded and wood split at night" (82-206/8); Elizabeth Power, a student from Frenchman's Cove on the Burin Peninsula, told me that if someone there wished to refuse credit for a favour quietly done, he might suggest that the fairies did it. A more enigmatic case of fairy assistance is found in two accounts of a brother and sister who lived alone on a small island off the Southern Shore (FSC71-34/66 and Q68-245). There they built a wall of huge boulders, and when asked how they did it would say only. "*They'se* help us," or "*They* always helps us." "No one was ever able to figure out who 'they'se' were," said the first collector, and according to the second, "*They* could be fairies or spirits." "They" could also be the invention of the strange couple (described by the first collector as "foolish," i.e., mentally abnormal), since the fairies might be invoked, explicitly or otherwise, by one who simply does not care to explain some untoward event. Mrs. Meaney tells about a girl who went missing several days, then professed amnesia in the face of her domineering guardian's queries:

A young girl, she lived with her — her father died when she was young, see, and this couple took and raised her ***. And one evening, Sunday evening, her mistress had a few friends in to tea, see? And when they were finished tea, she said to the girl, "Now take the tablecloth out and shake it out." So she took the tablecloth and went out, shook it out around the door. And just outside of the door was a little place raspberries used to grow. And she stopped to pick a few, you know, pick them and eat them, pick them and eat them. And gosh, she never came back. She never came back, and she never came back for two or three days. And when she came back — they searched everywhere for her — and when she came back, Missus said to her, [haughty tone] "Where were you to? Do you know how long you were gone? You were gone three days and a night." She couldn't believe it, you know. She was frightened. But they brought her back. She was none the worse for it, see? Now when anything like that happens, you're not supposed to take anything they'll offer you. When they takes you away. Don't take, don't eat, above all, don't eat anything belong to them.

BR: Why not?

MM: They'll have you then. You'll join them, you'll join them then, see?[29]

It is often impossible to know from a text alone whether intentional deception was involved, but there are some definite reports of purposeful invention. Fagan's parents told him:

> About thirty years ago, four or five families lived in the "Nord-East Pon'." Although the extreme end of the road is not a half mile from Riverhead, the people began moving their homes up to the main road in Riverhead. One old man, however, was very determined not to leave the Pon', but his wife played on his fear of ghosts, and particularly of fairies, that, as residents put it, "she frightened poor ole Paddy out of the Pon'." For example, if he were in the yard sawing up firewood she might ask him, "Who were all them saucy little young ones that were here throwing your wood around?" He didn't see anybody, and she concluded they must have been fairies. Another day she might ask him who was the strange man that came down the road with him.

He would assure her that he was alone, but with a sad or frightened voice she would say. "Oh, that must have been poor old John Mason, the Lord have mercy on him." [The dead are referred to as "poor."] When the old man was almost frightened out of his wits by fairies and ghosts (of his wife's making), he finally built a new house on the main road. (FSC67-4/84)

Mrs. Meaney and her family (a dozen children) lived "by the salt water, down by the Pond" (79-374/5), and it would be useful to know more about neighbourhood distinctions and whether they may have played a part in fairy tradition, as in Mrs. Meaney's mother's admonition, "Don't go over on the north side any more — that's fairies!" After his interview with Mrs. Mason, Fagan's mother asked him, "Didn't she tell you any stories about over in the Lane? Sure that was the real home of the fairies!" The Lane is where Mrs. Mason lived before her marriage (67-4B/6). Riverhead's physical division by water may have contrived to make the parts mysterious to one another at times. Mike Lee recalled the advent of electricity in 1965: "That night we spent a great deal of our time looking across at the other side for this was really the first time at night that you could distinguish the houses on that side of the water" (80-296/29).

There were many things I would like to have asked Mrs. Meaney, but I was not able to make myself understood much of the time. Our conversational difficulties had the single advantage that she pursued her own line of thought mostly uninfluenced by leading questions. On my first visit she would conclude a fairy story with something like, "Well, that's all I can tell you. Still, a lot of queer things happen." She would then go on to tell about some of these "queer things," so although it was not clear whether she was separating them from "fairies" proper or had just thought of something new, the natural narrative flow was apparent. "Something," for example, "a little woman," was often seen along the road; Mrs. Meaney passed her one day as she was returning from a neighbour's house with scraps for her hens. Another time a man greeted this woman, thinking he knew her; but Mrs. Meaney knew that it could not have been who he thought, for that woman was nowhere near the road at that time. Hearing this prompted "young" Mrs. Meaney (the daughter-in-law) to tell about strange headlights behind her car one night, which mysteriously disappeared; others have seen the same thing on the same part of the road near the Bay Roc Lounge, so "you do wonder." (On another occasion, the late John Meaney — Mrs. Meaney's son — told about an experience with a mysteriously stalled car, and about a token of his father's death.)

The most frustrating aspect of my communication problem with Mrs. Meaney was that I was never able to gauge her attitude toward the fairies and her stories, and all I can say with confidence is that she did not take the ones she told me very seriously. Fagan noted Mrs. Mason's offhandedness when he tried to establish a time frame for her tales: "I haven't been able to date them very well," he wrote, "to her the date was rather insignificant, and any attempts to get this information was dismissed with, 'Oh, that was a nice bit ago'" (67-4B/3). Perhaps belief is not a major issue for performance-oriented repertoires, as Mrs. Meaney's and Mrs. Mason's almost surely were; perhaps one accepts the tradition in its own terms for the sake of engagement with the narrative. One student concluded a collection of fairy narratives:

> When telling these stories Mr. Brendon didn't really commit himself as to whether he believed them or not. He just told them to me as they were told to him. In bygone days, he said, when people had fewer radios and no television, people would entertain each other by telling stories. He seemed to indicate that whether you believed them or not was unimportant, simply the fact of their existence and your knowing them seemed to create a bond between you and the rest of the people who were interested in hearing them. Now, as there are less people on Bell Island, the number at parties is lessened, not so many stories are heard because this is where you usually hear the stories. (72-95/17)

Colin Lee mentioned the "bond among all the communities in St. Mary's Bay" (82-205/12), and Mike Lee said that each community around Riverhead had its "own distinctive characteristics" (80-296/3); Riverhead, according to Colleen Meaney, was "famous for its get-togethers, scoffs, and sprees"

(79-374/7). The venues for the performance of traditional genres remained vital in Riverhead longer than in many areas partly because of the relatively late arrival of television (Mike Lee describes the breakdown of visiting patterns after its introduction). Nor was Riverhead torn apart by resettlement as many small communities were. The rich body of material from Riverhead, then, comes from a fortunate set of circumstances: a stable, performance-oriented community with specialist, long-lived narrators, and good students to record them.

Wayne Lee claims that fairy stories ended in Riverhead in the 1960s, with the coming of electricity (82-206/4). Fagan, writing in the 1960s, said, "The idea of being 'taken by the fairies' was very prevalent in the areas surrounding St. Mary's up to about thirty years ago. It is interesting to note that there are no ghost stories of recent origin either. The reason given by the older people — there are so many priests and nuns, and so much prayers being said" (FSC67-4/67). But the perpetual recession of the fairies may be at play here. "The most exciting story I've heard of fairies was alleged to have happened about fifteen years ago," wrote a Riverhead student in 1973. "It involved a baby swapping." She goes on to relate the classic form (73-169/29-30). "Night Kitchen" was prompted by a question from Mrs. Meaney's preadolescent grandson, who asked if she had ever heard of a cup and saucer in a cupboard that was broken by thunder and lightning when there was no thunder and lightning ("You haven't got it all," Mrs. Meaney said, and commenced). This grandson also told me of a personal experience involving Jack O'Lantern, who wrote "Jack" on a tombstone when the grandson's friend, on a dare, "cursed on him." So supernatural stories continue, but whether Mrs. Meaney is the last of the fairy specialists remains to be seen.[30]

POSTSCRIPT TO CHAPTER TWO

After the death of John Meaney in 1989, Mrs. Meaney came to live in a nursing home in St. John's. I have visited her there, but communication is almost impossible, not only because of hearing problems but because of the constant blare of the television set positioned between the beds on Mrs. Meaney's end of the room. She didn't have her songbooks, and when I brought a copy from the archive she didn't seem to realize that she had written them down (probably because they were typed and bound). She read with intense pleasure, however, stopping occasionally to declaim a verse with the clarity of a sudden strong radio signal breaking through the static of a stormy night.

3 | Bread, Wind, Old Paths: The Texture and Planes of Everyday Life in Fairy Narrative

Although they concern extraordinary events, fairy narratives are stories of ordinary life as well, as much about the narrators and protagonists as about the "fairies." They give beautifully detailed pictures of folklife, of people going about their daily round until it is interrupted by the intrusion of the marvelous. The retailing of this intrusion lights up the events surrounding it like the flash of a camera, and the sudden exposure fixes the moment in time, creating tableaux of people picking berries, digging gardens, or walking home after a dance. The projection of such homely activities on the fairies, so that they, too, are said to eat, play music, or conduct funerals, is one of the most intriguing aspects of fairy tradition in that some human characteristics are mirrored in the fairy world while others are denied them. The relationship of the human and fairy worlds explored in the last chapter continues with an examination of methods of protection — that is, keeping the otherworld at bay — and of some ways in which the infringement of the otherworld on this one is depicted in the association of particular times and places with the fairies.

Among the many byproducts of this discussion — or perhaps byways is the more fitting term — is a digression on the national derivation of certain traditions and their adaptation (or lack thereof) to the new environment. A more general, recurring question of evolution is how Newfoundland fairy traditions of the present — and as reflected in records of the last twenty-five years — are different from those of the past, not only in content and ubiquity but in immediacy in everyday life. Listening to fairy stories of long-ago events is a little like looking at old photographs — some faded, torn, steeped in a sepia of time through which one peers at shadowy shapes on a blurry background, others sharp as yesterday. Small details emerge: when Dan Costello of Avondale told me about seeing the fairies as a boy, he spent as long describing the new overalls he had been wearing as in describing the fairies. Colour streaks the images — in Avondale the fairies have been seen in red scarves, white dresses, multicoloured gowns — but the overall tone of long-ago events is difficult to envision, and it is hard to guess the extent to which images and ideas of these otherworlders coloured life then.

A photographic analogy does not work in all respects, for a photo is an unchanging document freezing the physical facts of the instant it was taken, whereas there are almost no contemporary records of Newfoundland fairy traditions prior to the 1960s. The difficulty (if not impossibility) of an "objective" portrayal of even the most "factual" history is well known, and increases exponentially for such vague and subjective matters as intensity of belief or experience. Indeed, the question is worth raising not so much in expectation of answers but as a reminder that fairy tradition has imaginative and emotional dimensions that may bleach out on flat paper, as oral texts lose inflection there. At the same time, inflation of past "belief" from a present perspective is always a danger. It is hard, for example, to evaluate the opening claim of this report from Conception Harbour, the community neighbouring Avondale on the north:

> When my mother was growing up the "fairies" were an accepted part of life. People referred to them as "the good people" and a surprising number of people really believed in them. If the cover was found off a well in the morning, it would be said, "Oh, the good people are around." When the wind blew, it was the fairies. Often those "squalls of wind" could mean perhaps bad luck since it meant fairies and my mother remembers being advised, "If

you throw a rock with the wind it will drive the fairies away." It was a sure cure and many people, especially if alone, would carry this out for their protection. By the action it would be assured that the fairies would never harm you. The only knowledge I have of fairies is whatever I hear from my parents, as it is recalled to me as "something of the past." (FSC73-64/18)

Here again is the idea that so struck me at the beginning of my study, that the fairies have gone from ubiquity to obsolescence in one generation. A profusion of MUNFLA accounts, notably a student collection by Tom Moore (71-42), confirms that Avondale and Conception Harbour are — or were — rich fairy areas, so I went there in March 1985 and got enough help, especially from Mr. Dan and Mr. Joe Costello, to make Avondale the base for this chapter.

Avondale — Salmon Cove until 1906 (Seary 64) — lies just beyond the opposite end of the Salmonier Line from Riverhead, and is about sixty kilometres from St. John's. Its location on the busy Conception Bay Road and its proximity to the Trans-Canada Highway (since the mid-1960s) have made it today a larger and more suburban community than Riverhead, and many of its 900 residents are commuters to St. John's. In 1971, Tom Moore wrote, "I could find no adult who did not know about the fairies ... generally thought of as devilish people with some magic power ... [who] were never known to use this power for any good purpose" (71-42/14). He identified most of his informants, including his parents, as of "mixed Irish and English extraction." In 1985, living and teaching in Avondale, Mr. Moore recalled that people had been delighted to talk about the fairies for his paper, and suggested that I visit Jack and Bride Parsley (Mrs. Parsley died in 1987 and Mr. Parsley in 1991).

When I explained my errand to the Parsleys, they were struck by the coincidence that just before I arrived there had been a "fairy squall," a sudden wind that took things up in the air. Mrs. Parsley and Julianne Lewis, a fourth grade teacher visiting their house, nevertheless agreed that "those things" aren't talked about anymore, though Mrs. Parsley was adamant that they certainly happened at one time. She herself had once met up with an unnatural dog that used to ply the road. Mr. Parsley, in his nineties, was too deaf to participate fully in the conversation, but occasionally offered something such as that the dog made a great rushing sound; one minute you'd think it was behind you and the next thing you'd hear it way in front of you. "Fairies," he said, would be something like hearing a train coming, jumping out of the way, and then there was no train. One of Moore's informants had used the term in a similar sense, describing invisible or "fairy horses," which raced down Lee's Pond and past him one evening while he was hauling wood. (A man near Western Bay made a distinction between "fairy" as a noun and adjective when he told me that there are "two kinds of fairy": one like his father once saw when he cut open a stump and little people ran out; the second, like seeing a ship on the ocean that wasn't really there.) Mr. Parsley told about a man fishing on the Labrador who said that he had been "home" overnight, and knew who had died there; when the crew returned in the fall, those people had in fact died — "He was a real fairy man." The Parsleys used this expression several times, mostly, I think, in reference to people who knew about fairy matters, although it might also have implied that there was something strange about them. Kevin Parsley, their son, came in part way through the visit, and hearing the discussion of one man, said that he had been "in the fairies so long" that he was "a fairy himself." He asked if they had told me about the fairy squall, so it seems the actual term was in use before my arrival.

At this point the kitchen had filled with children, the phone was ringing, and everyone was talking about something different, so it was hard to catch details of any one thing, but Kevin Parsley was telling about some friends of his hearing voices in trees, and how he himself was once followed at about three o'clock in the morning by "that fucking woman," whose high heels he could hear tapping along behind him. Ms. Lewis was reading aloud a copy of Tom Moore's paper I'd brought, and although she took an amused-but-tolerant attitude toward the project she told about a woman on Redmonds Hill who disappeared when she went out to bring in the clothes one frosty night at about ten o'clock. She was gone for weeks, but the parish priest told the people that if they watched on a certain night they would see a white horse with a sleigh, and she would be on the sleigh; they were to pull her off.[1]

3 | *Bread, Wind, Old Paths*

They got her back with the socks still in her hands. Mrs. Parsley said that Lee's Pond was the place for fairies, and that May and October were fairy months. She had never heard that you should not talk about the fairies, or that the fairies would take or change babies. She talked about how frightened people used to be of the dead, and how the night after a burial, a cup and saucer and food would be left out for the dead person. She did not tell about any personal experiences (other than the strange dog), but Mr. Parsley had an experience with fairies almost fifty years ago, according to one of Moore's informants.[2] He had moved his house onto a piece of land where there were many "old wood paths," tracks for the winter use of slides for hauling wood:

> It seems that he had put his house on a fairies' path. One night when Jack was at a dance his mother heard a young child walking back and forth along the front of the house crying. The child stayed there crying all night and when Jack got home she told him. Later Jack heard the crying himself while in the stable. He eventually moved his house again and had no more trouble from the fairies. (71-42/23-24)

Narratives about fairy paths and winds are especially suited to the depiction of everyday life, for in them the fairies' presence is invisible, and the listener's (or reader's) imagination is not automatically focused on a startling appearance; instead it sees the woman kept awake by the crying, perhaps nervously pacing the floor as she waits for her son, his later bringing the animals into the stables, and other such domestic scenes.

The Parsleys suggested that I see Dan Costello, who turned out to be a quiet, courteous man in his seventies (he was born in 1910). After I interviewed him, he took me to see his brother Joe Costello; I do not know if they are any relation to James Costello, an informant of Tom Moore's. Dan Costello told me about his father having to move the first house he built:

> But he had to shift out of it, he had to haul the house, he was took sick over there . . . the parish priest told him to move out of it.
>
> BR: Did he ever see or hear anything in the house?

> DC: Oh, yes, used to hear them walking around outside. Passing the road.
>
> BR: Was the house on a path?
>
> DC: Could be. And, this fellow lived there, now my brother went there after and built a shack, after he got married, they was only young people, my father gave them a piece of land, see? Same spot. And the little one, (no bigger than that?) she fell in the same place and broke her nose, had to go in the hospital. Right on the level ground. That seemed to say that she was knocked down by it.[3]

The fairy path is one of the major human intersections with the fairy world, and it is a dangerous one. The central image of path narratives is the house, the physical base of most people's lives, in which daily activities begin and end. Path stories suggest that if something is wrong there, nothing will be right anywhere. Often the inhabitants' bad luck involves their children. "I have heard stories all my life of the effects of people crossing the fairy paths," a Conception Bay student wrote, "and I interviewed an acquaintance of mine ... who lives not far from the fairy path" (77-162/1-9). Only one of eleven children born to a couple living in a house built on this path survived; the others died soon after birth, and after death had old, sunken faces.

> [Mrs. Butler] and everyone else in the community blamed the fairies and thought that in some way or other Mrs. Butler had displeased them. Mrs. Butler told the story of how sometimes in the night she would hear the table being set. When she would go downstairs all the dishes would be placed on the table ready for a meal. This was thought to be the presence of the fairies in the house. Mr. and Mrs. Butler finally realized or believed that their house was inhabited by the fairies and that their lives would always be affected while they remained in the house on the fairy path. While the Butlers were considering moving, Mrs.

> Butler died. Mr. Butler then moved out and built a house at the other end of the community. He remarried shortly after his first wife's death and he and his second wife had six children all of which were normal healthy children. Mr. Butler always refused to talk about his first family.

Mr. Butler was nevertheless able to sell the house to another couple, who then had two children unable to walk or talk; they moved the house into the next garden and had a third, normal child.

> They still live in the same house and believe that they have safely escaped the fairies. Behind the house is a large cliff and on the other side of this mountain is believed to be the home of the fairies. On certain days goats can be seen running — or could be seen, in those days — down from the mountain as if being chased by the fairies. This occurrence was usually followed by a heavy wind or rainstorm. This was attributed to the fairies who were upset. Several other families moved across the road so they would not be affected by the evil of the fairies. Sometimes during the summer rocks would fall down the side of the mountain for no reason whatsoever. This, according to Bill, was the fairies driving people away from their home. Today in Butlerville the foundations of the houses can be seen. The remaining houses near the area have been boarded up and have not been lived in since. Many of the people in the community are familiar with the story and believe in the power of the fairies and do nothing to get them upset.

If the fairies were really thought to cause storms, they must have been ubiquitous — and irritable — indeed. A flash of fairy anger even blazed a trail in one account:

> There is a path in Torbay cut through the woods which is still there today and which was caused by the fairies. They were so angry at one man that they caused a lightning bolt to strike the

house, go down the chimney, out the other side and through his garden, cutting a path right through the woods. (72-181/8)

One might reasonably, if fatuously, ask why the fairies don't just go around something in their path: if they have the power to affect the weather, cannot they make a little detour? One explanation is that in path stories the fairies are envisioned as a mindless inexorable force completely indifferent to anything "in their way." The answer, however, is probably not to be looked for in the nature of the fairies but in human nature. Clearly, many misfortunes could be blamed on "paths"; like changelings, they allow illness, particularly of young children, to be attributed to an external agency. The Butlers' children probably had a hereditary disease, but crediting the change of scene rather than a change of gene for the normal children of Mr. Butler's second marriage locates liability in impersonal fate rather than individual circumstances. There is also a metaphorical element to paths: although people everywhere are prone to attribute undesirable results of their own actions to bad luck, bad "luck" in the proper sense is the result of being in the wrong place at the wrong time, and getting caught in a current of misfortune.

In path traditions, the fairies' identity is very close to that of the dead:

> [In Brigus South], a house built on a "crossed path" will be haunted. A "crossed path" is a path that was once well-travelled, but is no longer used. My grandmother's first home was built on a crossed path. At night you could hear doors opening and people walking. It became so unnerving that my grandfather finally tore down the house and built a new one further in off the road. These things were never heard in the new house. (FSC70-13/139)

These travellers are not ghosts in the usual sense; they have not "returned" from the dead, nor have they any particular reason to harass the living. Rather they are there all along, going about their own business, so to speak, unless injudiciously or inadvertently interfered with. They are not always explicitly identified. A couple in Avondale lived peacefully in a bungalow until one night they heard a great racket; the man went downstairs to find the front door, normally unused, swinging open. The next night it was "as if some crew were travelling through the house," so they got the priest:

> The pastor told him to check old paths to the bog behind his house. He found an old path and sure enough when neighbors had put up their new picket fence it crossed the path and the fence joined on to his, which went to the corner of the house, thus blocking off the passageway of the path to the house. Immediately Bill took down the obstruction. This solved the mystery of the racket and the swinging doors. (79-410/10-13)

The house on the path is like the "haunted house" of ghostly tradition in some ways, but is different in that the latter is usually depicted as old and resounding with some tragedy of the past, while the former is often brand new, and the noise only the humdrum traffic of an earlier time. "I often heard a saying to build a house on a path the people in it would never be at rest," said a woman who heard the rumbling of a horse and box-cart going through her new house on top an old road in Harbour Grace. "They'd hear the people that once traveled over the road at one time. So now I'm beginning to believe it." The path-house is a superimposed image, a kind of double exposure in which the shadows of the past move behind the transparency of the present, their sounds echoing through the newly defined space. Either house type might be cleared by a clerical exorcist. The Harbour Grace woman called a priest who blessed the house inside and out with holy water, and the sounds ceased (76-138/1-21). On the Southern Shore:

> A newly married couple built a house in the community of Tors Cove. Every night at bedtime they would hear an ungodly racket downstairs which stopped when they checked it. They had a priest come in and the house was exorcised. The priest told them that their house was built over an old pass, and it was thought that the noise came from the spirits of the dead who used the pass. They never returned after the priest's visit. (FSC70-11/80)

Path narratives implicitly recommend an awareness of and respect for the past. Older people often advise the builders against a certain site:

> It was a belief in Cape Broyle [Southern Shore] about fifty years ago that it was bad luck to build a house on an old path. It was believed that the souls of the dead people used to use these paths and that the faries [*sic*] also used them. If a house was built on a path the people in it would never be happy. The man who told me this said he knew of an incident where the foundations of the house had to be removed because they were on an old path. He said, "The Walshes were building a house up there near where they live now. One day old Mrs. Walsh went up to have a look at it. She said that there used to be an old path running along right where the foundation was. She made them take up the foundations and start building somewhere else."[4] (FSC68-16/61)

Conflict over land use and customary rights of way might have been factors in path lore. Property rights seem to have been at the heart of an incident in Trepassey:

> [Mr. Sutpin] built a bungalow on a piece of land he secured. On this land there had been an old footpath greatly used at an earlier time. When the house was finished, the back door was situated directly opposite the front door, one at each end of the footpath. Tradition has it that every night, approximately at midnight, Mr. Sutpin would hear a rap on the back door. He would open it, and although he couldn't see anyone, he was aware that a long line of people would walk from the back door, across the floor (built directly over the footpath) and then through the front door which he would have to open for them. This went on for about three years; everyone in the settlement knew of Mr. Sutpin's visitors and they said it was because he had stolen the property. He was told that he would find no peace until he moved his house. This is what he did eventually, and in his new house he heard no more ghostly visitors. (71-41/75-77)

Two informants told the collector that when they bought a house in 1970:

> the man who sold it did so on the condition that they put gates in the fence they were planning to build around it. The reason for building the gates was that the fence would cross a path believed to be used by the fairies. As a result the Days built two gates where there wouldn't normally be any. Mr. Day didn't take the gates very seriously, but Mrs. Day was determined that they were going to be built into the fence. Mrs. Day knows of one family who built the house right on top of a path which came from the woods and over their plot of land. They had a lot of hard luck thereafter. They had retarded children and lazy children. Mrs. Day did not want to mention the name of this family as they were still living in Port de Grave. (70-26/56-57)

Taken as a whole, "path" texts demonstrate an unequivocal identification of the fairies with the dead, and specifically with the ordinary, pedestrian dead (surely an excusable pun in this context). Such an equation does much to "explain" the fairies: how they might be good or bad; why they are so often in groups (as opposed to the solitary purposeful ghost); why their actions, and even emotions, so often shadow ordinary human activity.

The identification is borne out by the concession of all rights of way to the fairies and dead on All Souls' Day. On Holy Souls' Day in Avondale and Conception Harbour, "it was believed that the souls were loose and people would never walk in the middle of the road to prevent them (souls) from passing" (FSC73-64/19). "On All Souls' Night, people on Fogo Island say that one should remain on the right side of the road when walking," wrote another student, "this is done to insure oneself against meeting the spirits of the dead. It declined about twenty years ago" (FSC70-34/50). A woman who threw out water one All Souls' Night had it come back in her face, and was told that it was because "on this night the souls were passing along on their way to heaven and nothing could cross their paths" (FSC74-116/4). One student reported:

> Years ago people used to say if you went out after dark on All Souls' Night, you would be likely to see a crowd carrying a coffin

up the road. If one of the crowd happened to see you watching them, you would have to go along with them whether you wanted to or not. They say that these were the fairies out on All Souls' Night burying their dead. (74-212/30)

Fairy and phantom funerals might be encountered at other times as well.[5] A young St. Phillips man who went into the woods one Sunday "either to go hunting or cutting wood, both ... [not] done on the Lord's Day," heard the "sweetest music he had ever heard in his life," and hid behind a bush:

> What the man then saw was a lot of little people singing as they carried a tiny wooden box directly ahead of him: it was a fairy funeral. The "little people" saw the man and he began to follow them. They treated him very nice and he really liked to be with them.

He was "simpleminded" after this, however, and his account is supposed to have been pieced together from his "disconnected ramblings" (Q68-403/3).

The size of the fairies much interested early students of fairy lore, and one theory advanced to account for their small appearance was that it reflects ancient conceptions of the soul as a small being inside the body, which emerges at death or sometimes during sleep.[6] The small fairy funeral processions would support this venerable concept and theory, as would the explicit ideas about the separable soul found in "fairy" areas like Riverhead or Avondale. Tom Moore's father recalled that when he was a young man:

> the older men often spoke about the spirit in the body. Mr. Johnny Nolan said that the spirit is in the body like a man in prison. When the body is asleep at night, the soul leaves it to roam in freedom until morning. This is why you should never awaken a sleeping person quickly in the middle of the night, for the soul may be far away from the body and not be able to get back. The result is death for the awakened person. (FSC71-42/26)

The mirror-imagery in fairy funerals is made explicit in a text about a Fogo Island man who had just left the funeral of a friend when he saw "a bunch of miniature people" carrying a "miniature coffin":

> He stopped, stepped aside, and let them pass by, out of shock, bewilderment, and what you could almost determine an inner sense of respect. When he explained what he had seen to the people upon his return to Seldom-Come-By, some old person told him that "depending on the time and the place, there is usually a fairy funeral for every human one that occurs." (77-160/25-26)

"It is customary for people to project their own mode of life onto the spirits supposed to live in their immediate neighborhood," Felix Oinas (1) writes. The same cannot be said of Newfoundland fairies on the whole (there are, for instance, no fairy weddings), but James Costello gave Moore an account of the fairies as needy but obnoxious neighbours, which has an intriguing historic element:

> [He] told me that as he heard it, over one hundred years ago the fairies lived around the settlement. They lived on what they could, often depending on the people of the community for food, and were often to be seen around the houses. Mr. Costello told me that they behaved very badly towards men with their evil powers and finally Father Rowe of Harbour Main (an adjoining community) "banished them to the woods" because of their evil. (71-42/15)

This text calls to mind the turn-of-the-century theory that fairy traditions derive from folk memories of conquered aboriginal peoples such as Picts or Britons, scattered bands of whom survived outside the supplanted area and made occasional forays for food or goods.[7] (According to this theory, the small size of the fairies comes from the displaced persons' appropriation of old barrows or caves as quarters: people seeing the small openings would conclude that the inhabitants must be small.) Could the presence of the

Indigenous population have helped fuel fairy traditions among the early European settlers in Newfoundland? A Placentia Bay boy playing with the fairies had to be forcibly removed from them by his father; the informant (who did believe in fairies) thought "it might have been the remains of an Indian band who were in hiding" (80-328/36). Macpherson Eveleigh told me that the settlers in New Harbour (Newstead in Notre Dame Bay) in the late 1800s found a clearing about a hundred feet across, with a tree in the centre over a hundred feet tall; "they say that Indians had this encampment just inside this harbour, but the people nicknamed it the Fairyground." The association strengthens the view of fairies as strangers.

"In the eighteen and early nineteen hundreds, people believed that the fairies lived in Stoney River, Back River, Bar River, and St. Shott's, and that they would come to Trepassey in the night" (FSC75-48/87). As among humans, the fairies' nocturnal assemblies might be boisterous or genteel. Tom Moore wrote:

> In 1888 or 1889 Mr. [James] Costello's father saw the fairies in his own house which was then on the main road through Avondale. One Sunday evening he returned to his own house and heard many young people's voices inside as he stepped into the porch. He didn't think any of his family were home but then figured they may have invited some people in. He opened the kitchen door a little and peeked in. "A young girl was sweeping the floor." They were all happily making fun and did not see him. "A beautiful music could be heard from the kitchen." He said they were all normal size. He made a noise before coming in so as not to interrupt their conversation. When he opened the door again, they were all gone. Also around 1884 some man in Avondale was in bed when his wife woke him saying, "They're breaking up everything downstairs." He heard terrible noises coming up from below. Tables and chairs were crashing around and dishes were breaking. As he rushed down the stairs, "a whistle blew from over on O'Kelly's hill." They had all disappeared when he reached the kitchen. Mr. Costello

explained that "they had been called back to the woods by the whistle." (71-42/24)

Sometimes their partying became habitual and a nuisance. The late Tuce Framton of Bay Bulls told me that when his parents lived in Freshwater Bay just outside St. John's, they would hear the stove rattling and the fire crackling in the kitchen after they had gone to bed; they could even see light flickering through the crack at the top of the door, but if they went to the kitchen to check, the stove would be cold. This house burned down in the fire of 1892, and although it was supposed to have been built on a fairy path, they never heard anything in a new house on the same site. Joe Costello said:

> Sure, out here, going out to Harbour Main, 'tis a pond, Black Duck Pond. 'Twas a man living there, Penny was his name. And his family was growed up and gone, and himself and his wife was living there, just like us [his late wife and himself]. And every night they [the fairies] used to come. Make a big racket in the kitchen, downstairs in the kitchen. 'Twas no electric lights or nothing then. And he used to get up and light the lamp and come down and start cursing on them [laughs], he thought he'd drive them that way.
>
> BR: Did it work?
>
> JC: That never done him any good. Do you know what he had to do? He had to go to the priest. It was a priest in Harbour Main, Father Rowe was his name, he had to come and say mass in the house. The last place they heared them was across the pond, on the other side to the mountain, they'd hear them over there in the night, they'd be picking and shoveling in the clift. That's where they went when the priest banished them.

The Parsleys told me that a Father O'Donnell banished a devil from Matt Penney's house, although they didn't say what the devil did there. The fairies' pre-eminence in raising kitchen rackets, however, is venerable.[8]

The fairies are seldom depicted as having dwelling structures of their own, although in the midwife-to-the-fairies story mentioned in Chapter One, the midwife is taken by "a lovely gentleman" to a house that is "spotless . . . everything was spic and span in it," where she delivers a baby boy (72-95:C1280/m.t.). More common is an association with topographical features such as hills or caves. A student from Englee (described as a "mixed" ethnic settlement) gives an odd account according to which children were regular seasonal "guests" of the fairies:

> Fairies, Green people: As children we were always warned not to go in the woods because the fairies would carry us away. There was supposed to be a girl in our family who had been carried away for the whole winter with these people, her father found her the next spring one evening when he went trouting. Her name was Dulcie. The interesting thing about this is that every family had a boy or girl who had been carried away by these green people but were always returned. The green people were supposed to do you no harm. You would become small like them and in the spring you would return to your normal size. There is a hill home called Manuel's Hill where these people were supposed to have lived. Nobody dared to go near that hill by themselves for they would, without question, become a part of these small people. (FSC70-12/100)

Tom Moore wrote, "I could never get a story on houses in which the fairies lived, but some people recollect it was underground" (26). Dan Costello said that he often heard, "years ago," that someone lost might be taken to the fairies' "residence" where "they had all kinds of nice stuff"; if he ate the bread there, he would never return. "You'd never think of that, would you?" he added, a question I took as a kind of musing on the remoteness of the idea. It may be that stories in which fairies and humans enter one another's dwellings represent an older strain of tradition that has fallen into disrepair, like many old houses themselves; perhaps the fairies' association with the bogs, barrens, and woods reflects their recession from everyday reality, a banishment from centre to periphery. If fairies and humans were at one time considered to have been more interactive — although I am inclined to think that in 1889 James

Costello's father talked about what *his* father saw — then the nature/culture dichotomy I see in fairy tradition might be a relatively recent development. This would be logical in that as people become less immediately at the mercy of nature in most undertakings, it becomes more distant, receding as the primary consideration in day-to-day life.

Roads, gardens, and barns, as intermediate areas between the house and the wild, are the stage for many fairy encounters. In Dan Costello's house, there is a horseshoe over the inside back door, and another on the barn door, which does not bear one of the small painted marks — usually a circle, heart, or star — common in some areas, including Avondale. When I asked Dan Costello about these marks, he said they were for decoration, but some MUNFLA reports assert that the marks are for protection: "The purpose of this circle is to keep away 'the evil eye.' Of course 'the evil eye' refers to the devil" (FSC68-19/75); "A farmer told us that these would bring good luck. I've also heard the explanation that these symbols would keep the fairies away" (FSC64-4/52); "These designs are painted there to ward off evil spirits which may come and spirit off livestock" (FSC70-22/190); "To protect animals from the fairies or evil spirits, they often painted a heart on the door of the barn. This was supposed to frighten away the fairies who might harm the animals" (FSC74-212/*); "This symbol was to ward off all evil, devils, etc. from entering a house" (77-168/n.p.); "The white spot will keep any evil spirits away . . . they were said to be the cause of a cow not being able to produce milk" (FSC75-13/*). A Carbonear woman used to find her two horses sweaty and with their manes plaited in the mornings:

> One night my grandmother decided to stay awake in the barn to see what would happen. Around eleven o'clock the fairies appeared, plaited the horses' manes, jumped on their backs, and with a cry that could raise the dead, rode through the side of the stable and flew across the yard out of sight. The stable was left intact and grandmother could scarcely believe her eyes. At twelve o'clock the horses returned, but no one was riding them. They made their entrance as they had left, through the side of the stable. . . . My grandmother blessed the horses, hung a horseshoe outside

the barn door, and drew a white circle with a spot of white paint in the middle. Since then there was never any trouble with the animals. (66-16C/24-5)

Narrative often finds humans in barns spying or trying some tradition, as above or in Rhoda Maude Piercey's memoirs of life in Winterton, Trinity Bay:

> There was an old belief that animals fell to their knees on Old Christmas Eve. One man was said to go to see if there was any truth to it. As he went to the barn door he heard one horse say to the other, "We have a hard day's work tomorrow, the master is heavy and the road to the graveyard is long and steep." The man died that night.[9] (88-032/27)

Those who spy on the animals praying are usually sorry, but in contrast to the usual interdiction on interference with the fairies, it does not seem to be dangerous to test them in this way, as one informant did:

> Once upon a time I had a horse when I was living alone at Gallants, about thirty miles from Stephenville. I used to hear a lot of stories about the fairies so I wanted to see if they were for real. Late one evening in the summer in the month of July I went over to my barn and plaited my horse's mane. I then went to my cabin and in the morning I went to the barn and found the horse's mane unplaited. This proved the stories I heard that the fairies came down in the night and unplaited the mane. I did this several times and the same thing happened. (73-107/44-5)

Wayne Lee interviewed the same informant, comparing his story to "a tale told by Riverhead residents regarding a man who nailed up his barn doors to prevent fairies from riding the horses and returned the next morning to find the barn covered in manure in retaliation" (82-206/12).

The "plaiting" motif seems to be particularly prominent on the west coast. Gary Butler says that in the French-Newfoundland community of Black

Duck Brook on the Port-au-Port peninsula, "lutins" are a particular kind of fairy that tangles horses' manes (personal communication). Ronald Labelle asked an informant in la Grand Terre on the Port au Port about them:

> ...when I asked her about the "lutins" who used to go into stables and tie the horses' manes into knots, she said she knew about them, except they were called "les fairies" or "le petit monde" where she lived. At first, she only told us that she had heard they went into people's houses and barns. Then her son Laurence, who has a strong belief in fairies, told us that he had seen horses with their manes braided by the fairies. He told us about the way fairies only came on certain years to certain places. Seeing we were interested in what he said about fairies, Mme. Chason then told us of the time Francis Louvet came over to see her husband Joe Carter. He told him that his horse had a braided mane some mornings when he went into the stable. She agreed with her son that fairies were very small creatures.[10] (76-79/11)

Perhaps the fairies' presence in stables can be challenged with impunity because there they are the trespassers. It is in their domain — woods, bogs, and barrens — that one must most beware.

Within this vastness and at the edges of community space are areas with special reputations, like Snow's Ridge near Clarke's Beach (where Frances Kavanagh says people go astray), a certain path in the woods at Portugal Cove (FSC64-5/216), or the berry grounds in North River, labelled "Fairyland" on a map by a student who notes that they are "famous for fairies" and that "a woman would not dare to go on these grounds unless accompanied by another individual" (91-182/16). Some communities even have places bearing fairy names, like "Fairy Hill" in Dunville, Placentia Bay, "where people were supposed to have been taken by the fairies" (80-328/24), or Brigus, where "Miner's Path is also called Fairies' Marsh" (FSC71-103/13). Many fairy places and place names are associated with their dance: in Victoria, they emerge from a crack in "Fairy Rock" to dance at night (FSC75-144/* and FSC76-25/*); Colliers also has a "Fairy Rock" where they have been seen dancing in May (Clara Murphy 110); in Oderin, Placentia Bay, they danced on "the fairy grounds" or Power's Green (FSC76-367/*). In Bumblebee Bight on Pilley's Island in Notre Dame Bay, Melina Whelan (age ninety-three) told me about Aunt Mary King, "a funny old woman," and the fairies:

> She lived down the road in a place they called Fairyland [chuckles]. Now. And she used to tell us that the fairies used to come out and dance around; and they were all dressed up, she said, and they'd dance around, the fairies would . . . all'd join hands, she said, and have a, make a ring, you know, and dance around. . . . They'd get all dressed up and go around in a ring. And sing . . . little small fairies, little-sized fairies, she said.
>
> BR: Were they tiny?
>
> MW: Oh, no no, just maybe like that child there, you know [my four-year-old son], danced around like that . . . we always call it Fairyland. I do. [chuckles]

"There is a road in Carbonear called the 'Fairy Run' . . . because people said they saw fairies running on it" (FSC76-112/*), and Upper Island Cove has the "Fairy Path," where "some people had claimed they saw the fairies" (80-314/83); in Trepassey, "people believed that there was a Fairies Field on the Lower Coast . . . because some mornings when they went to this field the wood was platted" (FSC75-179/*), and in St. Joseph's, St. Mary's Bay, people avoided the "Fairy Ridge" after dark (75-250/33); near Fermeuse, people went astray in "the Fairy Break" (72-73/8), possibly the same "fairy brake" I heard about from a man in Portugal Cove South.[11]

In addition to such "mapped" areas are unmarked pitfalls into which one can blunder as into a trap. An informant from Lumsden in Bonavista Bay told a collector how his father once went to look for berries; he was gone for hours, and his friends found him in a valley "walking around and around in circles in a trance." They shouted and shook him until he snapped out of it:

> As soon as he did, he told his friends that he had been in fairyland, and he couldn't get out no matter how hard he tried. He

said the fairies had been holding him captive. As soon as he came out of this trance he recognized where he was and walked out with his friends. (FSC74-121/49)

In Lewin's Cove, another collector's father told how his father once lagged behind as the two of them were returning from the woods. Turning back and calling, he found him "walking around and around":

> He called out again, and this time his father saw him and came. His father said it was like he was in a ring and couldn't get out. He would walk around and end up in the same place he started. He said then he often heard people talking about fairy rings but it was the first time he got caught in one. When my father called out to him he was able to walk out of the ring. (FSC74-11/15)

"Fairyland" can be a place or a state of mind, or both. A three-year-old boy, who was "very wild," got lost in the woods several days, and died two weeks after he was found; his mother "believed the fairies had taken his mind to fairyland" (75-53/15). Around 1944, a ten-year-old boy in Comfort Cove, Notre Dame Bay, "was taken on the fairyland, it was called then, but now is called the pond path" (FSC74-129/38).

In Avondale, many strange things happened in the place from which Dan Costello's father had to move his house, although it was only four years after I interviewed Dan Costello that I learned from his daughter-in-law that they call it "the fairy patch." It was there that Mr. Costello saw the fairies himself. His sister had just made him a new pair of overalls, and he had gone to await the return of the rest of the family from berry-picking:

> When she had them fitted and put on me, she pulled them down, buttoned them up, she said, "Now you're a sport from the west." And I ran over to the road several times, and they wasn't coming. The back road, over through the field. The last time I went over it was getting late, and the clouds was closing in, getting duckish, and I stood up on the fence, and I sang that: that I'm "a sport from the west." And looked down in the other place across the

road, and I saw six big men with gray suits on. They had a stool and all, 'twas sitting on, 'twas three used to stand up. And they had a big book, oh, way bigger than that [gestures to my notebook], and they used to haul that up and one would read and sing, and then would sit down and the others would get up and do the same thing. And I looked at them a while, but I had sense enough to know that it wasn't right. I started to get the cold shivers. And I hopped from the fence, and started to come out through the field. I didn't go over again, though, right? And I come in and told Nelly, my sister, and she said, "Stay over out of it, don't go over any more," she said. "The fairies would have you. . . ." And now, I can remember that as well as the day I saw it. Can show you the place it was at, and everything.

Another time, someone (I think his brother's wife) was cutting hay there:

She had the hay spread out, tossed down on the field. She came over here to get a lunch. And she was just leaving when she went out to the door. And what do you think she saw? The hay was passing over here. All in a cloud. Right up, away up, like as far as that — the helicopter goes. . . . And I went down over — did you ever hear tell of Lee's Pond? Where the Lee's Pond mountain is at. And the hay went along just as high as if it were a plane, went aback of the hills, and that's the last sight she saw of it. When she went over the meadow was cleaned. 'Twas just a bit of straws left around here and there . . . fairy squall, they used to call them here.

Mr. Costello spoke with animation, jumping up and going through the motions of holding a book for the first one; and definitely using the first person — "*I* went down over" — in the second story, before switching back to the third person. On the day we recorded this, I had had coffee with his daughter-in-law Florence, who lives next door, while waiting for him to return from an errand. Ms. Costello said that she had never heard of the fairies

Dan Costello

while growing up in nearby Holyrood, that Mr. Costello's stories were the first she had heard; she emphasized his and "the old people's" complete belief in them.

On another visit almost four years later, Ms. Costello said that not long ago her husband was working in "the fairy patch" when a swirling wind came along, taking rocks and dirt high in the air. He was amazed, and came home and told everyone about it; he had always heard of the "fairy squall," but had never seen one. Ms. Costello also said that last summer Mr. Costello's sister (the one who had made his overalls, now in her nineties and living in New Jersey) visited; I should have heard the fairy stories then, she said. One, according to Ms. Costello's sixteen-year-old son, was about one of their sisters being carried off by a whirlwind until they pulled her down with a rake. She was luckier than a Conception Harbour girl who disappeared when "overtaken by a strong wind," and was returned after refusing to eat fairy food, but left with a permanent speech defect (FSC73-153/28).

There are certain complementary contrasts between the fairy wind and fairy path. Their linkage in the account above highlights their commonality as a horizontal flow over the earth. But the wind is a sudden phenomenon, marked by its occurrence on an otherwise calm day, while the relentless presence of the path with its undeviating travellers is its essential characteristic. "Wind" and "path" encounters are acute and chronic contacts respectively, with corresponding narrative structures and protective practices. "Path" stories usually involve a number of incidents over time, culminating in the dawning recognition of the problem and its solution through house-moving or an exorcism ritual. In "wind" stories, the critical incident is a single episode (although there may be an aftermath in illness or derangement). Being abrupt and unforeseeable, suspect winds demand instant action, so there are verbal formulas and magical acts for ready response. A Conception Harbour student described a berry-picking expedition during which a gust of wind shook the trees around his sister; the father "flung his bucket of berries into the path of the wind and shouted. 'Take this, in the name of God, and leave us alone!'" The trees stopped shaking, and the mother concluded, "We must have been picking on some old path that the fairies used" (FSC73-153/27). A Colliers informant said:

> Grandmother used to always tell us, they [the fairies] used to take the big pooks of hay. You'd see the big pooks of hay rise up in the sky and land right down in another fella's garden. Well, whatever you had in your hand, you'd throw it to them and say, "Bring back my hay," and they'd bring it right back to you. (74-150/11)

Aly O'Brien, who with his brothers operates one of the oldest farms in St. John's (and who holds an honorary degree from MUN for his studies in Gaelic), said that "fairy whirlwinds" at harvest time could carry cocks of oats a hundred yards into the air; on sighting a small whirlwind, one would throw a wisp of straw after it to placate the fairies (74-118/5).¹²

Joe Costello said that a fairy wind "used to take all the dust and all the grass and everything with it; if you was in their way, you'd go too." This is confirmed by a story recorded in 1989 from eighty-year-old Jack McCall:

> Geez, I saw a woman going in a pook of hay, Bride Hall in Colliers. Uh, meself and Ann, me sister Ann, went in for a load of dry boughs — wanted them to make a flake to dry caplin on — and coming down the hill, we're coming right around the garden, it was handy out to the road then, and — the end of Whelan's road — and there was a lot of pooks of hay made up in the meadow. And she was over raking up hay. And all of a sudden this squall of wind come and rolled all the pooks together, took them all in one, *. So I come home to tell Mother, I said, "Bride Hall's gone in a pile of hay." "Ah, nonsense." Sure that night, sure enough, Aunt Mary come down, and sure enough she was looking for Bride Hall everywhere. Couldn't find her. Well, geez, they got the priest in and everything, and the next day they found her in to the side of Three Island Pond knitting stockings. So where'd she get the needles, where'd she get the wool to knit a stocking? And she was seven years in bed, then, never spoke after that. And so what was that? Geez, it had to be fairies. What was it? If a squall of wind was hard enough to take you, it wouldn't give you a set of knitting needles and a ball of yarn. *******. No, my son, as sure as you are there, there's fairies. Because I saw Bride Hall twirling up in the hay and gone. Geez, she was gone three or four days before they found her, and she was in to the side of Three Island Pond, sat down knitting a stocking. She said there was a crowd of horses got around her. Chasing her. And she said there was a woman there with her hands up getting them away from her. [long pause] Oh yes, there was fairies, I want to tell you that. . . . Where'd she get the needles, and where'd she get the wool? She had a hay prong in her hand when

> I saw her. I'm sure the hay prong never turned into a set of knitting needles and a ball of yarn. Yes, as sure as Christ made you, there's fairies.[13]

The transformation of homely objects is one way in which fairy narratives achieve transcendence of everyday life even as they remain grounded in it. A haystack becomes an aircraft, knitting needles are freighted with ominous significance. Mr. McCall's preoccupation with the unnatural knitting needles is one of those subtle cues, or clues, that seem odd unless recognized as a recurrent motif (well, they are still strange — that is their point — but they are not as idiosyncratic as they sound on first hearing). Chapter Five includes the motif of the fairies skewering berries on knitting needles; needles also thread accounts of "the blast," a fairy-inflicted injury known in the literature as "elf-shot," as when "the good people" speared a man in the side with a darning needle when he was trouting at dusk, because they "didn't want him there that hour in the evening". (76-350/20). Like the teacup in "Night Kitchen," an innocent implement of everyday life becomes a noxious dart. A still more common blast missile is straw, as in another account from the emphatic Mr. McCall:

> But there's one thing I believe in, that's fairies. They WAS fairies. My mother was going picking marshberries one time. She got up on ** to go pick marshberries, and she was sat down eating her breakfast . . . and when I come in through the door — "My God," she said, "*** pain in the leg." "Oh yeah, you got a pain in your leg it's not from picking marshberries." "No," she says, "I am not." And before noontime she was in bed. And she was in bed seven or eight days. And all of a sudden the leg got sore, right on the side of the leg. And Dr. Jones from Avondale come over to her. And he took a straw of grass right out of her leg, *** straw of grass, and geez, where'd the straw of grass come from in the leg? I'm sure it never growed in there. . . . It was inside the sore, when the sore broke, that come out on the plaster, a straw of grass. And geez, it was that length. And it was all coiled up.

So where did it come from in the sore? You know there's a lot of things happened, people just didn't stop to realize what it was, what was happening. Some thought it was simple, and more thought it was nothing. But there's a lot of things happen in this world and it wasn't just real, I'll tell you that.

Needles and haystacks, and things common as grass are the stuff of metaphor and fairy lore ("thick as grass," people say of the fairies).

Making hay, once an important outdoor job, is a natural focus for fairy narrative; the importance of wind at that time makes the narrative connection inevitable. A St. Mary's Bay woman noted a fading element of personification when she said that "while she would be out during the summer months making hay a 'gang of fairies' would come and take the stack of hay and spread it all over the meadow," but now "people in around home do not refer to it as such but they call it a whirlwind" (FSC74-102/38). Predictably, the fairies might do the opposite and lend a hand. A collector said:

> The man next door to me home told me of an experience his uncle had [*c.* 1921]. He was tossing his hay one evening down in Argentia. He heard some funny noises and when he looked around he saw about fifty little men dancing around a pile of hay. They were about six inches tall, dressed in red suits with a black belt around it. The language was a foreign one. He ran to get his wife to show her the fairies and when they came back the fairies were gone, but all his hay was dry and stacked in piles. Jim Smith, my informant, says the story is true. (FSC74-123/35)

Even tinier fairies lugged potatoes, ant-like, in another tale. "There is an old man at home who told about fairies that appeared on the windows and streets when his mother was young," wrote the Bonavista collector:

> His mother told him about one of her relatives who came upon some fairies one night as he was walking along with a bag of potatoes. They appeared on his back on the bag of potatoes and he soon noticed that the bag was getting lighter. When they saw

him looking at them, the fairies dropped the bag and ran. He said it took a couple dozen fairies to carry one potato. They were only about three inches long and looked just like a man. When this happened to him the man was about fifty years old so naturally everyone believed him. In fact this old man who told the story said that both he and his wife believe that there are fairies. (FSC74-98/41)

These industrious fairies are reminiscent of those in a Hampshire tale of a farmer who, in hiding, watches fairies remove hay from his barn straw by straw through the keyhole; when one says to another in a small voice, "I weat, you weat?" the farmer leaps out, shouting, "The devil sweat ye. Let me get among ye," whereupon they fly away in fright (Keightley 305–06). In 1990, Macpherson Eveleigh told me:

Well, my father said when he was a boy one time on Fogo Island, there was a certain man went into his store, or his barn, where he had some hay for his animals, and he said when he opened the door there was fairies dancing on the hay. And he said one of the fairies said, "I sweats!" Newfoundland talk. And this man said, "I said, 'the devil sweat 'ee'!"

"I suppose they heard the stories from Ireland, you know, about these little people," he continued, an ironic comment to follow this distinctly English narrative type, recorded mostly in the West Country. There, a farmer spies on fairies (or pixies) threshing, messing up, or thieving his corn, and hears them saying variously to one another: "I twit, you twit" (Crossing 59); "See how I sweat! See how I sweat!" (Charlotte Latham 28–29); "How I do tweat!" (Avon Lea); "I twate" (Briggs *Folk Tales* 1:186); "Tweat you? I tweat?" (Northcote 214); "I tweat. You tweat. Tweat I too" (Northcote 214). "I tweat! You tweat?" (Hazlitt 1:147); "How I do tweet." Farmer: "So thee do tweet, do 'ee? Well then, I do tweet and double tweet, looky zee" (Tongue *Somerset* 118; Whistler 49). In one version the farmer drives them away with a gift of clothing, at which they exclaim, "New toat, new waist-toat, new breeches; you proud, I proud; I shan't work any more!" (Crossing 66). (The reduplicative lispings typify the childlike quality often seen in the fairies, and the farmer reacts much as an exasperated parent might.) This narrative explains the fairies' speech in a text from Old Perlican, Trinity Bay:

> There was one man there, Uncle Tommy Becker, he used to have to tie up a bit of hard bread in his shirttail to keep the fairies away from him. I heard Mother say that when he was across the bay the fairies would be so thick as the grass, pitched on the trees, but if he had the hard bread, he was okay. The fairies used to have a favorite saying, too, for they always said, "I twit, you twit, I see twitweg" to one another and to other people. (72-25/16)

The "I-you" construction also appears in a text from Trinity or Bonavista Bay (the collector is unclear as to the location):

> Similar to the jackie-de-lantern is the fairies. These are little people . . . who are dressed in red and also tow people "away." They are said to offer a cup, saying, "I drink, you drink," whereupon, if you do, you too will become a fairy.[14] (77-238/2)

Direct West Country provenance is also evident in a text from Newman's Cove, Bonavista Bay, in which the collector describes "co-pixies" who "had the appearance of young boys" or "miniature children" who would lead people astray in the woods (77-144/50-57), for the West Country has not only the term "pixy" but "cole-pexy" and "colt-pixy."[15]

Because they are specific, small linguistic clues like "I twit, you twit," and "co-pixies" offer more conclusive evidence about antecedents than comparison on a larger scale, as fairy lore cannot be neatly divided into "Irish," "English," or "Scottish" in the first place, and the quality of sources is uneven in any case. I suspect, for example, that carrying bread comes from old West Country custom, but I base this on a bare handful of allusions.[16] To be sure, the carrying of oats and other staples is well attested in Ireland and Scotland, but more often in connection with critical times than as a routine protection.[17] Nor does the actual deployment of protective substance seem to figure in Irish narrative as it does in Newfoundland, as in a story Joe Costello told about a man working in his garden one evening:

> He was sat down boiling his kettle. It was two women come up, dressed in red, he said, red dresses on them and white flyers on them, and some kind of dark stuff on their head. And he come up and sat down alongside of them. So he never — he wasn't afraid or anything, you know, he never bothered, and after a time, he took out a slice of bread and he broke it in two, reached a piece to each of them. They disappeared right away. They went right on off, he said.

Whatever its derivation, the reason for the prominence of carrying bread in Newfoundland is clear: the likelihood and dangers of going astray are much greater here than in the old world. Dan Costello told of his cousin who disappeared when he went to his rabbit snares on the last day of October: "they said that was really a bad day to go, real fairy time." The searchers finally gave up when the snow came, and the next spring his body was found by trappers who were forced by high water to cross the river in an out-of-the-way spot. Although he knew the woods intimately, he had somehow crossed the Salmonier Line without even knowing it. (Moore had this story from his father, who said it happened in 1938 and that "Jim Costello was a real hunter and knew the woods well.")

It is seldom stated how or why bread affords protection. Some say it is a sop or a substitute, which the fairies would take instead of the person; some that it was for captured persons to eat so that they would not have to eat fairy food. Religious symbolism offers another explanation, since the fairies are supposed to be repelled by religious artifacts: one student said that her mother always called bread "blessed and holy bread" (FSC80-282/*); another, citing its use against "fairies and other creatures," said that "the bread was supposed to be blessed in that it resembled the sacred Host" (FSC80-295/*). One student wrote:

> Bread in a number of Newfoundland families had great religious significance. A housewife when making the bread would make a cross in the rising dough, then make the sign of the cross over the bread. On Good Friday a small loaf was made and this was kept until someone became sick, when a small piece was fed to the patient. Often I have heard one of the family say when someone was wasting a piece of bread, "That's blessed bread you're mauling there." The people in the household would be worried about me and consider me ignorant unless I broke a slice of bread in two rather than cut it.[18] (FSC67C-3/57)

Even without religious associations, bread provides a talisman of domesticity (and culture) against the perils of the wilderness. Its association with everything human is encapsulated in the metaphor for pregnancy, "bread in the basket" (FSC80-289/*) — and why else would the fairies be satisfied with it instead of a baby? Bread's protective essence lies — like all charms for everyday life — not in some rare or singular virtue, but in its very mundaneness. In a magic analogous to the fairies' transformations of everyday artifacts, bread, salt, and coins are invested with supernatural strength.

The salt in bread probably contributed to its prophylactic properties, and salt alone was a protective and saining agent.[19] Virginia Dillon gives a detailed description of its use on the Southern Shore:

> When a person has seen fairies, heard or seen a ghost, or has had a supernatural experience of any kind, he is given salt and water. The salt is stirred into the water and the Sign of the Cross is made by both the "victim" and the person administering. Three drops of the salt water must then be taken.... The salt and water was usually mixed in a cup and after the three drops had been taken, the rest would be thrown into the fire in three parts, in the name of the Father, Son, and Holy Ghost ... I have never actually heard anyone say why this is done but it seems to be considered as protection against some evil which might otherwise result from the experience. (FSC64-1/81-82)

She adds that it was not necessary to have seen or heard anything "not right," but merely to have been in a "place where there were fairies" after dark. She also mentions her grandfather, who lived with her family in his later years:

> He had had a stroke and his mind was not quite right. He came from Witless Bay, two miles away, and he didn't like to be in Mobile. He was always talking about going home. He'd say to my mother, "Give me some salt, I'm going traveling." My mother says that "the old timers wouldn't go anywhere without a bit of bread and salt." (FSC64-1/82)

Several of Moore's informants recalled an Uncle Peter Moore, who had died forty years before, saying, "There's no salt in the fairies' grub." James Costello explained to Moore, "They never can eat salt; just as you never eat their saltless food, they never eat human food with salt in it" (71-42/25). The explanation raises interesting if insoluble questions. Does it suggest that the customs of the past were part of a fully articulated belief "system," in which they had an overt rationale? Or does the explanation's association with an individual suggest that the explicitness was unusual and therefore memorable? Was Uncle Peter simply more articulate or better versed on generally shared concepts than most? Most information about the supernatural is found in narrative rather than abstract propositions or discussion, and even fluent narrators do not necessarily give much attention to the underlying premises of their tales; but this is not to say that native exegesis does not, or did not, exist. A Southern Shore informant was eloquent on the lost meaning of certain customs. "Some of the things old people used to do used to have meanings but you don't understand all of them," he told the collector:

> For instance, going to the well. I minds my grandma making us take a stick with us if we were going after sunset. But she'd make in the fire first and get a stick and put it in the stove. She'd put the stick there and hold it. Now the stick would catch fire. Grandma, she'd just blow off the blaze and she'd say, "Come on now, and go to the well." If you had to go to the well after sunset you had to take that stick. Yes sir, grandma never let us go unless

we bring it too. I suppose, Aubrey, blessed fire, you take Holy Week, the fire is blessed and you got to get a little bit of blessed fire and bring it home and put it in your stove. So it all leads up to something about the fire, see, the fire is blessed.

Collector: But why would you have to take the stick with you?

Mr. C: You know one needs protection. That's what it's for. Yes, it was for protection. One time if you walked in a meadow in the night time, you could get what you called a blast. You know, if you walked in a meadow in the night time, a child could get a sudden pain in your arm or leg or you might be crippled for life after that, see. That was why the old people used to bring the fire.

Collector: Do you know of anyone who got the blast, Mr. C?

Mr. C: Well, I don't know how well to believe this, but grandma told us a story about a young lad who got the blast. He was coming home one night and dark was here. It was dark you know and he was going all he could to get home. And then it happened. Yes, the blast hit him. He took a pain. It was a bad one, too, so grandma says, right here (touches upper arm). He was laid up for two or three days, he was only laid up for a few days, you know, he wasn't crippled for life or nothing. But you can be. Yes, that blast can be mighty awful.

Then if you washed your hair, I minds this well enough, if you washed your hair after night, the pan of water had to be put under the bench and salt put in. You had to put salt in it and leave it be until morning. I minds poor Tom Hersey, Lord have mercy on him, he's dead now, he threw out a pan of water through the door in the night and he come back, and, you see, he was going over and getting a tumbler and he says to his wife, "Where's the salt to, Mary, where's the salt to? They're after me, they'll catch me out there," he says, "I'll banish them now, I'm gonna banish them. Hold on now." He gets the salt and water and puts in it three drops, "In the name of the Father, Son and Holy Ghost," he says. "Now," he says, "I'll throw it out now and all the harm that goes with it."

Collector: What was he trying to banish, Mr. C? Was it fairies?

Mr. C: No, no, child, not them. It was those bad spirits. You had to put salt in the water cause that would keep them off and they'd do no harm. Poor Tom must've forgot what he was doing and threw the water out after night. Now he knew some bad would come. He had to fix that, you know, and salt could do it. Yes, salt is the only thing to banish those spirits. It wasn't fairies, bread is what you need to banish them. (76-82/90-97)

This informant, who himself encountered the devil in the form of a dog, a pig, and an amorphous black shape ("before the cars came, shocking queer things went ahead"), considered the fairies to be relatively harmless:

Mr. C: Now let's see, what will I tell you about today? I didn't say nothing about the dalladadas, did I?

Collector: What are the dalladadas?

Mr. C: Why, they're fairies. You know, little people.... This fella was going ducking, going in through the woods. And when he came to this meadow, it was an open meadow, he looked and about twenty-five of them came. Fairies or dalladadas came. They were little small men and they had tossle caps on. But they didn't do no harm. They didn't do no harm just went right off the path. This fella didn't know where they went. He didn't see them after. Fairies can run so fast, you know, they runs so fast that you don't know where they went.[20] (77-78)

Dan Costello's father was once taunted by unseen tricksy fairies:

We was in the country, logging in the winter. My father was smart then, he knowed every place we was through. He used to have the kettle boiled, and I used to come out with a load of logs.

> And when I'd go in handy to the place we was at, I used to see the smoke, fire place, they'd have the kettle boiled and ready for lunch, you know. And this day I went in, 'twas no smoke. And I said, "That's strange," I was outside of the place then, on another lake, gully we calls it, [with] the old horse and sleds. Went on up in the path, and never heard a [creak?]. No fire started or nothing. *** astray. And I tied on the horse and gave her something to eat, and went up over the ridge, and hauled out, and hauled out, and begar, after awhile I met him coming. He didn't know where he was to. The logs he had cut, was after cutting himself, used to come and pass by him, and say, "Some man's got a nice lot of logs cut there." And he had a scarf on, a woolen scarf, he took that off, and he never saw it after. He laid it down on the thing where he was cutting logs. He used to have that on for going in the morning, the frost and stuff, and put it on in the evening coming home when we'd be finished, and the topcoat. He never saw the scarf after.

A whole way of life is crystallized in this narrative. The frosty mornings, the smoke from the fire, the lunches that make the woods seem as familiar as a kitchen: the story of one strange day captures a hundred ordinary winter mornings in the woods.

When I asked Dan Costello if he'd ever heard that the fairies would take or change a child, he said that the same sister who had sewn his overalls heard about it, "time and again," from a Marysvale woman while living in Sydney, Nova Scotia. This woman said she was baking bread, and sent her little boy to the back of the house for some wood chips to light the fire:

> And he was so long gone she got tired waiting and she went to meet him. And hollered out to him, and when she went out around the house and the pathway, she met a little old worn man coming, right down low to the ground, and he with a pan of chips in his hand. And he handed her the pan. She didn't know what to say. And he came in, and boy, she said, they had

> him in bed for years sick, before he died, Almighty God took him. This little old worn queer person, she said. It was no way handy to the child went out for the chips.... And boy, she had to take and put up with it until he died.
>
> BR: Was that long after?
>
> DC: Yes, I don't know was it two or three years. Yeah, it was in bed, and she doing for it and tending on him, and washing him, changing him, just like the child.
>
> BR: Can a person become a fairy themselves, do you know?
>
> DC: Ah, yes.
>
> BR: How does that happen?
>
> DC: The child, now become a fairy.
>
> BR: So they had it with them?
>
> DC: Yeah, **** changed him. Took the child, see, and sent this old person.

It is curious that in a community apparently without a strong changeling tradition, the fairies, when seen, have a notable female bent. If one were given to the "composite" approach one might say that they didn't need to steal children since, being women, they could have their own; indeed, the notion would be supported by a story told by Bernadine Flynn of Avondale, given by one collector as follows:

> One day when Mrs. Flynn's mother was walking across the barrens to bring dinner to her husband (who worked on the railroad line) she stopped to pick a few strawberries.... Anyhow, when she looked up she saw the fairies with their babies. They were running across the barren. The fairies were dressed in beautiful clothes which had many bright colors. Mrs. Flynn's mother was very frightened but since she had her rosary beads with her she started to say it and the fairies left. The expression she used

> when she retold the story was, "I said to myself, the fairies won't get me this time."
>
> Mrs. Flynn told me that all the family believed that her mother had been bending too long and that when she looked up suddenly she was actually seeing something through blurred vision — not really fairies. However, Mrs. Flynn said that to her dying day [*c.* 1964 at the age of ninety] her mother always insisted that she had seen the fairies and actually had saved herself from them. (FSC71-9/28)

Tom Moore also had this story from Mrs. Flynn, who said that her mother, Mary Hicks, saw "young women in flowing gowns." When I visited Mrs. Flynn on Mr. Moore's introduction, she did not seem very interested in the subject; it was "all imagination," she told me, or perhaps high blood pressure. She said people used to tell a lot of fairy stories, but the only one she remembers is her mother's, having heard it many times. "Mother, you're crazy," Mrs. Flynn would tell her, but her mother would remain unperturbed and maintain that she knew what she saw, and that indeed there were such things as fairies. It might be expected that such a short narrative from an unsympathetic informant would show little variation, and the version Mrs. Flynn gave me was like those in MUNFLA — long bright dresses, babes in arms — but for one startling addition: when her mother said, "You won't get me today," the "swarm" of fairies "took off" for Lee's Pond, where they climbed into a boat; when she blessed herself a second time, they vanished.

This is one of the few instances in which the Newfoundland fairies are shown using boats on their own, so to speak. In contrast to parts of Ireland, where they are said to sail and even to fish,[21] in Newfoundland the fairies are largely angishores (in Newfoundland folk etymology, "hang-ashores" or land-lubbers), except for their vague generic relationships to mysterious lights and phantasms in general. Perhaps they don't like the salt water.[22] They do occasionally interfere with humans in the course of some sea-going endeavour, weighing down boats much as they do wagons or carts; "There's no one allowed in this dory only her own crew" was a formula Branch fishermen used "to keep ghosts or evil spirits from entering the boat" (FSC71-26/47). In 1963, a boat overturned in a storm near Portugal Cove, and all the men got to shore but one, who was found on the shore an hour later, where, according to one of the survivors, his previously black hair was white and "he had only four words to say before he died: 'the fairies got me'" (69-11F/8). His last words echo in a cautionary tale from a Torbay Boy Scout camp, in which a boy sneaks out for a midnight row on the pond, and is found the next morning with his hair, face, and "everything gone bleach white on him," repeating, "The fairies got me! The fairies got me!" So "they brought him into the mental hospital and they still couldn't do anything with him and he's still there to this day, and all he says is 'The fairies got me!'" (72-34/9-17).

The fairies do sometimes have rough magic boats, like the piece of wood upon which they ferried three Avondale children across a pond to an island where they fed them fairy bread (as a result two died young and the third was "never in her 'right mind'") (FSC71-121/13). Another makeshift vessel was "a boat which was made of birch rind and rolled up in the nose like a toboggan" on which a man was taken from a fishing camp on the Labrador to a house where there are "hundreds of small people," although he could not see them at first. Remembering "the old people telling not to eat the food," he abstained and was returned after three days, tipped out of the boat with a smack on the neck. An abcess rose and at the hospital in Battle Harbour "they took out bough sprinkles, old blasty [dry] boughs and stuff out of his neck" (67-32/42-43; also 76-292/7-10).

Another fairy sea story comes from Ron Maher of Flat Rock (near St. John's), who has written two versions of a tale he calls "The Fairy Knap" after a grassy plateau where people carried bread because "there were stories of people being 'took' by the fairies because they could not pay the bread ransom."[23] Around 1818, his story goes, a stranger was helping a short-handed crew bring in their fish; as they pass the knap, he looks up and says, "Many's the night we danced or played Buck-a-hurley there."[24] On landing he jumps from the boat and disappears. In the first version Mr. Maher says simply, "he was a fairy," but in the second he elaborates:

> The story of the stranger and speculation as to who or what was his identity, was soon a prime topic of conversation throughout the community. The itinerant priest was consulted and he allowed the stranger could be a fallen angel. It could be a fairy or it could be the devil himself, personified.

Just as there is the odd fairy boat there are occasional aquatic fairies. One boy thought that six girls swimming at the beach were his sisters and cousins, until he found them elsewhere with dry clothes and hair, and concluded that "the only possible explanation is that the girls he saw were fairies" (FSC67-21/124).[25] In Northern Bay, a collector's forty-year-old uncle was trouting before dawn, standing in four feet of water at the point where a brook entered the ocean, when he saw two men swimming in the water in front of him. When he told Johnny Hogan, "a real old woodsman who lived by himself," about it, Mr. Hogan informed him that the men were "the hollies," waiting to take any trout he might catch. Mr. Hogan knew about the hollies because two of them helped him load kelp every fall, when he would equip them with prongs and they would fill thirty or forty cartloads. In the summer they lived on the bottom; one smoked and the other didn't, and one liked the buns he would bring them and the other didn't (77-141/11-16:C2978/6).

The collector of the above text was unsure whether the "hollies" were "the ghosts of the seamen in the bankers disaster" who usually go by that name, ghostly "survivors" of the 1775 southeast gale that sank almost forty schooners anchored at Northern Bay and killed over three hundred men. But another student who interviewed Mr. Hogan himself said:

> the hollies were supposed to be the voices of the dead seamen who usually crawled up on the rocks in early morning and late evening crying out loud. Sometimes they helped an old sailor or fisherman to haul his trap or dory on the beach. Mr. Hogan, who fished alone, said he even saw them and fished with them for years. He says he was never happier than when he had a partner: the hollies.[26]

The shipwrecked dead are a special category of the dead with strong fairy affinities. One collector said that the victims of the Northern Bay disaster are still heard when the wind is southeast in August: "the cries and voices of the men and crew are now considered fairies" (79-378/13).[27] According to another, "people used to say that you should never go near Trepassey Harbour after twelve midnight because men who had drowned from ships became spirits and would take you with them" (FSC75-179/*). One collector's grandmother told him that around 1870 near Mortier Bay, her stepfather and some men were in the woods cutting, and pitched a tent on a path. That night they saw people walking through the tent; when they reappeared the second night, the stepfather asked, "What in the name of God are ye doing here?" The spirits told him to move the tent one foot to either side because they were in "the path that the shipwrecked dead used to use when they walked up from the sea" (FSC73-43/54).

Spirits plying their paths, fairies sporting in the sea: the otherworlders go about their business without concern for their human counterparts most of the time. As long as each world keeps to itself all is well; attraction of the inhabitants of the separate spheres to one another is the danger zone, as when people are drawn by irresistibly beautiful fairy music. A boy heard it while trouting at Lee's Pond and wanted to stay all night and listen, but "he finally got afraid and came home against his will" (71-42/21). Fairies in turn are drawn to human productions: a Bell Island student said that you should not whistle when walking alone at night "because the fairies are drawn to anything musical" (89-215/23). "Music is bad in the night," says Joe Costello, and tells about a young Avondale man who was walking home early one morning after a kitchen dance, still playing the accordion he had played for the dance, when "a big crowd of people" appeared in the road and started dancing: "It was women and men, he said; they was big, he said, some big and small." The musician fled to the nearest house, and was so ill with fright that they called the doctor and the priest in the morning. "You should never play music in the night, by yourself anytime at night," the priest pronounced. "Music coaxes them around."

Joe Costello never used the word "fairy" in the above account, or in any but the first narrative he gave me, and in that one his self-interruption to supply it suggests that it was as a courtesy to the outsider. I have emphasized the more common references in that account:

> *They* used to carry people away, sure, and everything. One time up here, not far away from here, there was a man went looking for his cow, you know, the cattle used to be out at that time, grazing, and he went looking for his cow in the evening, he got — *the fairies* took him, coming on night, and carried him away. And he was out all night with *those people*. And he said they gave him everything to eat but he wouldn't take nothing. They gave him all kinds of stuff to eat but he wouldn't take it. . . . He slept with them all night so in the morning they went looking for him and found him. The *good people* had him, that's what they used to call *them*.

What the fairies want with humans is seldom explained. Why they would wish to help haul fish or kelp, gather in kitchens, or ride horses is a mystery, unless one views this behaviour as reflecting the simple desirability of being human and doing everyday human things. The taken-for-granted value of the human state may explain why people seldom seem to wonder why the fairies "take" people in the first place.[28] The high regard in which humans hold themselves offers one explanation of the fairies' covetousness.

Another factor in the lack of explanation of fairy ways may be that they are simply accepted as part of nature, like the habits of animals or the changing of tides. This might also explain their relative absence on the water, for in accordance with this view, their natural habitat is the woods and barrens, and they would be as out of place at sea as moose or caribou. Since most Newfoundland settlers came from farming rather than fishing backgrounds, their fairy traditions would be land-based, and so replanted here. The exception, the fairy-like shipwrecked dead, are perpetually trying to get back to land, where the more "ordinary" dead still walk their old pathways, which prudent people keep clear. Smart people also carried bread, salt, or some other token of human culture when they went about the land, knew what to do if a wind seemed peculiar, and were careful at certain times of the year and in certain places. It was all part of living in a world that might contain more than usually met the eye. Only occasionally did one see a caprice of nature — giant hailstones, say, or the fairies.

When I left Dan Costello's house after our first interview, Mr. Costello went out one door to lock up, but made me go out another because I had come in that way and to do otherwise would "change my luck." In the car on the way to Joe Costello's house, he told me about Father Duffy's well, where Father Duffy struggled with an evil spirit, and overcame it when he struck the ground and water welled out. At his brother's house, he tactfully repeated his story of the men in grey to show the kind of thing I wanted, and left, saying "God bless you." (A year later Joe Costello and his wife moved into the St. Patrick's Mercy home in St. John's, where Mrs. Costello died in 1990). When I visited Dan Costello in 1989 to take his photograph, I was impressed once more with his kindliness, as he sat patiently in various lights while I fiddled with the camera. Afterwards he took me to see his horse, and then to his daughter-in-law's house, where he left us again with a benediction. Crossing the hundred feet or so between the old two-storey house and the modern bungalow that could sit on any California lawn felt like crossing a hundred years as well. It was not too hard to imagine the fairies rattling the dampers on Dan Costello's old stove, there in the low, beamed kitchen, the walls decorated with holy cards, horseshoes, and oil lamps; rather harder to think of them dancing on the dishwasher in the newer house! Ms. Costello contrasted her way of life, oriented to St. John's, to that of the old people to whom St. John's is a foreign place, visited only when someone is sick or dying in hospital. It is almost as if there are two Avondales, a new suburban community superimposed on the old self-contained one. The old Avondale was a complex place, with room for more than its momentary inhabitants; the otherworld lay just outside the thin membrane of everyday life, and the inevitable brushes of the denizens of the various worlds with one another are chronicled in oral tradition. To one used to such a wealth of possibility (however fearsome), an official world view that excludes such dimensions must present a rather flat and pallid prospect. Ms. Costello thinks that once

Dan and Joe Costello's generation is gone, it will be the end of fairy tradition. But perhaps her family or generation will remember their narratives, bringing them out occasionally like old photo albums and pondering the pictures they contain.

4 | *Tradition and the Interpretation of Experience*

This chapter considers how and why people decide that an incident involved "fairies," and some uses and results of such an interpretation. "How" includes "when," for interpretation is not necessarily a single definitive act, but can be a process that continues over time and varies according to narrative context; accordingly, "a" narrative is not a static entity but subject to re-evaluation and reworking over time and in different circumstances, and each performance or text illuminates the others. The uses of fairy narrative may be personal or social, or both, and like the fairies themselves range from positive and humorous to downright sinister; some are demonstrable, others speculative. The personal experience narratives on which this chapter is based come from three married couples from three different communities, who have several features in common: they are successful, active members of their communities, who can in no way be considered "marginal" or even unusual; they enjoy and support each other's narratives; and, they are kind and hospitable people who do not mind a stranger on the doorstep asking about fairies.

Roy and Mildred Kelloway live in Perry's Cove, a Protestant community of about a hundred people which relied mainly on fishing in the past, although as in most Conception Bay communities people travelled to Labrador, to St. John's and Bell Island, and to construction projects throughout the Avalon Peninsula. Mr. Kelloway was born in Perry's Cove in 1919 and has worked as a fisherman, miner, and carpenter. In two MUNFLA interviews he gave accounts of seeing the fairies, which I found striking for his unambiguous assertion that it was indeed the fairies, for his emphasis on the clarity of the memory, and for the visual detail in his narration of it. "There's no make-up to that at all," he assured the first student, "what I'm telling, I can really see it in me eyes now just as plain as I could then and I suppose that's what, that's over forty year ago" (76-330:C2884/6). Mrs. Kelloway, who grew up in nearby Victoria, also had a fairy experience, which was briefly noted by the students who interviewed Mr. Kelloway, but which she recorded herself for the first time in 1984.

The first two interviews with Mr. Kelloway were made in 1976 and 1982 by Eleanor and Cavelle Penney, relatives of Mr. Kelloway (76-330:C2884/1-6 and 82-383:C10340/m.t.). Eleanor Penney wrote that Mr. Kelloway was "eager to tell about this, and I believe he would like to get a chance to tell this story which many people had scoffed at," so in 1984 I asked Mr. Kelloway to tell it again. Taken together, the three versions (the Penneys' and mine) show the variation to which even a personal experience narrative may be subject over time, and how subtle differences within a basically stable outline can illuminate a single performance or text. Mr. Kelloway told me that one October evening when he was about ten years old, he and two brothers were pulling bog stumps in an area called the Droke when they heard women's voices singing the hymn, "Abide with Me":

> . . . and by and by we came to an opening out here, and looked over across in the marsh, and there were three women. So far as I was concerned there were three women, they was standing up. Big women. As big as the wife there, but not quite so fat, but they were so big as that. And they were standing up in this marsh. And everything that they had on was lily white. They had a big-brimmed hat on, each one of them, like straw hats, we'll say, you have on in the summertime. And their dresses were white; even their shoes, you could see down to their shoes, that was white. And we looked over and they stood up. And they looked over at us and they started to make some sounds like, "Whoo-hoo," you know.

BR: When they saw you.

RK: When they saw us, they started to "Whoo-hoo" like they wanted us to answer them back, you know. So anyway, we looked over towards them again, and they done the same thing again. So the youngest brother, he was only about, what, eight and a half or nine year old at that time, he wanted to answer them back. And the older brother said, "No, don't do that." So, he didn't do it anyway. Now we came on. So now it was getting dark. And we were coming on out now. And we had a little cart just in on top of the hill there, and when we got out to that, on the level, we put the turn [load of wood] and stuff on, put the three turns on and hauled it out. But anyway, my mother and my cousin's wife, they got uneasy, they were worried about us, see? So they came to look for us. And when we got out we stopped and we seen those two women coming in, almost dark then — this was my mother and my cousin's wife — coming in to look for us. So they came up where we was to and asked us what happened, you know, we was late. We said no, we was just working away and time went by and we didn't think about coming home, not then, you know. But while we was at that, this — those sounds came up over the hill again, alongside of us. And we all stopped and listened. The five of us. And they sang that hymn, the last part of that hymn again, the last verse of the hymn. They finished off the hymn. And Mother said, "That's fairies." She used to be telling us stories about fairies, years ago, when we were growing up, you know, "Watch what you're doing if you goes in the woods, don't cross the marshes," and so on, you know, and turn your pockets inside out if you happen to go in the woods, that would be a good thing to do to keep the fairies away, this is what the old people used to tell us, years ago, you know. Now whether there's anything to it or not I don't know; but I know I turn my pockets when I goes in the woods, if it's winter, summer, anytime, I always turn one of me pockets inside out, you know, just take it and pull it out, you know, that's all there is to it. But anyway, Mother said we'd have to go on home. So we left and come on out, put our bit of wood on the cart and come on home. And as we were coming along, they finished off that verse, anyway, or they disappeared out of our hearing. So when we got home — Mother didn't say too much, in there, about those fairies — but when we got home she started telling us a story about it, you know, about those fairies, and what they do with you, and so on, see. But I've heard other people talking about fairies, fairies as a — some people say, a small people. But those were three big women that we saw. And it was no one here in the Cove, we found out that much, there was no one in there that day from around here, this neighborhood, you know. So it had to be, uh, it had to be the fairies that Mother was telling about years ago.

Mr. Kelloway had his own tape recorder running as he spoke, making a tape for his grandson, so he was not tailoring the account for me. Nevertheless, certain small differences in the three accounts are probably attributable to an outside audience (me). The most significant is *who*, at the time of the event, identifies the figures as fairies. In Eleanor Penney's text, the youngest brother wanted to answer when the women hailed them, but Mr. Kelloway stopped him: "I had sense enough to say no, don't do that, you know . . . I had an idea there was something different about this" (C2884/3). In Cavelle Penney's text, it is Mr. Kelloway who wants to answer, but is stopped by his brother: "My brother said, 'No, don't sing out to them,' he said, 'don't do that because they might lead us astray'" (C10340/m.t.). In his version to me, Mr. Kelloway puts himself in a more neutral role between brothers, by having the oldest brother stop the youngest from answering: "I suppose he had more understanding, and maybe heard more stories about it," he explained later in the interview. The appeal to tradition and authority, rather than to personal acuity, is strengthened by his mother's ready diagnosis ("and Mother said, 'That's fairies'"), which does not appear in the Penneys' texts. Thus, in his

4 | Tradition and the Interpretation of Experience

version to me, Mr. Kelloway slightly distanced himself from the original identification, at the same time supporting it by showing that it was not his personal fancy.

It would not have been surprising if Mr. Kelloway had been even more reserved about his own opinion; I was, after all, a stranger, and my position in terms of belief unknown. In contrast, Eleanor Penney was in clear sympathy with the idea, having herself experienced something unusual when playing as a child on the same spot where the women in white stood:

> I never spoke or told anyone about it, but I can remember getting an odd, eerie feeling. However, fairies never entered my mind. My aunt, with whom I stayed, had often mentioned how Roy had seen the fairies, but I did not know exactly where. (76-330/5)

Possibly it was her aunt's version of Mr. Kelloway's experience, or her own imperfect recollection of it, which this student reported on a Survey Card *before* her interview with Mr. Kelloway:

> [Mr. Kelloway], along with his two brothers, went berry-picking late one afternoon. They went to a place called "the Droke." This one brother saw three women, whom he at first thought were members of the community. Upon getting closer he knew he had never seen them before. They were strangely dressed and were singing a hymn, "Abide with Me." They were holding hands and dancing in a circle. He even remembered that the soles of their shoes were white. Since then he has always sworn that he had seen the fairies. (FSC76-140/*).

I was taken aback when I found this card after my interview, for "dancing in a circle" — kicking up their heels, even, to reveal the soles of their shoes — seemed inconsistent with the strong visual emphasis in the taped accounts. Moreover, my impression was that, although Mr. Kelloway enjoys telling "old cuffers" (as he says), he does not consciously embroider them.[1] He feels that stories should be true to be worthwhile; for example, he said that he knows someone who could tell me fairy stories, but they would all be "lies." "What

I'm telling you is really true," he insisted, "if it didn't happen to me, I wouldn't be able to tell it, you know what I mean, it's not a story I heard someone else telling because it really happened to me, you know." There is nevertheless some latitude from telling to telling, which Mr. Kelloway at one point acknowledged himself, when Cavelle Penney asked if he had any other experiences with the fairies:

> Not too much with fairies after that. I never went in the woods without turning me pockets inside out. . . . The fairies won't bother you if you got some of your clothing turned inside out . . . I'd turn meself inside out, rather than they'd carry me away, you know. [laughter] But that's the experience I had with the fairies now. [pause] That is true, too, I mean, I tells about a [few?] things, but *most* of it is true, you know. (m.t. and emphasis)

Recognizing a small degree of elaboration on a basically true story, then, and leaving aside the fourth text (dancing in a ring) as dubious reportage, two more variations are worth noting as likely adjustments to audience. One is that Mr. Kelloway told Eleanor Penney that the youngest brother saw, not women, but "with him telling it, 'twas little people was around him," a differential vision implied in his words to me, "so far as I was concerned there were three women . . . big women." He also told her that when he got an accordion years later, he immediately played "Abide with Me," which came to him "just as natural as if I was playing a gramophone." The fairies made a deep aural as well as visual impression, then, with a melody that might also be taken as a small musical gift from them.[2]

A final notable difference between the first and subsequent recordings is probably not due to audience but to laws of oral tradition: it is almost inevitable that the number of women in the marsh should change from two to three, three being the standard for characters in folk narrative and for mysterious women in particular, from the weird sisters of *Macbeth* (fairies in some sources) to the "three sisters of fairies" whom a sixteenth-century charm invokes to appear "in forme and shape of faire women, in white vesture" (Ritson 27).[3] A more recent triad appears in an 1888 Irish story of "three beautiful ladies, all in white," who assault a girl for refusing them milk (L. Wilde *Legends* 97), and in 1932 a Dartmoor peat-cutter described the fairies: "They'm like white ladies dancing along-like, but it doant do to speak to 'em, aw no!" (Fielden). The Kelloway boys knew it didn't do to speak to them; as Mr. Kelloway concluded his account to Cavelle Penney:

> So I always believed in fairies after that. We had no trouble getting out, though, just the same, now, because we didn't answer the fairies back.

"Women in White" is one of a set of stories, mostly humorous, that Mr. Kelloway told in all three interviews. In contrast, the following account is not part of an established repertoire, but was elicited by my question as to what kind of stories his mother told about the fairies. It might be termed "passive" or memory lore in that he does not perform it like the others, but it is active in that he remembers it clearly and in that it silently informs his understanding of his own experience:

> So now I'm going to tell you this story, I suppose it's, oh that's a long time ago. Mother used to be telling us when we were smaller boys, you know, about the fairies. So she told us one about — she had a twin sister and an older brother. And they lived in Spout Cove, just down below us here, next settlement [now deserted]. So they went up on the railway track one day to — just went up to have a look around, to see the train coming or something like that, some amusement, you know. And her sister started to run away from them. Started to go in over the railway track, all she could go, and they couldn't catch up to her, and they started to sing out to her and she wouldn't, she wouldn't stop, she didn't hear them, or something. But anyway, the older brother, he thought about what his mother used to tell him years ago, you know, about if anyone was fairy-led or anything like that and they couldn't get no sense into them, call their name back-foremost, see? So her name was Jessie, Jessie Trickett. And it came in his mind, and he sang out, "Trickett, Jessie." And she stopped. So

they went up to her and asked her what happened and how she come to be running and so on. Well, she said she was in contact with a lot of little people, surrounded by little people. And they had green caps on, high green caps with tassels on the top part of them. They was only little small people. And they were going, and she was following them. And she couldn't, she didn't know anything about her brother and sister she left behind at all, she was just going with these people, you know. And she said she was very happy. Going along with them, you know. But when they stopped her and got her back, she got sick, then, after that ... for a few days. I suppose she realized what was going on, you know, and what happened to her and so on. So, that's what happened to *her*. So that's a true story now, that Mother used to tell me, and she used to tell lies no more than I do.

Linda May Ballard, citing an informant who believes his aunt saw the fairies because "she wouldn't tell a lie," writes that "respect for the previous holders of a belief may, in itself, be a sufficient reason for sharing that belief" ("Authenticity" 38); certainly this is true for Mr. Kelloway. When something happens that conforms with the outlines of tradition, belief is reinforced through personal experience, which confirms its validity. Stories offer models for action and interpretation, and even for experience itself. In crisis, Jessie's brother "thought about what his mother used to tell him," and called her name backwards; Jessie, also in accordance with the traditional script, stopped.

Lauri Honko points out that "a person who has experienced a supernatural event by no means always makes the interpretation himself; the social group that surrounds him may also participate in the interpretation" ("Memorates" 18). Mr. Kelloway's mother joins Mrs. Meaney's mother and Mr. Dan's sister in the narrative role of naming the fairies; the comparison of different versions from Mr. Kelloway and Mrs. Meaney, however, shows that this is one of the more variable elements. Honko also observes that the interpretation may be made long after the event, "as a result of later deliberation." This is illustrated by an account Mr. Kelloway gave me of being lost in St. John's

4 | Tradition and the Interpretation of Experience

thirty years ago. Although he told the second student he had had no further fairy experiences, it seems that since then he has decided that there was something unusual about the day he became confused in well-known streets. He describes his repeated attempts to orient himself:

> But when I'd go around that bend, I couldn't get no sense, see nothing — everything was changed to me, the houses, and the shops — everything was different, you know. So when I looked across the street towards Prowse Avenue across Pennywell Road, on the opposite side there was a little store there, a little knick-knack store where you can buy a few apples, or ice cream, and so on, you know, I think it's still there on the corner. But anyway, this man was there standing on the corner looking over across where I was.

Eventually he asked the man for directions, which instantly set him straight ("everything come right clear to me, I could see everything in a glance"); it transpired that the other man had been in a state of confusion as well, and Mr. Kelloway gave *him* directions:

> ... that's all I thought about it after that, it never come into my mind to — but I often thought about those strange places I saw on Pennywell Road that didn't look like the places I was used to. 'Cause I traveled there, I suppose, fifty times before that, you know.

"You were fairy-led," concluded Mrs. Kelloway.

The mutual support of one another's interpretations is apparent in the following recording of an experience Mrs. Kelloway had when she was about thirty-five years old:

> My sister-in-law and I went berry-picking. Anyhow, come the rain, we got in over the hills, come the rain. So she said, "We'll go out this way now," she said. So I said, "Well, you'll have to get ahead of me because I don't know this place very well," you know? So me sister-in-law went on, we got in this narrow path, and all in around here, she led and I went behind her, we talking

away, you know? So boy, we walked and walked and walked, and by and by we got to this place — everything looked so strange, and it was a little bit foggy, but not very much. So anyhow, we got to this place, 'twas a big running brook, was no way to cross the brook because the water was too high. And on one side was a big field of cabbage, and on the other side was potatoes and carrots and everything like that. Two big fields on both sides of this big brook, oh, way wider than this kitchen.

RK: No way you could get across it.

MK: No way could we get across it. Well, it struck me right quick. I said to me sister-in-law, I said, "We're astray. We're gone astray."

RK: It was foggy out, wasn't it?

MK: A little bit foggy. So anyhow, she stopped too, "Yes," she said, "we're astray." "Well," I said, "I often heard," I said, "when you goes anywhere and you thinks you're astray, turn, and go back, again." So anyhow, there's a place in here over the hills that when me other daughter was young she used to go swimming, they used to call it the Dark Hole. And I was only in there once, that's all. So anyhow, I said, "If we could get back," I said, "to the Dark Hole," I said, "I'd find my way from that. I think." So anyhow, between where we stopped and this place they call the Dark Hole, there's rocks and hills, and trees, and everything in the world; it'd be hard to get through, but anyhow we turned and we went back and we never had a bit of trouble — I don't believe I seen one tree to go through, that's the truth.

RK: Those trees and rocks is really there, too, you know, they're in there right now.

MK: Yes. And all of a sudden we got to this place I knew was the Dark Hole, see? So I said, "This is it," I said to my sister-in-law. I said, "Come on, this part here," I said, "I knows." We only just had to go then a little ways and we could see the houses, you know, over on the other side of Perry's Cove. So we was okay, then, we got home okay. But we often talked about it, and we've trampled in over the hills a hundred times since that, and we never ever seen this big running brook, and we never ever seen the gardens where the vegetables was to. It's not in there! No, even —

RK: Oh, no, there's no way it's in there.

MK: Even the gardens is not in there. So I don't know — we must have been fairy-led that day, that's all I can say.

Mildred and Roy Kelloway

This account highlights several factors that may usefully be borne in mind for the many stories about women, berry-picking, and fairies. First, like Mrs. Kelloway, many women married away from their home communities and were thus on unfamiliar ground when they ventured away from the new community. The sister-in-law might have been expected to be more familiar with it, but even she was in alien territory in that berry-picking was the only time of the year that most women spent appreciable amounts of time in the open, away from the home, community, and gardens. (Queen Maloney has written that berry-picking in the past involved travelling longer distances than it does today, because foraging animals would have grazed the bushes over around the roads and settlements.) It is hardly surprising that they got lost. But in contrast to men who go astray cutting wood or hunting, who typically go to great lengths to establish their intimate knowledge of the area, Mrs. Kelloway freely admits that she didn't know it well, and that she and her sister-in-law were "talking away" as they walked.

A home-centred view of women should not be exaggerated, however. A Ferryland collector interviewed a woman "known as a great storyteller" who was also "a great berry-picker.... She travels for miles in the country." Mrs. Clover (also described as exceptionally well educated) always carried bread, which several times saved her from the fairies, once when she was lost all night along with her eight-year-old son, and another time when she "fell and knocked herself out":

> Mrs. Clover said that when she woke up she had a strange feeling about her which she couldn't understand. She felt the fairies were there and found the bread so they left her alone. (75-53/14-18)

Experience in the woods provides raw material that can be fashioned to various ends. For anyone who took pride in his or her knowledge of the woods, the fairies could provide an explanation for having become lost, and a skilled narrator could convert the potentially embarrassing event into a heroic — or at least comic — exploit emphasizing his knowledgeability and bravery in the face of understandable bewilderment. Some of these accounts are dramatic indeed, like one from a Colinet man:

4 | Tradition and the Interpretation of Experience

It was March 1940. It was raining hard that night. Now I had no oil clothes or nothing, but still I was as dry as I am right now sitting here at this table. I left Mt. Carmel four o'clock in the evening and never reached home until one o'clock in the morning. I came to Colinet and travelled across the ice to John's Pond. I was on my way home from John's Pond to North Harbour and it was at the Beaver Ponds that the fairies attacked me and took control of the horse. Whatever way I'd turn her, she'd head back toward John's Pond. The fairies would not let the horse leave the pond. So I tied the horse to a stump of a tree on the side of the pond. And you should hear the gibberish and singing all around me. It nearly set me batty. No man would believe the singing, dancing, and music of these fairy characters. They were so handy they were within reach. When the cloud left, I put my head close to the water, and I saw little things on the side of the bank, around eighteen inches high, like rabbits. I tried to catch them, but they played all around me. They were teasing me. So I said, "Have your way, ye damn things." I left them alone and went back and lay on the sled. I was going to stay there the night. I stayed for so long and couldn't stand it anymore. No prayer was any good. So I made oaths and swore on them. It was just like an orphanage when I started swearing. Such crying and screeching you could hear as the little creatures left and went eastward. The horse's eyes lit up the pond. When I finally got home, I untackled the mare from the sled and instead of going to the barn she headed right back up the hill again. I was from four o'clock to one o'clock in the rain, but still my cravat didn't have a speck of rain. After that the horse couldn't be held going across the pond. Others wouldn't ride her at all on the pond because she travelled so fast. Once she got off the pond, she was back to her own pace again. (74-210/37-41)

Another man was walking in the woods wearing pot lids on his feet like "rackets" when he met the fairies: "I had to chop them off my feet, they got around me that thick" (64-13:C55/m.t.), he said, and although it is not clear whether he had to rid himself of the improvised snowshoes to escape, or he had to hack the fairies off them, the image is all the more alarming for being left undetailed.

Compared to such graphic accounts, Mr. and Mrs. Kelloway's experiences are mild, and readily explicable in naturalistic terms to anyone so inclined. There is nothing extraordinary about a cabbage patch and brook, except their being, like fairy trees, where they never were before. The claim that they are "not in there" should not be discounted too readily, because despite what I have just said about unfamiliar places, people did know cultivated spaces well. Similarly, Mr. Kelloway's assertion in "Women in White," that "there was no one in there that day from around here," cannot be summarily dismissed, as people in a small community do note the whereabouts of its members and the presence of strangers. Strangers unexpectedly encountered may, in legend at least, be taken for supernatural personages. A "strange man" in St. George's was assumed to be a ghost as there was "no report of a stranger" in the community that day (81-491/32); a St. Bride's woman, "having never seen this man on a bicycle before," rushed to her husband crying, "Oh Sacred Heart of Jesus, John, the devil is gone down the road on a swivel" (FSC80-315/*). On Fogo Island, a woman saw her friend's son playing with another young boy on a marsh:

> The strange boy was a mystery. The community was rather small and everyone knew everyone else. Visitors were such a rarity that everyone would know if there were strangers in their midst. Mrs. Jane had not heard about any visitors to the Island, so who was this strange child?

She hurried the reluctant boy away from the stranger, whom he could not remember as soon as he "came to himself" some way from the marsh. At his house the woman informed his mother, "He was a fairy boy ready to take Allen away. It was a good thing I came when I did" (79-411/24). Even unfamiliar animals might be suspect: "Most wild animals were looked on suspiciously to be fairies," claimed one collector (72-181/7).

4 | Tradition and the Interpretation of Experience

The core of Mr. and Mrs. Kelloway's stories is realistic in that neither of them saw or heard anything impossible to explain in non-fairy terms. To see their experiences as fairy-influenced is a choice: they *like* to think they had a brush with the fairies. One informant was explicit about choosing a fairy interpretation over other possibilites, when he told about hearing voices and laughter coming from the face of a cliff:

> Now the logical explanation of these voices were that I was on a high elevation on a clear sunny day. The children were out to recess at the school at Great Paradise and maybe their voices were echoed in the cliff at a distance of three or four miles. I prefer to think of them as the voices of the little people, or maybe they were poltergeist. (79-340/6)

A supranormal interpretation turns an everyday event into a remarkable one, and into a good story that attracts and engages other people. (The student wouldn't be interviewing the man quoted above if he said he heard schoolchildren's voices, and I wouldn't have met the Kelloways if it had only been local women in the Droke.) The narrative impulse is often overlooked in the study of "belief," although Richard and Eva Blum make it a working hypothesis in *The Dangerous Hour* that supernatural narratives "provide an aesthetic and social opportunity for narrator and listener" in illiterate village culture (7). One need not be illiterate, however, to enjoy or employ an oral art form, just as one need not be unaware of alternative explanations of a strange event. The desire for a good story is surely as important as other psychological and sociological factors, all of which combine with traditional models and materials to determine how the narrative takes shape: a choice in favour of the mysterious coins' valuable currency for social exchange.

Individual choice is an important consideration, too, in which aspects of a body of tradition are accepted for "belief." People do not unthinkingly accept a whole "set" of traditions, but evaluate them according to experience, authenticity, and other criteria; they are selective in what they take from the reservoir of available ideas and how they use it. Most use "tradition" creatively even when they consider themselves to be merely reporting, and personality and circumstance influence how they fit it to their own ends, whether consciously or unconsciously. This view may help to explain the wide variation in character imputed to the fairies; why, for instance, the genial Kelloways have not heard of the fairies doing anything really bad. Perry's Cove did have grim fairy traditions, for one informant recalled an event of 1932, when he was sixteen:

> ... [the informant] remembered seeing a girl being "taken away" by the little people. She was out sliding with a group of children one day — she was probably about nine at the time — and her slide tumbled off the route into the marshland. Several men who were working in the area heard her frantic cries and hurried to help her, although a short interval elapsed before she was reached. No amount of persuasion could coax her away and finally physical force had to be employed while she kept crying out that "she wanted to go back." They brought her to the priest who blessed her and tried to allay her hysteria, but she was never really the same afterwards. All she would do was chop wood and keep it piled up in the kitchen. You couldn't get her to say anything and she even had to be told to sit down, otherwise she would remain standing and staring vacantly before her. She was just a young woman when she died, only in her thirties, and in all that time she never got any better. (70-20/53)

Mrs. Kelloway did say she read about a woman who found a "different baby" in the cot one day, but got her own back in a few days.

> MK: I only read this, oh yes, I read that in a book. But this happened — that did happen to — like seventy or eighty years ago, you know, perhaps in my grandmother's time, you know. It happened, according to the book, it really happened, you know.
>
> RK: I don't think anyone would make up these stories, I don't see how they could, you know what I mean, there's something almost impossible to do, to make up a real story like that, you know.

4 | Tradition and the Interpretation of Experience

> MK: And sure it really happened one time way back in me grandmother's time into Victoria that there was three women went bakeapple-picking in the marshes. And they was never found after. And never heard tell of them. I don't know what did happen to them, you know.
>
> RK: Well, that's what happened, fairy-led, I suppose.
>
> MK: I suppose the fairies carried them away somewhere, yeah. That's only, now, what I thinks, you know.

The Kelloways' scrupulous self-restriction to narration of their own experience would help them to rule out parts of fairy tradition they found unacceptable, and their dispositions probably incline them to a benign view as well. To Mr. Kelloway:

> There's something about those people, those fairies we was talking about, there's something about it that's always happy. You know? 'Cause my mother's sister, she was saying how those little people was happy, the ones she saw was small fairies, little ones — I suppose it's fairies, it was little fellows with green caps on, you know. But the ones I saw were big women. Tall women, you know, like an ordinary woman, we'll say. All dressed in white with this stripey wide-brimmed hat on. So they was a happy lot; when you're singing a hymn you've got to be pretty happy. (laughter)

Most of Mr. Kelloway's stories reveal a humorous turn of mind and a nostalgic view of the past (the exception is his frightening encounter with a ghost on the road one night). In the first MUNFLA interview, when asked what they did for entertainment while fishing on the French Shore, he said, "We had no worries about that down there, there was always something to see to make you laugh. Them was the good old days, the happy old days." In all three interviews, he talked about the intense cold of winters in the old houses: how when you opened the hall door to go upstairs the gale nearly knocked you down, and how the boys, all in one bed, heaved everything they could find over themselves for cover. Once he woke with his lip frozen to the quilt, it wouldn't come loose until the heated kettle was applied. "'Twas hearty old days, happy days," he concludes. "Everyone used to be happy," he told me, they didn't have much but were content; it would be sad if people never knew what life used to be like, which is why he is making tapes about it for his grandson. I think that for Mr. Kelloway the fairies are emblematic of this vanished happy past.

As with most of my other informants, the Kelloways' interest in the fairies coincides with an interest in the past and a wide knowledge of other traditions. On one visit after our interview, we discussed blood-stopping, toothache charms, worm knots, wart cures, and the like. Mr. Kelloway can "put away" warts himself, having been given a charm at fourteen by a man in his twenties; he cannot disclose it without losing it. Mrs. Kelloway thinks that a good doctor has to have a charm and that perhaps they get one in medical school (she speaks of it as a thing tangible as a textbook, and indeed some charms are inscriptions requiring no special powers on the part of the owner). When she told the doctor that Karen, their daughter, had been having the "old hag" (a certain kind of nightmare), the doctor said that, being from Spaniard's Bay, he knew what she meant, but if she told that to a doctor in the U.S., he would laugh his head off. Mrs. Kelloway's sister (I think it was) told her to put Karen's slippers outside the door every night, which worked.[4] Mr. Kelloway gets the old hag as well, waking in a "vat of sweat"; he says it happens when you're on your back and is caused by blood stopping up or something like that. Mr. Kelloway also says that he "died" once, and found himself in a huge red plush room with brass plates on the wall. There were all kinds of people there, all happy, and he was happy himself; he wouldn't have cared if he never came back. But the Kelloways are bound to find good company wherever they go, amiable as they are.

In January 1988, after a hiatus from fieldwork, I found myself missing the storytelling sessions that had sparked my earlier efforts; so I placed a short piece on the fairies in *The Seniors' News* requesting information from readers. I received a call from Mr. Nick Shannahan of St. John's, who has a summer cabin in Bellevue, Trinity Bay, where he has heard Jim Lynch tell "enough stories to fill several books" about spirits and other strange things, including being "carried away" by the fairies. So I went to Bellevue and found Mr. Lynch in his yard, building a small ornamental bridge. (Later, in summer, the yard was full of fantastically decorated and painted furniture of his own design; he built the house himself, too, cutting every board.) Mrs. Katharine (Kitty) Lynch invited me in. She is in her seventies, and Mr. Lynch was born in 1905.

It took some time and persuasion to get Mr. Lynch to talk. He said that you had to be in the mood to tell stories, that it was one thing to be sitting around having a bit of rum and a game of cards (apparently the situation in which Mr. Shannahan heard him), but another to tell them "cold." Mrs. Lynch, on the other hand, was very forthcoming, and after she talked a while, Mr. Lynch got interested and told some stories himself. As usual, I did not tape on this occasion but asked to come back a second time. On the second visit, Mr. Lynch once again demurred, saying that I wouldn't understand a lot of the words he would use, because I didn't understand what life was like then; it would be no good because I "wouldn't be able to picture it." He was also put off by the tape recorder, but we (Mrs. Lynch, Martin Lovelace, and I) encouraged him, and finally he was prevailed upon to tell how he'd gone to cut wood for railway ties in the deep snow of a February morning, in a place he knew well since he "spent all his time in there":

> And anyhow, the first thing I knew, I was down into a new path, that was never there where I was to, I didn't go very far out of the mish [marsh]. And I thought it was a queer thing for a new path to be down there. So anyhow, I said, I'll go down the path and have a look, see? I went down the path so far, and there was a narrow path across the main path. I know it was strange, 'cause ne'er path, I know there's ne'er path there. I said I'll come back now, and try to see where I was to. And when I come back, I was around the back of a hill. I come up to a square cliff, about ten feet high, end of the path. And I knew then, something wrong.

> And I could see the houses over on the other side of the bay. New Harbour, and Green's Harbour and all along there. And how I got down there, I don't know, I guess I got lifted up and brought down there. I never walked down there, sure of that.
>
> KL: It would be a long time before you could get through that far.

"So anyhow, I knew there was something wrong," Mr. Lynch continued, describing his repeated attempts to orient himself and find the familiar path.

> I come back down along by the side of the pond again, and still no path. And I said, strange thing. So, the pond was only about a quarter of a mile up from the marsh, up from Samson's Pond, see? So I says I'll go up through the woods, now, I'll have to cross the path somewhere. So I was nearly up to the marsh when I comes across the path. And I went back to where I left from in the morning, it was only a quarter past ten then. I went over four mile of ground. And after that, when come four o'clock, *** in the thick woods, the dark came over like it was four o'clock, see. It's hard to believe it. So there was something strange about that, wasn't it?
>
> [All agree and talk at once.]
>
> ML: So there's no way you could have travelled that far.
>
> JL: 'Cause if I'd had to travel it, it'd take me half a day.
>
> KL: But the strange thing to me is those two paths, and nobody working them. One path going one way, a wide one, and then there was a small path, he calls it a hand-slide path, going the other one. And there was nobody in there doing any work.
>
> JL: I looked across there, the other side of the bay, New Harbour, Green Harbour, and all down the shore, I could see the houses.
>
> [KL assures me that he knows the woods inside out, it is "plain truth" that he's telling.]

> BR: And you never saw them after that.
>
> JL: Never saw nothing, never heard nothing.
>
> KL: Never see nothing, never heard nothing. But he told people about it, they told him it was the fairies playing tricks on him.
>
> JL: Played tricks on me alright!

Here is a reverse "supernatural lapse of time in fairyland," as scholars like to call it when someone thinks he has been in the fairies only a short time, while years have passed in the real world.[5] The subjective sense of time seems to be the "strangest" aspect of the experience to Mr. Lynch, while Mrs. Lynch fixes on the objective fact of the paths that were not there before.

Like Mr. Kelloway, Mr. Lynch has strong family tradition upon which to draw in making a fairy interpretation. The fairies played a trick on his father once on the Ridge, a long, thin piece of land jutting into the bay, now the Bellevue Beach Provincial Park (where one of the Lynches' sons is chief park officer) and the site of the original settlement.[6] The elder Mr. Lynch was chopping wood, and "the fellow started cutting way off from him, see? And every chop he'd make, the other fellow'd chop handier." The "other fellow" was a fairy, or a fairy manifestation; when the sound got too handy (i.e., close) for comfort, Mr. Lynch decided "he'd leave it, he knowed about the fairies on the Ridge":

> KL [aside]: People used to see them.
>
> JL: So anyhow, he put the wood he had cut on his back to bring out to the beach, see? And when he started travelling, he got into the biggest kind of woods, big birch, and big dry rampikes and all that never grew on the Ridge. And he travelled until he got tired, and said he knowed he was astray, so he hove down carrying the wood, you know, until he tried to get out of it his self, you know. Hove down the wood and axe, and tried to get out of it. So he got out to the beach, anyhow, it was there, got home. He told the wife about it, and they all had a laugh over it, see. After they'd got done dinner, they said they'd go up and see where the wood was to. And they got the turn of wood right

> against, laid to the water, the landwash. ****** the woods. Heh heh. Strange, isn't it?
>
> BR: Did you say people saw them? Did people ever see the fairies?
>
> JL: Oh yes, the one, Minnie Pine, the fella took her, see, he come out with a red cap on.

Minnie Pine disappeared while playing around a doorway with another child, who said that a man in a red cap took her by the hand and led her away. The next few days there was "rain in reeves":

> KL: And the third day, his [JL's] uncle was coming down from up the Broad, somewhere up the back of the Ridge, with a boatload of wood. And she — it was a little girl — she was scooping up water with a mussel shell.
>
> JL: Walking by the edge of the water.
>
> KL: And when he got in where she was to, she was asking for a drink. And the first thing he did was give her a drink. So he got her aboard, and he brought her down, anyhow, and she couldn't tell a thing about where she was. But everything on her was as dry as *****. She wasn't wet. That was funny. They said it rained awful hard, and where was she to when it rained?

Where indeed? The obvious answer is that she was in a house, or at least a building, but fairy tradition offers another explanation: like the informant quoted earlier whose "cravat didn't have a speck of rain" even though he was out in it all night, someone "in the fairies" can be insulated from the physical conditions of the everyday world (perhaps Minnie's request for a drink reflects the aridity of that world). Minnie's story was recorded in 1972 from an informant who said:

> A little girl by the name of Pine, she was about twelve, thirteen years old, and she leaved home to go picking up shells. She didn't come home and in the night they made a search. And she wasn't found — eight, nine days before they found her. And

> there was a man going along, going along in a boat, and she was in the beach, still picking up shells. So they got her and brought her home. The first thing she asked for was a drink of water. They asked her where she was to, and all ever she told, she was away with the pretty women. . . . They blamed the fairies for — she had been with the fairies. Still now they were dressed in black. And they said, a lot of rain while she was gone and she was so dry as when she left. (72-51:C1175/15)

The striking feature of these two accounts is the stability of the minor motifs of playing with shells and wanting a drink, in comparison with what most people would consider a major motif, the abductor. In a third, more recent account, the girl has a different name, but it would seem to be the same incident as she was lost during the "worst storm of the year":

> Finally they found her, sitting alone on a rock humming a little song. Her clothes were bone dry. She wasn't even dirtied, nor was her hair "mussed" up. Everyone was shocked to find her so clean, dry, and happy. She didn't even seemed scared about being lost. When they asked her what she had done for the two days, she replied that she had been picking berries when the nice fairy came and took her by the hand and played with her. When they asked her if she had been scared when it rained, she asked, "What rain?" People accepted her story without question. The few who doubted at first also grew to believe her story; after all, what other explanation could be offered to describe the weird happening? (84-370A/18)

It must have occurred to people that the girl was with other people — humans, that is. The possibility that she was abducted (by humans) might have been hidden from children; the use of a "fairy" explanation as a put-off for children could explain the difference in the appearance of the "fairies" in the different accounts, as this would be an individually supplied detail. Even if the adults had little conviction in the likelihood of fairy abductors themselves, their children might grow up insisting that they "really believed." In any case, both collectors of the accounts above indicate firm belief in the past. The first wrote:

> To this day it is believed that the fairies took her. Those old people around home actually believe there were fairies. I've often heard my grandmother talk about them. She said they were tiny creatures who lived in the woods and came out in the late evening. When she was a child her parents and others around warned their children not to go very far from home alone. I once asked my grandmother where the fairies are now. She said, "Oh, after everyone moved off the Ridge, the fairies must have left and gone somewhere else." (72-51/6)

According to the second, who had the story from her mother, "One thing they believed very strongly in was the Fairies. The Fairies were little people, two to three feet tall, dressed in green tights, suits, and caps" (84-370A/18).

Minnie Pine was not harmed by her experience, but grew up to be "the best kind" and married an Avondale man; Mrs. Lynch recalls her visiting Bellevue as an old woman: "Grandad told me, that that was the one, now, was brought away by the fairies when she was a child." Mrs. Lynch never heard of the fairies while growing up in nearby Chapel Cove, but was fascinated and listened avidly to the stories she heard when she married Mr. Lynch and came to Bellevue. She attributes the difference to the Englishness of Chapel Cove versus the Irishness of Bellevue; but her own example shows how quickly traditions are assimilated by a receptive new community member. It also underscores the importance of the movement of women upon marriage as a major factor in their dissemination. Mr. Lynch's mother, for example, was from Fox Harbour in Placentia Bay, and told Mrs. Lynch of an incident there that Mrs. Lynch remembers, even though the meaning is partly unclear to her:

> But she said those two little boys come out from school, Saunders, their name was. And it was in the fall of the year, the evenings were short, and they went in to their rabbit slips [snares]. They wasn't going to be gone long, their mother was getting supper, and they were gone to the slips. So anyhow, time passed

away, the boys didn't come. By and by everyone started looking for them. And they were never found. Somebody come to her house and told her they had them, one time, she said, and she had clothes up warming to put on the boys, thinking that they had them found; but they never were found. Nobody never found them. But they said the priest called three lots of fairies, three groups, and they wasn't in either group, the boys wasn't in either group that they called. Now I don't understand that part of it either, you know, I don't know.

Mr. and Mrs. Lynch's knowledge differs slightly: she knew about carrying bread but not turning a cap or clothes; Mr. Lynch never heard of carrying bread but knew about turning clothes. When I asked about changing babies on my first visit, Mr. Lynch said he never heard of it, but Mrs. Lynch said promptly, "The Smiths raised a child that wasn't their own." When I asked about this on my second visit, with the tape recorder running, Mrs. Lynch suddenly became uncharacteristically vague and evasive: "That was a long time ago. It might be true and it mightn't be, you know, I don't know. You hear a lot of old stuff, people tell you." The most interesting difference between the first and second interviews was in the account she gave of her two sons and their friend getting astray in 1964. The first time, I am almost certain, it was simply that they had gotten lost; the second time, there were subtle but distinct indications that there was more to it than that. And on a visit in 1990, she referred to the incident, saying, "The boys always said, 'the fairies had us that time!'" Thus over three tellings the fairy identification (half-joking in the last) became more explicit, perhaps as Martin and I became better known.

In the second telling, the key phrases were so casual and unemphatic that I almost missed them; indeed, it was not until I listened to the tape later that I realized their significance, buried as they are in the homelier details of the boys' adventure. The transcript is too long for inclusion here, for Mrs. Lynch vividly recalled how the boys set out for a walk on a warm day which gave way to "a gale of wind" by late evening, when they had not returned; she went up the hill behind their house and called, but heard only "the woods cracking, trees renting," and returned to the house to get help. Before a big search party could be assembled, however, a man drove up to tell them that the boys were in Thornlea, where they had been taken by fishermen who had been out checking their traps and found the boys on a cliff "back of the point," the same place Mr. Lynch had been "carried." Mrs. Lynch then shifts to a boys'-eye-view of events as she describes their attempts to cope with being lost. The suggestions of fairy influence are emphasized in the excerpts below:

> KL: . . . they took off their big jackets up on top the hill, threw them down when they started walking, they got warm, and they threw them down not very far from our fence. And they went on the path: *they never left the path, they said.*
>
> JL: *They never walked over there.*
>
> KL: They say they never left the path. And when they got walking so long a time, they discovered they were astray. So they said they were on the path, now, they'd come back home. So I don't know whether they — what they done, but anyhow, *when they come to theirselves*, they could see the lights of the homes over on the other side of the — same place that he [JL] was, I suppose. So they made a shelter for themselves. And Jim said it was so cold, he thought that he'd get to haul off his long rubbers and emp [*sic*] the water out of them. But he said he couldn't get them off, he was too numb, too cold, to get the rubbers off. So the other boys lay down, they wasn't stirring, Andy said all he was afraid, he wasn't going to see "Danger Man" tonight, "Danger Man" used to be on the radio that time — the television (chuckle). Anyhow, they wouldn't stir for Jim anyhow.

Jim, the oldest at thirteen or fourteen, heard a motorboat engine, but had to force the others up to go to the cliff; on the boat, only one man heard their calls, and that was a man who had only at the last minute decided to go out (a decision Mrs. Lynch considers the answer to her prayers). With difficulty they got the boys into the boat:

And the men took off their oilclothes and gave them to them to wrap themselves up in, you know, to keep the cold air, the wind off them. So they were shivering like a leaf when I found them over in Thornlea, brought them home. I put them in — I said, was he hungry, "No, that woman in Thornlea gave us a wonderful meal." Jim said she had sweetcake and everything, they loved sweetcake, you know. So anyhow, they went to bed. And I mixed up a drop of gin that I had there, made two parts to it, and I gave it to them hot, and I said, "Go to bed." And they never got a cold out of it. But the next day they done some talking about it, you know. Oh, my, did they ever talk about that. Andy said, "I bet I blaze a trail the next time I goes up in back of that stable." The stable was only right there in the garden, you know. *But that's what they figure, they were brought away....*

BR: I bet they never forgot that.

KL: Oh, they'll never forget it. They'll never forget it, and I won't either. But I think it was an answer to a prayer that they were found. Because Jim [the son] had his self give up, he said, "When we were going up the hill, we looked out around the Broad and they were digging" — my aunt's grave, my aunt had died that week and they were digging her grave — and he said, "when we were so cold and wet and miserable," he said, "I thought to meself, well, if they finds us, they'll be digging three more graves tomorrow." That's what he thought about. Now I had some old gray blankets that everybody hated, they were, I suppose you could call them horsehair blankets, but they were woolly, they were wool blankets, and they were dark. Nobody liked them, everybody hated them. "Oh, Mom," he said, "what would I give to have one of them old gray blankets." (laughter) Well, I said, you got to be in a position like that to appreciate stuff, a lot of times, you know. (end of narration)

Katharine ("Kitty") Lynch and John Rieti-Lovelace

4 | *Tradition and the Interpretation of Experience*

Jim Lynch

The "supernatural" elements of this story lie in cracks between the bigger blocks of prosaic detail with which it is built; perhaps they are unemphatic because this is not primarily a "fairy" story; more important elements are fear, the cold, wind, the near-miraculous rescue, and the rediscovered delights of safety and home — sweetcake and blankets — contrasted with the open grave. It is every parent's nightmare with a happy ending, the inverse of the story of the Saunders boys of Fox Harbour (no wonder Mrs. Lynch recalls the poignant detail of their mother warming their clothes on the stove when she thought they were found).

Mrs. Lynch recounts the episode as if she had been in the woods with the boys, with an intense sympathetic participation in her family's experiences that is also shown in a story Mr. Lynch tells about nearly being lost at sea in a storm: although Mrs. Lynch was in the hospital at the time, she "saw it all" as it happened in a dream. Mr. Lynch tells of many mishaps and close calls while working in the woods and on the water, and his fairy experience fits this genre and repertoire. For all these near escapes, Mr. and Mrs. Lynch say that there were seldom serious accidents ("not like you hear about today"), and Mrs. Lynch says that although they had little money they "lived like kings," always with plenty to eat. They had eight children, including a boy who died at fifteen months and a daughter at thirty-six years. In 1988 Mr. Lynch was still digging potatoes (he got thirty-two barrels the year before), but by 1990 a bad heart slowed him down.

Like the Lynches, Mary and David Nolan raised a large family — twelve children — and continue to work hard at personal and community projects. Mr. Nolan, born in 1913, began fishing at the age of five and stopped at sixty-four; he says matter-of-factly that he was the "best fisherman in Green Cove" (one of the larger communities toward the northern tip of the Avalon), and he still spends part of each day at the wharf in an advisory role. When a film crew set up in Green Cove several years ago, Mrs. Nolan (also a native of Green Cove) organized their food and lodging. Although they are not in the least apologetic

4 | Tradition and the Interpretation of Experience

or abashed about what they told me, I have used pseudonyms for them and their community (and omitted identification of related MUNFLA material) because they were concerned that I not use real names for any of the people they talked about; because they told me in confidence about experiences of several of their children with spirits; and because they were the only informants to express the fear that their stories might be laughed at. I visited them after hearing a tape made in 1985 by one of their young relatives in which Mr. Nolan talks about spirits, ghosts, fiery dogs, and strange lights. I guessed that he would know something about fairies as well, and within ten minutes of knocking at their door was seated in the kitchen hearing how Mrs. Nolan's mother had once been "towed away." As she told it on the second visit:

> I suppose I'll start to tell you, the best way I can, anyway. I guess I was about thirteen year old, and my mother went berry-picking one morning. She went in with her friend, a Mrs. Butt. She didn't live too far from our house, so they took their bucket and their containers and they went in. So they were picking berries together, I don't know how long, she didn't have too many berries picked. So when she — when Mrs. Butt went back to empt [*sic*] her container, she couldn't find my mother. So she went all through the woods everywhere and she couldn't find her; she didn't pick any more berries herself, she was worried too much, she was looking for her. She went all over the woods everywhere. So in the evening she had to give up looking for her, and then she came home. So when she came home, somebody come to the house and said how Mrs. Butt was out, and we wondered where my mother was to. So we went down to her house and asked her, and she said she couldn't find her. She said she strayed away from her, and she was looking for her all day and she couldn't find her. Well, of course we all got worried, and my father said, "We'll wait for her awhile, now; if she don't turn up we'll go to look for her." So he got ready, he had his lunch, his tea time, and he went down to some of his friends, and I was there alone in the house. Now I was the oldest, see? So I used to go from window to window, looking

for me mother, no sign of her. So by and by, me father wasn't back either. So after a while, nine o'clock came, and no sign of me mother, and nine-thirty came. And when nine-thirty come, the door opened and in she come. "Well," I says, "in the name of God, where were you to?" I didn't know her. And she said, "Wait for a while, now," she says, "and I'll tell you." And she was all down over double, you know, and her hair all over her eyes; one shoe on and the other foot bare. And she looked right gone, you know; oh my, I couldn't describe to you what she was like. At them times you wore your hair up in a ball, it wasn't cut off. So my mother used to wear hers up in a ball, but that was all down over her face every way, you know? So she came in and she sat down, and she says, "My darling," she says, "I'm astray all day." I says, "Where did you go astray to?" She says, "I don't know. I was picking berries," she said, "and I got me container filled and I went to emp [*sic*] it in the bucket, and," she said, "something happened to me," she says, "and I don't know what happened to me. So," she said, "that was early in the morning, and we were only in the woods about an hour," she said, "when that happened. And," she said, "I was gone all day, and didn't know where I was to, and I didn't know I was walking. But," she says, "I came to myself laid down by a brook. Now there was no brook where we were to picking berries," she said, "neither one to be seen. And when I came to one of me boots were gone," she said, "one of me boots were gone, and my container was gone, and I had nothing on, my sweater was gone. So," she said, "I got up, and I pushed my hair back, and I started to walk." Now on Gray Cove she was picking the berries, but when she came to she was on Old Perlican barrens. Well, that was ten miles from where she was picking berries to. So she started to walk, she said, and walked, and walked, through bushes and trees and woods and everything. So she came to a high clift. And when she went on the edge of the clift she looked down, and there was two women there, boiling the kettle where they were berry-picking. And they started to run, they got afraid of her. She said, "Don't run, my dears," she says, "I'm not going to hurt you," she said, "I'm astray all day. Where am I to?"

"Well," they says, "M'am, you're in Broom Cove." Now Broom Cove was a long ways, wasn't it?

DN: Yes, it's way above Old Perlican.

MN: Yeah. So anyway, they asked her down and they gave her a cup of tea. And when she got — they wanted her to go to a house and stay all night, and she wouldn't go. And they didn't have nothing to give her to put on one of her feet. So she said, "Put me on the road now, and I'll walk home." So anyway, they walked her to the road. And they were in the ***, they wanted to go down and phone my father and them to the house. She said no, she said she'd try to do it. So she walked a long ways, and then she came across a car. Well, the man was in the car used to buy salt fish here in Green Cove, his name was Captain Perry, he belonged to Carbonear. He was always visiting our house, and come up and have a lunch and everything when he was buying the fish, and he knew all of us real well; he knew my mother because she was always tending on him, see? So she stopped the car, she put up her hand and stopped the car. And she says, "Will you take me home," she says, "Captain Perry, I'm astray all day." And he says, "Who are you?"

"My," she says. "You know who I am," she said, "you visits my house every day," she said.

He says, "No, I don't know you."

She says, "I'm John Woodruff's wife." She said, "You visits my home every day and haves a lunch."

"Oh no," he said, "you're not John Woodruff's wife," he says. "Move from the car," he said, "I'm not going to pick you up," he says, "I don't know you."

So that'll tell you that she was disfigured, see? That'll give you an idea what she was like when she came home. So anyway, she kept on the road and walked seven mile with one foot with nothing on it. She used to tie something around the foot to try to help it along, her scarf or whatever she had there, so when she — that's what she told us. So when she came to the house then, she was almost gone. She was really disfigured, you know, she wasn't like herself at all. But she was in bed then for almost two weeks. So she told us, the fairies took — brought her away, and she was gone all day. The fairies took her and she didn't even know they were taking her. And she was — must, she must be asleep all day or something that they did with her, that she never came to until in the evening, by the side of the brook. But I often heard my grandmother saying that fairies would never touch you if you were near a brook. Fairies would never cross a brook.

BR: So that must be why they let her down there?

MN: Yeah, that's why they let her down. They came to the brook, see. Now that's really a true story. People may not believe it, but that was really true.

Mrs. Nolan shows the same empathy in her narration of her mother's experience as Mrs. Lynch in her sons', with recreation of dialogue and verbalization of her mother's thoughts.[7]

Mrs. Nolan does not doubt that the fairies had her mother. To one disinclined to this explanation, alternative theories present themselves. One is that her mother experienced some sort of blackout, in which she walked for miles in a somnambulistic state or seizure. If so, it seems to have been a singular occurrence, for Mrs. Nolan doesn't mention anything like it happening again. Another, more sinister possibility (as raised in connection with Minnie Pine) is that she was assaulted or taken away, not by fairies, but by humans. This would explain one of the most puzzling parts of the story, Captain Perry's refusal to give her a ride. Surely even if he did not recognize her, a man would

4 | *Tradition and the Interpretation of Experience*

not refuse assistance to a woman in such obvious straits. If she had been a victim of violence, however — as her appearance would suggest — his refusal may have come from a fear of being implicated, an impulse commonly enough observed today. The stigma attached to being a victim is equally well known, and Mrs. Nolan's mother may well have been reluctant to report an attack. The social repercussions of any deviant behaviour or incident might be felt by an entire family for a long time, no matter where responsibility lay. One woman, for example, felt called upon to cloister herself when her son abandoned his family:

> In the community of Green Cove, there is so much belief in folklore, that it would be almost impossible to name them all. One of these beliefs is connected with the fairies, and there are many stories about them. No one would be caught out "on the barrens" on a foggy night, for this is where the fairies were found. In most of the stories, the belief was that if the fairies got you, all you had to do was turn your clothes inside out and they would leave you alone. I am told that this happened to my uncle one time, but since the expression "the fairies had him" also has another meaning when older folks talk of drinking in front of children, I'm not sure if the *real* fairies *really* had him.[8] However, the old woman who told me this swears that it really happened to her and some friends, one evening, when they were off picking berries. Mrs. James Nolan, my great-aunt by marriage, is the typical community busybody. Everybody rushes to her with news and to get it. She is about seventy and hasn't been outside her door in about fifteen years, since her son deserted his family and was never heard of. However, "Aunt Annie," as she is known, is extremely pious and holy, so I would believe anything she told.

If the fairies could be used as a euphemism for drinking, as this account states, they could also be used to keep worse behaviour from children's ears.

Community members might intervene in unacceptable behaviour they found extreme. The student who heard about the girl taken by fairies in Perry's

Cove wondered "how the fairies could be called 'good people' when they did such awful things":

> [The informant] looked calculatingly at me for some time before saying anything. Finally he began, "Well, sir," and went on to tell me about a man in North River who had mistreated his wife and spent many of his nights drinking. One time as he was making his way home, the fairies took him and gave him a ducking in the harbour. Now it was a cold winter's night and the poor man was almost gone. They pulled him out again and sent him home to his wife, bidding him tell her what the "good people" had done. I was satisfied enough then, and so were the others who sat around smiling at the old man and winking at me. (70-20/53)

The good citizens of Plate Cove, Bonavista Bay, set the priest on an "old lady" who declined to share her business with them:

> A certain Mrs. Drayton would disappear in the wood and would remain there for two or three weeks or even a month. When she would return she was well and unharmed, and the people were curious to know how she lived during this time. People could never find her in their search for her. They used to say the fairies had taken her. They begged the priest to find out from her where she was and what she ate but he did not succeed. He told her the next time she would not return and it happened exactly this way. After the priest's visit the next trip to the wood was her last one, but her body was not found until three years later by her nephew, and [the informant] said it was just over a hill down between two rocks, a place where people had been many times.

The informant explained the woman's behaviour by saying that "she had had an illegitimate child, and in those days, especially in a small community, this was a disgrace so it affected her mind" (FSC71-95/19).[9]

Mrs. Nolan accepts the fairy interpretation of her mother's experience and therefore does not think Captain Perry's refusal to help remarkable,

4 | Tradition and the Interpretation of Experience

because in the terms proposed by fairy tradition, it makes sense. She was unknown to him, not only in her everyday identity but in her essential humanity. If it is unlikely that one person would refuse another as he did, then the implication is that she was not a person, but something else: a fairy. She had almost become non-human, her near escape symbolized by the loss of one shoe (according to folk tradition, shoes may come off a person's feet at the moment of a traumatic death).[10] Mrs. Nolan's mother had had one foot in fairyland, or the grave, but did not cross the river, the ancient symbol of the boundary between life and death.[11] The more cynical may wonder whether Captain Perry knew her only too well.

Some people are on more comfortable terms with death and with the fairies than others, but they are apt to be perceived as eccentric (at the least). Mrs. Nolan describes a "real old woman," Mrs. Copper of Green Cove:

> She'd go around every day, now; she'd visit so many houses a day, and ask you for cookies, or a piece of bread, or a sandwich. Well, everywhere she went, everybody gave her what she asked for. She used to wear a great big white apron, you know, and she'd take the apron up here like this here, you know, gather it, and all the cookies and everything would be down in her apron. And then she'd go way in over them hills over there, you know, go up over all these hills every day. Now her husband was dead for years; his name was Mike. And she'd be up there all day sitting down talking to Mike, as she said. But everybody used to say, here, that she was talking to the fairies.

Whether "she was talking to the fairies" was derisive or not (as "in the fairies" sometimes is), Mrs. Copper's asocial bent seems clear. While this chapter — indeed this study — demonstrates that perfectly ordinary people have had fairy experiences, the accounts above show that in certain cases there is an association between the fairies and personal peculiarity. The difference seems to be one of chronic connection with the fairies, whether self-proclaimed or attributed, as opposed to a one-time or occasional experience; the latter may even serve to emphasize a person's normality by her successful

145

extrication. The reputation acquired by regular association with the fairies was not necessarily bad, but dubious. Mr. Nolan's mother knew a woman in Gray Cove (next to Green Cove) who went with the fairies every October:

> They said she could do anything. You know, she'd do anything for you, if she wanted to cure you, if she wanted to do anything with you, she could do it. But she always kept herself to herself. *** she'd say, "My darlings, I'll soon be going away, now, you won't be able to visit me no more for a little while." That was it, she was going away, and she'd go away, nobody would know where she'd go to; nobody knew when she left the house or anything. ******* two weeks, she'd come back again. When she'd come back again, then she'd be — they said she was right thin, you know, right — even her face would be changed.
>
> MN: She was with the fairies.
>
> DN: **** back to herself again. But they used to ask her where she was to, she went, "I was with the fairies." That's all they would get out of her. . . .
>
> MN: Yes, she'd cure people and she could put a wish on you.
>
> DN: Yeah, she could cure you, yes. She could foretell things, you know, was going to happen. . . . She could meet someone and tell their fortune. She'd meet someone and look at the palm of their hand, and tell them about their future.

Links between the fairies and witchcraft are not found in MUNFLA, although it may be an unexplored connection. The Nolans did not call the woman above a witch, although she has the characteristics of one; but an even more classic portrait in the person of Mrs. Farmer, who was "just like a witch" and who put "wishes" on people (including Mrs. Nolan's mother), included no fairy connection. Nor are there many MUNFLA accounts associating the fairies with other personal supernatural powers, but one informant's grandmother "was endowed with supernatural powers after a strange happening when she was only a child":

> Her father and herself were picking flowers in a field back of their house on the Southern Shore, when the little girl was picked up and swept across the meadow at a very fast pace. She wasn't touching the ground but the heels of her feet brushed the daisies as she swept past. The father turned to see his youngest daughter "taken away by the fairies," as he suspected, and yelled the girl's name backwards, three times. Immediately the spell was broken and the young child was placed on the ground without harm. Since that time she has had special powers: predictability, an ability to read tea leaves, ESP, all unnatural but stemming possibly from her being "taken away" that afternoon in the meadow. (FSC76-24/*)

In Marystown on the Burin Peninsula:

> They said [Jim Martin's] house was built on the path of the fairies and so was Mr. Frank Brades's. And they said that the door would open on opposite sides of the house, the windows would open and close. Believed this was the fairies on the path. Everyone would go to Jim Martin's with a toothache. He would always be sitting on the chopping block because no one would go into his house. He would open your mouth and put the sign of the cross over the tooth and mumble something like, "On your tooth I place my thumb, from now on, it will be numb." Everyone believed that the fairies had something to do with it as he was an odd man. Whether or not it was the fairies it seemed that the toothache would be severe pain for a second and then no more. (75-251/58-59)

The house next door to the Nolans was plagued with fairies and ghosts. One day their neighbour had to help her husband at the fish flake and tucked their baby into the cot while she went out; she returned to find him under the bedclothes, "turned black — he wasn't the same baby at all." She revived him by dipping his head in basins of cold and warm water, but "the features of the baby never came back":

And that house where that woman lived to, 'twas always something heard there. They'd be sitting down in the night, you know, and the knob was on the door would be turning back and forth, you know, yet nobody would come in, and nobody would go out. But 'twas always a ghost heard in that house, wasn't it?

DN: Yeah, right.

MN: So that's what she claimed, that the fairies took the baby while she was gone, and changed it. So the features of the child never came back. It was always a queer-looking child, you know —

DN: Yes, only ten years of age, just like an old man of sixty.

Mr. and Mrs. Nolan agree that not much is said about fairies these days, but "it *was* fairies, that was really true years ago." They believe, however, that spirits of the dead are as frequently encountered as ever. One of their sons quit a good job, for which he had specialized training, and took up fishing because he saw the spirit of a man he knew at his workplace one night. Another son picked up a hitchhiker; when the boy jumped out of the back of the truck after the ride, he recognized him as one who had been killed by a car not long before. One of their daughters left an abusive husband and went to stay at the house of a man who had died who had always been good to her. (Mrs. Nolan was shocked that she could do this the day after he died, but explained that in living with her husband, "all fear left her.") She would hear the man walking and whistling, sometimes at the stove, but she wouldn't go to the priest as Mrs. Nolan wanted her to because she knew he wouldn't do any harm, and because she did not want his daughter to know he was not "at rest." When her brother spent a night on the daybed there, he saw the dampers on the stove rise up and down, and heard footsteps on the stairs, but it was not until her children started seeing the man that she finally allowed Mrs. Nolan to get the priest to put him to rest.

Spirits appear because they need help getting to rest, which is why, Mr. Nolan says, you should ask them what they want. Mrs. Nolan says she is "fearful," but Mr. Nolan (who has had supernatural encounters himself) says that he is not afraid, and that if he had been in his son's place (the one who saw the spirit at work) he would have asked, "What the hell do you want?" Usually the spirit wants a priest, to conduct the offices necessary to allow it to rest. It is common for miraculous powers to be attributed to priests in Newfoundland, from curing to cursing and exorcism. A Father Mackay once cured Mrs. Nolan's mother as she was on her deathbed:

> So, years after, he would always come to the house, and he used to look at her, you know, he'd say, "I brought you back from the grave." And he'd say, "I suffered for it myself. I really took you back," he said, "from God. And I suffered for it myself." That's what he used to say to her. So, he really could cure, though. If you had anything wrong with you, and he crossed you, my dear, you'd really get better.[12]

However, Mrs. Nolan does not think the priests have the same faith, and therefore the same power, that they used to. Given their strong religious orientation, the absence of priests in the Nolans' fairy narratives is striking; but priests' attitudes varied just as their parishioners did, and perhaps the Green Cove priests discouraged the idea. One Green Cove informant did mention "a priest of the community who used to visit us would tell us ghost stories at night," and a Green Cove collector had a priest as an informant for ghost and fairy stories. The Nolans said that the priests would be angry if anyone said that they didn't believe in spirits, but they consider spirits different from fairies: "A spirit won't tow you away but a fairy would," according to Mrs. Nolan, and Mr. Nolan added that "some spirits is wicked. If they got anything in their mind, you know, and you don't stop, they're liable to do something with you, strike you or something, cripple you or something." Only Catholics seem to appear after death, they said, and only Catholics seem to see spirits (Green Cove has both Catholics and Protestants). The fairies seem to have become historical figures in the still vital otherworld of Green Cove.

Interviewing the Kelloways, Lynches, and Nolans as couples showed the importance of mutual reinforcement in the development and perpetuation of fairy traditions. Each partner took an active role in the other's narration, prompting, affirming, clarifying. In contrast to this marital accord is a 1984 interview with Mrs. Margaret Ennis of St. John's. I contacted Mrs. Ennis after reading her and her sister's contributions to a Folklore paper (73-74) on fairy lore, mostly from Outer Cove, where she spent summers as a child. It turned out that most of what Mrs. Ennis knew came from an uncle; although her mother believed in the fairies ("always that kind"), she never said much because Mrs. Ennis's father had "no time for it." Mrs. Ennis recalled an incident (not in the paper) illustrating the rift: she and her mother and father had gone berry-picking in the White Hills and couldn't find the path when they wanted to come out, although they tried every direction (Irv Winsor, a dental hygienist, says that as boys he and his friends would say there were leprechauns on Sugarloaf in the White Hills, just east of St. John's). Mrs. Ennis's mother turned the sweater on her shoulders, but her father said they should get on their knees and pray (both parents were "very religious"), and they soon found the way out. Later, her mother would tell people that the fairies had them, but she would only say this if her husband were not there to call it "a pile of nonsense."

Mrs. Ennis did not give her opinion of the incident (although the collector stated that she "still believes in the fairies"), nor did her husband, who was present at the interview, offer any comment. Mr. Ennis also remained silent when Mrs. Ennis told of seeing something that might have been "a ghost or fairy" one night when she and some friends were napping in a car on a lonely road while returning from St. Pierre. She suddenly woke to see a woman in white, with a baby in her arms, standing, then kneeling, in the road. She got her "prayer beads" out of her pocket and crossed herself, but the figure was gone by this time. Warming to the topic, Mrs. Ennis began to recall other details about the fairies, such as that it was "always nice" with them, but Mr. Ennis began to talk about "people's imaginations"; the interview became a polite disagreement over "lies" and "things that really happened," and somehow wound around to television coverage of the local election. It would seem that Mrs. Ennis's marriage mirrors her mother's in respect to fairy belief, then, and it is perhaps significant that one of the stories in the paper was a personal experience narrative she heard from a woman on a bus, whose own husband thought she was "half crazy" (30). One can only wonder whether, if Mrs. Ennis had married someone with an interest in the supernatural, she would have maintained her fairy lore instead of allowing it to atrophy into vague recollection.

The Kelloways, Lynches, and Nolans all heard fairy stories from and about family members while growing up, with the exception of Mrs. Lynch, who embraced fairy stories on coming to Bellevue (perhaps replacing Mrs. Ennis in the ranks of tradition bearers). Their narratives show that family members are a major influence both in the general transmission of fairy lore and in the interpretation of particular incidents. It is harder to document "community" influence in action. Most of the narratives I recorded for this chapter are family folklore, performed in the family. In the precipitating incident, there was not much potential for community involvement, as the threatening situation was resolved quickly: the Lynch boys and friend were found; Mrs. Nolan's mother returned. Had search parties been mounted, the possibility of "fairies" would likely have been raised, and the tentative elements (as in the account of the Lynch boys) would acquire more definition through repetition and aggregation; debate, if not consensus, would throw them into prominence, and for all the dissenters there might be, the incident would be well on the way to becoming a "fairy" story. If the missing persons stayed missing or were found dead, disabled, or deranged, it would almost certainly become a fairy story, at least in some people's eyes.

A fairy interpretation, then, might be placed on an event or situation at a private or public level, and there are many reasons it might be done. Some are artistic or sociable: to have a good story, to make things exciting, to make one's self interesting. A fairy encounter can do all those things even as it provides a time-honoured excuse for getting lost, or showing up where one should not be, or not showing up where one should. One would not wish to be too interesting, however, nor to have many fairy encounters, for those who made a habit of it do not seem to have been pillars of the community, although they might have had useful skills like the magical power of charms. And there is the distinctly unsavoury possibility that "fairies" could be used to cover up violence, abductions, or other deviant behaviour.

It is ironic that these latter, darker possibilities should arise in a chapter in which the fairy experiences of the informants were mostly harmless or even comical; death and disability, which loom so large in an archival "portrait" of fairy tradition, play little role in these personal experience narratives. Yet as soon as comparative material is brought in, they are back: the Perry's Cove girl who lost her mind, the Saunders boys, the Nolan's neighbour's baby. The apparent discrepancy may have to do with the worst cases becoming public property, instead of fixing at a private level as more inconsequential incidents might. It offers an important perspective on the use of archival and field texts, for it shows that one would get quite different pictures relying on either source alone. One might, with archival data alone, assemble a falsely coherent overview, and make connections that do not actually have much meaning in context or performance, that is, in real life. It could be equally misleading to depend completely on field research, for it would be possible to conclude from the texts recorded for this chapter (and, for that matter, the earlier chapters) that fairy traditions have mostly to do with strange but harmless experiences of mischief or illusion.

Although tales of dreadful fairy fates do not figure in these informants' personal experiences or repertoires, they nevertheless form the backdrop for stories of the most innocuous nature, a potential for disaster that imparts a necessary tension to such close encounters. If there were no danger inherent in the situation, the stories would lose their dramatic edge and their structural hinge, which is the knowledgeable response or the fortuitous circumstance that short-circuits the fairies' design: Mr. Kelloway and his brothers knew not to answer and so were not led astray; Mrs. Lynch's prayers were answered and a man who would normally have been at home went to check his traps and found the boys; the fairies were forced to abandon Mrs. Nolan's mother by a brook. The effectiveness of countermeasures or counter-events that stay the danger is taken as confirmation of the "fairy" nature of the experience. The deliverance from harm allows the narrators, today, to relate the tales with a zest and enjoyment that the written transcription cannot convey.

5 | *Fairies, Devils, and Other Impostors in Bishop's Cove: Tales of a Trickster*

*W*hen the chief informant for this chapter decided he did not want his real name used, it was completely in character that he suggested I call him "Uncle Joe," for around his community "Uncle Joe" is the apocryphal, archetypal jokester who had a ready answer for everything, sometimes true and sometimes not. I have chosen instead, in view of his deep knowledge of local tradition and history, to call him after John Smith, who he tells me was the first settler of Bishop's Cove. This chapter adjusts the focus more closely on context and performance through an analysis of Mr. Smith's fairy traditions, their relationship to the rest of his narrative repertoire and style, and the possible influences of personality and biographical circumstances on their development. John Smith was born in 1922 in Bishop's Cove, Conception Bay, and was described in 1972 by his nephew, Gus Smith, as "the finest storyteller in our place." His "hobby," according to Smith, was "telling stories to young children" who flocked to his shop: "You can go there at any time of the day and you will always find several children there" (72-262/4, 22-23). When I called on Mr. Smith in March 1985, he had closed the shop, married, and had a young child of his own, Steven. He did not seem to find my inquiries particularly unusual, perhaps because he is accustomed to being sought out and listened to; within half an hour he was telling chilling tales about "those people."

Although Bishop's Cove (once Bread and Cheese Cove) is only about thirty kilometres further north than Avondale, its fairies have a distinctly different character, possibly deriving from a predominantly English/Protestant background that links them with the devil and witchcraft. Just off the main highway from Spaniard's Bay, it is contiguous with Upper Island Cove, also English/Protestant; as one student put it, "the only thing that makes them two distinct communities is the sign which is put right in the middle dividing the two."[1] There are about three hundred people in Bishop's Cove and eight hundred in Island Cove; most men worked on Bell Island and construction projects around the Avalon since the decline of the fishery in the 1930s (74-218/3, 80-322/20).

Mr. Smith's main occupation was always his shop; possibly he was kept from more typical pursuits by a leg disabled by polio contracted at the age of three (72-262/21). Everyone said he would never walk again, but when he was fourteen a Catholic man gave him a stinging nettle and told him to pray to it, or to something else; it didn't matter what, as long as he believed he would walk, and didn't tell lies (the serious kind) or kill anything. After that, he says, he got around as well as anyone (and was even stronger in the arms than most), but even as a child he had been determined to do everything everyone else did. Nevertheless, he did not attend school, and he is proud that his stories do not come from books but from other storytellers and from his own experience. So their formal quality owes little to literary influence (as Mrs. Meaney's probably do), and lies less in wording than in performance: his narratives are polished products set apart from ordinary conversation, with a strong sense of structure, movement, opening, and closure. Mr. Smith opened our second interview (the taped one) with a description of protective practices, leading to a general statement of his own position on belief in the fairies:

> Well, see, it was this way, that when a child was born, they put bread onto the cut [from the umblical cord], in case that anything would happen to the child. And when the child got a bit bigger, they'd remove the bread, pierce a small five cent piece, and put it on the neck of the child so it wouldn't be changed back [pause] to those people. So after awhile longer, they'd take

5 | *Fairies, Devils, and Other Impostors in Bishop's Cove*

away the bread. So when they'd leave the house, they'd go and they'd take an onion. And they'd chop en in two pieces; they'd put one half to the back door, and one half to the front door, so that no evil spirits could enter the house in that form. So in order to reinforce and make it a bit stronger, they'd take and sprinkle salt to the back door and to the front door, plus the onion and the small five cents so the child would be safe. Now that was old people would do that with the younger children. So in order to keep the luck of all that, they'd get a horseshoe and they'd nail it on the door, but be sure the horseshoe was bottom up, so the luck would bide into the horseshoe and wouldn't tumble out. You see, because that was the way of the old people in Bishop's Cove in them years. So right now it's passed away, an awful lot of people do believe into it and still carries on some of that tradition right now. I knows I do, I believes in that kind of stuff, in putting up me horseshoe. Do you see, you was speaking the other evening about [pause] fairies, or so-called fairies; good people, some people calls them good people. Some people calls them bad people. Do you see? From my point of view, probably they don't exist, but I wouldn't say they don't.

Off tape, he said that some people call them "devil's angels," and that Dr. Cron, a Harbour Grace physician about whom a number of fairy legends circulate, called them "sons of bitches."

Abusive language towards the fairies is an alternative to the flattering "good people," but it is harder to document "obscene" language because of polite restraint in front of strangers and, probably, women. Jack McCall's discourse to his male interviewer (partially quoted in Chapter Three) was peppered with vigorous expletives on the "motherfucking fairies," although this seemed to come as much from general saltiness of speech as from fairy tradition: "Well, I saw one that I was frigging well sure, it couldn't be anything else in this world, only a fairy," he declared at one point. Mr. Smith refers to "that damn thing" twice in the following story, and I am sure that his emphatic deployment of the term "fairy" was mainly for my benefit; in conversation he refers simply to "them" and "that crowd." In any case, this is how he went on to justify his view of "their" existence:

> Because I'll tell you a story now about a young man, two young men that, the two of them was the one age, they was born to two sisters. One's name was Joe, and the other was Joe. But the only thing to distinguish one from the other, they called them "Little Joe" and "Big Joe." So one day in the spring of the year they decided they'd go in the country to bring out a load of firewood. So they went on, they went in the woods about four or five miles from home. They cut down their wood together, they lugged it together. But when Big Joe come back, Little Joe was gone and he was nowhere to be found. And when he come back, his horse, wood, and dray was also gone with the load of wood. So thinking to his self that Little Joe was left to come home, but he thought it funny that his cousin'd leave him in the woods. So that evening about five o'clock when he come back with his load of wood, Little Joe's mother come out and asked where Little Joe was at. But he said, "Little Joe is leaved, he wasn't there when I come down, he come away and leaved me." So when the mother looked, the horse was to the door, the dray was to the door, and the wood was to the door, but Little Joe wasn't home. So they waited and waited. Nine o'clock come, ten o'clock come, eleven o'clock — and no Little Joe. And the night passed away, and no Little Joe. And he never returned for two days. Two days passed, and in the evening they looked out, and there was this man, presumably 'twas Little Joe, as she thought, was out to the door. So she opened the door and let him in. So he came in, she give him his supper, he eat it very savage because he was hungry. And on looking at him, she knew it was something wrong with him, but she still thought it was her son. And proud that he returned. But sometime that night she sent out for an old lady [a midwife in the first telling] to come out to see Little Joe. And when the old

lady come in and looked at Little Joe, "By God," she said, "that's not Little Joe you got there, if that's what you call that damn thing to the door," she said, "that's not Little Joe. That's a *fairy*." And she said, "I'm going to drown him. Because it's not Little Joe." So the mother begin to screech and bawl, about what she said about her son after gone two days and returned to the woods; the old lady said she was going to make away with him. "Oh, yes," she said, she was going to get another old woman, they were going to heave him in the pond. "Because," she said, "that's not Little Joe you got there. Little Joe went away this morning," she said, "and he was a good-looking young man, smart. And that thing you got there sot down feeding it," she says, "is about seventy years old. So," she said, "I'm going to heave it in the water. Because it's not Little Joe. And Little Joe'll never come back while that's here."

"But," she [the mother] said, "he got his jacket."

"I don't care," she said, "what kind of a jacket he got on. That's Little Joe's jacket, but that's not Little Joe."

So she sent for the other old lady, and the other old lady come in, she said, "No, that's not Little Joe. That's a fairy you got there. And we're making away with him."

So they went ahead, took a blanket — with the woman screeching and bawling — they wrapped him up in the blanket, and they took him. They carried him down, they put bricks, or rocks into the blanket, they heft in the pond with him. And that's where he drowned, or that's where something happened to him. And the next day, about nine o'clock in the night Little Joe come back. With ne'er a jacket on because the fairy was after taking his jacket and putting it on ***. But he come back. Little Joe, just the same as he went in the woods four days before. Sat down, and eat his supper, and the old lady come back again. "Now," she said, "that's Little Joe you got there. Who in the hell was the other fellow," she said, "that come here," she said, "the fellow who drowned?"

Now that is true. Because [it was] handed down generations to me.

BR: His mother didn't recognize, his mother thought the first one was Joe?

JS: Thought it was Joe, because she was proud her son come home. So she was willing to accept anything. But the old lady was accepting nothing, only Little Joe. That's why she took this and hove it in the water. And Little Joe returned, safe and sound, the only thing his jacket. So he said, "The funniest thing that ever happened," he said, "was last night around about twelve o'clock when I was in the woods, I thought," he said, "that the old woman next door hove me in the water. And I come to meself. And jumped up out of the woods. Come back," he said, "and walked home."

Now that, it really happened, about 1900; anyway, 1896, 1900. Because it was told to me by a man that went to see him. He seen the first ugly machine they brought there, and he seen — he knowed what the old woman done, and he seen Little Joe when he come back.

BR: Was he okay after that, Little Joe?

JS: He was the best kind, lived to be eighty year old. Always happy-go-lucky.

"Little Joe" is an elegant illustration of the set of themes that I have suggested lie at the heart of fairy tradition. First, it turns on the question of identity: the impostor does not simply impersonate Little Joe, but has actually become him — Little Joe felt himself "hove into the water" even as he "came to himself" and jumped up to go home. Then, a play between nature and culture appears not only in Joe's dazed suspension in the woods, his

5 | *Fairies, Devils, and Other Impostors in Bishop's Cove*

humanity siphoning into the fairy, but in details like the jacket (culture), which the mother finds so convincing. The term "machine" ("he seen the first ugly machine they brought there") is especially apt in this regard, since in Newfoundland usage it means "a device, contrivance or contraption, especially one without a specific name; an object or phenomenon; thingumajig" (Story et al. *Dictionary* 318). In "Little Joe" it combines indirect reference to the fairies with the suggestion of an automaton stuffed into Joe's jacket and sent in to take over as Little Joe. (The broom-in-place-of-a-body motif works the same way: a bunch of twigs bound up on a stick is "culture," but just barely.)

In 1974 Gus Smith, Mr. Smith's nephew, recorded "Little Joe" from an informant who acknowledged that it circulates in different versions:[2]

> Well, there's thousands of stuff on the go about spirits and stuff people seen. The one I suppose everyone remembers around here is about old Mina Cross out here on the shore and her son. There's different stories about what happened but I'll tell you the one Father told me, alright?
>
> The story goes, see, that Mina Cross, who was a widow, had a little boy who one day went in the woods cramming around about something. I believe he was in trouting. Anyway he got astray in the woods and was gone for a week. My son, we had every able-bodied man out looking for him but one trace of him we couldn't find. After five days the Mounties told us to give up. He was gone for sure, so we thought, anyway.
>
> Well, the next day who in the Christ should pop his head through Mina's door but her young fella. Mina just about fainted. The boy seemed to be different though. His features had changed a bit and he wouldn't speak. The doctor said, "I'll come around later. Don't worry, Mina." She wasn't worrying, of course, only too glad to have her little one back home.
>
> Everyone thought it strange though. Before he went away he was some bright, me son, let me tell ya. Now he was different, see? He wouldn't even talk, sure. He would just sit there with his

feet in the oven and a blanket over his shoulders and he wouldn't eat a bite.

After a few days anyhow Mina got worried. She went down to Island Cove then to have a talk to an old midwife that was down there, I believe her name was Bertha Deaver. I knows she was a Deaver anyway. This midwife said she'd come up and have a look at the boy. Well, my son, as soon as she saw what was in the chair she just about screamed her head off. Mina ran over and grabbed her and asked her what was wrong. "Mrs. North," [*sic*] she said, "that's not your son, that's a small devil. If we hurrys though we might be able to save him yet. Take that thing on the chair and throw it in the pond." Mina thought now that this old midwife had gone off her rocker. People had a lot of trust in her though. She had strange powers, see. Anyway the men that was in the house at the time took what was suppose to be her little fella and throwed him in the pond. My son, they say he sank like lead. Never seen it after.

Mina started screeching now. They had some job trying to hold her. Took four or five men, I suppose.

When they got back to her house who should they see on the chair by the stove but Mina's real son. You talk about a woman glad. Bertha, the midwife, told her that, see? Drown the devil and your son will come back. She was some glad.

The boy should have had a five cent piece around his neck, see? That would keep off evil stuff. Piece of bread would have done the same trick. Yeah. Fairies. I daresay you can believe in 'em. (74-218/18-23)

Fairy or devil, the identity of the impostor does not seem to be a central concern here, nor in "Little Joe"; if stability can be taken as an index to importance, the more meaningful elements are the anxious search for the son, the mother's relief at having him back, her willingness to turn a blind eye to certain peculiarities, and her terror at the midwife's proceedings. It is significant that these should persist even into a second generation; the narrator of "The Small Devil" is, after all, using the first person for performance of the tale as he remembers it from his father. (Besides suggesting that these were the affective points around which tension and attention revolved, it is another demonstration that removal in time fosters elaboration as well as disintegration.)

MUNFLA contains only a handful of parallels to "Little Joe." MacEdward Leach recorded one in 1950 from someone who heard it in Spaniard's Bay in 1918: Jack is supposed to leave with his brother for the Labrador the morning after a dance, but during the evening he goes to bed sick; the brother has to leave without him, and Jack lies in bed all summer tended by the brother's wife, who writes to her husband that he "was able to eat all she could give him but still he was sick." When the brother returns in October,

> First thing he asked is, "Where's Jack? How is he? Is he dead, or what about him?" "Oh, no," she said, "he's in bed yet." So he ran upstairs, and I believe he reddened the shovel in the stove, and he ran up with it, and he told him to get out. And he threatened the shovel with him — on him, and he jumped out of the bed and went through the window. And about two hours after, his brother came back. "Well," he said, "'tis a wonder ye didn't keep him all the winter. I'm out there," he said, "the whole summer not a stitch of clothes on me." His beard grew down a foot long, they hardly knew him. He said, "I'm out there in the woods the whole summer," he said, "and I couldn't get clear of them. I was surrounded by about ten thousand fairies and I couldn't get away from them," he said, "until that fella came back. When he came back," he said, "I got clear." He said, "I went out that night by the house," he said, "and when I went out there was about ten thousand fairies around the house. They took me," he said, "and they brought me away. And they left this fellow behind," he said, "the fellow went up and got in the bed. They left him behind and they took me away," he said,

"and I'm out the whole summer. My," he said, "if he hadn't got to drive him out," he said, "I'd be out all the winter." So that's the story, believe it or not. (78-54:C3295/m.t.)

This text has a close affinity to folktale in the person of Jack, who in Newfoundland folktale, Martin Lovelace suggests, may be characterized as a lazy trickster. There is an interesting tendency in Newfoundland folktale to have brothers as protagonists, and sometimes antagonists. One brother spies on another in Mrs. Meaney's "Night Kitchen," and the other flings the teacup (in the Irish analogues the cup is flung at a girl by the fairies themselves). In the tale "Daddy Redcap," Jack goes underground with a small red-capped man and gets gold and women, which his brothers haul up out of the hole; when it is Jack's turn to be pulled up, he ties a rock to the rope that the brothers pull halfway up, then drop. "Huh! I knowed darn well what they were going to do alright," says the narrator, "you can't trust your brother."[3] The longest Newfoundland version of the international tale type "Gifts of the Little People" departs from the classic pattern in which the fairies remove the hump from one man's back and put it on another's by making the hunchbacks brothers, and by freeing both of their humps in the end (73-102/31-45).[4] In Leach's Jack tale, there is a hint of sexual duplicity in Jack's being tended in bed by the brother's wife. There is a suggestion of betrayal, too, in the seemingly irrelevant opening about identical cousins in "Little Joe": they are supposed to do everything together, but Big Joe thinks at first that "he come away and leaved me." It seems that tensions arising from the crucial working relationships between male kin (outlined by Firestone in *Brothers and Rivals*) find expression in folktale, where they are usually happily resolved.

There are no women among the "Little Joe" changelings, which retain a strong family resemblance even spread over space. In Rock Harbour in Placentia Bay, Anita Best heard about a seventeen-year-old man who was stricken dumb and lame near a waterfall "where the fairies used to dance." At home in bed, he wouldn't eat when anyone was in the room, but "even if they just left the room for a second, he'd devour everything that, you know, they managed to bring him up." So they called in a clergyman:

> ... and he said, well, that's not your son lying down there. The only way that you're going to get your son back is to, ah, is if you red-hotten a shovel, that is, you know, heat a shovel up until it's red hot, stick the shovel under him and heave him outdoors under the sun. So the mother didn't want to do that, because she really believed it was her son, and he was just sick or something, but eventually her neighbors talked her into it, and they red-hottened the shovel and hove him out ... he was himself after. But funny thing, even when he was himself, when he come back to himself and he used to go around, he was always a little bit touched, you know. (71-53:C984/15-16)

(Note again, "the mother really believed it was her son.") A South Coast version reverses the usual role in diagnosis when a woman whose son is missing for three weeks finds "this fellow" she doesn't recognize lying on the daybed in the kitchen. He won't speak to her, but the neighbours come in and say it *is* the son. Over several weeks he becomes more "friendly," but he "wouldn't eat while they'd be looking at him, and as soon as they turn their back he'd clean off the plate in a minute." A priest tells the men to throw him out on two shovels, and the real son turns up three hours later, saying that he had been out on the barrens in a "big company" that was "chipping and chatting, but he never knew what they were saying. He knew all the boats and everything that used to go in and out to Marystown and he knew their names and everything like that ... but he still couldn't get clear of the bunch he was entangled with" (72-27:C1105/m.t.).

A huge appetite, a standard motif in international changeling lore,[5] does not characterize child changelings in Newfoundland, but food figures prominently in this comparatively small corpus of adult changeling stories. If eating is symbolic of social integration (hence the taboo on fairy food), the impostors try to gobble their way into human society — Little Joe ate "very savage" — although they are not able to do it normally, that is, in company; the exception is the "small devil," who betrays his nature partly by not eating at all. The importance of commensality as a symbol of normalcy is shown in the happy ending of the version of the "hunchback" story mentioned above, when the brothers and their wives (gifts from the fairies) sit down, "laughing and talking, to eat their supper." More pragmatically, the motif may express resentment about food consumed by a non-contributing member of the household, as these fairy-afflicted young men might have been ("always a little bit touched, you know").

In 1635 in England, Heywood wrote that the fairies could "eat, drinke, sit at table" and "may be easily tooke for some friend or acquaintance."[6] In 1988 in Upper Island Cove, Harold Short wrote that they have "the uncanny power to change themselves into someone you know to get you to follow them" (91-232/2). An Island Cove woman "thought she was being led away by a member of her family" while berry-picking one day, but it was the fairies; she was ill for months and "never returned to her old self" (75-79/30-31).

Mr. Smith tells of an impersonation that was never exposed, despite the impostor's brazen announcement of his identity. A young man, whom we learn is unmarried only from the aside that he locks the door when he leaves the house, seems to have had no one to redden the shovel and pitch the usurper out:

> The fellow that I'm telling about, that happened right in here in Bishop's Cove. A beautiful young man, about eighteen years old. And he was a beautiful young man. And one night — we used to, all hands would go to a certain marsh, to go, well, boys and girls, just to have some fun. And this night he thought it was someone on the marsh. But he went up himself. He went alone. And he told me the yarn over: he said when he got there, he thought there was people there, but there was no one that he knowed anything about, he didn't see anyone. And when he turned around, he seen an old man, as he thought, he said, but he was a very small old fella popping around on the ice. So he went up to bid him the time of the night, 'cause he thought it was one of the other boys just trying to scare him off. And the old man had a whip in his hand. And he cut him across the leg, he always said he cut him across the leg. And the young man

come out, and he took sick. And there was a piece of bass rope come out of his leg about three months after that, but he was always crippled after that, he could hardly get around. But they took a piece of bass rope — he said the whip was made out of bass rope, which was used to moor a boat — so he cut him across and about three months after that when they took it out, he never did come to himself to be right after. Because, one day I went in myself to the house he was living in. And when I went in — this is the truth — when I went in, he was sot on the bench. So I bid him the time of the day, called him by name, and this fellow looked at me, he said, "No. I'm not the fellow," he said, "that you thinks I is." Well, we'll use the word Joe, but 'tis not his name, because — so, I said, "Good morning, Joe."

He said, "No, I'm not Joe."

I said, "Who in the hell is ya, if you're not Joe?"

"I'm the Joe," he said, "that used to be."

I said, "You're what?"

"I'm the Joe," he said, "that used to be. But I'm not the Joe that you knows now."

"Well," I said, "that's funny. Who are you trying to scare?"

He said, "I'm not trying to scare anyone, because Joe is coming up the street there, up the road there now."

And when I looked through the window, sure enough, Joe was coming up the road. But who was the fellow I was talking to? I don't know. So, Joe come up, and when he come he unlocked his door, and he come in and he said, "How did you get in?"

I said, "I opened the door and come in, which way do you think I got in?"

"But," he said, "that door was locked! I locked the door before I went out," because he wasn't married. He said, "I locked that door."

"But," I said, "the door was unlocked."

He said, "The door wasn't unlocked, because the door was locked when I just come there."

"But," I said, "when I come there the door was [un]locked, 'cause," I said, "I'm in here. I come in and the door was still locked?"

"Yes," he said, "I just unlocked the door."

"But," I said, "I was just talk —" and I said, "I was just talking to you." And when I turned around the bugger I was talking to, he was gone. And the other Joe was come home. So he said to me, he said, "Now, this is what I'm telling you." He said, "I'll be one place, but this —" he was very wicked then, he said, "this fellow that *is* me," he said, "I'm not [real name] —" but that was his right name, but 'tis, you know, I use the word Joe — he said, "I'm not Joe." He said, "Although I'm living here with you, and I'll do you no harm. But," he said, "I'm telling you that Joe, he is not — he's a fairy, he's turned into a fairy now. I'm the fairy. The other Joe is gone." You know, he could frighten you in that sort of a way. But then after I sized him up, he died a few years after.

BR: So he was young when he died.

JS: He was only a boy, a young man around thirty-eight or forty. But they knowed, when he did die, that it wasn't the right fellow that died. Because when he died, he come right back to a beautiful-looking young man. You could see the young man then. He come back to his self. Because there was not a blemish on him. But the other fellow was going around was all scriveled up. So they claims that when he died, they sent back the right man. And *they* went on. Because they never dies, they say.[7] And that is right. I seen that meself.

Joe, a kind of perennial mummer, seems to have enjoyed his ambiguous identity. I do not know whether Mr. Smith really meant his own claim — "I seen that meself" — to withstand close scrutiny, for I doubt that his pride as a narrator would let him give a denatured performance that does not include the appropriate certifications of authenticity. The skilful teller of fairy and ghost stories aims to induce feelings of wonder, fear, and amazement in his audience (perhaps as Joe did with his odd conversation), and he can hardly do so without displaying conviction himself (unless he adopts the opposite tactic of utter neutrality, and claims to be reporting only facts upon which the listener can make up his own mind). In Mr. Smith I sometimes sensed a certain conflict between literal and artistic truth. Still, he believes in the reality of certain fairy incidents to the extent of refusing to speak of them on tape, and I think that in terms of belief "Joe" and "Little Joe" fall somewhere between these serious matters of which he can hardly be induced to speak, and the tall tales and legends he relates in exactly the same manner as the "Joe" stories. He has "yarns" and "lies" (as he calls them) about winds so high that gulls were stuck in the ice by their beaks, and a man was blown home from the Labrador in a barrel; a rope made of squid; and liniment so powerful it chased a pain through a man's body until the pain shot out of his toe across the water, leaving a hole in his toe and boot ("they don't make that kind of medicine anymore!").[8] One morning it was so cold that Mr. Smith's grandparents donned mufflers and gloves — in their photograph on the wall. (In the midst of these yarns, he owned scrupulously if unnecessarily, "I say 'I' because it sounds better, you know.")

Mr. Smith also tells stories about tricks he has played, some of which were elaborately arranged and sustained over time. One involved a rubber spider put into some made-in-Korea boots, which had the town hysterical over an imagined plague of foreign spiders. Another was about how, on a bet, he got two fellows who had fallen out speaking to each other again through a faked telephone call. I was not unduly disconcerted, then, when I found this Survey Card:

> John Smith claims that he was whipped by the fairies when he was a small baby. His mother left him in the crib while she went out to the clothesline. When she came back John was gone. They looked for him for three days, before he was found. As a result

> of this John, who was born a normal child, has been a cripple ever since. (FSC80-322/*).

Nor was I too surprised when, on my second visit, Mr. Smith and Vera, his wife, told me how after I left the first time, they "laughed and laughed" over what he had told me. Upper Island Cove has a reputation for wit, part of which is the putting on (or down) of outsiders. "It was always one up for the person who could pull a good one on anyone from outside the community — the minister, the boss, the salesman, the policeman, the magistrate or storekeeper," wrote one student, noting that the cycle of "Uncle Joe" jokes (Uncle Joe in court, Uncle Joe goes shopping, Uncle Joe on Bell Island) originated from this tradition (72-103/7). The story that particularly amused Mr. Smith and Vera, however, was not "Joe" or "Little Joe," which Mr. Smith continued to maintain are true, but one that was obviously fictional anyway. We recorded it on the second visit:

> Well, see, a long while ago in Bishop's Cove there was an old gentleman and his old lady. They lived together for all their lives. So one day the old woman — it was late in the fall of the year — she said she didn't have a partridgeberry for to boil a bit of jam for the winter. So the old fellow decided — they was very happy — decided, he said he'd go and get her a gallon of berries. Now he was born in the world, he never had a brother, and he never had a sister. And he had no known relations in the world. So he took the bucket, his gallon can, and he went off to get a *** of berries. Reached the berryground, picked his gallon of berries, sat down on the rock to get a smoke for himself. Proud enough that he had his few berries for his old woman. So, in a few minutes there was an old gentleman come along, a stick in his hand, and he sat down on the rock. Spoke to him, . . . "have you got any relations? *******?"
>
> "No," he said, "I got no one in the world but myself. My father never had a brother or sister, and," he said, "I got no brothers or sisters."

"Oh, yes," he said, "you got a lot of relations."

"Oh, no," he said, "I haven't."

"Oh, yes," he said, "'Cause I'm your Uncle Krinkle."

"Well," he says, "If you're me Uncle Krinkle, that seems to be a very funny name, I never heard me father tell about Uncle Krinkle."

"Oh, yes," he said, "I'm your Uncle Krinkle. And," he said, "you've got a lot of cousins, but you can't see them right now."

"Well," he said, "that seems to be funny."

So he said he talked away and he said, "What about me aunt?"

"Well," he said, "she's here."

So he said, when I turned around instead of being Uncle Krinkle on the rock there was an old woman. "Well," he said, "that's a damn queer thing because me uncle was just here. He told me he was Uncle Krinkle."

"So he is," he said, "I'm here." So when he looked, he said, he was still there. So the two of them. So he said a few minutes after that, he wanted to come home, picked up his can to come home, and when he looked, he said, there was all his little cousins going off with the full gallon of berries: every man, and every child, had a berry put on the hat-pin. And the gallon of berries was lugged away by the fairies, going off through the woods, he said, with no more than one berry on a pin. He said, there should have been thousands, he said, walking along. So he said, "That's how many cousins I had."

An extraordinary feature here is the fairy couple, prolific parents at that, for the fairies seldom appear in twos, but in larger groups or singly. Even the occasional appearance as a pair is not male and female, although it may embody opposites of some sort: a man met two fairies, one laughing and one crying, and took the "good one" on his lap (64-13:C74/14). In the parallel world of "Uncle Krinkle," the fairy couple mirror the "happy old couple" who, typical of folktale, open the story, but "corrects" their lack of family by producing numerous children and siblings. Like "Little Joe" and "Joe," "Uncle Krinkle" may be read as a text *par excellence* about recognition, on knowing or not knowing people, particularly one's own relations; indeed, it makes little sense in any other terms. And one might well have a horde of unknown cousins in Bishop's Cove and Upper Island Cove, where there is a limited number of surnames. Gus Smith, describing the necessity for nicknames, says that ninety per cent of Bishop's Cove are Smiths (74-218/3); Barry Smith lists more names than that but adds, "most all of these families are somehow interrelated" (80-322/7). Short wrote that Dr. Cron nicknamed the families in Island Cove so he could tell them apart (the Lynches, the only Irish surname among them, were "Faries" [*sic*] or "Denies") (FSC91-233/*).[9]

"Little Joe," "Joe," and "Uncle Krinkle" are about tricks and impostures, and so fit Mr. Smith's bent in this direction; perhaps that is why, out of all his fairy lore, he chose them to develop for performance, at least for my interviews. The influence of this personal proclivity is nevertheless limited, as the archival material shows for "Little Joe" and "Uncle Krinkle." Although Mr. Smith says he picked the latter name "out of the air," his claim to wild invention is tempered by a 1974 text from the Bishop's Cove area (the only identification offered by the collector):

> There was an old man who lived on Harbour Grace Ridge, he was called Uncle Stickly. Uncle Stickly used to buy berries. Another man, Uncle Ned, from the same place, went marshberry picking in amongst the rocks. Uncle Ned was picking berries when he looked up and saw what appeared to be Uncle Stickly. Uncle Stickly took Uncle Ned's berries and began to string them on straws. When Uncle Stickly finished — Uncle Ned still thought it was him, so he cursed on him, saying, "God damn you, Uncle Stickly." Uncle Stickly then took the berries on the straws and disappeared with a lot of little people chasing him. (75-79/5-6)

Skewered berries seem to be a local comic motif. James Green of nearby Tilton told me "a yarn" (his term) about a man boiling up (making tea) while picking marshberries, who looked around to see that the fairies had all his berries "skivered up on knitting needles." (I was not admitted to Mr. Green's house until I produced identification showing I was a student; he thought I might be a spy, because "you never know," with all the Europeans around. Mr. Green is a student of military history, an interest perhaps reflected in another "yarn" he tells, about a man who was refused participation in some local event by a woman; he somehow amassed a bunch of fairies and let them loose in her house, where they swarmed about wreaking havoc until she relented.)[10]

The fairy's disguise as Uncle Stickly, a local merchant, fits nicely with the following usage of the term:

> Uncle Ray firmly believes in fairies and spirits even to this day. For he says, "What would you call that old merchant who wouldn't give you your cent for the flake bough, if you wouldn't call him a fairy or an evil spirit of some kind?" (81-314/22)

The metaphor works because in essence the fairies are robbers, their pilferings ranging from trivial (berries) to tragic — children, health, sanity. In "Little Joe," "Joe," and "Jack," they are bent on theft of a human niche; they want a spot by the stove and plates of food, but they don't want to work for it.

Mr. Smith was cheated as a child of the mobility that made full participation in the life of the community possible. His dual roles as storyteller and prankster restore power to him: as a narrator he draws people to himself, and as trickster he sends them running about at his bidding. He uses cunning to triumph over more simple-minded types, at least symbolically. Gus Smith gives the following:

> Before you go in the woods put a hole in a nickel and tie it around your neck to keep away fairies. The fairies will see the bright nickel and be frightened away. This was not believed by my uncle [Mr. Smith]. As a boy he would wait behind a rock for some young person to come along. He would steal their nickel. (FSC74-218/11)

Since Mr. Smith probably did not have the physical ability for mugging, this sounds more like a compensatory fantasy than fact. He does, however, successfully perpetrate long-standing falsehoods. In 1987 I met Daniel Claybourne (a pseudonym), a student from Bishop's Cove who told me that it was only recently that he learned that Mr. Smith lost the use of his leg to polio, not in the war or in the mines on Bell Island. He described going to Mr. Smith's shop with his friends to hear stories, and said that the closing of the shop and his marriage somewhat curtailed Mr. Smith's former audience's access to him. He also said that Bishop's Cove consists of four parts, each with a storyteller who would gladly kill the others. An informant, describing the importance of storytelling, said that "whenever a time [party] was being held at a neighbour's home they wouldn't even call it a time unless they had a few good storytellers there" (74-218/34). Storytelling, then, was an arena in which Mr. Smith could compete on an equal basis. Perhaps the lessened opportunities to go out and get raw material in the form of experience made him especially attentive to traditional sources, hence his extensive repertoire.

Mr. Smith also lays claim to various psychic powers. He says that people used to say that "things cast their shadows before them," and he is sometimes able to foresee things. One morning several years ago he thought the sea looked funny, and told Vera that by nightfall "part of Newfoundland would be under water"; that day there was a flood in Argentia. Another day a series of numbers flashed into his mind, and he told Vera to get a lottery ticket with those numbers; she did, but then changed them, only to discover that the original numbers would have won them a million dollars. He can also "see" backwards: sometimes he goes into a kind of trance and events of two hundred years ago "come to him." Vera confirmed his predictions, as well as his claim that he can make people tell him all about themselves, whether they want to or not; he did that to her, she said. He said this ability is "handed down" (I am not sure whether through teaching or "gift"), and he got it from his grandfather, who could stop horses with his mind and could make people think that a pencil was a snake (Mr. Smith often saw that himself). Vera, a robust woman in her thirties, rushed in and out of the house during our interviews, offering comments and suggestions, checking to see whether I'd

5 | *Fairies, Devils, and Other Impostors in Bishop's Cove*

"John Smith"

gotten everything on tape. She says that Mr. Smith sometimes "scares her to death" with his stories, but she clearly takes pride in them, and it was she who brought out a photograph of Mr. Smith accepting a car that he won on the "Cream of the West" television quiz show in 1963.

A concern with control can be seen in Mr. Smith's claim that he is hard to knock out. Once he pulled some of his teeth with pliers, and when he went to the dentist to have the remainder removed he refused anesthetic because it wouldn't work anyway. (I thought he was joking about this, but Vera, coming in just then, said she'd found him in a pool of blood in the yard that day.) He does not normally drink, but when challenged to a drinking match one time he remained unaffected while the seasoned drinkers reeled. As a child, he said, he never slept more than two hours a night, and his mother predicted that he'd never see thirty. (One night, while roaming about, he saw a huge hovering object with bright lights; the next day, when a young boy who also saw it was accused by his parents of lying, Mr. Smith came to his rescue by confirming it.)

Mr. Smith is, then, by his own portrayal, "a hard case," who must find it irresistible to practise his wiles on an itinerant folklorist. Nevertheless, some stories can easily be seen to be entertainment tales (like "Uncle Krinkle"), and others, without a doubt, are not. In the former category are tall tales and legends for which he employs the same style as that of "Joe," "Little Joe," and "Uncle Krinkle," with dialogue and the repetition of words and phrases almost like refrains. Two of these, which he tells as he heard them from "comical" storytellers, concern local landmarks. Bishop's Cove was the last place founded by the devil, he says, when the devil got mad and kicked the two Tolts apart, rested in the Devil's Hole, had his dinner on Dinner Hill, and hurt his foot kicking a quarter-mile hole into the cliff at Garman's Gulch. Presumably much later, a thunderbolt cracked one of the Tolts; they dragged the hundred and twenty-seven foot bolt out of the ground with horses, and "every man in Bishop's Cove had a grapple [anchor] made out of the thunderbolt that split the Tolt in two pieces."

The characteristic regional association between fairies and the devil shows up in topography. "The Devil ate his dinner" on Dinner Hill, one collector wrote, and so did the fairies (70-25/85). Another makes the familiar Irish/fairy connection:

> The first inhabitants that came to Bishop's Cove were from Cork County, Ireland. These people believed in fairies. There is a big hill directly over the settlement. The settlers named it Dinner Hill because this is where they believed the fairies came and gathered each day for dinner. (FSC80-322/*).

The same student wrote of the famous thunderbolt:

> Many years ago before electricity came to Bishop's Cove it was believed by the local people that the fairies lived on a hill called the Tolt. One night a thunderbolt fell and the Tolt split and rocks were sent hundreds of feet in the air. The people believed that this thunderbolt was sent by God to destroy all the fairies. Fairies have not been seen since this event in 1901. (FSC80-322/*)

5 | *Fairies, Devils, and Other Impostors in Bishop's Cove*

Of course, it was not really the end of the fairies, for elsewhere the same student wrote:

> "In the days of darkness" when there was no electricity people used to use the oil lamps. During this period (1940s–1954) many people had encounters with the fairies. They also saw ghosts and weather lights. . . . There are no fairies here today, they all moved away when electricity came. (80-322/21, 26)

Mr. Smith took issue with several points in the above accounts, saying that "there was never an Irishman in Bishop's Cove," and that Bishop's Cove had electricity in the 1920s, and lights were "blooming by 1945." But just as that collector did, Mr. Smith casts the fairies in the past in one breath and resurrects them in the next. About sixty years ago, he says:

> the last fairy was seen in Bishop's Cove. He was seen on Dinner Hill. And he was supposed to be getting his dinner too. That was the last one, until the other year that woman I was telling you about, which I'm not telling, because that's an actual fact, and the people are still alive today.

The latter reference is to an incident that is among those he treats seriously and refuses to speak of on tape, or at all, when pressed. It concerns an "educated, clean-living" woman who was picking berries one day when a strange, well-dressed man — "one of them" — appeared and tried to get her to go in a direction "she knew wasn't right." She ignored his coaxing and sat down on a rock reciting scriptures to herself, where she was found, unharmed, in the morning. It takes strength to resist the devil and the fairies, both of whom threaten personal volition. Two Bishop's Cove men were "led astray," and "when they were found they were supposed to be fairy-flicked — a sort of hypnotism" (FSC74-218/7). "The older people," wrote one student, "believed that the devil lived in "Devil's Hole Hill"; young men on the way to fight in World War Two would spend the night there and put their names on the wall: "the purpose of this trip was to show their bravery and when they returned home they were praised for outsmarting the devil. If they were weak the devil would have taken them" (80-322/13). Another student says the names were supposed to have been carved by the devil himself, and "when anybody died in the town the family would go to the cave to see if the name was still there or if it was gone. If the name was gone then your soul had gone to hell, if your name remained then your soul had gone to heaven" (FSC 91-233/*).

Being taken by the fairies consigns one to a more living hell. One of the stories Mr. Smith declined to record was about a woman who ended up in "the mental," or psychiatric hospital, as a result of seeing a strange old woman on the road. This somehow affected her so that "her mind stopped where it was," and everything now is as it was thirty years ago to her; she doesn't recognize her grown son, insisting that her son is only two months old. But even for such serious matters, Mr. Smith shuffles the various elements and motifs like a deck of cards, displaying them in a different configuration each time. Several years after telling about the time-stalled woman, Mr. Smith told of a "beautiful young woman" who met an identical fate when she entered an empty house formerly inhabited by a hunchbacked man who had moved to Vancouver. "Something bad" happened to everyone who went into this house; the woman felt "hundreds" brushing against her on the stairs and in the rooms, even though she could not see them. She, too, ended up in "the mental" with time standing still. It is useful to observe an individual performing the reshuffling that is so clear at a general level, that is, in aligning texts from different informants in an area. Another constellation of the above motifs, for example, can be seen in a recent account:

> A girl from Upper Island Cove was believed to have been "whipped" by a fairy. When she was just a school child on her way home from school one day, her friend threw her mitten into a deserted house. Since it was winter she went to get her mitten. When she went in she saw a little man who "cut her with a whip across the legs." After this she became sick and crippled. The doctor came to see her and performed surgery on her leg. He removed bones, bits of cloth, and other strange things that did not belong. While she was sick, her grandfather came to see her.

> When he was going to her room upstairs, there were many little people coming down the stairs. The house was full of them. After a long time the child recovered, but was never the same. Scars and marks remain on her legs today.[11] (91-232/17-18)

The bodily extrusion of foreign matter, long a hallmark of bewitchment, is in Newfoundland (as in Ireland) blamed mostly on the fairies, but Bishop's Cove harboured a lone late human practitioner of the missile-injecting art:

> A woman told me one time of an incident in her childhood which she will never forget. She and one of her friends were laughing at a poor old man who lived in an old house. One day he ran after them and her friend fell. She injured her leg and a doctor was called. An operation was made on her leg and bones (fish) and straws of grass were taken out of it. That woman is now in the mental but this happened long before she entered the hospital. How the stuff got into her leg is unknown. The old man was then believed to be behind it.[12] (FSC70-25/94)

The continuous recycling of narrative components seems to enhance their credibility rather than detract from it, all the "whipping" and "flicking" being taken as instances of proof rather than narrative variation or elaboration. Although one student described fights between "Ridge Goats" and "Cove Goats," rival groups of preadolescent boys from different sections of Bishop's Cove (70-25/23-4), he does not mention them as a possible explanation for a friend's misfortune:

> When I was about twelve years old [c. 1960] we went skating on a pond (marsh). There was always talk of things being seen there. For some reason or other I had to leave my friend alone for a while; upon returning I found that he had fallen down and couldn't get up. He fell on his stomach. He said that someone whipped him on the back. Sure enough there were about a dozen whip marks across his back and they are there today. His parents and others said that it was the fairies who did it. It is very strange

and unexplainable. Even a bruise would disappear after eight years. (FSC70-25/80)

When the victim's brother described the same incident ten years later, the "someone" who whipped him on the back had become a bunch of singing, dancing, little men (80-322/22-23). On the subject of violence, the first student also described the now-defunct "Teek" or "Tag" day, January 6, the last day of Christmas and of janneying when "people used to dress up and go around cracking others with sticks" (70-25/79). An acquaintance's father was once beaten by two men for "devilment." He wrote, "I heard one man say that men used to await others for hours on the roofs of houses. He said it was the risk of one's life to go outdoors on Teek day" (FSC70-25/50). (Mr. Smith confirmed that the adult "teeks," usually dressed in oilclothes with black stockings over their faces, were dangerous; his grandfather once jumped into the water to avoid them.) But when Mr. Short of Island Cove was lost one January night and returned bruised, frostbitten, and trouserless, the spectre of human violence was not raised (at least according to the collector); instead, since "Mr. Short was a man well-noted for his honesty as well as being noted as one who positively refused to believe in ghosts, fairies or superstitions," his explanation that he had been led into the woods and stripped by six small fairies was accepted, and "many people believed that such an experience happened to Mr. Short because he refused to believe that fairies existed" (Q68-259/2-5).

The recorder of Mr. Short's misadventure explicitly distinguished "old fairies," who "are good and will often help you when you are in trouble," from "young fairies" that are bad, and do things like the harrowing of Mr. Short. "Childish" fairies in a text from Victoria are downright diabolical:

> This is a story my Uncle Dave claims to be true. The story is about an old man. One night this old man was walking down the road when he came across a group of children who looked terrified. When he asked them what was wrong they said that there were some little men down the road and they were afraid to walk any further. The old man said there was nothing to be afraid of and he proceeded to walk down the road. The next

5 | *Fairies, Devils, and Other Impostors in Bishop's Cove*

> morning they found the old man dead and his hair had turned a silver white. It was said that the children were little devils in disguise who had tricked the old man into getting killed. (FSC75-144/*)

Yet, malevolent "old" fairies abound in Bishop's Cove. Mr. Smith's narratives are full of aged fairies: there is the "old man" or "small old fella" who struck "Joe" with the rope, after which Joe becomes, or is replaced by, a "scriveled thing"; the counterfeit Little Joe ("that thing you got sot down there feeding it is about seventy years old"); Uncle Krinkle, "an old gentleman"; and the strange old woman the sight of whom put a young woman in "the mental." Frightening old figures may be solidly material, like Aunt Victoria, an "old lady" who dressed in black and was considered a witch by some (FSC80-314/*), or insubstantial, like the "old man" who terrified Gus Smith's grandfather on certain mornings by walking across the stage into the water, or out of the water and across the stage (74-218/24). Even the Old Hag in Bishop's Cove is thought of as an "old person" ("over sixty") who returns after death to "hagg" someone who has spoken badly of him or her (FSC70-25/78). The fairies' apparently opposite guises as old people and small children suggests that the very young and the old have more in common than the broader middle range; perhaps they are in the same cognitive category, according to the theory that the far ends of a spectrum sometimes meet.

Young or old, the fairies are a powerful crowd that, perhaps out of envy, threatens individual human personality. Trance and possession are particularly strong elements in Bishop's Cove fairy lore:

> Many years ago it was believed that a person could be possessed by the fairies. One man, Harris Smith, was led away by the fairies and he wasn't found for three days. When the local people found him he was naked from the waist up. He had gotten hungry and eaten his sweater. (FSC80-322/*)

He lost his memory and was "never the same after" (80-322/23). "Fairies are supposed to be little men about two feet tall who wore red suits. They usually led night walkers away on a parade in which the fairies danced around the person as he walked," said one student; they "took control of a person's mind and led him astray," as in the case of a man who failed to return from a trouting expedition:

> They found him walking along an old grassy road. He seemed to be talking to little fellows around him. It was no use to talk to him so one man smacked him in the face. He came out of it but didn't remember what he had done. He was said to have been "in the fairies." (FSC70-25/79,81)

The Bishop's Cove Old Hag acts much like the fairies:

> The hag doesn't let the person beset rest. The hag usually is supposed to lead the person, or place him/her in a frightening position such as in a graveyard at night.... The person who was beset would be struggling to get back to reality but couldn't. He knew that he was asleep and that by waking everything would be solved.... One could be hit by the hag and wake up feeling the force of the blow.

Or the "hagged" person might become "lightheaded" and talk in his sleep, and would be said to be "in the ditties" (70-25/104-5). The paralysis that renders the hag victim helpless also immobilizes the will of the fairy-stricken, who might be literally petrified: in Upper Island Cove, "one of your limbs would become wooden instead of flesh and bone" if you are "flipped by the fairies" (FSC71-41/19).

The term "flicked" seems to be peculiar to the area from Clarke's Beach to Harbour Grace. Two Spaniard's Bay informants were discussing the fairies:

> Informant 1: They used to call them little people, you know. They was all dressed in white and they be only about three or four feet high.... See now, the wife's brother down there, look, when he was small he was supposed to be lugged away by the fairies.... They took a bone out of the calf of his leg ... just like fish bones....

> Informant 2: When he was getting over the wall he felt a belt flicking him across the legs. And then he took sick, you know, took sick and his legs started to swell. And sure Dr. Cron come up and he said, "Miss," he said, "Miss, where now has this boy been flicked with the fairies?" (75-163/18-19)

Today's doctors seem to be less acute in their fairy-linked diagnoses than Dr. Cron, who "always told his patients to curse the fairies and the devil and they would recover from their illnesses much quicker" (FSC80-322/*). A few years ago, Mr. Smith said, a man in a boat was surrounded by a swarm of "busybees" (bumblebees); he got sick and was taken to the hospital where he died although there was not a bite on his body (when I later asked if he'd ever heard of a "blast," he said that's exactly what this man had gotten). It was also recently that a boy "lost his mind" and the doctors didn't know what was the matter with him; Mr. Smith knew, because he could recognize it from the old stories about that kind of thing, but when I asked what it was he shook his head and refused to say more.

Reserve in speaking of disease or tragic events combines with ordinary caution in speaking of fairies to create formidable obstacles for field researchers, even cultural "insiders." A student in my 1989 summer class said that a woman in her home community in Trinity Bay was supposed to have been "fairy changed" when the fairies "towed her away" and replaced a bone in her leg with a feather or a straw, but that no one in the community dares to ask the woman herself about it (FSC89-287/*). Gus Smith observed both reticence and joking in Bishop's Cove:

> One thing I did find strange while I was collecting was that some people were frightened to talk about omens and fairies. This is especially true of anyone who had seen some of these. An example of this type of person is Aunt Rachel. She was willing to talk about anything someone else had seen but there was no way to get her to talk about some fairy that I knew she was in contact with. Grandfather Smith [Mr. Smith's father] was negative on this point also. In fact he was frightened to talk on

anything to do with this. Some of the people home believe that these spirits are still here. If you happen to laugh at these they would get frightened to death ... my father says that his great grandmother didn't want him to build a house where he did. The reason for this was that it was two feet too far to the south which meant it was on fairyland. Dad answers, "That's okay, I have a spare room built on for them." Aunt Sarah (Dad's great grandmother) replies that she wouldn't say that for all the money in the world.[13] (72-262/14-16)

One Bishop's Cove man "saw something on the gate post" one night at the stage that so frightened him he was sick in bed for three days after. "He has never told what he saw," writes the collector. "Now and then I hear of this type of story in the community — of seeing something and not telling what they saw" (FSC70-25/93). A Bishop's Cove informant told about some men who went to cut wood on Good Friday; when they put the axe to the tree, "a gush of blood" poured out. "Well, they lived through the fright somehow," he said. "They never talk about what happened. No. Not to anyone. Queer stuff happens sometimes you know" (74-218/17). The taboo on speaking of frightening or sinister subjects makes it hard to know when the full range of supernatural tradition is represented, and underscores the importance of "native" collection. Even "ordinary" lore might not be offered freely to a stranger; Daniel Claybourne (the Bishop's Cove student I met in 1987) said that his father, on hearing of my work, expressed surprise that anyone would tell me anything at all.[14] On my first visit, as Vera left the house at one point, Mr. Smith cautioned her not to tell anyone who was there or what we were talking about. (Possibly he wanted to keep this information to be given according to his own inclination, after curiosity was aroused. When Vera returned she reported, rather gleefully I thought, all the questions about my visit.)

It is unlikely that I exhausted Mr. Smith's repertoire, as every time I visited him I learned a little more (on my latest visit in 1990, I even learned how to put a spell on my enemies by driving a nail into a board in a process called "pinning"). In 1986 he gave my six-month-old son a Newfoundland nickel,

5 | *Fairies, Devils, and Other Impostors in Bishop's Cove*

which led us to talk of its protective power. I mentioned an incident in the news that week, about a young boy in Nova Scotia who had gotten lost; even though he was spotted by searchers several times, he fled, and was found some days later dead. "Something crossed his mind," said Mr. Smith; some "force" had him, because there was no way he could have eluded adults like that. They were looking all over for him, he said, and he may have been under a stump all along. He said that in the old days they would have thrown bread all around and it probably would have worked.

He also told me that his grandmother would put a child born with "retardation" on the doorstep at midnight, and take it in later. Eighty per cent of the time it would be normal, he said, and it might even come back "with more power than before." He had mentioned this cure before, but not that his grandmother did it; and during a visit in November 1987 he went even further, saying that his grandmother once wanted to put a child out, without its clothes, so that the "real child," who was "out in the woods," could be brought back. The child's father wouldn't allow it, even though the grandmother told him "what they had could be anything, could be the devil"; eventually the girl had to be kept in a "pound."

On this visit, Mr. Smith also said, for the first time, that the reason the fairies took people was to get their souls, that this would make them "wiser." This was not an interview-induced generality, but was in fact a correction of the friend who was visiting with me, who asserted that fairies usually took children; Mr. Smith said that they preferred adults for this reason. The separable soul, an object as thievable as an apple, is depicted graphically in one Bishop's Cove narrative:

> My father told me one night that he saw a big black dog running along the road; by the time it got to where he was standing it shrank to the size of a kitten. When he arrived home his grandmother was dead. The shrinking animal was her soul. (FSC80-322/*)

Despite their lack of soul, the fairies are not just amoral but wicked, and the Bishop's Cove version of the fallen angel legend links them directly with

Lucifer by saying that "the fairies had *caused* war in heaven" (FSC88-311/*) (emphasis mine to contrast this with the versions that say they were merely neutral), or that they are "angels driven from heaven because they were bad" (80-322/21). Their devilish nature explains why the ringing of church bells at midnight scared them away from their efforts to take a Bishop's Cove woman (80-322/24).

This diabolical strain extends even to healing; Bishop's Cove is the only place I know of where "being able to charm away warts, etc., was said to be 'Satanic Power'" (FSC70-25/68). However, Mr. Smith tells about a number of charmers and healers with no indication of such an association. One blood-stopper was probably schizophrenic, for he was completely normal sometimes, uncontrollably wild at others; he died in the mental hospital without passing on his charm. Mr. Smith had a wart charm himself (involving tying a string and saying "In the name of the father," etc.), but it was overheard one day and thus lost. Mr. Smith's views on religion are iconoclastic by traditional standards: referring to the Bible, he said, "I suppose you should believe it." He once shocked his grandmother by saying that the moon was only a rock, while she saw it as a light put there by God.

In November 1987 I asked Mr. Smith about the expression "in the fairies," which made him and Vera exchange looks and smile; he embarked on a story about an Island Cove man who had been in bed for years. The day his mother died, the people returning from the funeral found him at the kitchen table. "Now why was he in bed so long?" Mr. Smith asked, and I never did find the answer to that; I gathered that the man is simply slow, and he now gets on well in a group home in St. John's. Later that same day, Elsie Drover of Island Cove (whom Janet McNaughton was interviewing about her midwife grandmother) showed us a picture of a woman about three feet tall who used to keep a shop and who was very clever. "Would people have said she was a fairy?" I asked, thinking of her size. "No, my dear, she was not in the fairies!" said Mrs. Drover emphatically, the implication being that she was much too smart for that. Mrs. Drover also said that there is now a housing tract on the old cemetery where people used to say the fairies had their funerals, and that "you never hear of them now."

5 | *Fairies, Devils, and Other Impostors in Bishop's Cove*

Harold Short's 1988 collection from Island Cove suggests otherwise. The eighteen narratives from thirteen informants also confirm the essentially bad character of the area's fairies: two of the encounters are "neutral," that is, there seems to be no threat of harm to the persons involved; five are near escapes; and in the rest the human protagonists meet with injury, madness, or death. The familiar themes and motifs are there: people compulsively follow "jackies" and little red men into woods and ponds, or follow voices they think belong to relatives or friends; a little man pulls straw out of a woman's knee ("so it would not give away the secret of their little hiding place"), and a boy's leg exudes paper; a young girl is greeted in the road by a strange little man and dies the next day. Very corporeal fairies like those in the "Joe" stories appear in two versions of a tale unparalleled in MUNFLA:

> A young girl from Upper Island Cove while sitting in her house one night was captured by the fairies and dragged away. As the fairies were leaving the house, one was captured and chained to the same chair that the little girl was taken from in order to make the fairies give back the little girl to her parents. A few weeks later the girl's parents heard a noise in the living room. When they went to look they found the girl in the chair with her clothes turned inside out. Later they discovered she was crippled. Until the day she died she could not walk due to her experience with the fairies.
>
> "Captured Fairy Version 2": There is a story of a young girl from Upper Island Cove who in the late 1800s was taken by the fairies. She was taken from the back porch of her house and replaced by a fairy. The girl's family would leave the fairy in the porch each day after the event, hoping that the other fairies would return the girl and take back the fairy. The girl, however, was never returned.[15] (91-232/16-17)

"Two hundred years ago or less," said an informant in Bryant's Cove (next to Island Cove), "there were many towns and villages in Newfoundland swarming with ghosts and fairies" (75-5/n.p.). The late 1800s seem to figure in folk tradition as a time when fairies were still so common that no description of their appearance was necessary, as they commandeered kitchens in Avondale or bodies in Bishop's Cove. Referring to the general run of phantoms and fairies, Gus Smith asked one informant "why such things as a 'Drummer' or a 'Headless Dog' were not seen around here now":

> He replied, "There's too much noise and rackets going on now, sure. So many cars and stuff. Years ago, when the sun went down and it got dark sure everything was still. Now people don't move until after dark. They're around, boy, you just don't hear them." (74-218/35-36)

"I also feel the old fellows like to brag a little," Smith adds, "a good many times I heard the comment, 'Nothing happens now like we had in the good old days!'" Mr. Smith tells me the reason fairies are not seen now is that "these things" — fairies, UFOs, phantoms, and the like — go in twenty-five-year cycles, and we are in an "off" cycle at the moment.

On one of my later visits to Mr. Smith, I remarked that I would like to have a time machine to go back for just one day and see what life was really like in an outport of the past. "You wouldn't want to come back," he said; once I got on a hill berry-picking with a bunch of women, I would know how fine it was compared to today. I was surprised to hear Mr. Smith say that modern life is "poison" to him, for despite his intense interest in the past, I had not sensed a strong nostalgia in him before. But Mr. Smith has had several heart attacks since I first met him, and has been in weakened health ever since. He can't understand it, he jokingly tells his doctors, since he is only thirty-five. And he is notoriously a hard man to keep down.

Mr. Smith's repertoire (by which I mean not only his stories but all of his knowledge about the fairies) has several implications for the reading of archival material. By showing that it is possible to have fairy traditions too sensitive for discussion with an inquiring stranger, as well as jocular tales and entertainment legends, it recommends caution about generalizing from the archival data alone; if one were to find in the archive, say, a set of funny fictions, one could not necessarily draw conclusions about the narrator's overall attitude

5 | *Fairies, Devils, and Other Impostors in Bishop's Cove*

toward the fairies or about the character of the fairies themselves. Another contribution of Mr. Smith's repertoire to the interpretation of archival material is that his performances exemplify the dynamic observed in Chapter Two whereby events of long ago are retailed in a more detailed, animated fashion than those of more recent occurrence. Further insight into narrative processes is afforded by his different performances at different times, in which he juggles a stock of themes and motifs into different combinations. This building-block approach is not often observed on the part of an individual, because most informants are recorded only once; and those who are recorded over time are not usually creative narrators like Mr. Smith.

This chapter shows that for all the similarity of fairy tradition throughout the province, there are differences in the general cast and overall character of the fairies in different areas. This is evident not from a single text but from a corpus; a set of legends from Bishop's Cove would not be confused with a set from Avondale, although only a stretch of road separates them, and most of the same motifs and concepts are found in both. If you see strange women in gowns that billow in a sudden wind, you are probably in Avondale. If a little old man flicks you on the leg with a whip and you go mad, you are in or near Bishop's Cove. Or, you might meet one of "them" there and not even know it.

POSTSCRIPT TO CHAPTER FIVE

In July 1991 I went to Bishop's Cove and, with some trepidation, read this chapter to Mr. Smith and Vera. It was a great relief when Mr. Smith said that I had "put it all together very well" and gotten most things right. He did not contradict anything as I read, but in conversation over tea midway through, he indirectly addressed some of the things I had said. He talked about how active and strong he had always been despite his leg, so I inferred that I have perhaps overplayed its effect on his life. Yet his very insistence on his ability to do everything that everyone else did (and then some) confirmed my impression of a person who hates the thought of seeming anything less than master of a situation. He simply "would not accept" any limitations, he says, and recounted yet more mischief in proof of his incorrigibility: how he trained a cat to jump on people's shoulders in the dark so they would think the devil had them; how he once drank the altar wine when sent to ring the church bells in place of his grandfather, "a wonderful churchman" (a sexton), who was ill. His grandfather never suspected anything, because he thought John was "an angel," but others in the community knew better and put a nickname on him: "the Devil." He and his best friend, also named John, were so awful together, "tormenting" people in one way or another, that one man dubbed them "Antichrist Number One" and "Antichrist Number Two": "Don't let them both in together, whatever you do," people would say. That friend is dead now, and Mr. Smith feels that his own time is short, for he has been in the hospital a lot lately for problems with his heart and leg, which now keep him housebound. But he can project himself onto the hill facing his house if he concentrates (Vera says she even saw him over there once, when she glanced into the kitchen mirror); and he can still help people with his psychic gifts (when a young woman recently came to him with unspecified emotional troubles, he was able to divine their cause and cure). "You'll laugh at the devil," he says people used to say to him; with luck he is still too contrary to go gently anywhere soon.

6 | *UFOs: Urban Fairy Oddities, and Some Modern Influences on the Genesis and Evolution of Fairy Tradition*

𝒜lthough ancient and remarkably stable, fairy traditions do show syncretism with "modern" legend and current ideas, which come not only from oral tradition but from print and electronic media as well. The association of fairy and UFO (unidentified flying object) lore is a notable example, and raises questions about analysis and classification. Does it make a difference, conceptually speaking, whether a crowd of little people are supposed to have come from another planet or a nearby bog? When a person has an experience or tells a story that is recognizably (to one acquainted with fairy tradition) a "fairy" one, but does not make that identification or interpretation himself, is it still a "fairy" story? In other words, does one take what David Hufford calls an "experience-centered approach" (*Terror* 14–15) and concentrate on the experience itself rather than the label?

The stereotype that fairy traditions thrive only in remote rural areas is exploded in this chapter, which takes many examples from the St. John's area. The related notion that old and isolated communities best foster fairy lore is dismissed through an examination of Bell Island, once one of the most heavily trafficked places in the province and still one of the best for fairy lore. Although it might be hypothesized that such "urban" regions[1] would show a tendency toward amalgamation of fairy lore with modern or "urban" legend, in fact fairy narratives of the St. John's region and Bell Island are not much different from those of the outports, except for their setting. Finally, on the question of the decline of fairy traditions, I examine legend cycles about two individuals that establish a definite point in time for their active development and transmission on a large scale.

The three chief informants for this chapter have in common an extroverted, expansive personality. The first is Mr. H. Miles Furlong, who contacted me in response to my article in *The Seniors' News*. A lifelong resident of St. John's, he is nearing retirement from his position with the Roman Catholic school board, and says that because he is "Irish and Catholic," he "believes in miracles"; so if I were to tell him, for example, that I saw St. Patrick's Hall across the street from his house turned upside down, then as far as he was concerned, I did see it, and I was not drunk or crazy either. ("Whether it happened or not, is something else. A person tells me something, I believe that person is telling me what he honestly believes. And you can sense between what a person believes, and when he's pulling your leg, 'cause I have that kind of experience.") This was the attitude he took toward the story told to him six or seven years ago by Ron Ennis, a former policeman (now deceased). They were standing on the steps of the Basilica after Mass "swapping yarns," and Mr. Furlong told Mr. Ennis that the sacristan of the church once told him about seeing a black, well-dressed gentleman (the devil) on a staircase:

> And he [Ennis] said, I'll tell you one now, he said, when I first joined the police force. A young, raw recruit, do anything the sergeant told me, the lieutenant told me to do, I'd do it, no matter what it was, I was a policeman, I was going to be *the* policeman, the best policeman that ever was. And there wasn't any school for that sort of business, you had to learn the hard way, on-the-job training, sort of, from day one, you see. [He is sent to investigate the theft of some lumber from Holy Cross School] ... and Brother Ryan [the principal], his reaction to the policeman showing up was that this was good enough, now, to let the people know that they were sailing on thin ice. So, he said, "Ron, look over there in that garden," he said, "do you see anything

over there?"** Looked over the garden to see if anyone was lurking about, so to speak. And he said, "What do you see, Ron?" And he said, "A garden, trees, not a very well-kept garden, it's toys there, kids playing, I suppose there, and grass is not cut; a few trees growing wild and uncared for. And there's a ****** at the back of the house, steps coming down." He says, "No, Ron, do you see anybody?" He says, "No, Brother, I don't." He says, "Do you see that little fellow at the top of the steps?" [Pause] Turned around, and said "What the hell's going on here?" ***** He said, sure enough, there he was. Little short fellow. Very short, and sprightly. And he says, "Yes, I do see him." And he says, "Do you see any more?" "Hmm, by gosh, you're right, Brother, there's three or four of them, three or four of them there." And *** goes back and forth and after awhile it was getting on towards dusk, and Ron wasn't feeling very comfortable, so he says, "Okay, Brother, I'll go back in the morning and report to the assistant chief," I think it was, "very good," he said, he couldn't get out of there fast enough. So he got home and didn't anticipate, didn't think about it, he had his notes, and when he went in in the morning to report in the morning to work to the chief, he told him that he'd gone up and inferred from Brother Ryan that the main purpose was that someone should see a policeman walking around there looking at the lumber, and obviously there was something being done about the thefts up there. But, he said, he didn't seem to be very concerned about losing a few planks, whatever it was. But he said, "I saw another strange thing up there," he said, "he pointed out to me in the garden adjacent to the school, ah, that there was — he showed me, he pointed it out, that the fairies were out there. And," he said, "I did see them. There was probably five, six, seven, eight of them there." And started to describe them, he said, "The old chief made a roar at me, bawled at me, 'Get out of here, Ennis, you've been at the — you've been into the sauce again. So you get out of here now, and I won't send you up there anymore. You can leave all that business alone, forget it'." And that was the end of the story. But we laughed hearty over it, the two of us, but Ron was not telling me a fabrication. What Ron was telling me was what he — I believe that he honestly thought, honestly believed he thought. Now whether that's power of suggestion, whether it's fact or fancy, or maybe he was in the hooch, but he said he didn't, hadn't had a drink, he wasn't drinking style (?) at the time. But that is the story that he gave me.

BR: And he was perfectly serious when he told you. I mean, you knew him, and —

HMF: Well, he was sort of matter-of-fact, telling me this. He was not trying to impress me, he knows me better than that. . . . He was a typical policeman type, you'd tell him nothing that he could hang you with, because he would.

BR: Did he say what they looked like?

HMF: Small people, very small, within a range of — well, what I infer *** — maybe a foot, two feet in height. Very sprightly, as I say, and quick of movement, and rather — he didn't describe their garb, but the way it was — he talked to me as if I should know what a fairy looked like. And, for that reason, then, I didn't press him on the matter, and he was well into his story, and this is what they **. So, in that way, I can only infer, the way he described them was sprightly, and very small little people. Nothing grotesque about them, or anything like that. Their garb was, I suppose, whatever fairies should wear, whatever fairies would wear, or should wear, in that case they were wearing. But I think he mentioned something about a tasseled hat, or something. And that was — he's the only person I've ever known who told me about that way, uh, described them, tried to describe to me in a general way. They were playing games of some sort or other, or bring *** something. They had music, he didn't say who played what or what they played, but there was music there, they seemed to be quite happy, and very jolly.

This incident could have happened anywhere; if Mr. Furlong had not mentioned that it was on Patrick Street, the only clue that it was not some small outport would be, perhaps, the figure of the policeman. The "sprightly" fairies are identical to some of their outport cousins, as can be seen by comparing the text with two recorded by Virginia Dillon, which share other features with Mr. Ennis's story as well. Just as the Patrick Street fairies were no fleeting impression, the men in Dillon's first account watched the vision in leisurely calm detachment:

> When my grandfather was a young man, probably in his early twenties, he was walking home to Mobile from St. John's with some other men. They were on their way home from "the ice" [the seal hunt]. It was just about sunset when they came to Witless Bay. Just before they entered the settlement one of the men happened to look into a meadow which was near the side of the road. A group of small figures were dancing around in a ring. I think they are described as being dressed in red and green, but I don't think my father is sure. The men stood there looking at them for maybe half an hour. An interesting point about the story is that only some of the men could see the dancing figures. The figures were called *fairies* by the men who told the story. (64-1C/26)

In the second account, attention is directed to the sight, as by Brother Ryan. Some children were sliding on a frozen marsh when "someone cried out something like, 'Look at the fairies,'" and they saw "strange little figures" dancing among them on the ice:

> Some of them, including my uncle, saw nothing, but several of the children saw them and could describe them to the others. All of the children of course went home immediately. Those who had seen the figures could vividly describe their dress and behaviour. (64-1C/27)

Sometimes strange sights can be made "contagious" by touch: "If you see something and someone else doesn't, you just touch the other person and he'll see it too," explained a Colliers woman who communicated her vision of a fairy woman to her husband this way (74-150/17). Frances Kavanagh told me that "there are such things that some people will see and some people won't. Like ghosts — everybody don't see, but some will.... They claims it has to do with the time of the day that you're born. If you're born between two lights [between day and night] you're apt to see things."

Mr. Clive Tucker, a wildlife officer from St. Phillips (just outside St. John's),[2] would explain the difference in what people "see" in terms of psychic ability. My article in *The Seniors' News* reminded him of two experiences he had long ago; he also thought that I might share his interest in dowsing. Mr. Tucker divines the location, depth, and quality of water through a process he cannot explain, but that does not require that he be anywhere near the site (although he does use rods at the site as well). He can also screen houses for radon gas, and applies dowsing experimentally to other objectives, such as treasure, bodies, or poachers' guns, with varied results. On his second visit to my home, Mr. Tucker brought a diagram he had made of the house, showing two veins of "positive energy" running through it. (Coincidentally, I had just rearranged the furniture to facilitate tape recording, and had set a chair for Mr. Tucker in the spot where the lines converge.) We had already recorded his strange experiences on Three Pond Barrens, on the northwest edge of St. John's and now part of Pippy Park. The first took place when he was about eleven years old, trouting with a friend. It was just after dark, and he and his friend were heading home when they saw lights in a marsh about five hundred feet away: "first of all, we thought it was people with kerosene lanterns, looking for something that was lost ... a lot of people just wandering around the marsh with little lanterns looking for it." But this was the first year of the Second World War, and after they watched for a while, "then we begin to think, that it was German paratroopers or something after landing. And we got afraid, and we just booted out of there as fast as we could." At home he told his father about the lights, "expecting to call out the troops and everything; and he told me, go to bed, it was only Jack O'Lanterns." When I later — off tape

— brought up the subject of UFOs, Mr. Tucker said that he and his friend had in fact been watching for UFOs, and that just before they saw the lights they had seen a glowing orb go across the sky. Had I not expressed an interest in this topic, this would probably not have emerged, just as he has kept his second strange experience to himself for almost fifty years. Several years after seeing the lights, he was near the same area near dusk and decided to take a shortcut across a bit of marsh and pick up the trail on the other side.

> So I tried it, the first time I tried to get through, and I ended up right back where I started. Well, I just figured I got threw off the course. So I started again. I took my bearings a second time, and I ** started to come through again. The second time it was similar. I ended up right back at the point. I started off again, ** so I took a hard look at it, and I said, "Really, this time I'm really going to do it this time, this is it, this is it, third ***." So I really set off with determination. And I come up, and I pressed on it, and I tried to get through, get through and get over to the road that was on the other side of that marsh and the third time I ended up back, and by that time it was dark, and I didn't know how long I had spent there, it could've been ten minutes or a little bit more, ten or probably twenty minutes, or half hour, could be an hour, 'cause it's gotten dark in this length of time, I had no watch, no means to tell time.

So he took the regular route; the next day he went back and walked over the marsh with no trouble at all. But the evening before, "I was going around, but I wasn't going anywhere," he said, "there was a barrier just keeping me out." He compared it to what someone coming to a plexiglas shield who didn't know about plexiglass might feel, but says that it might not have affected everyone, that some people might have "blundered through" it "like an elephant walking on daisies." He considers several possible explanations, both natural and supernatural: "So it could have been a magnetic set-up that did it, or there could have been some other reason to keep me out of it, or for some reason I would've went through it, I would have saw something there that maybe you wasn't supposed to see at that particular time." As an analogy to the experience, he tells a story he heard as a small boy from a man who had been setting rabbit snares on the Windsor Lake watershed (Windsor Lake lies at the top of the Three Pond Barrens and is the water supply for St. John's):

> And he was going for years and years and years. And he was a level-headed man. And he went through, and this evening he came home, and he told about this little small grove of woods and he tried to go through, as he had done for a thousand times before; he just couldn't seem to get through. He tried, and he tried, and he tried, and finally he gave it up and he went around it. And he went on about his business, finished his snare lines and stuff, and he came home. And he told my father about it, and I was sitting down listening to him. So a couple of days after that when the time came to go back to his snare line, he went back, and when he came home that evening, he dropped into our house and was discussing it again with my father — I was still, listening, all ears — and he told that he had gone back through the same area he had gone through, and he had no problem, like he had several days previous. There was some reason that he just couldn't, or wasn't allowed to go in that little area, that spot, at that particular time.[3]

As in his own case, Mr. Tucker considers a number of explanations, but leans toward the idea of protective intervention:

> Now whether it was some sort of psychic barrier, or whether it was methane gas or something coming up that was affecting people — they could be breathing it, and thrown off that way — there's a lot of things, eh? . . . So probably, it was to keep him away from harm . . . around here, people always say when children are born there's a guardian angel comes with them. That's why little kids have been known to walk out in places where really, they should be killed and gone. But they don't, they survive and they push through, and they come on back out of it again,

William Clive Tucker

eh? And they don't get injured, they don't get harmed. Sometimes they'll fall out of a four-storey window on a sidewalk and get picked up, and they don't even wake up sometimes, they're asleep, eh? So, if a person do have a guardian angel, there is some truth to that, that could be the force that was keeping you out, that something in that marsh would harm you, that you'd breathe the vapours that could be there, or could be, like I said before, could be — if it's the spirit world or whatever, could be involved.

Another direct traditional precedent for his own experience came from his father, who was mysteriously saved from disaster as a young man in the late 1920s. Seeking work at a lumber camp on Grand Lake (near Grand Falls in central Newfoundland), the elder Mr. Tucker arrived at night only to learn that the next morning there would be hiring at another camp twenty or so miles away. So he set out for that camp on a footpath, until he came to a small rise in the path which he could not mount. He tried running up several times, even starting from the hill behind him to gain momentum, until suddenly he lost consciousness. He awoke in the morning covered with snow but only slightly chilled despite the frigid temperature, and walked up the slope to discover a sheer cliff on the other side, over which he would have plunged had he been able to continue the night before.

Mr. Tucker has had strange experiences as an adult as well. Once he was in a canoe on a large pond when a storm came up and threatened to swamp him. He paddled furiously toward a lighted house on one shore, only to find upon reaching the shore that there was nothing there. Another time, he and a friend were driving through a snowstorm in a two-ton truck when there was a bump, and to their horror a man's arms cleaved the snow on the windshield like wiper blades, and a face pressed up against the glass. They pulled over, but when they got out there was no man and no tracks either. Mr. Tucker has no explanation of this, but notes that there was a river running under the road in that place: he connects many strange occurrences with the presence of water. On another occasion, he was camping with another man on one side of a valley, when he saw lights like "little lit-up needles" or "tinsel off a Christmas tree" going up the valley. This went on for a while, and finally he mentioned it to his friend, who said he had been "sizing up the same thing":

> I didn't mention it to the other person, because I thought — well, I wouldn't want him to think I was weird. And he didn't mention it to me for the same reason. [chuckles] So sometimes people see things similar, they say nothing to each other. It's only once in a while to mention something, and find out the other person had a similar experience.

Some experiences and opinions, then, might be kept private unless — or until — one is assured of an appropriate audience with a shared perspective. A familiar tradition creates an automatic audience, whatever the individual differences in attitude or belief. If it becomes attenuated so that it no longer offers ready categories (such as "ghost," "fairy," or "old hag") or comparative data for someone experiencing something out-of-the-way, that person may keep the experience to himself for fear of seeming "weird." One implication in this for the collection of folklore, especially folk belief, is that an informant may feel isolated in his or her own culture or community and more in sympathy with "outsiders" who express an interest. Mr. Tucker, for example, says his family is not interested in his dowsing (his daughter even disapproves); for a sense of collegiality, he subscribes (and contributes) to *The American Dowser*, the journal of the American Society of Dowsers, and is the Maritimes editor of the more recently established *Canadian Dowser*. The subjects of both journals range from standard on-site well-finding to psychic applications in diverse areas such as health, archaeology, and creativity, and Mr. Tucker feels more in tune with these innovative ideas than anything offered by his immediate culture, in which his attempts to discuss technique with fellow dowsers have met with resistance on their part.

One day Mr. Tucker brought me an article from the *National Enquirer* of December 1988, "UFO Experts Claim: Fairies Throughout History Were Really Space Aliens":

> The fairies described in folktales were actually alien beings from another planet! That's the conclusion of two UFO experts — who declare that the accounts of fairies throughout history closely resemble the modern reports of ETs or extraterrestrial creatures.

The "astonishing similarities" pointed out include small size and green colour; the power to disappear at will, to make humans see things that aren't really there, and to levitate themselves, objects, and human beings into the air; the "missing time" experienced by fairy and UFO abductees; and the circular patterns made by landings of UFOs (Ruehl). A more extensive comparison was made in 1969 by Jacques Vallee, who contends that "the modern, global belief in flying saucers is identical to an earlier belief in the fairy-faith" (57), and it seems to have become a commonplace in recent extraterrestrial abduction literature that the aliens and the fairies are kin (Strieber 68, 90; Fowler 207–14).

Such parallels have not escaped Newfoundland observers. "My grandmother said that in her childhood days they would tell stories of fairies as we would tell stories of space men," wrote one student (FSC74-1/14). Mr. Smith said that a woman in Bishop's Cove thought that the reason a changeling was put outside was so that the space people could retrieve it. In Heart's Content:

> People say they saw jack-o-lanterns which were little people from another planet or elsewhere who stood on the water. These little people held lanterns in their hands. My source [father] never saw one but those who did usually had a buddy to corroborate the story. (FSC71-119/8)

Jack McCall (the man who saw Bride Hall carried off in the pook of hay) told about a man who was crossing Graveyard Hill in Brigus alone in a slide when a bolt broke, forcing him to stop and make a repair; "a woman passed him the key in his hand," and disappeared:

> It had to be a fairy. Had to be something enchanted or something — alien, well, there was no aliens then. Probably that's the aliens now, coming back in the shape of aliens.... That's what it is, boy, the aliens now, that was the fairies then.[4]

Sometimes, though, striking similarities pass unremarked by informants. When a Carbonear student asked his mother about a spot that "was once haunted by ghosts or fairies," she told him that an old woman of her acquaintance used to see a big light by a brook in a certain garden each night:

> ... so she went over in her yard this night, and when she saw the big light she said there was a bird flew over, bigger than a house, she said the bird flew over and landed on the middle of the road. So she had a big dogberry tree in front of her house, she went out and sat in under the dogberry tree and she said she watched this moving out the road and she said it frightened her to death.... The next morning she got up and for curiosity she said she had to go out on the road to see if there was anything happening. She said it was just like somebody came and took the boughs and hauled them all over the gravel road and cleared it off as clean as anything. This is what happened to it, the big bird came and cleaned off the road.

Collector: What did she think it was?

Informant: She said it was a big bird!

Collector: Just that?

Informant: Just a bird. (76-133/11-13)

Mr. Tucker thinks he might have encountered something extraterrestrial, if I take his meaning correctly (for he does not say so outright). Often he sees lights in the wilderness, which he long took to be poachers; after a while, however, he realized that there was a pattern to their appearance, and he would know ahead of time when they would be seen. But if he were to take anyone along to see them, "they" would seem to "know" and fail to appear. Once he and another man were parked on a pinnacle when they saw a light coming toward them about fifty feet above the ground. As it neared them the radio, phone, and lights of their truck went out, and the truck would not start; it suddenly began to snow, even though it was only early fall. Somehow they finally got the truck started, and went down the hill to where it was not snowing, and saw the light disappearing in the other direction. The night before a great bolt of lightning — or something — struck Bell Island in the late 1970s,[5] Mr. Tucker saw a light circling over the island, but did not think much of it at the time. But later he heard of someone who saw two lights "fighting" above the island; one finally shot the other, which plunged to the ground (it was a UFO battle). Mr. Tucker thus retains the youthful interest that led him to look for UFOs on Three Pond Barrens, although he keeps it mostly to himself. I can never help thinking of the seeming incongruity of his private interests and his public persona — as he put it when we were talking about people's looks one day, he is "not the kind of guy you want to meet with a moose steak in your pocket." Who would suspect that this down-to-earth officer of the law has an eye on the sky for unearthly visitors?

Mr. Ed (or Ned) MacDonald of Kingston, Conception Bay, also considers extraterrestrial influence as a possible explanation of "fairy" phenomena. Perhaps about ten years younger than Mr. Furlong and Mr. Tucker, he is like them in his expansive, confident personality and open-minded interest in supernatural tradition. Like Mr. Tucker, he possesses psychic abilities and has had a number of strange experiences, several of which he described for his niece, Louise Mullaly, for a term paper she called "Facts on Fairies: Rules and Stories in the Area from Kingston to Northern Bay." When I phoned Mr. MacDonald in 1984 to ask if I could come talk to him about these experiences, he interrogated me briskly: Did I believe in ESP? Prophetic dreams? Tokens? Apparently my answers — along the lines of "certainly something to it" — satisfied him, as he told me I could come by anytime. The first day I went, he was busy in the carpentry shop adjoining his house. Over the pounding and sawing, he also told me that his fairy experiences were not a matter of "going astray," which he has done through carelessness, with no fairies involved; rather, there was a "sense of presence," of "something there," and the environment, though familiar, was somehow different. (He noted casually that there is a presence in his shop that has sometimes pushed him aside.) He suggests that "fairies" — which the old people called "good people" or "little people" — is just a convenient term for a certain experience or sensation that can happen to anyone anywhere, whether they have fairy traditions or not; no one knows the real cause, which could be, for instance, an investigative source from another planet that puts people in a hypnotic state in order to study them.

Whereas Mr. Tucker's strange experience involved not being able to get into a certain space, Mr. MacDonald's involved not being able to get out. Since I never did hear about all of the experiences directly, his niece's paper is used for these accounts. Once, he was cutting a Christmas tree near Mt. Pearl (a city adjoining St. John's) in a small patch of wood near a new subdivision. When he wanted to come out, however, he was suddenly unable to find his way. He could no longer hear dogs barking and children playing, but only a whispering:

> I could hear voices but there was nobody there. I said, what I'll do is walk back, backtrack, now I left tracks in the snow. So I backtracked — I knew where I came into the woods, I came in through a clearing, I got back to the clearing, I backtracked and sure enough the tracks were going backward all the ways until I came to the middle of that clearing, and you know the tracks

> stopped right exactly in the middle of the clearing. Now I couldn't just come down out of the sky and make the tracks, right? Started to get a little bit frightened then, so I says okay, the tracks stop here and I'm about fifty feet from a fellow's house; I knew right where I was, but I walked for an hour and I was still in the woods; now I got a bit panicky then — Christ, I'm going to die here in the woods. So I started walking, I walked for two and a half hours and I came out to this strange place I never seen before in my life.

He stopped a car and learned he was in the suburb of Glendale, but he walked on, still hearing the whispering, until he recognized a house and "snapped out of it" and arrived home hours later from "a patch of woods that either way you'd walk out in ten minutes" (79-378/17-18).

On another occasion, he was staying with friends in St. John's, sleeping on their chesterfield in the living room, when he awoke in the night needing the bathroom but was unable to find the door:

> No, no, I wasn't drunk, because I started in the corner and counted the corners, 1-2-3-4. Now if that door there is open and I'm walking from corner to corner groping around, I got to find the door, right? I couldn't find it but fortunately he had the fireplace there. . . . But I mean you don't believe in it because you don't believe in fairies, but I faithfully believe in fairies. (79-378/19-20)

A third experience happened when he was much younger, and his father sent him to the barn to give the horse some hay. He couldn't find the hatch and was "trapped" in the loft until his father came looking for him several hours later, and the hatch reappeared (79-378/21).

Just as Mr. Tucker tells stories of other people's experiences that parallel his own, Mr. MacDonald's repertoire includes stories with bouts of impeded movement. One involved his grandfather (his niece called it "Grandfather's Encounter with the Fairy Power") who was unable to get his cart into the woods in Western Bay one morning: "there was a force pushing him back; the nearer his destination he got, the harder the force got, and finally he had to give it up and turn back." Later that evening "the cry went out that Bill Lench wasn't out of the woods," and search parties set out for the place they knew he had been cutting — where Mr. MacDonald's grandfather had been attempting to go. Among the men who found him was Dr. Dunn, who said as they neared the spot, "We're too late, his spirit just crossed the pond." They found him dead, but his body still warm, under a toppled load of wood.

Dr. Richard Dunn was probably licensed under the "grandfather clause," which recognized physicians whose experience matched the formal training of younger counterparts. Mr. MacDonald told me:

> The amazing thing about Dr. Dunn was he used to make his own medicine. Now he was a firm believer in fairies. In fact, at that time, the mode of transportation at that time was horse and buggy, right? They say Dr. Dunn, being a kindly old gentleman, he'd pick you up, you know, if you were hitch-hiking at the time. I don't think they used to use that term at that time, "hitch-hiking," I'm not sure. But he'd stop and give you a lift. But if he had a wagonload of fairies, he couldn't pick you up. He'd say no, he'd stop and tell you, "I can't pick you up 'cause I've got a wagonload of fairies here." But he used to make his own medicine, he never bought any ingredients for his medicine. And apparently he had some miraculous cures. He wasn't a doctor, by the way, he didn't have his M.D. But he was recognized by the Newfoundland Medical Association — he was allowed to call himself "Doctor." I'd say he was the only quack in Newfoundland who was allowed to practice. Right now he'd be prosecuted, right?

(Later Mr. MacDonald directed me to the Kingston cemetery to see that Dr. Dunn's tombstone includes the title "Doctor"; I couldn't see the dates for the snow.) When I asked an old man near Western Bay about Dr. Dunn, he told me that he used to say, "Come on up, boys!" and the fairies would pile on his wagon.[6] According to tradition, both Dr. Dunn and Dr. Cron encouraged stories about their fairy connections. A Bell Island informant claimed that he heard from Dr. Cron himself how he had to walk to a patient in Upper Island Cove when his car was stalled by the spirit of a murdered woman (the next morning the car started immediately) (72-95/13-14).[7] In another Bell Island version, an unnamed doctor with a stalled car "cursed the fairies and said they could have the car and off he trod over the hills to his patient"; when the car started easily the next morning, he concluded that "the fairies just wanted to use it" (73-171/11).

The easy familiarity of Drs. Cron and Dunn with the fairies no doubt enhanced their authority and their patients' confidence in their ability to effect a cure. Whether they cultivated the role or not, the image of doctors and priests as intercessors with otherworldly powers makes them natural figures for the accretion of supernatural legends. Their travel at all hours, often in relation to life-and-death situations, would provide much raw material for potential conversion to legend. Indeed, anyone who regularly travelled alone might have legend-worthy experiences, such as a butcher who, according to Louise Mullaly, felt the fairies climb on his buggy or slide every time he passed Heart's Content barrens (79-378/9). The fairies readily transfer their attentions from carts and slides to automobiles, which are prone to harassment by extraterrestrials as well. Cars have even replaced horses as registers of supernatural presence, stalling out instead of balking, as when Mr. Tucker's truck went haywire at the approach of the mysterious light.

Mr. Tucker and Mr. MacDonald seem to pick up interesting experience and items wherever they go. (Mr. Tucker brought me a list of potential informants from all over the Avalon Peninsula, with suggestions on what I might ask them about.) Both, as younger men, did stints as orderlies at the Waterford Hospital; it was there Mr. MacDonald heard about "padlocking," a curse put on by a "bad widow" that could only be removed by a "good widow," and where Mr. Tucker received the electric shock (not electroshock!) he thinks may have tripped his psychic abilities. With the exception of John Ashton's work on lumber camps, the role of large employment centres in the transmission of folklore in Newfoundland has been neglected in comparison to that of small communities, but as Mr. Tucker's and Mr. MacDonald's conversation shows, they provide a forum for narrative exchange and opportunities for new experience.

Proof that migration and admixture are a powerful creative force is offered by Bell Island, that great iron-ore magnet that drew people to work in the mines from their opening in 1895 until their closure in 1966. Bell Island also provides an even better example than St. John's of fairy traditions thriving in an industrialized, if not exactly urban, setting. About nine miles long and three miles wide, it rises out of Conception Bay on sheer cliffs, which afford landing in only a few places. There were no inhabitants in the second half of the seventeenth century (Seary et al. 7), but by 1794 Aaron Thomas observed that there were residents on Bell Isle, "reckon'd to be the fertilest spot to be met with on the northern coast" (66); it remained an important agricultural area long after the mines opened. During the entire period of operation of the mines there was a continual flux between the island and "mainland" communities. The *Newfoundland Royal Commission 1933 Report* describes the early seasonal arrangement of two six-month shifts, one made up of those who fished in the summer and worked in the mines in the winter, and another of those who worked in the woods in the winter and in the mines in the summer; and even at the height of operations, many miners commuted on weekends to homes in Conception Bay (Seary et al. 36). It is not surprising, then, that many stories collected on Bell Island are about other places. However, there is also a large body of indigenous fairy lore, that is, of fairy incidents on the island involving island residents. Their abundance in MUNFLA attracted me to Bell Island, where, as mentioned in the Preface, I heard my first fairy story. I was not the first to be so drawn: one student set out purposely to collect "fairy tales" there because he "heard that there are very many on the island" (72-144/2). Bell Island's reputation for fairy lore even borders on *blason populaire* (regional slur) in one account:

> A friend of mine knew a woman living at Sandy Point who used to live on Bell Island. When Jennifer went to visit the woman after not having seen her for a few years, she asked the woman where her husband was. The woman said the fairies had taken him away. When Jennifer expressed disbelief and asked if he had died, the woman said no, he wasn't dead, he had been taken away by the fairies one night and she hadn't seen him since. The

woman got most upset when my friend continued to express disbelief. My friend said people from Bell Island are known to be strange anyways, so she passed it off and didn't mention it to the old woman again. (70-6/19)

Bell Island is the only place I have heard of having a special fairies' day, other than October 1, May 1, or Halloween: "A night in February, Fairies' Eve, it is claimed that one can see the fairies dancing on the West Dam" (74-43/11).

Overall, Bell Island fairy lore differs little in its outlines from that of the "mainland." It does not appear to have adapted particularly to the presence of the mines, although one informant and her friends did count a hundred men emerging two by two from an abandoned mine one day (they disappeared, leaving no footprints behind) (72-95/48-49). There are no reports of "knockers" or mine spirits as found in Welsh or Cornish folklore, and in general the mines seem neither to have deterred the fairies nor to have afforded new narrative possibilities; the fairies appear just as they might in the woods, for example, in this account:

> One of the men who worked up to No. 4 compressor claimed that one night when he was on duty the fairies visited him. He said that they were little men about three feet tall and they were all wearing red stocking caps on their heads. He started to cuss and they went away. At a certain time each year on Bell Island in a certain area near the mines numerous people have seen a fairy celebration, dancing and making merry. These people have sworn to what they have seen. (71-75/22-23)

As elsewhere, the fairies were associated with the woods (the east end and Lance Cove according to 72-97/8) and other natural features. One man was unable to cross Perry's Brook (now Main River) at certain times of the year for the "hordes of little people" that were crossing it themselves (72-97:C1284/5). "The older people," according to one report, said that the eastern head, a supposedly unscalable column of land rising from the sea at one end of the island, "belongs to the Good People"; in foggy weather they would be seen singing and dancing and building a bridge to the "mainland" (72-95/10). Another wrote:

> There were marshes nearby on the front of the island where we lived and stories were told about fairies which lived there. There was one particular piece of marshland which used to shake like jelly when we would run across it. Stories were told that it would open up and swallow us up like it had done to other people. This particular place would never freeze over and stories were spun about the evil that dwelt there. (71-109/29-30)

Bell Island has the usual reports of the fairies' banishment. Monsignor Bartlett blessed a rock where the fairies danced: "This was around twenty years ago and there have been no reports of fairies since" (73-123/10-11). As usual, this is not quite the case, as reports continue to come into MUNFLA.

One of the most interesting recent accounts, recorded in 1989, is about David (Davy) Mercer, the stories of whom form a veritable catalogue of fairy motifs; it is the first one I have read from someone who was actually involved in the original event:

> My grandfather told me of a fairy happening that he had seen himself. One day in the early 1920s, Poppy and his friends were playing near the woods. They were afraid to go in the woods because they had been warned of fairies. Suddenly they heard a giggling noise, one that sounded very unusual. Poppy and his friends ran as fast as they could to the nearest house. When they got there they realized that one of the boys was missing: Davy Mercer. They were afraid to go back and look for him, instead they went to the Mercer home and told Davy's parents. Mr. and Mrs. Mercer gathered up a few more older folks and began to look for Davy. They had no luck in finding him. It was a week or so when he found his own way home. His parents were shocked: their darling little boy, who was completely normal before, was now practically deformed. They pulled sticks, rocks and things from the lumps in their son's skin. Davy was now mentally and

physically disturbed. From that time onward, he was never the same. As he grew older, he became stranger. He walked around crimpled [sic], wearing a long coat and a top hat. He always carried a brief case and tried to sell things; however, no one ever saw what was inside the briefcase.[8] (89-215/15-17)

Mr. Mercer died around 1960; there does not seem to be a consensus as to whether he was mentally normal or not. All accounts agree that he was taken by the fairies, but the age at which this happened varies, as do the details of the encounter. Some describe his condition on emerging from, or being found in, the woods: he "was unable to speak plainly and was limping, one leg was shorter than the other" (73-123/12); "one leg had a malformity, his face was 'acned,' and he had a strange fairy-like voice (a high-pitched nasal voice)" (71-109/43); "he had a limp and his face was pulled to one side" (72-117/9); "he was all disfigured and scared and simple-minded" (71-75/21); "they found him wandering around in the woods all crippled up deaf and dumb" (74-43/14); "he had twigs in his nose, his body was slashed and bruised and ever afterwards, although he was very intelligent and quite normal formerly, his speech was impaired, his intelligence seemed to have diminished, and he became hunchbacked" (FSC67-3/37); "they took ribbons of green grass out of his leg" (72-95/11). Most accounts say he cannot recall what happened, but several purport to give Mr. Mercer's own explanation. In one of these, some friends ask the normal Davy Mercer where he is going one night; he tells them that in a previous encounter, the fairies told him he had to come to the woods every midnight:

> Well, this night his friends held him and wouldn't let him go. The next night he went and never came back for three days and three nights. After he returned he could only say a few words and appeared to have gone silly. (FSC71-22/30)

One informant claimed that Davy Mercer "wrote about how he was let go because he was so cute [local — "acute," i.e., smart] and small that they took pity on him, but they struck him deaf and dumb so he couldn't tell where they was living" (74-43/14).

Apparently, as an adult Davy Mercer did odd jobs for a living, and some suggest that his skills were learned from the fairies: "While he was with the fairies he learned how to carve figures from wood" (71-75/22); "he was afterwards . . . renowned for his beautiful penmanship, the like of which no one had ever seen" (FSC67-3C/37). He did carpentry, and many informants mention a model church he built: "He wanted the fairies to come to it," claimed one (74-43/14). He "sold portraits for some company and took pictures as well" (71-109/43), and "sold little things around the neighborhood and took measurements for clothes" (74-43/14). (My neighbour, Alexander Parsons, was once measured for a suit by Mr. Mercer, who ordered them in from Montreal.) "Davie Mercer was extremely skilled with his hands and had an almost fanatical love of flowers," wrote one collector, "he would love [my informant's] lilacs and would come to the house when they first bloomed. He went from door to door asking for odd jobs, like framing pictures. . . . [He] was very affectionate and generous and hated to be given charity" (FSC67-3C/38). This last description contrasts rather poignantly with the frightening figure he cut, especially among children. "There goes Davie Mercer, he was took by the fairies," they would whisper when he passed (FSC67-3/37). He must have been used extensively by parents as a warning figure. One informant considered his case proof of the fairies' existence:

> I still persisted to question my father as a non-believer of fairies. He next told me about a man who I personally had known. He was a Mr. David Mercer who lived on Bell Island. He was a short thin man. He walked with a limp, his face was very white and wrinkled, his speech was not a stutter or a stammer but a mixture of the two, and he had a perpetual grin which was horrifying. He was a very awkward and even frightening individual. To see this person would quickly lead one to believe that he had experienced a great shock of some sort. The look of terror was painted on his face. Dad explained what had happened to turn a perfectly normal man into such a horrible specimen. One evening just before darkness Mr. Mercer went into the woods to look for his father's sheep. It soon became dark and he didn't

> return home. The next day a search party went to look for him. He was soon found curled up by a tree in a fit of terror. He was crying and mumbling, his clothes were torn and he seemed to be in pain. The sheep he had gone to look for were all dead. They had been torn apart but not eaten. Many of the people who were present when he was found believed it to be the work of the fairies, Mr. Mercer was taken home and a doctor was called. He was baffled at the condition which this man was in. He treated his broken leg but couldn't revive him from his state of shock. He later had Mr. Mercer admitted to a mental institution where he received the necessary treatment. After he returned to Bell Island, Mr. Mercer couldn't recall any part of that dreadful night which had rendered him so. However[,] many of his friends and neighbors who were present at the time can't be convinced that it was not the work of the little bad ones and would never think about returning to that fatal spot at night. (Q68-259/6-8)

The efforts of the doctor and hospital belie the commonplace that a "fairy" diagnosis is made in the absence of medical models of disease; indeed, "doctors baffled" is a motif used to reinforce a supernatural interpretation, and confinement to "the mental" a common result of fairy affliction. On Bell Island, health care was once more accessible than it is now. "At no time were you short of a doctor," said one informant, comparing 1971 unfavourably with the 1930s, when you could get one of three doctors within half an hour of a call (72-97:C1285/13). Yet I have found no reference to a natural malady such as polio or a stroke in connection with Davy Mercer's condition, although most accounts point to a single traumatic incident rather than a chronic condition.

In 1983, Arthur Clarke of Bell Island told me a story that cast Davy Mercer in the role of a powerful outcast. During a card game Davy Mercer entered the room, and one of the players said, "Go away, Davy, you'll bring me bad luck." "You'll always have bad luck after this," said Davy (Mr. Clarke's voice rose in squeaky imitation). Sure enough he always did. And so the small, unlovely, but apparently respected figure recedes into legend, marked by the crueller forces of the world for a place in history he probably would rather not have occupied. After death he was granted the normalcy he never enjoyed: "I have not been able to talk to anyone who saw Davie after his death," said a collector, "but it is rumored that he went back to normal shape" (FSC67-3C/38).

Davy Mercer had a St. John's counterpart in Stuart Taylor. An informant who lived next door to him on Cabot Street said that he had been "carried away by the fairies," and that "after the fairies brought him back, he was unable to work in the daytime" (FSC74-6/20). "Every night he would go off to the woods and generally people thought he was a fairy himself," wrote another student, whose informant said:

> Mr. Taylor was building a chimney for Mrs. Hayes on Cabot Street but they found that they had run out of bricks before they were finished. They needed a hundred and fifty more bricks but neither Mrs. Hayes nor Mr. Taylor had the money for these. That night Mr. Taylor went into the woods again and the next morning at five A.M. when Mrs. Hayes looked out her window she saw a neat pile which contained exactly one hundred and fifty bricks stacked below her door. It was believed that Mr. Taylor had gotten his fairy friends to bring them. (72-181/13)

"It was said that wherever he was at midnight he would have to leave because the fairies called him or had some claim on him," reported another:

> It seems he did not claim this himself but people said it because he had some strange ways, was tiny and elf-like in appearance, and was frequently noticed leaving the church service at odd times. He played the violin in the Salvation Army services. My [second informant] adds that the man was partly blind, and was often seen to go and sit on a certain stone in a certain field. This stone was known, at least to the children, as a fairy stone. [A third informant] says that this man was believed to have been changed into the short elf-like man that he was when he went into the

woods one day and the fairies got him. His appearance before this had been quite normal.⁹ (FSC71-86/22)

Mr. Taylor was said to have uncanny abilities:

> [My informant] has been told about a man who was a real fairy or will-o-the-wisp. His name was Stuart Taylor, a very small and tiny man. He was reported to be able to get out of any room, no matter how many locks you had on it. They decided to test him one night. They put him in a room with no windows, only one door, locked from the outside, and the men stood guard so that there was no possible way he could get out. Within a few minutes he proved them wrong. They say he was "not of this world." (81-186/13)

In his 1931 *Paths to Yesterday: Memories of Old St. John's, Newfoundland*, John Maclay Byrnes mentions Stuart Taylor, "known to the small boys as the 'fairy man' or 'changeling,' who played incessantly on a tin whistle" (76). This was in a section on "quaint St. John's characters," toward whom Byrnes notes that "genuine kindness . . . tempered what otherwise might be possibly considered a regrettable attitude of levity towards their really pitiable misfortune" (64). One "character," his neighbour, was often pelted with stones and rotten vegetables by children; perhaps understandably, he could be overheard shouting "savage imprecations" against people in his nightly prayers (67). The idea that an abnormal person might possess supernatural powers would be an important tool for gaining the respect compromised by the abnormality. As an unidentified writer said of Stuart Taylor, "to say we were scared stiff of him is only putting it mildly. There were stories about him saying he could turn us into goats or cows, whatever" (unattributed quotation 72-116/32).

The stories about Davy Mercer and Stuart Taylor circulated mainly in their own communities, although reports of Davy Mercer come from various locations in Conception Bay as well. But the most famous figure associated with the fairies was known all over Newfoundland, her story spread at first not only by word of mouth but by newspaper and radio. Many accounts found their way into MUNFLA. For example:

> In New Melbourne, Trinity Bay, a little girl got lost in the woods and was given up for dead. Several weeks later she walked out of the woods completely safe, unhurt, and well-nourished. She was asked how she had managed, and she said that the fairies had taken care of her until she wanted to come home again.... [The informant] said the little girl it happened to is alive now but is an old lady, so it must have happened some time ago. (70-6/18)

[The informant] remembers hearing about a young girl named Harris who was cared for by the fairies. This happened about twenty years ago in New Melbourne. The girl was about seven or eight years old. She disappeared in the middle of winter and was said to have been taken away by the fairies. The young girl eventually turned up safely and the child herself said that she had been fed berries by the fairies. (70-26/56)

In March of 1985 I was unaware of the Lucy Harris story (in any variant), although the name rang a bell when Hubert and Ethel Burke of Victoria told me that a long time ago she was lost for a long time (they didn't know exactly how long), during which she was taken care of by "little men and women." There was something like a bear, too, Mrs. Burke recalled, and Mr. Burke thought it was a big black dog that lay down by her at night and kept her warm.[10] I should go there, they said, and "ask anyone," so I did. In New Melbourne, I wandered near the beach until four teenage boys came by, and I struck up a conversation (well, actually I waylaid and then grilled the taciturn fellows). When I asked if they had ever heard the "old legend" of Lucy Harris, they replied to my amazement, "Why don't you go ask her?" I had been under the impression that it had all happened so long ago she would now be dead or at least ancient; but when I went to her house — unable to think of a good reason not to — I found she was in her sixties at the most. As I prefer not to recall the most embarrassing episode in my fieldwork, and do not trust myself not to downplay the awkwardness of it if I elaborate, I reproduce my field notes here:

> Ms. Harris seemed offended at my probably bungled explanation of my visit. "Fairies?" she asked scornfully, "I don't believe anything like that!" It happened when she was about ten; she

was gone ten or eleven days, and didn't eat anything; and to my great embarrassment, her sister or sister-in-law (?) came in and informed me that she had lost both legs as a result of their having been frozen. I bumbled rather lamely on about how interesting the legend process was since *other* people attributed it to the fairies, etc. etc. "The Lord above protected me," she declared firmly, and I apologized for bringing it up and dropping by unannounced like that. She said it was alright, she didn't mind. Still, although they relented a bit at my discomfiture, I don't think she or her sister (?) were too pleased; I had the impression that I was not the first to ask about it. Her brother (?), who had greeted me very kindly, said nothing the whole time and I left after about ten minutes. As I drove out of New Melbourne, I noticed that one of the old churches has been converted to the "Pentecostal Church," and I wonder if she could be a convert whose new views do not take in fairies?

On 1 April 1985 — three weeks after my visit — the *Evening Telegram* carried an article by Michael Harrington in which, drawing on the *Evening Telegram*'s original reports, he recounted the events of 1936 when Lucy went astray (the edited article is now in his *Offbeat Mystery of Newfoundland and Labrador*). When it was discovered on the evening of March 26 that Lucy had not been seen since that morning, when her sister left her in the woods near their house, a search party set out. Over the next week, during which snow, fog, and rain alternated with clear freezing days, the number of searchers grew to over two hundred. Most gave up after a week, but her uncle and a few others continued to search, and on April 6 her uncle, three miles from the house, heard someone say "Hello." He turned to find Lucy sitting upright against a tree: "I'm the little girl who is lost in the woods," she said. She was taken to the Old Perlican cottage hospital and then into St. John's; on April 9 an editorial headline in the *Evening Telegram* read:

"I'm the little girl who is lost in the woods" greets searchers for nine-year-old Lucy Harris who spent eleven nights in the open

— saw rescuers but was too weak to call out — birds sang all day and kept her from being afraid, she said.

(Variation was creeping in even at this early stage, for the article itself says that she *heard* the searchers, not saw them.) It went on to describe how she sat down under the tree the first evening and did not move the whole time, ate snow, and slept at night. In the following days the *Telegram* followed her progress, and when it was found necessary to amputate her legs, launched a subscription appeal; there was also a benefit concert, and Harrington mentions that the story was "featured in the fledgling radio broadcasting service" (*Mystery* 48).[11]

On 10 April 1986, Don Morris resurrected the story once more for the *Sunday Express*. He used mostly the old *Telegram* accounts, but he did phone Ms. Harris, who told him that the incident is "still vivid in her mind." (He also reported that she is a devout member of the Pentecostal Church, confirming my earlier hunch.) A more informative interview had run in the *Evening Telegram* for 21 December 1961, in which Ms. Harris (then thirty-four) described how she had wandered absent-mindedly until she realized she was lost, and began to run in panic, losing her shoes. She sat down and went to sleep, listening to the birds. "Today Lucy remembers this all as a dream," the article continues, "but she does recall that she received hundreds of dolls and toys from all over the world.... She was a favorite with both doctors and nurses in the hospital where she kept telling the story of her experiences" ("Lost" 48).

But what story did she tell? Did she really say anything about fairies? It is only to be expected that legend would have her do so, since otherwise there would be no "story," only surmise. The narrative embellishments afforded by putting the story in her own mouth are illustrated here:

> This event happened in New Melbourne, Trinity Bay, about fifteen to twenty years ago [*c.* 1950]. It involved a woman, and my grandmother thinks her name was Lucy Harris but doesn't really remember. This woman was supposed [to have been] "led away" by the fairies into the woods in the late fall, at a time in the season when extreme exposure to the elements would cause

death. My grandmother said that the woman was gone for several days, and after this length of time was found deep in the woods, sitting up against a tree trunk, unbelievably, alive. She had been frost-bitten, though, and as a result lost a limb, either an arm or leg, my grandmother doesn't remember this either, and said she wouldn't guess because she didn't want to give me any false information. The story that this Lucy Harris told was that she was led away by the fairies maliciously, into the woods until she was lost. Then when it became cold and she couldn't find her way out of the woods, Miss Harris said that the fairies took pity on her, changed their attitude, and hovered around her keeping her as warm as they could until the search-party found her several days later. Miss Harris said that she did not imagine she saw the fairies — she really did! She said that they were little people but my grandmother does not remember how they were supposedly dressed. (FSC74-1/14)

Lucy's sense of companionship — if that may be taken as the core of her experience — is well-known among mountaineers. William Thomson recounts the experience of two climbers descending Mt. Everest who camped in a snow hole and later "told of a curious sensation that a third person had been sharing the hole during the night," and of a German climber who "was aware of a companion advising him that he had dropped his gloves," although there was no one there when he turned to speak. Thomson points out that since the experience often occurs in company, it cannot be explained by the need for companionship alone (194). Sir Ernest Shackleton writes of an Antarctic expedition:

> . . . during that long and racking march of thirty-six hours over the unnamed mountains and glaciers of South Georgia it seemed to me often that we were four, not three. I said nothing to my companions on the point, but afterwards Worsley said to me, "Boss, I had a curious feeling on the march that there was another person with us." Crean confessed to the same idea. (209)

The mountaineer Frank Smythe was once comfortably seated on a ledge, when out of the corner of his eye he thought he saw his partner climb up:

> I turned towards him, remarking: "Hallo, you've come up very quickly," but, at the same moment that I said this, I saw to my astonishment that there was no one there and heard his voice a long distance below. . . . I at once told myself that I had only imagined that I had seen him, though I was wholly unable to rid myself of the impression that I had seen *someone*. No doubt I would have forgotten about the incident if many hours later when we were talking about the climb Graham Brown had not said: "You know, Smythe, throughout the climb I had the most curious feeling that there was a third man on the rope, and I couldn't rid myself of it all the way up." (125)

On another, more stressful occasion, Smythe carefully divided a piece of cake and offered half to his "companion," even though he was alone (208).

Although William Thomson suggests such experiences are "an accepted phenomenon of mild hypothermia," cold weather is not requisite for the disconcerting effect. R.U. Sayce (noting their affinity to fairy belief) gives some non-mountaineering examples, including that of a South African native soldier, who while crossing the desert suffered from thirst and fatigue: "When in this condition everything appeared small; a man looked about the size of a fowl."[12] An early Newfoundland example comes from a 1919 pamphlet by P.J. Kinsella, *Some Superstitions and Traditions of Newfoundland*:

> The sailor has one strange fear, a fear that attaches itself to him, and makes his "watch" a dread, particularly in the lone hours of the night. This dread is the peculiar belief that whilst he is guiding the ship a spirit stands by his side. He cannot tell you just what this "fetch" may be, or who the lonely watch keeps there. (39)

Given the apparently common experience of a "sense of presence," then, and that Lucy must have been half-conscious or delirious much of the time, it would be surprising if she had *not* seen or felt anything. Oral tradition would quickly act on an ambiguous statement, easily jumping from birds to fairies, for example, since fairies often appear as birds. Religious imagery could be expected as well, as in the account that says that "Lucy told them that each night a woman came and put a blue cloak around her. This was supposed to be the Blessed Virgin, of course" (86-23/10).

Whatever form the supernatural guardianship took, it had ample traditional precedent. The well-known story of a small Colinet girl is often conflated with Lucy's. Michael Harrington couples the two in his book, in which he writes that between 1905 and 1911, a four-year-old girl named O'Keefe went missing for ten days, and was found by Simon Nolan of Salmonier, lying on her back, her mouth full of leaves and grass; she survived unhurt, and the "older generation" thought that "the good people" were involved (*Mystery* 46–48). In 1950, folklorist MacEdward Leach had the story from an informant who heard in 1918 how an eleven-month-old girl was lost in Colinet and found twelve days later, sitting under a tree playing with dead leaves and laughing. "So that's the story," the informant concludes, but when Leach asks how they accounted for it, a voice from the background pipes, "the fairies." "Oh, the fairies," replies the informant in what sounds like mild surprise that Leach had to ask, "oh, yes, the fairies was supposed, it was supposed that the fairies took the child and kept it alive" (78-54:C3295/m.t.). One Simon Nolan of Salmonier said that another Simon Nolan — no relation to himself — was returning from the States around 1914 when he found the girl in a sand pit; although it had rained during the nine days she was gone, she was neither wet nor hungry, and "everyone says up to this day that the fairies had her" (FSC74-102/41). In another version the girl's rescuer is her uncle, who was in the States when he "had a dream telling him to come home to Newfoundland and look for her in a certain gravel pit. He found her there. She told the searchers who found her that 'the little people fed me'" (FSC70-14/117). But "she could never tell where she was," according to another informant, who said that three-year-old Minnie Keith was lost in May and found in October wearing the same pristine pink dress and hair ribbon (81-207/97-100).

A sample of versions from other locations shows how easily they localize and blend. A Petit Forte girl was gone for a week, and "said that she was with the good people, they were the fairies, see, and they gave her stuff off the hills, they picked berries, and that kept her alive" (76-350/21). "Years ago a girl disappeared from [the informants' community, Cupids]. She was eleven years old, and after searching for over a week, they had given up any hope of finding her alive. However they did find her in a clearing of wood sitting alone. She explained that she had been fed and sheltered by a group of small men" (83-39/7). Around 1955 near Seal Cove, a girl named Anne was lost and given up for dead but found twenty-one days later: "she claimed that the birds and fairies had brought her food in the morning and evening. Just after sunset, she said, they would cover her with leaves and this kept her warm" (79-455/13-14). In St. Joseph's, a small girl who was gone for a day said that "she was in the company of some nice friendly people all day and at evening a lady in blue came and took her back and put her in over her own fence" (71-93/2). One informant said that when his aunt in Bonavista Bay was about five, she disappeared for nine days and was found paddling in a brook; she said she had been "with a crowd of girls having a good time," was given berries to eat, and finally taken safely home; "I suppose 'twas the good people had her, that's it, you know," the informant concluded with a laugh (64-7:C13/6).

Only occasionally is the protected person male or old. A St. John's man went fishing one Victoria Day:

> He and a companion got lost when the fog came in and were lost for approximately fourteen days. When they finally managed to come out of the woods they said that the fairies had saved them. He said that every time that they had wanted to lie down and go to sleep because they were exhausted, a little man with a green suit and red cap would make them keep walking. Otherwise they would have undoubtedly died of exposure because the weather on the 24th of May here in Newfoundland is never too warm. (FSC74-6/21)

Around 1910 in Grate's Cove (not far from New Melbourne) a woman in her seventies was lost for a week in the late fall, and found "abnormally well, considering":

> She was later asked how she had survived this period and her answer was that someone had been taking care of her. The local people were surprised at this and asked her what she meant. She said that she didn't see them but she felt them, at which point the locals seemed to understand. My grandmother says that opinions on the source of this "care" were divided. Some — most — thought that the fairies were the source, while the remainder thought that she was taken care of by those who had been praying for her. It was themselves, they thought, that she felt but couldn't see. Those who had thought she was saved by the fairies did not change their opinion of the old lady because of the event.

The collector adds an important explanatory note as to why the people might have changed their opinion of the woman: "the fairies were evil and might have changed the old woman for the worse, or they might have thought she was wicked, for them to want to save her in the first place" (FSC71-46/37). The girls cared for by the fairies seem to be exempt from this suspicion, as well as from the usual taboo on eating fairy food; the fairies are good in these accounts, which hopefully propose that children will be protected even when human support breaks down, and that they can emerge unscathed from traumatic experience.

Lucy Harris's role as heroine — her courage was much celebrated in the media — may also explain why the fairies are so often said to have helped her, in spite of her grave injuries. One collector did report that she returned with "no hands and feet," and that "people believe she was taken away by the fairies" (76-41/3); another that when she was found she was like an eighty-year-old woman with snow-white hair, and was very sick and lost her legs, but "she told them that she wasn't lonely there, the fairies were with her, the little people, the fairies she called them, and they fed her and kept her warm, they fed her little berries" (72-72:C1117/6-8). The relative consistency (with the emphasis on help) suggests that the story was put forth by Lucy herself, and eagerly accepted by a public as a happy ending (hence, in legend, the amnesia as to the loss of her legs).

The "babes in the wood" theme appealed to city literati as well as the "folk." One student had the story of the Colinet girl from his grandfather:

> Of course, this was another case of the fairies. Grandfather then went to the bookcase and pulled out a book entitled *Sea Room* by R.A. Parsons. He opened the book to a poem entitled "The Gloucesterman" and invited me to read it; when I did I found that it was the story that I'd just heard. At first feeling disappointed I asked him if this is where he had heard the story, whereupon he said, "Of course not! I was told this by old Mr. Taylor not long after it happened." (73-55/6-7)

The finding of Lucy Keefe is a subplot in R.A. Parsons's 1963 poem about Matthew Rorke:

> And there were those who said, and yet who say,
> Of their belief unto this very day,
> That fairies led the little girl astray
> And nourished her in their mysterious way;
> For we have old and wise men, who agree,
> That there be little men, we cannot see,
> Who yet inhabit forest land and hide
> Amid the valleys of the countryside,
> And ancients now, who solitary make
> Long journeys through the woodlands take
> Some little offrings in meat or cake,
> The gnomes and fairies to propitiate
> And leave these here and there by boughs of green
> Observed by none, save the little men unseen. (43–44)

Parsons may have been inspired to name his character "Lucy" by Lucy Harris, or by Wordsworth's poem "Lucy Gray," about a small girl who disappears in a snow storm. The Newfoundland novelist Margaret Duley, who based her 1939 *Cold Pastoral* in part on Lucy Harris's story, has her characters reciting "Lucy Gray" as they sit in the kitchen awaiting news of the lost heroine (41).¹³ One winces at the liberties these "creative" writers take with folk tradition. Certainly Parsons, a St. John's lawyer, is the only person I have ever heard suggest that meat (!) was placed about the woods as offerings,¹⁴ and it is amusing to hear him echo the conventions of his illustrious predecessors in assigning fairy customs to "the ancients." On the other hand, there is a note of authenticity in his description of how "Rorke told his tale again, and o'er and o'er/One hundred times and like a hundred more" to listeners who came round repeatedly, "perchance already bent/to get the best in future argument." Duley's use of folk tradition is more disturbing, perhaps because of her stature as an important writer. Clara Murphy, from the perspective of a Conception Bay upbringing, calls *Cold Pastoral* "an urban perspective on rural Newfoundland belief in fairies and indeed on the rural Newfoundland way of life" (113). Drawn from the beginning as too sensitive and ethereal for outport life, the heroine, Mary Immaculate, imagines fairies with "spangles, wands, wings, and tiny silver bells" (28), and is lost after purposely omitting the "ceremony at the door," a preposterous ritual for protection against the fairies enacted by her family each time they left the house. Found after three days (when searchers are led to her by a "changeling" whom she had befriended), she is taken to hospital in St. John's, where she recovers completely, is taken up by a wealthy New York philanthropist, and is adopted by a doctor's family into upper-class St. John's society. Duley, of course, was licensed by literary tradition to make what is even called in the text "a Cinderella story: coaches and horses, rags to riches" (60), but it is annoying to see her invention take the direction of stereotype. "Pure Irish, I'd say by the sounds of her. I know the shore she comes from," whispers one of the nurses outside Mary Immaculate's hospital room, "I was there once and it took me back to Grimm" (53). Most of Trinity Bay, including New Melbourne, is neither particularly Irish nor Catholic; the Trinity Bay coast of the Avalon is the only place on the Peninsula where Irish family names are not found (Seary 472). Duley seems to have drawn less on real life and observation than on her own "townie" folklore of the outports as bastions of outlandish, if picturesque, customs and beliefs.¹⁵

It has never been necessary to leave St. John's to hear a fairy story or have a fairy experience, and a few more examples in proof of this will close the chapter. A paper on "times" opens:

> A St. John's lady went to a dance with her husband. Across the room there sat a woman with a vaguely familiar face. The lady ventured over to her table and inquired, "What do you do when the fog comes in?" The lady immediately responded with, "Get in before the fairies get ya." Instant friendship. What created this bond between them? They were both Southsiders. (84-539/4)

On the northern boundary of St. John's are the Three Pond Barrens, "a well-known faery place" (67-20), where people have had experiences even stranger than Mr. Tucker's (72-72:C1116/1-2, for example). Bewildered in the central urban wilderness, a visitor to St. John's left a house on Circular Road for Belvedere Street one midwinter's day:

> And here I walked into this, this summer place. Nothing but the straight road and I never found that place since. 'Twas straight road as far as you could walk and I was meeting people — baby carriages, youngsters with ankle socks on them, lovely bows in their hair, and the tallest kind of people — men and women. No one speaking. They all walking, and the trees on the side of the road were right tall. You couldn't hardly see the sky. No houses or nothing. And I said, "Where am I to at all?" . . . And I said, "I'll never get out of it" . . . when just as quick as you'd snap your fingers, here I was right by where I was going, and here was the youngsters digging in the snow, the big piles of snow piled up.[16] (81-207/106-7)

One informant's aunt started out for Holdsworth Street but walked compulsively until she found herself in woods; a man came along and told her to turn her gloves inside out and make the sign of the cross, and she was able to return. "The only explanation anybody could give was that she had been taken by the fairies," and despite the apparently harmless experience "she never was really the same afterward" (74-9/12-14). This story brings us full circle to the stories that opened the chapter. Unlike that of Lucy Harris, most "fairy" experiences are unspectacular, private affairs, unaccountable little slippages in space or time, oddities pondered from time to time by the people involved, maybe shared if someone asks. Small people dance in a Patrick Street garden, an invisible wall rises in a marsh, a scrubby patch of trees becomes a boundless wilderness: little fairy tricks, and suddenly everyday reality is open to question.

If present governmental plans are carried out, a four-lane highway will soon bisect the Three Pond Barrens. The fairies have literally lost ground all around St. John's: the "Sand Pits," once "the home of the fairies" (72-181/9), is now the (rather inauspicious) site of the Health Sciences Centre; the fairy lights that Aly O'Brien's father and cousin used to see at a certain spot on Kenmount Road have been replaced by traffic lights for the Avalon Mall (74-118/6-7); the "Water Line" fairies of Major's Path (76-269/17-21) must not mind the roar of jets if they are still there. Still, strange things can happen anytime, anywhere, even in the city.

7 | *Fairy Tradition as Discourse on Time and Change*

By this point it should be apparent that fairy traditions, whatever their decline in relationship to a former status, are hardly extinct. They do, however, frequently serve as a vehicle for discussion of the past and for reflection on how times have changed. Their perceived recession makes them an evocative symbol of the past, and conveys an image of a time when the way of life and world view were more amenable to fairy tradition than today. Most of the informants for this chapter feel that the present is uncongenial to fairy lore, being inimical to the fairies themselves (as when prayers, lights, crowds, or roads are said to have driven them away), or non-conducive to narrative and belief (people are more unbelieving now, they do not tell stories anymore). Most of them, even the most active narrators, consider themselves to be telling stories from a past tradition, even when their repertoire includes recent events. One would give much to know if this has always been so, or if this is a function of fairy lore in late twentieth-century Newfoundland, a transitional phase on the way to its demise. In any case, the idea that fairy narratives mostly concern the "old days" makes them a natural medium for talking about change, and almost paradoxically, about contemporary culture.

This chapter concentrates almost as much on the conversation or situation surrounding the fairy stories as on the narratives themselves, which will by now be very familiar to the reader. For all the caution necessary in working with archival texts, singly and as a body, their ultimate reliability is shown by their high predictive value: when someone is flicked in the eye by a branch, one knows what is coming next. Still, there are always surprises, and that intriguing difference between areas will be finally exemplified by a juxtaposition of material from Bay Bulls and Marysvale. This chapter is also intended, in part, to ameliorate some of the drawbacks of my research methods. Most of my interviews were conducted in carefully arranged conditions in which I led the discussion and kept it to a fairly narrow focus, that is, "the fairies." The natural context in which fairy stories are told and custom enacted would, of course, be different. But while it is theoretically desirable to record or analyze "real situations," in practice there are obstacles to this beyond the obvious fact that one cannot hang about indefinitely, hoping for them to occur. In my fieldwork, I often found that the more "natural" or spontaneous the occasion, the harder it was, later, to work with the material. When a discussion becomes lively and several people begin to talk at once, it is impossible to attend to more than one of them at a time, and even if recorded, the conversation is impossible to transcribe. In the interest of obtaining clear texts, performance dynamics such as audience interaction and reaction, evaluation, and debate have perhaps been given short shrift.

A more serious shortcoming of the formal interview is the isolation of the subject from related topics. The separation of fairies from ghosts, tokens, and so on is an arbitrary one, as in narrative practice a vast array of mysterious experiences and events flow together without pause. This narrative complex is exemplified in an interview with two informants, which has the further advantage of being conducted largely by one of them. To preserve the integrity of this interview as well as its natural rhythm and flow, it is presented here in modified transcript form. I have summarized in brackets the "non-fairy" narratives, and it is impossible to transcribe all the expressions of agreement and mutual affirmation that characterized this conversation. The informants are Queen Maloney and Annie Hayes of Bay Bulls, a town of about twelve hundred people twenty-one kilometres from St. John's on the Southern Shore. Mrs. Maloney ("Queenie," b. 1908) knows about the discipline of folklore through Gerald Pocius, who sometimes takes students to her home; this is how I first met her in 1983. She is a keen local historian and writes a regular

7 | *Fairy Tradition as Discourse on Time and Change*

Queen Maloney and Annie Hayes

column, "Down Memory Lane," for *The Seniors' News*. When I visited her in search of the fairies in January 1985, she mapped a campaign with the efficiency of a general, and we descended on several households demanding information in a way that would have been unthinkable for me on my own. Several weeks later we made another foray, and did the following interview with Mrs. Hayes (b. 1910), who taught school for many years in Brigus South on the Southern Shore, and who has taken folklore classes herself. Mrs. Hayes began by talking about the fairies' path:

> AH: It's supposed to be a path in the woods where nothing ever grows. And nobody walks there, but still, nothing ever grows there. And now, I remembers as a youngster, hear tell of one man had a dog, and he brought the dog in and he did everything

possible to get the dog to walk on the path. No way. That was the fairies' path. And then they used to have what they called the "fairies' ring." Did you ever hear tell of that, the fairy ring? It's kind of a circle. Now this is supposed to be where the fairies danced in the night. And it's a little grassy place, and every place else was covered, but this place was bare. And the old people used to say, well, the fairies danced there last night, and that's why there's nothing grows there. So they had the fairy path and the fairy ring. Well, then the fairy bread, remember? If you were going anywhere in the night, you'd always take a bit of bread with you.

QM: Right.

AH: 'Cause I remember my youngsters now, when I'd be going down to Brigus [South] in the night, my mother would say, "Don't go without taking a bit of bread, fairies will get them." So you'd take the bread with you. But can you imagine, now, giving bread to anyone?

BR: How was the bread supposed to protect you?

AH: I don't know, it's supposed to be fairy bread. Now, remember, there's fairies, and there's good people. Did you ever hear tell of the good people?

QM: I heard it out to Bertha's the other day [on a visit with BR].

AH: Well, the good people are supposed to be the people that were in heaven, when St. Michael rebelled against Our Lord. And Our Lord turned out St. Michael and these people went with him. Now they were called the good people, see? But the fairies were only small, little, tiny. But the good people were the same as any adult. But they used to wander the earth, looking for some place to go, you know, the good people. But I remember hearing my mother saying that her mother — that was years and years ago — was cowhunting. And it got dark, you know,

7 | *Fairy Tradition as Discourse on Time and Change*

foggy, in the evening. And she was going away in the woods, she was going astray, maybe, and she heard voices singing out, "Go back, go back," you know, to her, telling her not to go any farther. So she stopped. And she could hear a lot of talking, but this one person's voice was singing out over all the rest, "Go back." And she recognized the voice, she said, as her godfather, and he had been dead a number of years. But she went back, and no time after, there was people came to her, you know, looking for her. And they said to her, "You shouldn't have gone any farther, 'cause that was the good people."

QM: I see.

AH: You know, they were singing and that. But now, up where I lived in Brigus, they used to — I suppose it's true, anyhow, everybody told it. This old lady, she was eighty, I suppose, Mrs. Gregory. And she went picking berries, not very far from the house, now, like we'd go out there, picking them. But when night came there was no sign of her. All the men went looking for her and everything. And they found her in Tierney's Marsh, that's about eight miles from Brigus. And they said there was no way the old lady could walk there, 'cause there was marshes and bogs and everything, you know, it was not like now, no road or anything. But they found her in there and they brought her out. So when she got better, a few days after, somebody was talking to her and she said, when she got in there, she said, there was like children, little children, playing around. And one child came up and offered her something to eat, a bit of bread or a bit of cake, but she said an old man shook his head. And he said, you know, that — she didn't take it. And they were saying that if she had to take [had taken] the bread the fairies would have her.

QM: Yeah, that's right.

AH: The old people — and they were saying another little boy, up in Admiral's Cove, he was about three or four, about like the little one of Molly's. He was out playing around the door. And it was in the evening, and when they went looking for him they couldn't find him. And they found him down on Brigus Road, that's four miles away. But the story they told about him was, when he grew to manhood, every year on that day, he'd be gone for a day and a night. It seems like he had to go back to the fairies. People never found out where he went, but he was, you know, gone for a day and a night. But now that's the stories the old people used to tell, I don't know what credence you can put in them, but that was it.

QM: I don't know, there must have been something to it.

AH: Yeah.

BR: Was he alright otherwise?

AH: No, they said he was never right after, you know there was always some little thing —

QM: [Knowingly.] Yes.

AH: Yeah, something wrong with him after. But that could be now, like we explain that you got astray, and you got afraid and all that, wouldn't you? But the old people used to say the fairies took him. But the Irish were really superstitious that way, you know, they really believed in the fairies.

QM: Yeah, that's really where it came from. A lot of Irish people were here.

AH: Now, see they had ghosts, and they had good people, and they had fairies.

BR: And the good people and the fairies were different.

AH: Different. The fairies were small little things. Like a lot of children, you know. But the good people were the size of average adults. They were supposed to be turned out of heaven, and wandering the earth, looking for a place to go. In there now, you

7 | *Fairy Tradition as Discourse on Time and Change*

know the White Horse going into Brigus? Well, always up on White Horse there was something seen. You know, nobody could pass there, everybody used to be afraid. But I remember being small, now, my mother and — this evening, three ladies were come out picking berries and it was right late. And Mom asked them, she said, "What kept you so long?" "Well," they said, "we couldn't pass White Horse. Because there was people there dancing." And Mom said, "Dancing! You know there's nobody —" "Oh, yes, we saw them. And we couldn't pass. We had to sit down and wait 'til they went away." And she was talking about it after to the older people and they said, "Oh yes, that's where the good people are." So I mean there must have been something to it.

QM: Yeah, there was something.

AH: Yeah, something to it. And I remember between Cape Broyle and Calvert, there was a place, Three Rocks, there was supposed to be something seen there. But this old man used to drive the priest then in a horse and carriage, no cars or anything, he told the priest about it, he said, "Everybody sees something there, a certain time of the night." "Well," the priest says, "when you comes to it, you tell me, and I'll get out of the horse and carriage." So when he came to the spot he said, "That's there, now, Father, where they see it." He said, "You go on." So the priest got out, he put on his stole, and he took his book. And he walked up the hill, all the ways up. And when he came up he said, "Yes," he said, "they won't see anything there anymore." But they never saw it. Now what they used to say then was, so many people dying without seeing the priest, that they had their Purgatory there. And I heard an old man — well, he was my great uncle. He said he was walking home from Calvert to Cape Broyle, and it was dark and the night coming on, and he said he thought he heard horses' bells and he stopped. He stepped off the road and stopped. And he said a *** funeral passed him, the

233

horse and the coffin, and all the men behind them. And nobody ever spoke. But this was the place now where the priest said they could have seen something, you know.

QM: Did you ever hear it said, in regards to ghosts, if there's three people, or two people walking along, and it was a ghost, it's only one will see it?

AH: Yeah.

QM: The other won't.

AH: The other won't.

QM: Or, two out of three. Now, I'll tell you that. [She and her brother saw shadows near a graveyard, although her mother didn't; later, three sailors' bodies are dug up there.]

AH: Well, my, I don't know, years ago they used to tell so many things, I don't know if half of them are true or not, but they used to tell an awful lot. That's how they spent their nights, wasn't it, recreation. Telling ghost stories, and telling things like that.

QM: Gather in houses. There was no television or radio.

AH: I remember a Mr. Johnny Morris, in Ferryland one time, he told me that this girl was working with the priest over there, an old priest. But she went out twelve o'clock of a Saturday night to the well, to get a bucket of water. She was passing by, right by the church, Ferryland church, 'cause the priest's house was near it, and she saw lights on. And like he said, she was so curious, she went in to see what was going on. But when she went in, she said, it was a rush, like people coming out past her. So when she went home she told the priest, and the priest said, "Well, you have to go back there the same time next Saturday night." "Oh, Father," she said, "I can't." He said, "You'll have to." So the next Saturday night she went back a bit earlier. And this priest came out on the altar. And he said, "Anyone here to serve Mass?" And

7 | *Fairy Tradition as Discourse on Time and Change*

of course she fainted with the fright. She went over, she told the priest again, he said, "You've got to go back again." And he said, "If he asks the next Saturday night, you say yes." So she went back again, she was frightened to death, she went back, went in, the priest come out, he said, "Anyone here to serve Mass?" And she said, "Yes." And she said with the same, there was a big noise like people standing up, you know, the congregation standing up. But the priest told her after, must be a priest died, and wasn't after saying all his masses. Now Mr. Johnny Morris often enough told me that, he said it was really true, it really happened. 'Cause he knew the girl well that it happened to. So I mean there's such things, you know.

QM: Oh, yeah, right.

AH: The church is a lonely place in the night, there's something about it, you know.

[QM talks about poltergeists.]

AH: There was, up there in Cape Broyle where Frank Halen lives there now, Mr. Greg Button, his daughter's now in to school with me — they told me that when they go to bed in the night, downstairs they hear the furniture being moved, the doors would be open, the dishes would be rattling in the cupboard, and everything. So that was alright, anyway, Mr. Halen didn't want Frank Halen to build there, you know, he said, "Now everybody in Cape Broyle knows about it." But Frank Halen built, and he had a basement. And they said they had to move out of the basement. They never let on, but he lives upstairs. They had to move out of the basement. People coming in all hours of the night, doors banging, and dishes, and everything, you know. So there must be something, there's something to it.

QM: That can happen.

[BR says it reminds her of a person she and QM visited last time.]

QM: For instance, we asked Tuce about fairy stories, and he said, you know, in regards to just what you're telling, in other words, between fairies and haunted houses were so much alike.

AH: Yeah.

QM: But he told exactly the same, didn't he?

AH: Well, these girls were in school with me, Mary and Jean. And they used to tell us when they come to school, you know, everything in the night, they said they wouldn't get a wink of sleep. But some people don't mind. More just can't take it, you know, their nerves can't take it.

QM: And some people don't believe, but —

AH: I'm shocking superstitious, Mrs. Queen, ****, I'm shocking! [Three knocks preceding death.]

QM: Yes, see, there's people psychic, that's what it is.

AH: I'm shocking, oh my —

QM: Yeah, that can be, that doesn't mean you're crazy!

AH: No, but it **** people up.

QM: Yeah, you're psychic. For instance now, this is a sad story. [Tells about tokens preceding her son's death in 1966, which she told me once before only in great confidentiality.]

AH: That's a token, that's what they used to call a token. Oh, I'm shocking that way. If anything is going to happen, I'll know about it beforehand. So now, lately, I don't say anything, because Molly's always after me, "Don't be telling them old things, Mom." But there's something, because you'll know beforehand there's something going to happen.

QM: Oh, yeah, people are — do you read your horoscope?

AH: No, I never look at that at all.

7 | *Fairy Tradition as Discourse on Time and Change*

QM: [Surprised.] Well, it's a wonder you don't.

AH: No, I ***. Now, my daughter, Terry out there, she looks at that all the time. I never bother about that.

QM: It don't always apply, to, we'll say, one person. But there are times it's so true. For instance, [examples.] But things *are* foretold.

AH: Oh, yes. I'm definitely sure of that, they're foretold to you.

[QM reiterates about horoscopes.]

AH: Oh, we're shocking superstitious folks! [Laughter.]

BR: Do you think that people used to be more sensitive to things like that?

AH: Oh, yes, the older people. Oh, yes, yes. The older people were. The young crowd don't believe as much as we did, indeed they don't. Like now, another thing, if they saw a crow, that was a sign of death. [Daughter Terry sees crows as sign of her father's and uncle's deaths.] But now, there's none of that in Molly. Molly said, "I got no Irish at all in me." She don't believe in nothing like that, you know, like we're talking about. But there's some kind of a —

QM: Oh, yes, the black crow. And the three knocks. I used to hear Cyril's [her husband's] mother tell about the three knocks.

AH: Oh, yes, when you hear the three knocks.

QM: And sometimes a man, for instance, lost on a ship, and we'll say his wife or his mother or someone home knows what happened even though —

AH: Yeah. And you remember those three girls were lost up the Head here?

QM: Yeah.

AH: Well, Mr. Will Power in Brigus, he was down LaManche and it was in the wintertime. And he was coming up on his horse and slide, himself and his son. And he said when he was passing along there, he said it was just like someone got on the horse. The horse couldn't haul it. Could not, he said, no way. And that horse, he said, he beat him up with the whip, said everything, and the horse couldn't haul, right until they got up past White Horse. But when he came home, the son came in and called for the Rosary. And they said that's the last thing he'd ever do because he wasn't religious like that. But there was *something* got on that horse and slide, and right in that spot.

QM: [Emphatically.] Yes, right.

AH: Yes, often heard it, he used to be telling us about it, whatever it was. And then they used to tell too, about people lost at sea, the people in the house would hear people walking with oilclothes on.

QM: Yes!

AH: Coming in with, you know, oilclothes on and all that. Well, this was all the older people, they always knew about those kind of things.

QM: Yeah.

AH: But I don't know if everybody's going too fast today or what it is, they don't believe in anything.

QM: Well, you know, the way everything has, well say, advanced, it is impossible to think there could be anything like it now. Because everything is lit up, you know. After all, it was darkness then. I can remember in the night, going over my grandmother's with a lantern in my hand.

AH: Yeah, right, I can remember that too . . .

[Frightening sound of loons in the marsh.]

AH: But I don't know, the fairies were the main thing. They had you tricked. "Don't stay out after dark, the fairies'll get you."

QM: Yeah, right.

AH: "Be sure and put bread in your pocket, the fairies'll get you." And this sort of stuff.

BR: Were they ever good? Did they ever do good things?

AH: No. They never — they used to take people away, is the only thing I remember, you know, if they got in the way the fairies would take them, wouldn't they? I remember, Mrs. Queen, a fairy squall. Everything would be right calm, there wouldn't be a breath of wind. And all of a sudden a big fairy squall would come up in one part of the woods, wouldn't it?

QM: Yeah.

AH: Blow everything. And the old people would say, "That's a fairy squall."

QM: I heard my father tell about in there on a marsh. And a red hat going up the marsh and he following it.

AH: Yeah.

QM: And then he thought on what he had been told about the fairies.

AH: Yeah, the fairies used to wear red hats, I often heard that too.

QM: He followed a red hat. I heard him tell that.

AH: And up there on Brigus Road, now just above Brigus crossroads, there was a Mrs. Winter lived. She used to sell liquor. [The priest tells her to desist, but she doesn't; not long after she falls off a ladder and is killed.] When we were youngsters we were told, "Don't go by Winters', it's after dark." But the man that I boarded with when I was teaching [saw an old woman with shawl who disappeared]. But they used to say then that's where you have your Purgatory, you know, the old people. They wants a prayer or something like that, they'd say, *****.

BR: What was it, that if you were seen, you were in Purgatory?

AH: Yeah, and that you wanted a prayer to get to Heaven, that was where you were to. Yeah, I don't know how true, but — But poor old Father Kennedy, you know, Father Mike?

QM: Yeah, right.

AH: When his sacristan was sick one time I was doing the altar, and it was in Lent, I think. Anyway, I was coming out, and I was going ahead of him. He said, "You'll wait. You'll wait," he said, "and lock the door behind me." And I was afraid for my life, the church in the night, you know. I said, "Father, I'm afraid." He said, "You let me go ahead of you." He said, "You know the Devil," he said, "is after the priest more than anyone else." He would not come out of that church last. And I heard lots of people say the same thing. He'd never let on, but he wouldn't come out. Sure, Father Maloney, we used to have rings around. Years ago, when Father Maloney was studying for the priesthood, I used to tell him, you know, about certain things were seen on Shore Road and Brigus Road, and —

QM: Yes.

AH: "Ah," said Father Maloney, "That's a crowd smuggling. There's nothing seen there." He'd be arguing with me. But when he went up to Parker's [?] Cove up to St. Joseph's, he used to sleep in the sacristy of the church, he'd go over and have Mass, and that's where he used to sleep. So he wrote me a letter, and he said, "I'm after changing me mind an awful lot. Last night," he said, "I had to leave the church." Whatever came there, he never went back to sleep in the sacristy after, Lizzie Power told me. Something drove him out of it in the night. But he changed right over, he was a changed man, he believed. He said to me, "Yes, there can be things like that." But he saw something in that church, whatever it was. So I say there's a something, whatever it is, I don't know.

QM: Right.

BR: Would the priests ever say anything about fairies?

AH: The old Irish priests would. Dean McCarthy, up in Renews, Monsignor McCarthy. Now he used to say, "the children shouldn't be out after night, the fairies might get them."

QM: He was right from Ireland.

AH: Yeah, he was right from Ireland. And he told me when his people died at home in Ireland, he always knew. He said he used to hear, you know, a horse and carriage would drive up to the door and he'd get up, think there was a sick call, nobody there.

QM: Yes.

AH: He was, oh, right Irish ***. Oh, yes, he believed in it, because he used to be saying, "I don't know how people can let little children go out like that. Don't they realize the fairies will get them?" And the other nuns would be laughing and everything at him, but he was right Irish. He believed in it. Well, I was listening there one day to some doctor, Mrs. Queen, he was talking about depression. And he said there's more depression in Newfoundland than any other province. And that's because the Irish were so superstitious where they came out of. You know, they were always picking at things. One morning there was a doctor on was talking about that. Well, it seems it's only the older people, the younger crowd growing up, they don't —

QM: No, they —

AH: They don't believe in anything like that, you know.

QM: With television and radio and all that, how can they believe? And the streets, everything lit up.

AH: I used to know a lot of stories, but I'm forgetting a good many, you know. Down through the years. But I used to tell one to the youngsters up at school, I used to be known for telling stories. I said, "Now, this is a true ghost story," you know, I said, "if the rest of them aren't true, this one is." [Mock ghost story.] Well, the youngsters used to get some kick out of that. And they'd be telling me about the haunted houses in Cape Broyle. "Miss, you don't know about them. You were born here but you're gone a lot. There's three haunted houses." . . . I said, "Don't be so foolish, no such thing as a haunted house." "Oh, yes, Miss, they're haunted." See, now their parents must be after warning them, I suppose, these houses are empty, don't go near them, you know. So the youngsters grew up with the idea they were haunted, and they stayed clear of them. Sure, heavens, you wouldn't keep them clear of them now, tell them they're haunted. No fear, they'd go in anyway. [Laughter.] But they don't believe in things like that. I suppose it's good in one way they don't believe in certain things.

BR: I guess it meant a lot of fear.

AH: Yeah, it did that. [Frightening figures: Boo-man, Mac woman in Admiral's Cove.]

[Mock ghost stories, wakes and pranks — "Look, if it was today, they'd be calling the mounties every day."]

QM: [Her brothers hide behind a tombstone and recite rosary to scare a woman.] So, Mary wasn't long taking in the clothes, she went in, "The souls were out."

AH: Oh, yes, that was a common thing. The souls were out. Oh, that's common, to say the souls were out.

BR: They were different from the fairies and good people?

AH: [Chuckles.] Yeah, they were the souls. [Laughter.] All Souls' Night, sure, Mrs. Queen, my, it used to be an awful night, they were afraid and everything, wouldn't they?

QM: Oh, yeah.

AH: They'd light candles and they'd open the doors of their houses let the souls pass through and everything. Like Molly says, must have been warmer than it is now. [Laughter.] Oh my ... It was a real solemn night, not like now, people were so much afraid. And it was supposed to be that the souls of the dead returned. You know the old people had that feeling, that somebody belonged here died, they'd return. I remember my grandmother dying [apparition as forerunner; steps precede news of death; light shining into house is visitation of dead woman].

[QM talks about people gathering in houses for storytelling; one man used to read to people, substituting whatever came to mind when he couldn't read a particular word, since the others couldn't read at all.]

AH: That's the way it was everywhere, then, you know. People were more united.

QM: Oh, they were more united.

AH: They were a lot more united than they are now.

QM: Yes, people gathered together.

AH: Sure, they hardly know anyone now, from one end of the harbour to the other, do they?

QM: Oh, no.

AH: They hardly know anybody.

The discussion moved to a lamentable present in which everyone is off to bingo, people don't even know their own relatives, and kids, who used to be nice, will "drive you mad." But the tone of the litany was light, and I did not get the impression that Mrs. Hayes and Mrs. Maloney are really nostalgic about the past; they are perhaps too well aware of its limitations for that. (Once, as we were driving along the highway to Trepassey, Mrs. Maloney remarked wistfully how much she loved to travel and how little opportunity she had ever had to do it; now you see young women going all around with big backpacks, she said — that would be her if she could be young again.)

Nowadays, Mrs. Hayes keeps any foreknowledge of events to herself "because Molly's always after me, 'Don't be telling them old things, Mom'." Another daughter, Terry, reads her horoscope and has had experience of tokens, but "there's none of that" in the hard-headed Molly, who declares that she has "no Irish at all" in her (using "Irishness" as a measure of "superstitiousness," not in reference to actual ancestry). Mrs. Maloney validates Mrs. Hayes's experience directly in modern terms ("you're psychic") and indirectly by describing her own experience with tokens. Both see their generation as distinct from the preceding generation in regard to folk belief but also from the young people of today who "don't believe in anything like that"; perhaps the position of "something to it," which runs like a refrain through their conversation, represents a middle ground between the perceived deep belief and cynicism of the surrounding generations, a point from which one can swing in either direction on various topics.

The prominence of religion in Mrs. Hayes's and Mrs. Maloney's accounts reflects the strongly Irish/Catholic composition of the Southern Shore. The role of priests in folk religion is a natural outgrowth of their position as custodians of supernatural knowledge, although in the realm of folk belief they are not necessarily considered infallible nor is their word always gospel. Everyone is equal in the debate over the existence of folk supernatural phenomena, and personal experience rather than official edict sanctions the authority. Thus we see Mrs. Hayes arguing with Father Maloney, who is later converted, through experience, to her view: "He was a changed man, he believed."

Although widespread, reports of clerical involvement in folk supernatural traditions vary considerably, as presumably clerical attitudes themselves would. When I asked Ellen Keough of Marysvale, Conception Bay, whether the priest would ever say anything about the fairies, she dismissed the idea: "No, no, no. I don't suppose the priest would fool with anything like that, boy." The fairy traditions I recorded in Marysvale, compared to the Bay Bulls material, show the same divergence and similarity that characterize Newfoundland fairy lore as a whole. For example, in contrast to the distinction Mrs. Hayes makes between good people and fairies, Mrs. Keough says they are the same, only that "good people" is a later term; it is the one she uses herself, "but most says fairies."

Mrs. Keough was born in Labrador in 1898 to a family that had been in Marysvale at least as far back as her grandparents; originally the family was from Ireland. Mrs. Keough was in three shipwrecks in the course of her work on the Labrador fishery before later work as a maid at Government House in St. John's. These details come from a "life history" written by Ferdinand Jones, a student who boarded with her for several years who also wrote that "her house has become a place where passers-by stop in" (81-016:C8724), so I enquired after Mrs. Keough in 1985. I was directed to the house of Mr. and Mrs. Joseph Ryan, where she stays winters, her own house having no plumbing and only a woodstove for heat.[1] As Mrs. Keough's hearing was poor, it would have been impossible to do the interviews without the help of Mr. and Mrs. Ryan, who know a good deal of fairy lore themselves. Mrs. Keough first told about the time her brother was coming home from school around three o'clock, and thought he saw his friends coming to meet him; but it was not children but the good people, who "beat him up" and moved his heart from the left to the right side. He was in bed for three years and three months, until his side "broke out in nine holes" and hair and "everything come out of it that you can mention." This, added Mr. Ryan, was a "blast."

In Bay Bulls, Bertha Deagon's aunt got a "blast" when she went to the well one night; her finger swelled so much she had to wear a man's shirt, until she went to a "half-doctor" in Petty Harbour, who lanced it, and "pieces of bough, bone, every kind of thing" came out. The "doctor" told her she'd "gotten in somebody's way," perhaps some poor soul who wanted a drink.[2] Mrs. Maloney and Mrs. Deagon also told about a woman who, sometime around 1953, went astray and somehow got through miles of trackless wood and bog to end up at the lighthouse. They said that she used to tell how she dropped her rosary beads, and felt herself lifted into the air when she bent to pick them up. She was returned the next morning, in tatters, by the lighthouse keeper. "There had to be something miraculous about it," said Mrs. Maloney, and although she and Mrs. Deagon didn't know if it was fairies or what, they stressed that it was humanly impossible to have gotten where she did on foot.[3]

Roughly the same thing happened in Marysvale (even to the same time, late afternoon) to Clara Ryan. Mr. Ryan said that she was picking berries, when she found blueberries so profuse "she never seen the like of them": she walked along, picking, and the next thing she knew she was in Colliers, "down against the salt water":

> . . . can't remember leaving the other marsh, getting to Colliers, 'til she came to herself. When she came to herself she found out she was up there. They just took her, b'ye. She must have started picking their berries, see?

Fairy teleportation seems to be particularly prominent in the Colliers area. Jack McCall said that around 1980, Tim Hunter of Colliers, who had been an invalid for years, was found drowned in a dam three miles from his house: "Nobody knows how he got in there, he never walked."[4] Clara Ryan was unharmed, "they never actually caught hold to her face or anything, they left no marks on her," said Mr. Ryan, "but most people, if they had any dealings with them, they left marks." They twisted Will Kane's mouth and ruined Joe Barter's leg: "When they touch you, they done the job on you."[5]

Despite such recent occurrences, Mrs. Keough states flatly, "*They* be gone now, because of cars." "Too much light now, eh?" amplified Mr. Ryan. "And so much excitement." In Bay Bulls, Bill Joy pondered the fairies' disappearance: "But what happened to them these past forty years is what I'd like to know. That garden used to be full of them." His grandmother saw them once but it didn't do her any harm, as she died in 1956 at the age of ninety-three. "What did she see?" asked Mrs. Maloney. "Oh, the same as the rest of them — little blue suits and red caps." On a later visit, he reiterated his skepticism, saying that if there were such things he surely would have seen them in sixty-four years. He wondered how the details in those stories could be so precise, and Mrs. Maloney suggested that untreated high blood pressure made some people see things. "It would take more than high blood pressure to make me see little people in blue suits!" he laughed, adding that the only fairy tales you hear now are the ones in the election campaigns.

"How did they used to be dressed, Nelly?" asked Mr. Ryan, "all in little red uniforms, didn't they?" "Little, down like that," replied Mrs. Keough, "red caps on them." When I asked if they were male or female, she said, "we don't know that" because "they all dressed the one way." The yard near her sister's house "used to be fulled up with them, yes, fulled up." She said that they were always "a big lot together" and they didn't go into houses, but Mr. Ryan then called to mind a story about a man who was in the woods when a bird jumped on his horse, which was "sweating mad" by the time it got home. The bird flew up into the loft, and that night "appeared as a man." They had to get the priest to bless the house, and take the bird back where it came from.[6] "That was an awful bad spot over there for them, too," he said:

> I often heard my mother saying about that, right. When Frank McHugh, now — he bought the land off Flanners — I often heard my mother saying, "He's going down with the fairies," hey, to live, because that's where they used to be known very well, in olden times, eh, at the particular spot.

Mrs. Ryan questioned whether the bird was really the "good people," and Mrs. Keough and Mr. Ryan were emphatic that it was. Although Mr. Ryan says he has gotten all his information from the "yarns" of the older people, his ideas about the nature of the fairies are quite firm. He is definite that they will never get back into heaven: "they were in Heaven, then, they had more opportunity than me or you. We'll probably have to go to Purgatory, right? But they were in Heaven, and banished out, and banished to earth." That is why "they hate to be cursed," and "they hate anything holy" (prayers, or artifacts like rosaries, scapulars, or miraculous medals). And there was nothing anyone could do to heal a fairy-inflicted injury, although some healers could recognize it and say, "We can't do nothing for it, he was hit by a blast." Mr. Ryan clearly has some belief in the reality of the fairies, even if as a reality of the past. "Well, if there's no such thing as good people, how come there's something being written up in university about it?" he demanded, "There must be something."

Mrs. Keough never heard that you shouldn't talk about the fairies, and when I asked if it was dangerous to listen to the beautiful music they made, she laughed: "Oh no, they're not so bad as they used to be!" Her jocular attitude reminded me of Mrs. Meaney's, but was equally hard to judge because of identical problems with her hearing and my unfamiliar accent and idiom. It was frustrating not to be able to ask everything I wanted to know; folklorists joke about the familiar lament, "if only they'd been there ten years earlier ... ," but there *is* sometimes cause for regret; some things *are* lost, especially in conditions of rapid cultural change. As I mentioned in Chapter One, the only "midwife to the fairies" story recorded in Newfoundland is from Marysvale (in sadly garbled form), although I didn't know this until after my interview. On a third visit, Mr. and Mrs. Ryan were not there, and Mrs. Keough and I could hardly converse at all; she knew the informant, but I couldn't get across what it was I was after (its rarity having excited my butterfly-collecting instinct). Even more frustrating than the feeling of having arrived too late is to learn that the stories had gone on after one left an interview. Mrs. Ryan told me that Mrs. Keough kept remembering more and more after my first visit, but between then and my second visit they had both forgotten them again!

Still, any vestiges I might have retained of the notion that old people know the best fairy stories were stripped away by my visits to Clarke's Beach that same month. I began by visiting the Winters, an elderly couple who regarded my request dubiously if not distrustfully: "Lies," snorted Mr. Winter when I explained what I wanted. Mrs. Winter seemed more desirous of being helpful and more inclined to think that there were true unexplainable experiences, and told about a "reliable" woman she knew who saw a funeral procession of little people walking along the road between Cupids and Brigus about forty or fifty years ago. Mr. Winter, who occasionally added something almost in spite of himself, said there were often things seen there; walking along there as a young man his hair sometimes stood straight out from his head. Both stressed the importance of fairy and ghost stories as entertainment in the past, and how easy it was, when you had grown up hearing them, to imagine all sorts of things when you were out alone at night. But even as Mr. Winter was assuring me that "all these things" were in the past and "you never hear of them now," his adolescent grandson — whose presence was possibly an inhibiting factor — volunteered that he had just heard something about

Frances Kavanagh

little people with accordions accosting someone in a marsh; he didn't know if it was true or not. The Winters (rather hastily) suggested that I see Frances Kavanagh, across the road, who was "a good one for that sort of thing."[7]

At the time I interviewed her, Mrs. Kavanagh ran a school bus fleet with her husband, sat on the town council, and had several children at university. She is a confident person who takes pride in her knowledge of supernatural traditions, although she considers ghost stories her specialty and her fairy repertoire relatively small. "She can scare you to death," her daughters assured me admiringly. They prompted her at several points in our interviews, and Mr. Kavanagh sat by the woodstove and made the odd contribution; it was clear that everyone present had heard these stories many times. Mrs. Kavanagh does not "believe in the fairies" herself, which is why, she says, she can talk about them. Yet she asserts the factual basis of most of her stories, which she recounts in a low, serious voice.

Some incidents involved members of her own family. Her brother was on the way to a dance when he heard music he thought was coming from a house, but when he neared the house he saw that it was shut up and the music came from the marsh. So he "just went off," because:

> You're not supposed to stop and listen, that's apparently when they get power over you, it must be something like a trance or something. But that's when they get power over you, if you take an active part in what they're doing. And you are [taking part], if you stop and listen.

A young sister who died saw "them" in the likeness of her other sisters:

> She said to Mother, "What is Margaret, Mary, and Liza doing," she said, "out?" And Mother said, "They're not out, they're in the kitchen." She said, "I seen them out sitting on the fence." [Pause.] So, there's no alternative, there's nothing else she seen.

Mrs. Kavanagh's repertoire and clarity of expression suggested that she would make a good informant for Peter Narváez's radio program on the fairies,[8] and in December 1988 we visited and recorded some of the stories she had told me almost four years before. The wording of most was very close — identical in places — indicating well-honed performances. The internal stability of the narratives in the two interviews contrasts with certain inconsistencies in our unstructured discussion, just as her solemn manner of narration contrasts with her jocular attitude in looser talk. This may have been due in part to the way I pursued matters beyond their normal termination in narrative, as after a story about a great-aunt who decided to walk home from a dance:

> It was a beautiful morning and she figured, no, she would walk home alone, she wasn't afraid. So down from their house was a little running brook. And when she got near the end, she saw those — down around the brook. And she figured, "Well, what are they doing down around the brook at this hour in the morning?" And she watched them and she walked on, she watched them, and by and by, when she got up close enough, she realized

it was nobody belonged to her. [Pause.] It was the fairies! So she stopped, and she looked at them. And they started making a ring, going around. And when she watched them for awhile, she turned to go back. And when she turned to go back something hit her in the heel. That's alright, she went back, went to her friends up in the Goulds, and she stayed there the rest of the night. And the next morning she woke with pain, and her foot gathered and broke. And there was stone, and there was bits of wood, and feathers, and everything worked out of it. And she was crippled for the rest of her life....

BR: What did the people look like, did she say?

FK: They looks like ordinary people. Sometimes. But these did look like people, because she thought that they were some of her own family.

BR: You were telling me that they can take any form, or that they can take other forms.

FK: Yeah. Trees, birds; sometimes you hear of them whistling, really like birds. That's them.

BR: How can you tell?

FK: I don't know. People just know. It's them! It's not birds! [Laughter.]

But after a story about her uncle, she said they always look like small people:

He was making hoops, see, years ago, people used to make hoops for barrels and that, for the fishery; and he looked through the window and he saw them down dancing around the brook. And he went and called his wife to come and look. But they had hard hats on, and long-tail coats. And they were having a ring, they were all joined hands together and they were dancing around the brook. And when she got there, they were gone. That's the time that he left, went for her, and he got back they weren't there.

BR: Were they little?

FK: They were little, yeah. They *always* appear in the form of little people.

BR: Huh, always small?

FK: Yeah, always small.

When I asked about their gender, she said, "They were always referred to just as fairies … they were never distinguished between sexes, male or female." She also says that "they claim they are fallen angels whom God cast out of heaven because they were disobedient," and that "they expect pardon the last day, if not, they would destroy the world." They are repelled by religious symbols like scapulars or rosaries, and can be driven away by swearing; she mentioned that a man "got astray in the trees, and couldn't find his way, and cursed — the 'G-d fairies' — and next thing everything was gone." She also gave the following story about her father:

> Some do get astray, and it doesn't affect them somehow or another. Because I remember my father was surrounded by them, by little trees. And he took — it was in the woods — he took a turn of boughs on his back, and when he did — he was in the path when he put them on his back — and when he put the boughs on his back, he couldn't find the path, he was in a little thicket of trees. And he knew the trees weren't there. So he threw the boughs down, and he sat down on a stump. And he lit his pipe, and he said, "Where the heck am I?" He was astray, he didn't know. And that was in his own garden. And he lit his pipe, he sized the situation up, and by and by there were no trees there at all, there was the path! Maybe it's a figure of the imagination, I don't know. But, apparently, they claims these things happen.

It wasn't until my visit with Peter Narváez that, through the prompting of her daughter, it emerged that it was in fact her father who had cursed the "G-d fairies." This small revelation was a salutary reminder that even the

7 | Fairy Tradition as Discourse on Time and Change

apparently most forthcoming informant may not relate every detail of a personal nature.

Gardens into wilderness, the familiar suddenly strange: the threat of the fairies and nature itself. In Northern Bay, says Mrs. Kavanagh, a woman and her grandchild got lost in the fog while berry-picking; their bodies were found the following spring behind the fence of a garden right in the community, "the child was in her arms, they were sitting under a tree." A tug of war between nature and culture is explicit in Mrs. Kavanagh's two accounts of changed children. One, as a baby, was laid on the grass while his mother got hay in; when they got home, "he was all scriveled up, he looked like a sixty-year-old man," and the mother "figured that that's what she had, they had taken the baby and left a fairy." He died when he was twelve, and until then, "when he'd get out he'd always want to go for the garden." Another mother took her "beautiful-looking little girl" to visit a sick neighbour at night, and on the way home "had to come across this old road." The next morning, the child was "different entirely. The child was not the same after. It was weird-looking, it was strange-looking. And the child was never — she never got out of it, she is still living." She is about *forty* now, and although she falls about inside the house, banging the stove and all:

> let her outdoors, and she goes like the wind, not a thing wrong with her. And she always goes for the hills. But, oh, yeah, when she gets out, it takes three or four to catch her. She's really wild.

If, as these accounts suggest, the hapless changelings were confined to the house, their break for freedom can be understood without recourse to symbolic interpretation. However, it is clear in comparison to other accounts (such as Annie Hayes's story about the man who, taken as a child, had to "go back to the fairies" for a night and a day once a year) that this compulsion is part of the fairies' hold over them. Mrs. Kavanagh tells about a man who had a permanent "wild strain" after going missing overnight while hunting. A search party found him with his gun trained on a man who had spotted him up in a tree:

> So they talked and got around him and they finally got him down out of the tree. So he came home and he wasn't right, he

wasn't acting right. And they took him to the parish priest. Now he had food, but he never ate it. That time, they used to carry it in a red square like an handkerchief, they'd tie up their sandwiches in that. And anyway, the priest threw that in the stove, he said not to eat it. He threw that in the fire. And he told them they shouldn't have let him sleep. They should — no, because when you sleep, the fairies gets power. But he did what he could for him, but he wasn't the same after. Never. He had a wild strain about him. Crazy-like. That really — that's true, that really happened.

The despoiled sandwich seems to have absorbed evil from the encounter, as a person does who is polluted by the noxious natural junk of a blast. Mrs. Kavanagh knew of two men who got blasts: one was "flicked in the eye" and went blind, and another got a pain in the face when he drank from a brook in the evening — "His face gathered and broke, and everything worked out of it, they said, sticks, stones, feathers, hairs, everything. But his face never went back at all." She says that you are not supposed to drink straight from a brook in the evening, but must use a cup or a dipper. Perhaps the significance of this artifact (culture) is its separation of humans from animals, who drink straight — unmediated — from the water.[9]

"He's still like it," Mr. Kavanagh added of the man whose face "broke." I would have liked to have interviewed this man, but even my nerve has limits. I did, however, meet a woman in Long Pond, Conception Bay, who showed me scars on her legs as the result of a mysterious injury she received when she was nineteen. I heard about Mrs. Hackett (a pseudonym) when in June 1987 I accompanied fellow folklore student Julia Bishop on an interview with Mrs. Kenny (also a pseudonym), Mrs. Hackett's sister-in-law. When the subject of my research arose, Mrs. Kenny and her daughter said that Mrs. Hackett (now in her sixties) always said that the fairies hurt her leg. She might tell me about it, they said, but then again she might not as she has recently "gotten religion" (a conversion from Church of England to Seventh Day Adventism). I phoned Mrs. Hackett with some trepidation (recalling my meeting with Lucy Harris), not lessened when she spoke of "evil in the world" and "Satan," but when I visited her later that week she was extremely hospitable and seemed happy to tell the story.

One Friday in September (Fridays are bad days anyway, she said) she and her brother and a friend were berry-picking in Middle Bight Road near Penney's Hill, in an area where several people had gone astray. She and her friend got separated from her brother and were astray the whole day. The friend, who for some reason figured that the fairies had Mrs. Hackett, encouraged her to swear, but Mrs. Hackett could not bring herself to do that; eventually they found their way back. Three days later, on her nineteenth birthday, she was berry-picking on different ground. Just before leaving she got a drink of lovely, clear water, but when her friend went to get some (I don't know if this was the same friend), she couldn't see it. When Mrs. Hackett got home, she discovered a cut in her leg, although the cotton stocking and pant-leg were not torn; she thought she might have hit it on a stump, although she could not recall doing so. The leg was not painful at first, but it would not heal, and her mother and the older people said it was a blast. Mrs. Hackett said that like all the children she believed in the fairies while growing up, but had become skeptical by that time; she was frightened by this diagnosis, however, especially as the leg became painful and various remedies failed. A Mr. Sexton at the American army base in St. John's, who used to do first aid, put several things on it to no avail, and a Dr. John on Bell Island (who had "escaped from the German ships," and who Mrs. Kenny said was a doctor in Germany but had no credentials here) unsuccessfully prescribed a poultice of blue potatoes and molasses every night, and olive oil every morning. Although she was Protestant, she went to see a Father Bradshaw on Patrick Street in St. John's: he blessed the leg, and the pain went away but not the swelling. (On the way into St. John's the car turned itself around at the bottom of Foxtrap Road, so she knew "something was going on.") Three nights later someone (I don't know who) lanced it, and pus poured out. She went to Uncle Billy Cable, who had a charm, for nine days in a row, although he told her it was too late. The old people told her it was no good going to any doctor, and a woman who "read the cup" told her she would lose her leg. The leg was bad for three years, and I'm not sure what finally cured it, although I think it was the charm. For years afterward she "found her leg" every Friday.

Mrs. Hackett concluded that the problem was probably an infection from all the cures she tried, although she didn't say anything about the original cause. She did not make an explicit connection between the injury and the drink of water, and I did not recognize its importance at first, taking it as part of the circumstantial detail with which such accounts are typically filled. It was only later, making notes, that I realized that she actually told the story quite economically and that there was too much emphasis on the "lovely," sweet quality of the water, and on her friend's inability to see it, for it to have been meaningless. I recalled Mrs. Kavanagh's story about two sisters playing in a barnyard, whose way was blocked by a big pool of water when they tried to go to the house. The "delicate" one, Maggie, couldn't cross it, so the other went to get help. When she returned, Maggie was gone; she was found the next day, two miles away under a tree in the Birch Hills, missing one boot:

> So they presumed that's what happened to her, she was taken away — there was no water there! In the first place, where'd the water come from? The water wasn't there. They really only saw it. And she never lived. She was always sick, she never got the better of it. She was sixteen when she died.

Here it is clear that the water was a fairy illusion, but in Mrs. Hackett's account this is only apparent from its proportion in the narrative and from an understanding of other narratives in which it figures the same way.

Mrs. Hackett knows of other people affected by the fairies, but she does not talk about them with the same interest she does about her own experience. Her mother's cousin had a blast, and "they say that everything came out of it, fishbones and everything." This cousin lived in a house that they said must have been built on "a bank of fairies"; the priests and ministers had to come and pray at midnight to clear the house. The cousin had a child that they said got changed — the midwife told her it was not the child she had delivered, and that she should throw it in the river to get her own child back. This was not done, and the child grew to have a "woman's head on a little

7 | *Fairy Tradition as Discourse on Time and Change*

body," and was never able to get out of her cot. She died in her twenties, and they said that there was nothing in her coffin. Mrs. Hackett's mother also had a stepsister who was "taken" and was found dead with her boots off (another signifier, like illusory water). Mrs. Hackett said that "good people" and not "fairies" was the usual term, and that if you used the latter you had to mention whatever day of the week it was. Some people said they were short people with red caps, and some claimed to have seen them singing and dancing in the hills. She mentioned Lucy Harris, saying that she was lost for twenty-one days and that she was able to describe the "beautiful people" who took care of her; she was alright after it all, and the whole business helped her family, who had been very poor. Mrs. Hackett did not offer an explanation of the fairies, except to say that they could have been evil spirits and that perhaps evil is in the world in a different form today.

The case of Mrs. Hackett underlines some of the limitations of fieldwork as an outsider, and the limits on how far one can guess at private opinion. I only heard about Mrs. Hackett by accident; and had I only my conversation with her to go on, I would have concluded that she considered "the fairies" only one possible explanation for her leg, a remote one at that. But only a few weeks after my visit, I ran into her niece and told her as much. The niece assured me that the idea of an infection is a new development and that Mrs. Hackett has always been adamant that the cause was the fairies. Perhaps Mrs. Hackett gave me a different story because she didn't know me, or perhaps she has changed her ideas because of her change in religion. Maybe she changed her mind for other reasons entirely, or a combination of reasons, including what Yeats called "the spirit of the times." After we talked about the fairies, Mrs. Hackett brought out pictures of her three children and grandchildren, and her recent travels with them; it did seem incongruous to think that the woman climbing into a helicopter for a ride over Mt. St. Helen's, or smiling on the beach in Barbados, once had a run-in with the fairies.

Despite Mrs. Hackett's present naturalistic opinion about what ailed her leg, it is clear when she tells about it that she still thinks there was something strange involved. In this she is like Mrs. Kavanagh and a legion of other informants who reject the general proposition ("believing in the fairies"), but

257

affirm the particular ("*this* really happened"). And even though Mrs. Hackett has abandoned, at least officially, her former position (positive attribution of the injury to the fairies), her story has entered tradition as a "fairy" story, for her niece will have none of the change. In this it is a little like the tales of Lucy Harris, and shows how in folk narrative, even memorate, there is no authoritative version even when the "author" is known. It also shows how fluid, ambiguous, and contradictory a matter is individual "belief," a thousand permutations of which constitute the subject referred to so automatically as "folk belief." Most studies of such "beliefs" are based on texts recorded from informants on a single occasion, but an understanding of the dynamics of belief (and the processes of oral tradition) would be enhanced if the meanings of the "belief" in question could be documented at different points in the tradition-bearers' lives.

One valuable study of change over time was done in 1972 by Marie Burry, who wrote about three residents of her hometown who had gotten blasts, two of whom she had known from her childhood. One told her about getting "flicked" and expressed her conviction as to its origin:

> I believed my mother when she said it was the fairies and I still believe it, to tell the truth, and that was fifty-three years ago. I still find my leg and I had an operation on it two years ago. The fairies did it, don't you fool yourself. I never ever heard about the fairies doing anything good for anyone either.

But her son, daughter, and husband disparage her belief, and Burry writes:

> Her story has survived in spite of the disbelief of her children and her husband.... However, I am inclined to believe her story is changing somewhat these recent years. Maybe she does not want to appear too foolish in the eyes of her university-graduated son who recently has set up a professional business in the area. After his brief visit during our interview I detected a little bit of doubt creeping in — "Maybe if there had been doctors in those days..." Some of the details have changed as well. I used to play with Mrs. Ford's children when we were younger and I can recall

her telling the story several times and saying how all sorts of things came out of her leg, even straw and fish bones! Then too, when I mentioned this project to my mother she said, "Oh, Mrs. Ford would be a good person to go and see. She really believes in the fairies and tells how fishbones and straw came out of her leg after the fairies flicked her." Yet when I asked Mrs. Ford if anything came out of the sore leg she replied, "nothing that I can remember." (72-236/64-66)

In contrast to Mrs. Ford, the second informant had the full support of her family, who have had fairy experiences themselves, and related a story with a wealth of detail, including the three bones that emerged from her leg, and how her leg still "comes again" in May and October when the fairies shift their camp. "I believe it was the fairies who did all this, my dear, and I'll believe it until I dies," she said. "I think they are still around but there's so much traffic back and forth now that no one ever sees them." Mrs. Ford said, "I think there are still some around, but things are opened up too much for them to bother you."[10]

Burry's study shows the great usefulness of previous acquaintance with informants (or potential informants) and their repertoires, and with other community members, in undertaking a formal study. In the first chapter, I mentioned that I know two people who denied knowledge of the fairies when I first met them but who, it transpired, knew about them very well indeed. One was the late Alice Hayes of St. Thomas (1911–1991) (not to be confused with Annie Hayes), who assured me on our first meeting in 1983, when I stopped to photograph her yard art, that she "never heard anything about that." On a later visit I mentioned the subject again, and her daughter, unaware of our earlier conversation, said, "Oh, Mom can tell you all about the fairies." But Mrs. Hayes said nothing, and although I visited her several times to record songs, the subject did not come up again until I stopped in on my way to visit the Kelloways in 1984. Moved perhaps by a spirit of competition (I mentioned why I was going to see the Kelloways), she launched into a string of stories of strange events, ghosts, dreams, tokens, and the like. Still, no fairies proper, and by 1985 when I went to record music with Julia Bishop (Mrs. Hayes was a singer and accordion player), I didn't expect an answer to my almost automatic question — it was a joke by now — whether the fairies didn't play beautiful music. To my amazement she agreed that they did; someone heard it once, and what's more her father once saw three or four fairies, who wore red stocking caps and were only a few feet tall, and who made faces at him. After all the evasion I was taken aback by the rather unspectacular nature of this incident. I was even more puzzled when I later discovered that she had given the story to another student, unknown to her albeit a friend of her granddaughter's; she told her that they were brightly dressed and said "Ya, ya, ya, Tom, boy" (82-297/12).[11] A year later, Mrs. Hayes told me the story again, complete with the fairies' taunt, "Nyah, nyah, Tom, boy!" She also said that the fairies once took her uncle; they threw him over a hedge and gave him a "flick" in his neck, which was lanced so that "twigs, everything came out of it." Although I never did figure out for sure the reason for her early reticence, it was a good lesson to have gotten early on in this project, for it showed the need for caution in making negative conclusions about the existence of fairy tradition on the basis of casual inquiries.

I met my second reluctant informant the same day I met Mrs. Hayes, also by photographing his barn. Richard Murrin lives alone in Shoe Cove (a twenty-minute drive from St. John's), on a small farm that has seen little in the way of modernization except for electric wiring installed in the 1920s. There is no running water, and the kitchen woodstove is the sole source of heat; Mr. Murrin does all his own cooking and baking, and having no car, goes into town only occasionally for supplies. Although as a young man he worked for a short time as a policeman in St. John's, he has long subsisted on what he grows; he refuses to take the "old age" pension (he was born in 1916), not approving of dependence on government.[12] He is a solitary person disgusted by the modern world and his position in it. Nevertheless, he is always kindly and humorous; he says if he ever did see the fairies, he would gladly go with them.

It wasn't until my third visit that Mr. Murrin made this joke. We had been discussing edible wild plants, and he said there was a certain kind of mushroom called a fairy cap, and I reiterated that I was interested in fairy stories and had read a lot of them. "There's fairies," he said, as casually as if he had never said that there weren't. Sometimes children were gone overnight or longer and would be found safe, and people would say the fairies had taken care of them; on the other hand, there were "bad ones," like those that people said got a boy in nearby Pouch Cove, who was "foolish" — always laughing and grinning — and who died young. On a later visit, he said that his father had gotten a blast, which is when the fairies "shoot something" at you. He had been walking in a certain part of the barrens when he felt it in the leg; Mr. Murrin doesn't remember whether it worked its way out or a doctor took it out, but a rag emerged, and his father always walked with a limp after that. Mr. Murrin himself had experience with "spirits," when he came out of the barn three days in a row with one side of his face "blackened" with something like soot. Another day, he was telling Martin Lovelace and me about his father "limbing off" spruce boughs, when one flew out of his hand three times. "You often hear of the fairies doing that kind of thing," Martin remarked, and Mr. Murrin agreed — "maybe they had a nest in that one or something," a suggestion he almost surely would not have made if Martin had not brought the subject up. A certain obtuse persistence helps, then, although no doubt some of my "informants," pressed rather unwillingly into that role, thought at times I had a bit of a bee in my bonnet. Perhaps Mrs. Hayes finally gave me the story about her father just to shut me up; perhaps Mr. Murrin felt it polite to humour Martin and me if we wanted to think that the fairies made the wood fly out of his father's hand.

"You wouldn't see fairies around here now because it's getting too inhabited," says Frances Kavanagh, laughing, "When a place gets inhabited, they move to other places. They don't like too many livyers around!" She says that "it's only now, this generation, possibly is in doubt, you know, about them. There *were* fairies." I am not sure whether by this last remark (spoken hastily like so many revealing phrases) she meant that the fairies were real to people in the past, or that they once did exist. In any case, fairy narratives can be in no danger of disappearance as long as there are narrators like Mrs. Kavanagh and audiences for her tales. Nor are new supernatural experiences in short supply. In 1988, someone Mrs. Kavanagh knows (I think her sister) was driving past a graveyard late at night when she saw, across the road from it, at least five figures in white shawls, with hoods over their heads. One had its arms out, as if holding a large book, but she could not see what it was doing. There was also some kind of animal, bigger than a sheep and smaller than a pony. Mrs. Kavanagh had no explanation of what this apparition could have been, but she suggested to the woman that she note the time and date and go by there again the same time the next year. As Mrs. Meaney might ask, "Now, what was that but the fairies?" Or to put it more formally, only the lack of a label makes this incident any different from a fairy vision of old.

The fairies may be gone, but it is still not hard to find people to talk about them. After giving a guest lecture to a Folklore class in 1989, I met Elizabeth Power, a first-year student from Frenchman's Cove on the Burin Peninsula, who says unabashedly that she believes in the fairies. She heard hundreds of stories growing up, many from her mother, who uses the terms "ghosts" and "fairies" interchangeably. Ms. Power remembers details of behaviour rather than details of narrative, and told me some things that I had neither heard myself nor read in MUNFLA, such as that infants were protected by candles over the crib and a piece of white silk in it until baptism, after which they were "in the hands of God" and the measures discontinued. In her childhood, boys were encouraged to be brash and bratty (they would not be reprimanded for "talking back," for example), because the fairies only wanted "good, innocent" children. (It was not that they preferred boys, but that boys spent more time playing away from the house than girls and so were in more danger of being taken.)[13] After a death in the community, children were not allowed in the area of the house in which it occurred because the fairies would be wandering there, looking for the dead person's soul; they were also not allowed near graveyards at night because of fairies. Ms. Power stresses that although fairy stories were told for entertainment and were treated with varying degrees of seriousness, they were not merely cautionary tales for controlling children. Her testimony shows that fairy traditions continue to influence thought and behaviour, and that there is still much to learn about them and from them.

7 | *Fairy Tradition as Discourse on Time and Change*

So this chapter closes with a call for more field research, not only on the fairies but on all the supernatural traditions with which they have been so inextricably woven. It would be better to have verbatim conversational recordings, as of Mrs. Hayes and Mrs. Maloney, than to have to piece discrete "items" together like jigsaw puzzles and deal with all the problems of distortion to which such a composite picture is prone. Mrs. Hayes and Mrs. Maloney's conversation shows how closely fairy traditions have been allied with religious beliefs and practices, many of which are now discarded by official church doctrine. Fairy tradition, having never been part of the official creed, cannot be so excised and so should outlive many aspects of folk religion, but it will not be the same without them; good records of the relationships must be made now for a future understanding of both the fairies and folk religion.

The call for more research may seem superfluous in the face of Newfoundland's present economic crisis, in which the decline of the fishery, recession, and governmental cutbacks in health and education threaten the existence of hundreds of communities. But it would be too bad if a subject of such historical, literary, and ethnological interest should fade away marked only by a single monograph. It is true that if fairy lore is dying it is a lingering death indeed, but change is undeniable, and charting it essential for a full understanding of past and present meaning. Change in "a tradition" over time is the sum of hundreds of individual changes like those described in this chapter; and change is not only in content and form, but in the way people talk about and use the whole concept.

One use that has remained constant is to compare the past with the present. Discussion of fairy lore almost invariably includes reflection on the past, and changes are crystallized by attributing the fairies' disappearance to modern devices or conditions, as when Mrs. Keough blames cars, Mr. Ryan lights and bustle, Mrs. Kavanagh crowds, Mrs. Ford roads, or Mrs. Maloney television. In the seventeenth century, John Aubrey also blamed new media and technology:

> Now-a-dayes Bookes are common, and most of the poor people understand letters; and the many good Bookes, and variety of Turnes of Affaires, have putt all the old Fables out of doors: and

> the divine art of Printing and Gunpowder have frightened away Robin-goodfellow and the Fayries. (*Brief Lives* xxv)

In fairy lore, the agents of extinction are periodically updated — perhaps soon people will suggest that increasingly popular all-terrain vehicles will squash the last of the fairies flat — but the effect is the same. Thus the "old fables" remain ever modern, and it may be that the habitual assignment to the past is the secret of their longevity.

8 | *Conclusion*

Oblique allusions to "those people" and "them" nicely connote the simultaneous likeness and otherness of the fairies. "They" often look like ourselves, and are seen to engage in some of the same activities (dancing, picking berries, conducting funerals) and to want some of the same things (music, food, babies). Yet they are essentially strangers, "a different people apart," as Elizabeth Mullaly, a Northern Bay woman in her nineties, told me. They have their own language, their own inscrutable motives, and their own territory. Often they are viewed (as one culture often does imagine another) as undifferentiated, dressing and looking alike, so that even their gender (if any) is not distinguishable. Laws unto themselves, their behaviour and its effects on humans might be good or bad, and the outcome unpredictable. Although defensive measures were available in the event of an encounter, it was best to avoid one in the first place by heeding traditional wisdom on such matters as staying in at night or building a house on the right spot.

Amorphous and polymorphous, the fairies are eminently adaptable to many situations and ends. They make excellent scapegoats for human failings and problems, and have taken the blame for illness, violence, disability, and death, as well as for more minor puzzles like a misplaced thimble or a wrong turn on the trail. For misfortunes that really are beyond human control, the fairies give form to otherwise inexplicably cruel fate. In this they serve as scapegoats for God himself: it was not He who caused the baby to shrivel and die, but His enemies from mythological time, the fallen angels. People who met an untimely end might also be said to be victims of their depredations, and even not to have died at all but to be with "them" somewhere, not in the everyday world, but not in the ultimate human destinations of heaven or hell (hence, in Catholic tradition, the association of the fairies with the in-between state of Purgatory).

Containing such important ideas about life, death, and cosmology, fairy tradition is intricately bound with folk religion, and priests have a correspondingly prominent place in fairy narrative. Their role is usually a powerful one, diagnosing or banishing the fairies, blessing someone who has met them, sometimes communicating with the fairies themselves. (A few accounts show a midwife in a comparable role, determining the presence of a fairy and what should be done about it.) Whether priests were really so active or not, their presence in narrative removes primary responsibility for a fairy interpretation from "the folk" (by putting it on the priest) at the same time it supports it (he being the authority in supernatural affairs). But even when fairy lore is justified in terms of official religion, it proposes alternative or complementary tenets to those of the church. The mixed or amoral character of the fairies — good, bad, both, neither — offers a more realistic vision of ambiguous life than the absolute categories of good and evil. Moreover, the nature of the fairy world (and thereby of the human one) is something a person can judge for herself; there is room for individual judgement and opinion based on evidence, not dogma. And since all experience (personal, second-hand, and legendary) is useful in evaluating the spiritual world, stories of ghosts, tokens, apparitions, and the like flow together with fairy stories, although they are not necessarily interchangeable or even similar phenomena. Unlike church doctrine, the debate is something anyone can take part in, or ignore if it is not to his taste.

Beyond philosophical contemplation, fairy stories provide entertainment and have many secular aspects, not the least of which is their setting in well-trod ways. As art, they transform the familiar, imparting new dimensions and potential to its beaten path. People need to be taken imaginatively away from the workaday world and its strictures, and turn to oral literature more frequently in the absence of television, books, and other means of escape. Fairy narrative does not take them so far as folktale; indeed, it is the very propinquity of the fairy plane, and its sudden subversions of the mundane, that lend it power. It is all the better if the story is scary, for listeners can return relieved to comfortable normality, like moviegoers from a horror film. Unlike the movies, though, storytelling is a democratic and interactive medium; it has its stellar tellers, but it would be a dull person who never had a thing to contribute. The knowledge that an account of an unusual experience will be well received might encourage one to place a "supernatural" interpretation on it, or at least to stress its strangeness. A good story has social value that lets one in on the fun.

In contrast to the value placed on performance is the reticence some people display in the face of inquiries. Here the documentation by "native" collectors is crucial, although they do not always get the story themselves, for even "insiders" can become "outsiders" when they have a microphone or pen in hand. Without their attempts, it could not have been established that there *are* things people will not readily discuss. Even rebuffed, insiders can write from memory, and some of the best records come from students writing of their own recollection and experience.

The greatest deficiency in the archive, as in the historical and ethnographic record in general, is the under-documentation of women's culture, which makes it hard to say whether fairy traditions are different between women and men. Even when collectors are both men and women, as among the students (the professionals have been mostly male), the preponderance of informants are male. It seems that men acquire a reputation for storytelling more often than women, and are more likely to put themselves forward to be interviewed. All three replies to my newspaper query came from men; I learned about the three couples of Chapter Four through referral to the husbands, but it turned out that the wives had well-developed narratives as well. (It is frustrating that in my present work on witchcraft, which so deeply involves women, it is easier to find male informants than female; this is due in part to the referral chain, where one contact suggests another — a man tends to send one on to another man.) Some gender differences are apparent from content, in certain narrative roles: mothers leave babies unattended and they get changed; lost girls are cared for by the fairies, who are more likely to "beat up" boys and men. Such differences could be further catalogued, but without contextual data they do not show much about whether men and women actually used fairy tradition differently, whether it had particular meaning correlative with gender. Women's social roles suggest that they would be the prime enactors of certain traditions, such as placing bread on babies and coercing children into good behaviour with fairy threats (and exemplary stories to back them up). The relocation of women upon marriage was an important mode of dissemination, as was men's travel to work in the fishery, construction, mines, or lumberwoods. Smaller, private interfamily and intra-community routes of transmission — and women's use of them — are largely unmapped.

The gender of the fairies themselves — or the lack thereof — is interesting in relation to human gender habits. Does their frequent appearance in same-sex groups reflect the sexual segregation of the tradition-bearer's society? Or does it reflect the opposite, the saltless asexuality of the fairy domain versus the fertile human one (hence their thieving of humans, especially children)? Does the virtual absence of male/female fairy couples reflect the unimportance of the human "couple" relative to other groupings, or does it suggest sterile sexlessness as well? Do the common fairy forms as children and old people suggest the latter, too? Like humans, the fairies mix for parties and dancing, but even then they dance in a circle, not in pairs. Their egalitarian uniformity extends to their clothes, usually alike when they appear in groups. Descriptions of these groups call to mind visions of plants and animals, a bog of pitcher plants or a flock of birds, organic images echoed in expressions like "a bank of fairies" or "fairies thick as grass." As biological forms, they can presumably reproduce themselves; perhaps, as Mr. Smith suggests, they never die, or perhaps their numbers are maintained by a constant infusion of the dead. But this is the kind of question no one (but a folklorist) seems to ask. Why do they dance or wear clothes anyway? One may as well ask why the sky is blue.

Looking too closely at the fairies in any case distracts from the real *dramatis personae* of fairy narrative, the people in them — humans, that is. In oral tradition, people do not tell stories about the fairies alone; stories that have fairies as main characters are a literary genre. The objective existence of the fairies is accepted as a given in fairy tradition — even if temporarily for the sake of the story — but it is defined in relation to humans, as it impinges on their lives. The fairies may make startling appearances, but once they are banished from a scene they are dismissed from further contemplation as well; the narrative follows the *human* back to his house, detailing his reception and recovery or whatever happens, and is not concerned with where the fairies went. As the fairies derive their importance from the human sphere, so they take colouring from it, and are different things to different people: "happy" to jolly Mr. Kelloway, duplicitous to tricky Mr. Smith. Their general character also varies from place to place: devilish in Bishop's Cove, feminine in Avondale, ghostly in Riverhead. Stories may bear a narrator's personal stamp even when the plot is constant, as in Mrs. Meaney's and her protagonists' "fearful" encounters versus the triumphant ones of bold Mrs. Mason. Sometimes it is hard to know whether a narrative or experience can be classified as a "fairy" one or not. Can Mr. Tucker's invisible walls be considered a fairy phenomenon, although he does not call them that? If not, does fairy tradition cease to exist if the word is dropped, but people continue to get lost in well-known surroundings, have household disturbances after fencing an old path, or hear mysterious music? Will people continue to wonder whether the explanation for such strange occurrences could lie in an order of beings other than themselves?

The fairies' best chance of survival depends on their pliability. It seems reasonable to suppose that synthesis of fairy lore with "modern" folklore and "new age" psychic lore will increase, although it is possible that there could be a complete switchover from, say, fairies to extraterrestrial beings without much hybridization. In making such connections, people combine oral tradition with a variety of media (books, newspapers including the tabloid variety, television, movies, radio) and make accordingly eclectic interpretations of their own and others' experience. The study of evolutionary change requires continual fieldwork with a wide conceptual net. Given the special characteristics of Newfoundland legendry, in which ancient types, defunct elsewhere, exist alongside a completely modern corpus of wormy hamburgers and deadly suntan salons, an unprecedented profile of change over time could be built. Will the devil give up card games for teenage cults? Will the aliens drive out the fairies, or have they been here all along in that guise?

Predictions of the fairies' demise may be, as they have been for centuries, premature. From their long pedigree and transatlantic durability, and from the plethora of MUNFLA accounts, it may be concluded that fairy stories fascinate; they should not suddenly stop doing so even though the demand for them — as for many types of oral literature — has declined. Extraterrestrial aliens could neatly replace the fairies as strangers. But their flying visits from afar are unlike the fairies' proprietary inhabitation of the woods, bogs, and barrens; the aliens do not live next door, and so cannot inhabit the imagination in the same way. They are not the numinous neighbours the fairies have been, and their distant galaxies do not have the compelling immanence of the fairy world.

Notes

Preface to the First Edition

1. "Notes" 95. Although Wayland D. Hand in "European Fairy Lore in the New World" notes that "a considerable body ... has reached American shores," his citations, like the bulk of field reports — Halpert, Moses, Kelly, Farmer, Leach ("Celtic Tales") — come mostly from first- or second-generation Irish immigrants, a preponderance that probably led Baughman to observe that "belief in fairies has never at any time taken hold in America" (xii). In *Bluenose Ghosts* (first published in 1957), Helen Creighton includes a single fairy story from Cape Breton (Nova Scotia), adding, "I had often inquired for fairies but, until then it seemed that they had not crossed the water from the old land" (238), but by 1968 she had found a few more examples for *Bluenose Magic* and concluded that "the few instances we have prove that belief in their presence is not foreign to our soil" (102). They are perhaps not so rare as Creighton thought: in the summer of 1984, Martha MacDonald recorded several fairy stories on the Iona Peninsula of Cape Breton in the course of fieldwork for her Folklore master's thesis at MUN (86-89; personal communication); another Folklore student, Ian Mackinnon, mentioned a Cape Breton priest of his acquaintance who is a believer in the fairies (personal communication).

Chapter One

1. I devoted a chapter of my thesis to the printed record of the fairies' protracted demise.

2. Number 5070 in Reidar Th. Christiansen's *The Migratory Legends: A Proposed List of Types with a Systematic Catalogue of the Norwegian Variants* (91).

Chapter 2
1. He died on 27 March 1983 at the age of thirty-nine.

2. This is the only instance of this term I have encountered, although there is an Upper Island Cove reference to "jackies" (see Chapter Five). The St. John's *Daily News* for 16 July 1894 carried an article headed, "Very Uncanny: A Crazed Man's Actions Yesterday," describing a disturbance created by a man "roaring and crying at the top of his voice. It was one of those unfortunate men named Littlejohn." It is a common enough surname in St. John's and on Bell Island, however, and my late neighbour, Estelle Morris (long of St. John's), knew of no stigma attached to it.

3. The community is unnamed, but judging from the student's surname and the paper's content, it is almost surely Riverhead.

4. Ó Heochaidh summarizes an Irish text:
    > Narrator begins by saying that the "old people" believed that many of the dead returned to earth, some as they were when they were alive, others in the shapes of lambs, very often black lambs, and that those souls who returned were so numerous that every dock-leaf had a soul sheltering behind it. Furthermore, the lonely hills were so full of the "Good People" — the Fairies — that ordinary people paid no attention to them! ("Seanchas" 205).

    John Mannion describes the Riverhead area as settled primarily by Irish rural immigrants from the southeast counties of Wexford, Waterford, and Tipperary, brought by English Westcountrymen who called at Waterford on their way to the fishery; he also notes that migration to the area was "but a small part of the wave of southern Irish immigration that reached the shores of the Avalon during the first two decades of the nineteenth century" (*Irish Settlements* 19).

Colin Lee writes that "it is believed that all the Lees in Riverhead descended from three brothers who settled there from England over two hundred years ago" (82-205/informant data sheet), and Mrs. Meaney (a Lee before her marriage) told Colleen Meaney that the first settler, Henry Lee, a fisherman, arrived in Riverhead between 1735 and 1740, although she did not say from where (79-374/12). Mannion's case study of an Irish merchant family in Placentia shows the inextricable early ethnic mixture of the Placentia Bay fishery in which Henry Lee, whether English or Irish, was probably involved ("Transatlantic" 374–76).

5. Minor White Latham writes that it is "one of the earliest origins assigned to them," citing *The Early South-English Legendary* of the thirteenth century; he also quotes Christopher Middleton's sixteenth-century *The Famous Historie of Chinon of England* on "Such creatures as we call Fairies, whome some imagine to be those spirites that fell downe upon the earth, and since that time inhabit the severall corners thereof" (42).

6. Migratory Legend 5050 in Christiansen (89). For Irish versions, see Ó Muirgheasa (138–39); Croker (1:37–46); Gregory (*Poets* 109–10, *Visions* 240–41); Kennedy (*Fictions* 87–96); Bryan Jones ("Stories" 339–40). Killip gives a Manx version (31–32).

7. Baughman (122); it is D1960.2 in the *Motif-Index of Folk Literature* (Thompson 2:350), although it is a narrative type rather than a motif. Hardwick (164–69), Rhys (2:458–84), Hartland (170–73, 207–21), Briggs (*Dictionary* 370–73), Croker (3:266–72), and Bryan Jones ("Cavan" 321–23) give versions of what Thompson calls "Kuffhauser. King asleep in mountain," in which a culture hero (Arthur, Bruce, etc.) and his army are found asleep by someone who is led to their castle or cave (often visible only at certain times, often full of finery or treasure) by a stranger. Inside, the finder semi-awakens the sleepers when he partially unsheathes a sword, rings a bell, blows a horn, etc. (Sometimes he is warned against this, sometimes urged to do so.) He is frightened when the sleepers stir, and pushes the sword back; fleeing, he is attacked or pursued by the angry warriors, who would have been freed by his

unsheathing of the sword (or analogous act, such as "taking something" in the Riverhead texts).

Detail as well as structure show "Brass Castle" and "Twisted Ramrod" as unmistakably belonging to this type. The stranger, for example, may carry a rod with magical properties; the captives may be arrayed in rows. Dáithí Ó hÓgáin's study of D1960.2 in Ireland is especially useful for comparison (some of the fifty-one texts are in English). These show the legend blending with fairy tradition even when the culture hero element is relevant; and the latter is omitted in some. Other parallels include designation of the men as "enchanted," and the guide as a "well dressed stranger" (287).

Parallels can also be seen in "The Giant's Stairs," given by Croker (2:315–26), in which a blacksmith rescues a boy from rows of hundreds of identical children imprisoned in an underground cave. When the giant asks to shake hands, the smith holds out a plough-iron, and when the giant twists it the children laugh, enabling the right child to make himself known to the smith. The child has not changed in seven years, but grows up to be noted for skill in working brass and iron. The twisting of a rod proffered instead of a hand is found in some versions of ML5010, "The Visit to the Old Troll. The Handshake" (Christiansen 86), in the Irish tale type 726, "The Dream Visit" (Ó Súilleabháin and Christiansen *The Types of the Irish Folktale* 143), and in a Danish version of "sleeping warriors" (Hartland 213). In connection with the unexplained title "Brass Castle," it is worth noting that in one version, a man finds a cave full of brass vessels (Rhys 471–72).

"Brass Castle" and "Twisted Ramrod" might be related to what Cross lists as a motif in the *Motif-Index of Early Irish Literature*, "H1385.0.1": Unspelling quest: journey to disenchant (free) captives."

8. It is easy to imagine the influence of even one book on the repertoire of an individual or a community. A Colliers student described her grandmother, who died in 1970, as a strong believer in fairies and the community reader:

> Every Sunday afternoon was a very special occasion. People, usually the same people every week, would come to visit. With them they would bring a book. These people usually could not read. They came

to have my grandmother read for them. She was a very good and expressive reader. This special storytime was somewhat similar to our present day soap opera. When she would reach the climax or an especially exciting part of the story she would stop and continue the story the next week. This custom went on for years and years. She also read at wakes. She was sort of the official parish reader. (81-455/23)

In Ireland a great deal of fairy material made its way into popular print, which could have crossed the Atlantic along with oral lore. Yeats mentions chapbooks: "They are to be found brown with turf smoke on cottage shelves, and are, or were, sold on every hand by the pedlars, but cannot be found in any library of this city of the Sassenach. *The Royal Fairy Tales*, *The Hibernian Tales*, and *The Legends of the Fairies* are the fairy literature of the people" (*Fairy Tales* 7). "Lageniensis" (John O'Hanlon) said in 1896 that the "Tales of the Queen's County Peasantry," a column by John Keegan (d. 1849) in *The Leinster Express*, was read with avidity at ceilis (77–78). Croker's *Fairy Legends* was very popular and was reprinted repeatedly; it was available in abridged form as a volume in "Murray's Family Library," for example, and was extracted and rewritten in popular collections as well, often without acknowledgement. An item in the St. John's *Public Ledger* for 4 December 1838 refers to the connection between sneezing and the fairies "found in Crofton Croker's well known and amusing story." (Thanks to Clara Murphy for this reference.)

Printed collections of Irish tales were also available from the United States ("the Boston States," as they are sometimes called in Newfoundland because of the many Newfoundlanders who sought work in Boston). P.J. Kennedy's *Irish Fireside Stories, Tales and Legends* of 1900 contains a catalogue of the other offerings of the "Excelsior Catholic Publishing House" of New York; these include the 570-page *Fairy Folk Stories* (no author), *Legends and Fairy Tales of Ireland* ("over four hundred pages," no author), and *Turf Fire Stories and Fairy Tales of Ireland* (no author).

9. Mrs. Meaney allowed Julia Bishop and me to borrow these to copy for MUNFLA, and later I discovered that another student, Julie Hauri, had in 1978 planned to make Mrs. Meaney the subject of a master's thesis and had

copied some scrapbooks as well. In that set (78-279) there were seventeen songs, and in those that I copied (85-198), sixty-three more; each page was photographed and given a "P" (photograph) number for MUNFLA. The songbooks also contain recitations and clippings from newspapers and magazines, which are mostly locally composed poems or songs or pieces on local history and people. If the pages of songs show a concern with the preservation of tradition — Mrs. Meaney thinks today's songs are "no good" — the clippings suggest an alertness to new sources and materials. Many are of a humorous nature, such as limericks, and contrast interestingly with the tragic character of many of the songs. Some are on traditional themes, such as a beer advertisement featuring "An old island story: Kinchler beats the devil" (P4597). There are also notes of Mrs. Meaney's own, such as a list of deaths for 1973 (including that of Austin Breen at the age of eighty-five) and the rather lyrical observation, "On Monday night Feb. 17th two stars appeared together in the western sky, they were called Venus and Jupiter, they were travelling side by side" (P4669, P4614).

10. In one Irish version, for example, he is told, "If you had to pull out that sword Ireland was free, but you were too big a coward," but in another, "If you had to touch that sword or pick it up, that army would go out and kill every man, woman, and child that they met till they'd come to the place where they'd have to stop" (Ó hÓgáin 289 and 286). The variation argues against a single printed source for the Riverhead texts.

11. An example of what in ballad scholarship Wimberly calls "riddlecraft," whereby Otherworlders set riddles "in an effort to get mortals under their power" (301), and David Buchan calls "witcombat" ("Witcombat Ballads"). I do not quite understand the riddle, unless it means that a woman can only keep secret something that she does not know, that is, she cannot keep a secret.

12. A third version from St. Mary's retains the key utterance, although not as a fatefully broken prohibition:

> There was a girl up there to Liz's Point [in Riverhead]. They said the people, the good people, took her, you know, they used to live there

at that time. But they took her, what they used to call the fairies, took her. And be God, she got a chance one day or one evening or something, to her mother or father; she said, "I'll be passing along this evening," she said, "and if you don't catch me," she said, "at that time, you'll never get me back." Did you ever hear that? And be God, she was passing along and she said to her mother, she said, "Now or never." [Second informant: She was running?] She was running. So her mother never caught her, so they never seen her after. So that's why they call it Liz's Point. (73-107:C1814/m.t.)

13. For Irish versions, see Curtin (179), Kenneth Jackson (91), and Patrick Kennedy (*Fictions* 105–09).

14. "Indeede your grandams maides were wont to set a boll of milke before him [Incubus] and his cousin Robin Good-fellow, for grinding of malt or mustard, and sweeping the house at midnight" (Reginald Scot 48).

15. This is a widespread narrative type, for which E.B. Lyle gives many references in "The Ballad Tam Lin and Traditional Tales of Recovery from the Fairy Troop." (The shape-shifting of "Tam Lin," through which Janet has to hold on to the captive before he can be freed in his true shape, appears in this narrative and in "Liz's Point" as a physical struggle with the fairies themselves.) Walter Map gives a legend of a man who plucks his "dead" wife from "a great company of women" (Hartland 1923, 187–89). Padraig O Tuathail gives several Wicklow versions, in one of which the lost girl makes the characteristic final cry: "Gone, gone, for evermore!" (84–86). One of two versions in Kennedy's *Legendary Fictions* includes the "dead" wife's instructions to leave food out for her every night. More recent Irish versions may be found in Glassie (*Ballymenone* 543–51; references 779), and Ó hEochaidh (46–49; references 376).

The broom or other item is a "dummy" substituted for the stolen person. Archibald Campbell gives a changeling narrative in which a withered leaf is found in the coffin (71–72); Napier one with a wooden figure (41); A.A. MacGregor, an oak log (*Peat Fire* 93–94); and a green billet of wood is found in *The Fairies of Tomnahurich*. Yeats tells of a girl taken by fairies: "a villager was said to have long struggled to hold her from them, but at last they prevailed, and he found nothing in his hands but a broom-stick" (*Celtic Twilight* 36). William Wilde tells of the exhumation of the coffin of a fairy-taken woman "in the full conviction of finding only a birch broom, a log of wood, or the skeletal remains of some deformed monster in it" (127).

16. "Bibe" is the southeast Irish term for banshee, the English spelling of "badhbh," a term used in Waterford, south Kilkenny, and south Tipperary (Lysaght 34–36). In Newfoundland, "the Bibe was a spirit whose wail foretold death in a household" (FSC73-142/64), but both "bibe" and "banshee" can refer to a range of fairy-like phenomena beyond death portents. Neither have the specifically female denotation found in Ireland, nor are they solitary figures. "Watch out, the banshees will get you," older children would tell smaller ones in Harbour Grace, said a student, adding, "banshee meaning fairies" (FSC76-143/*). In 1968, a young Bell Island man encountered the banshee, "a sort of cloudy mist (human-like) which appeared only on the full moon of a Wednesday night, and sort of enveloped anyone who happened to meet it"; he banished it with the sign of the cross before this could happen (FSC73-31/31). An informant from Red Island described "bibes or spirits" that might sound like "a child crying or someone moaning," and told of one man who followed a light — "the bibe" — to a graveyard where he was immobilized (79-435/38). A Riverhead collector said that "strange noises like a dog or rooster when neither animal is present are considered an omen; the old people refer to this as a 'Bibe'" (73-169/4), and a Cape Broyle collector described "the bibe" as "a cry that people often heard years ago" that would lead one away in pursuit of it (FSC76-82/*).

17. McPherson notes that in Scotland, "an apparition might give 'the dead man's nip'," producing a spot or mark on the skin of someone who maligned the memory of the deceased (131).

18. Mr. Hayes said this to Martin Lovelace on 17 February 1985. I was in the next room with Mrs. Hayes, who would not tell me about the fairies until I knew her several years (see Chapter 7); by contrast, Mr. Hayes had never set

eyes on Martin until this occasion. A Branch collector says the ropes were cut so that "the spirit could rest," claiming that the practice originated in Ireland as a protection against theft of the corpse for medical experimentation (FSC71-26/33).

19. "If suspected children were heard speaking above the understanding of children, it was considered a proof that they were changelings," says Davies, "this was a widespread belief in Wales" (133). (They should then be thrown into the river or threatened with a red hot shovel.)

20. Hartland, for instance, commented on Pitré's study of Nicolas Pipe the merman, which traced the legend from Map in the twelfth century through thirty-three versions to the mid-nineteenth: "It may be said in general terms that the farther they were away from the alleged time of 'the Fish,' the more they knew about him, and the greater the wonders they told of him" (Map 205). Gustav Jahoda cites a "census of hallucinations" undertaken by the Society for Psychical Research in which "it was observed that the most dramatic cases tended to be those alleged to have happened a long time ago" (43).

21. In Sweden, according to Klein, Nicolovius found that people preferred to consult a klokgumma (clever woman) who did not live in their own village, because the one at home "lived too close to be regarded as truly klok." Klein also translates Tillhagen on the kloka, that "their reputation was the least in the place where they lived" and "belief grew ... with distance" (329). In her field research on witchcraft in France, Jeanne Favret-Saada found that "a serious crisis will never be taken to the local unwitcher. People prefer to choose their therapist beyond some boundary (in a neighbouring diocese or département), in any case outside the network of acquaintanceship" (20).

22. A lost boy's hair turned grey, and he was found "smoking a pipe, just as the fairies did" (76-269/21); another boy taken by the fairies was found with his nose stuffed full of straw; he "grew whiskers and a beard and smoked a pipe like an old man," stopped growing, and died a year later (86-67/6-7).

23. Leather 47. Robert Wildhaber has devoted a recent monograph to "der Altervers des Wechselbalgs."

24. Several cases were documented in court trials of the late 1800s (Croker 2: vii–ix; J. Cooke 300). Yeats discussed a Tipperary case with an old woman who told him that the man who did it was "very superstitious," since "everybody knew that you must only threaten, for whatever injury you did to the changeling the faeries would do to the living person they had carried away" (Gregory *Visions* 360). The practice, or at least the idea of rough treatment to restore health, is very old (David Buchan suggests that it prefigures modern medical treatments that employ shock). The penitential (handbook of penances) of Theodore, Archbishop of Canterbury (668–90), decrees that "if any woman puts her daughter upon a roof or into an oven for the cure of a fever, she shall do penance for seven years" (McNeill and Gamer 198); Bartholomew Iscanus, Bishop of Exeter (1161–84), prescribes forty days for "he who places his child upon a roof or in an oven in order to restore his health" (McNeill and Gamer 350). Etienne de Bourbon (b. 1195), a Paris inquisitor, gives in his "Preacher's Manual" a detailed picture of ritual proceedings undertaken against supposed changelings at the shrine of St. Guinefort (a greyhound), in which the mothers called upon the "hobgoblins" to take back the sickly children, "who as they said, belonged to the fiends," and return their own healthy ones (Coulton 93–94). (Jean-Claude Schmitt's study of the legend of St. Guinefort contains some interesting medieval material on changelings, including representations in religious iconography: 74–81.)

    "That the Fairies would steale away young children and putt others in their places: verily believed by old woemen in those dayes: and by some yet living," wrote John Aubrey in seventeenth-century England, but he makes no mention of getting the original children back (*Works* 203).

25. Susan Schoon Eberly, for example, correlates descriptions of changelings with various birth defects and congenital and other infantile illnesses, as Piachewski did in a 1938 monograph on "der wechselbalg"; and Lindow says that "J.S. Moller has convincingly demonstrated that the most common causes of such stories were idiocy, mongolism, hydrocephalus, cretinism,

rickets, and atrepsy" ("Rites" 42). Mrs. Mason referred to an article in the St. John's *Evening Telegram* for 9 March 1967, about a child suffering from progeria, or premature aging, as "an example of a changeling"; but whether she meant that the child would have been considered a changeling in earlier times, or whether it would still be considered fairy-afflicted cannot be determined from the context (67-4B/17).

26. Halpert discusses the visitation of parental sins on offspring in "The Cursed Child Legend." In her memoirs of work as a nurse on the South Coast in 1939–40, Ilka Dickman, a European physician, describes the birth of an anencephalic child. The midwife said they ought to name it quickly, and Dickman ran to get the teacher to baptize it:

> In the meantime, in the house of the newborn, there is the mother, crying in her bed; the father, sitting next to the dying baby, deeply shaken; the grandfather, utterly upset; all of them worrying themselves to death not because of the misfortune itself, but rather on account of the unknown sin they must have committed, to which the deformed child is ascribed. (27)

Usually maternal impressions or "marking" are attributed to "natural" causes, such as a fright or an unsatisfied craving during pregnancy; the unmet desire for strawberries, for example, might result in a strawberry-shaped mark; or a mother frightened by a mouse might have a child with a mouse-shaped mark on it (one woman frightened by a bird had a baby that was "half-bird" — 84-203/19). A pregnant Bell Island woman who opened the door to a fairy or "dwarf-like man with a smile on his face" gave birth a month later to a baby "with the same smile on its face" (72-117/9-10). My late neighbour, Estelle Morris, always maintained that she was afraid of cats because her mother had been frightened by a cat when carrying her.

27. One collector said that boys in Mall Bay (near Riverhead) used to wear plaid skirts until they were five or six, but offers no explanation (FSC80-296/*). This is one of those customs the true explanation of which is quite hard to judge; probably, like most fairy lore, it varies as to belief. There was a hot debate

on the usage in Ireland in *Notes and Queries* around the turn of the century: G.H. White cited *The Hospital* for 1905 that Connemara nurses often met adolescent boys in petticoats, which the mothers insisted were to prevent the fairies from taking them, "but the common-sense nurses often attribute the custom to motives of economy." In reply, R.A.S. MacAlister wrote that Aran Islands boys wore skirts because they were easy to make, and when he told a native of the "fairy" explanation, the man was astonished: "Well, there isn't a man, woman, or child on the island that believes the likes of that," he said, "but there was a man here with a notebook a while ago, and the people sent him away with it filled." Estyn Evans says it was done "to mislead the fairies," noting that boys were "preferred and cherished"; he also suggests the fact of their biological inferiority (being more susceptible to illness and death than girls) as reasons for the fairies' desire for them ("Beliefs" 42). Sam Hanna Bell also gives the preference for boys as the reason for petticoats (75). Parry-Jones claimed that in Wales "only male infants were stolen; there does not seem to be on record a case in which a baby girl was taken" (51). (I have heard no statements to the effect that the fairies prefer boys in Newfoundland, and there seem to be an equal number of each sex "taken.")

28. A Latin treatise compiled in France in the early fourteenth century includes a tale in which thieves disguised as women break into a house, where they sing, "Take one, give back a hundred," as they remove the most valuable items, unopposed by the occupant who thinks they are "good beings" who will increase his belongings a hundredfold (Cohn 214). In one of *The Royal Hibernian Tales*, a thief interrupted in a nighttime burglary impersonates a spirit in order to escape the awakened householder: "In those days people were more easily imposed on, than in this age, so that the gentleman, believing him to be a spirit, ventured up and unlocked the door, and he passed out quickly" (167). An 1814 Irish account tells of a woman who puts some food in her neighbours' house while they are out, "inverting at the same time all the little furniture of the place"; the "old woman of the family" takes the visit to have been from the fairies ("Irish Folk-Lore" 140). In Scotland, a "superstitious" old man — he once saw fairies riding cats on Halloween — thought himself harassed by "evil spirits" when two pranksters put a hook

down his chimney and yanked his hat off his head (Wilson 99–101). The 1734 edition of the chapbook *Round About Our Coal Fire* contains a narrative in which a woman insists she got a ring from the fairies, despite her husband's claim it belonged to another man. Adds the author:

> The fairies were very necessary in families, as much as bread, salt, pepper, or any other such commodity, I believe; because they used to walk in my father's house, and if I can judge right of the matter, they were brought into all the families by the servants; for in old times folks used to go to bed at nine o'clock, and when the master and mistress were laid on their pillows, the men and maids, if they had a game at romps, and blundered upstairs, or jumbled a chair, the next morning everyone would swear it was the fairies, and that they heard them stamping up and down stairs all night, crying, "Waters locked, waters locked," when there was no water in any pail in the kitchen. (Rimbault 481–82)

29. For references to the taboo on eating, see Hartland: "We touch here upon a very ancient and widespread superstition, which we may pause to illustrate from different parts of the world" (41).

30. In the interest of future research, it should be noted that on a third visit to Mrs. Meaney, to check that she had received a copy of the tape I had mailed, I found that the tape had been much in circulation among the neighbours and family; so people have heard the stories, whether directly from Mrs. Meaney or the tape.

Chapter Three

1. People recovered from the fairies are often, like Tam Lin of ballad fame (Child No. 39), pulled off horses — or last seen on them, if the rescue attempt fails (Eamonn Ó Tuathail "Sgealta 166; Pádraig Ó Tuathail 84–85).

2. It is not uncommon for several individuals in the same Newfoundland community to have the same name (hence the ubiquity of nicknames), but Tom Moore confirms that there was only one Jack Parsley.

3. Haddon says that an Irish child who fell down accidentally would be given salt because the fall might have been caused by the fairies trying to run away with it (358).

4. I know of no reports in MUNFLA of ways to ensure against inadvertently building on a path. In Ireland, tentative boundaries for the proposed structure might be marked out with sticks or stones, and if these were left undisturbed, the site was taken as acceptable (Duncan; Duffy; Ó Danachair; Mac Gréine "Longford" 267 and "House"). There are many Irish narratives about houses built on "passes": Mac Gréine gives several about people having to move houses, and notes that the passes were usually between fairy forts; Edward O'Toole gives an example in which a little man warns a builder that his prospective site is on a "pass"; Helen Roe says that tenants forced to take such a house in Laoighis always left doors or windows open for "those who wish to use the pass" (26). I have not noticed in Irish tradition the same idea applied to old (human) roads or paths.

5. Fairy funerals are common in English and Irish tradition. Briggs gives references and texts in her *Dictionary of Fairies*, including William Blake's vision of one; Redmond gives a Wexford example from 1894, seen by three men (363); for more examples, see Bowker (83–96); Robert Hunt (218–19); and Wiltshire (17–18, 31).

6. Lewis Spence outlines the theory of the "manikin soul" in relation to fairy lore in *British Fairy Origins* (68–70).

7. David MacRitchie (inspired by J.F. Campbell) was the chief proponent of this school, with his *Testimony of Tradition*. Lewis Spence summarizes the arguments in *British Fairy Origins* (56–59).

8. Heywood's Hierarchy of Angells of 1635 includes the passage:

> In John Milesius any man may read
> Of divels in Samartia honored,

> Call'd Kottri, or Kibaldi; such as wee
> Pugs and Hob-Goblins call. Their dwellings bee
> In corners of old houses least frequented,
> Or beneath stacks of wood: and these convented,
> Make fearfull noise in buttries and in dairies;
> Robin Good-fellowes some, some call them fairies.
> In solitarie roomes these uprores keepe,
> And beat at dores to wake men from their sleepe;
> Seeming to force locks, be they ne'er so strong,
> And keeping Christmasse gambols all night long.
> Pots, glasses, trenchers, dishes, pannes, and kettles,
> They will make dance about the shelves and settles,
> As if about the kitchen tost and cast,
> Yet in the morning nothing found misplac't. (Ritson 14)

Thomas Churchyard wrote in 1578:

> The Phayries are another kinde of elfes that daunce in darke,
> Yet can light candles in the night, and vanish like a spark;
> And make a noyse and rumbling great among the dishes oft,
> And wake the sleepie sluggish maydes that lyes in the kitchen loft.
> (M. Latham 51)

Earlier still — in the thirteenth century — Gervase of Tilbury described the "Follets" of England "who inhabit the houses of the simple rustics, and can be driven away neither by holy water nor exorcisms; and because they are not seen, they afflict those who are entering with stones, billets, and domestic furniture; whose words, for certain, are heard in the human manner, and their forms do not appear" (Ritson 16–17).

9. For an analysis, see Lovelace (1991). In Spring 1988 Kathy White of CBC radio told me that she keeps a horse near Kilbride, just outside St. John's. When she told the owner of the stable that she wanted to bring a stocking for her horse on Christmas Eve, he became upset and insisted she could not go into the barn that night; when she persisted, the whole family joined in dissuading her.

10. Both cyclical appearances and the braiding of horses' manes are documented in French tradition. Paul-Yves Sébillot wrote of "les fées":

> Mon père, dans ses *Traditions and Superstitions de la Haute-Bretagne*, leur a consacré plus de cinquante pages, il s'est livre a une enquête sur elles a une epoque (1880) ou nombre de sexagenaires avaient vu les fées. Une femme di 88 ans les avait même vues dans son enfance. L'opinion generale était qu'elles avaient disparu au commencement du XIX siècle. (7)

The idea is the basis of the story that some peasants, seeing an automobile for the first time around the turn of the century, took it for the return of the fairies (Sebillot 8; Schloesser).

Guillaume d'Auvergne, a bishop of Paris who died in 1249, describes spirits in the likeness of girls and women in shining robes, who frequented woods and stables, where they plaited horses' manes (Cohn 214).

Of course, neither idea is restricted to France. Rhys found the idea that "they had their periods" in Wales (1:277); an Armagh informant told Paterson in the 1930s, "it's speyed [foretold] the fairies will come again" (90); and a Donegal man told Evans Wentz that the fairies "were terribly plentiful a hundred years ago, and they'll come back again" (73).

As to braiding, a Dorset informant said that a carter would tell him, as a boy finding the horses sweaty and knotty-maned, "Oh, the fairies have been out again" (Begg "Witchcraft" 71). Herrick gives "a charm for stables":

> Hang up Hooks, and Sheers to scare
> Hence the Hag, that rides the Mare,
> Till they be all over wet,
> With the mire, and the sweat:
> This observ'd, the Manes shall be
> Of your horses, all knot-free. (375)

John Cousins reports in his MA thesis that braiding the horses' manes is "the last bailiwick of the fairies" on Prince Edward Island.

11. In Wiltshire, said Aubrey:

> Some were led away by Fairies, as was a Hind [farm overseer] riding upon Hakpen with corne, led a dance to the Devises. So was a shepherd of Mr. Brown of Winterburn Basset: but never any afterwards enjoy themselves. He sayd the ground opened, and he was brought into strange places under ground where they used musicall Instruments, violls, and Lutes, such (he sayd) as Mr. Thomas did play on. Elias Ashmole Esq, sayes, there was in his time a Piper in Lichfield that was entertayned by the Fairies, and had often-times seen them, who sayd, he knew which houses of the Towne were Fayryground. (*Three Works* 204)

12. Flying haystacks are well-attested in Irish tradition: one J.D.D. gives a Wexford narrative in which the "good people" transport one across a river to Waterford. For an English parallel we are again indebted to Aubrey, who records in *The Natural History of Wiltshire*:

> Anno 1660, I being then at dinner with Mr. Stokes at Titherton, news was brought in to us that a whirlwinde had carried some of the hay-cocks over high elmes by the house: which bringes to my mind a story that is credibly related of one Mr. J. Parsons, a kinsman of ours, who, being a little child, was sett on a hay-cock, and a whirlwind took him up with half the hay-cock and carried him over high elmes, and layd him down safe, without any hurt, in the next ground. (16)

13. Unaccessioned tape submitted to Marie-Annick Desplanques by David Abbott for Folklore 2000, Summer 1989. My transcription and pseudonyms.

14. Elidorus, whose visits to fairyland were recorded by Giraldus Cambrensis in the twelfth century, said that the fairies would say "Ydor Ydorum" to mean "bring water" and "halgein ydorum" to mean "bring salt" (391–92). According to Giraldus and other commentators, this was supposed to resemble Greek; could the double construction (with the "I-you" sound) and its association with drink be a remarkably persistent motif?

15. Keightley cites Brand for "cole-pexy" in Dorset, and an 1825 reference to the "colt-pixy" of Hampshire, "a supposed spirit or fairy, which in the shape of a horse wickers, i.e. neighs, and misleads horses into bog, etc." (305). Ruth Tongue gives the south Somerset phrase "cull pixying" for gathering the apples left after harvest, that is, gathering what was left for the fairies (*Somerset* 119); Gillian Edwards gives "colt-pixy" defined as a verb by Brewer, "to take what belongs to the pixies," and cites Halliwell on the Devon expression "colt-pixy" for beating down apples too high to be reached — "colt" being an "old cant term meaning to cheat," hence, cheating the pixies (158).

16. Robert Herrick, along with his fashionable Elizabethan airy-fairy conceits, wrote more authentic verses based on observation of his Devon parishioners:

> Bring the holy crust of Bread,
> Lay it underneath the head;
> 'Tis a certain Charm to keep
> Hags away, while Children sleep. (426)

Another:

> If ye feare to be affrighted
> When ye are (by chance) benighted:
> In your pocket for a trust,
> Carry nothing but a Crust:
> For that holy piece of Bread,
>
> Charmes the danger, and the dread. (426)

Clobery, another Devon poet, referred in 1659 to "Old countrey folk, who pixie-leading fear, bear bread about them to prevent that harm" (M. Latham 248). Much later — in 1874 — a Mrs. Whitcombe remarked that in Devon, "there are the wicked elves, who change the babies in their cradles, and to prevent this mishap many a mother in former days placed a crust of bread under the cradle pillow" and that Eucharist bread would be taken home from church by communicants "to preserve the house from all evil" (45–46).

17. Ó'Súilleabháin includes oatmeal, not bread, in his list of protective talismans (*Handbook* 462), and while the distinction is minor, he does not mention that they were carried habitually, that is, by persons not in vulnerable circumstances. Estyn Evans says that in Mourne County food, including oat bread, was carried in the mountains against the "hungry grass," a supernatural affliction closely related to the fairies (MacManus Chapter Eight, Lady Wilde *Legends* 183) that causes sudden intense hunger, weakness, and confusion (204). Oatmeal and salt might be sprinkled on children on certain days (May 1 or Halloween) or on journeys (Bell 75–77; Foster 30, 258). Oatmeal might also be carried to keep fairies away by persons travelling after nightfall in Highland Scotland, according to J.G. Campbell, who also says that midwives would leave a cake of oatmeal by the bed of a newborn (47, 38). Kirk says that "the Tramontaines [Scotch-Irish] to this day, put bread, the Bible, or a piece of iron, in womens bed when travelling [i.e., travailling], to save them from being thus stolen" (54). For northeast Scotland, J.M. McPherson mentions bread, the Bible, and cheese under the pillow at childbirth (110), and a birth celebration or "merry meht" at which all visitors had to partake of bread (35).

Bread or bread and cheese were carried on the way to a child's baptism to be offered to anyone met on the way (Wood-Martin 39). The offering sometimes had a special name: "blithe meat" or "blithe bread" on the Isle of Man and in Scotland (Killip 68); "Kimbly," "the child's fuggan" (flat cake), and "the christening crib" in Cornwall, where one informant said it was intended to ward off the evil eye and turn away envy (Courtney 157–58). Only a few Newfoundland collectors have specifically mentioned baptism: one said that in St. Joseph's, St. Mary's Bay, "many people would never take their babies to the church to be baptised without a slice of bread in their pocket to keep the fairies away" (75-250/32), and another that "company-bread" was put in the clothes of infants on the way to baptism around St. Mary's Bay and Placentia Bay, the idea being that the fairies would take the bread instead of the child (FSC64-5/221). (The *Dictionary of Newfoundland English* cites a 1924 reference to "company bread" as "bread carried when alone to ward off the fairies" — Story et al. 111.)

18. Gregor observes that in Scotland "old people looked with much reverence on 'bread,' as well as meal. To abuse either one was regarded as profane" ("Bread" 196).

19. In his essay on "The Symbolic Significance of Salt," Ernest Jones discusses the sexual significance of salt, bread, and money as used in their various combinations for protection against evil. To summarize his argument crudely, salt = semen = urine = the essence of humanity. If the lines of his argument were applied to fairy tradition, the fairies could be said to represent sterility and impotence, and are thus banished with "vital" substances. David Buchan's delineation of the strain of "sterile negation" in the interaction between humans and otherworlders in wit-combat ballads would support such an equation (390). It is interesting, too, to consider the "wet" and "dry" symbolism Alan Dundes finds in evil eye beliefs (life = liquid, death = drying) in relation to the fairies: people taken by the fairies are often prematurely old, shriveled and withered ("scriveled up"), that is, dried up. Not only major motifs — throwing water, leaving water out for the souls — but minor motifs gain significance in this light: for example, Dundes's suggestion that toasts ("drinking healths") really mean, "I drink, but not at your expense. I am replenishing my liquid supply, but I wish no diminution in yours" (267–68) is intriguing with regard to the fairies' invitation, "I drink, you drink." Their claim to sweat ("I tweat") can be seen as a pathetic pretension to (salty) humanity. One would expect, incidentally, not only in accordance with this code but simply from its prominence in Irish tradition, that spitting would be an important aversion technique. I have not found it in MUNFLA, but perhaps informants considered it too rude to mention, or maybe no one asked.

20. In *English as We Speak it in Ireland*, P.W. Joyce gives "dallag" as "any kind of covering to blindfold the eyes," and "dallapookeen" as "blindman's bluff," both from the Irish "dall," blind, and "dalla," blinding (245), which fits well with the flitting fairies of Mr. C.'s narratives, who move too quickly for the eye to follow. (Mr. C. also uses the Irish term "bibe.") I have not encountered "dalladadas" in the English-language Irish material on fairies; Yeats (*Fairy*

Tales 75, 99) and Croker (2:98) give "dallahan" and "dullahan" as a "headless phantom." There might also be a linguistic connection with the "dubhdael" or "daradael," a black insect of reputed "demonic character" (Cavanagh).

21. "The sea and seafaring has permeated the fairy beliefs of Teelin and Tory" writes Maire Mac Neill in an introduction to Séan Ó hEochaidh's collection of Donegal fairy lore (19). A Galway Bay informant told Lady Gregory, "They are on the sea as well as the land, and their boats are often to be seen on the bay, sailing boats and others. They are like our own, but when you come near them they are gone in an instant"; another said, "I know they go out fishing like ourselves" (*Visions* 27).

22. A Cornish band of smugglers evaded small red-capped people by taking to their boats, "because none of the fairy tribe dare touch salt water" (Bottrell in Briggs *Dictionary of Fairies* 132–34), and a Scotsman once escaped the fairies by heading for the sea, "since neither ghost nor elf can penetrate seaward beyond the contour reached by the highest tide." In the latter story, the fairies complain as they chase the fellow, "Not so swift would be Luran, but for the hardness of his bread"; Luran was, however, eventually spirited away during a boat journey (MacGregor *Peat Fire* 9–10). (J.G. Campbell gives several versions of "Luran," with equally enigmatic references to bread — *Superstitions* 56.)

23. The first version was written for Peter Narváez and published by him in *Lore and Language*; the second was published by Mr. Maher himself in *The Seniors' News* March 1989.

24. Aly O'Brien says the fairies played "pucka-hurley" (74-118/3), and a small girl on Merasheen Island was taken to a fairy feast where they played "a game called hurley" (69-8E/24-26).

25. Mermaids (pronounced "meer-" or "maremaids") are different and I would not consider them fairies, although they are obviously related. Their appearance usually presages a storm or disaster. A woman in Lanceo "swore on the bible" that before the tidal wave of 1929, she saw "a stream of mermaids"

swim toward land, beach on the cliff, and swim back to sea: "she knew that something terrible was going to happen" (FSC74-11/40). "A crew on one ship saw a mermaid sitting on the rock combing her hair near the shore. One man pointed a gun at her. She screamed and took to the sea. After, some of the men were lost when their ship was dashed on the rocks in a storm" (FSC74-11/41). "Mermaids are generally regarded as being evil or being able to entice sailors to a watery grave," but they might also lead mariners to safety (FSC68-3/153). They are sometimes associated with the motif of three wishes; one man so favoured described his benefactor as having long hair, a pretty round face, and tiny white hands, and "from her waist down she was only a fish" (FSC71-37/34). More narratives may be found in 71-14/33, 75-252/27, 73-71/45, and FSC71-43/45.

26. Page 18 in "A History of Northern Bay," written for a history class in 1972 and deposited in the Centre for Newfoundland Studies at MUN.

27. Similar spirits, wailing during storms or on the anniversary of a wreck, are found throughout the province, but have attained such fame in connection with the Northern Bay disaster that they are mentioned on a plaque at the provincial park there. The term probably derives from "holler" or "howl"; in Sandy Point, for example, the ghosts of men from a shipwreck "howl" to be rescued after midnight (82-208/44).

28. The apparent lack of motive has often puzzled students of fairy lore. Dean Baldwin, discussing "Fairy Lore and the Meaning of 'Sir Orfeo,'" points out that "in spite of the individuality of each version, there is this curious similarity among them: all fail to specify the reasons or motives behind the major events in the story," and that "we are never told why the queen is taken away. In fact, none of the versions even mention that the abductors are fairies until after Heurodis has been rescued by Orfeo." He considers in turn the reasons most often advanced (by scholars) for fairy abductions — to gain spouses, midwives, or nurses, or to pay a tribute to the devil (the "teind to Hell" of Tam Lin) — and decides that none of them apply, and "we are left with an apparently capricious kidnapping." To these reasons can be added one

advanced by O'Sullivan: "The fairies, who are said to be bloodless try to get some blood by abducting humans into their world" (*Legends* 47). I have not seen this in MUNFLA, although it might explain why "red attracts fairies" (FSC72-129/17), or "the fairies especially went for people who wore red clothes" (FSC66-7D/66). For a discussion and references for the tithe to hell, see E.B. Lyle, "The Teind to Hell in Tam Lin."

Chapter Four

1. I took his meaning at the time to be old humorous stories; the *Dictionary of Newfoundland English* gives "cuffer" as "a tale or a yarn," "a friendly chat," or "an exchange of reminiscences," and as a verb to mean "to converse, usually about old times" (Story et al. 128–29). One student defined "to have a cuffer" with the example of a "gossip session" between two women "in which a lot of information was exchanged" (FSC71-9/39), and Mr. Tucker (of Chapter Six) told me it means a good talk on any subject.

2. The idea that people might get melodies or musical ability from the fairies (prominent in Scotland in connection with certain families of pipers) seems to be uncommon in Newfoundland. One student reported that an Irishman named Dick settled a few miles from Branch in what came to be called "Dick's Path":

    > He knew many unfamiliar songs and the people believed he learned these songs from the fairies. He let them believe that the fairies talked to him and his songs came to be called "fairy tunes" ... [My father] remembered his uncles and other older men requesting the fiddlers of the place to play "fairy tunes." These were tunes that were passed down from father to son but had been first learned from Dick the Irishman (FSC71-26/45).

    This collector doubted that anyone knows them now, but another collector recorded the continued existence of at least one. Dick English, according to this student, lived in the woods about ten miles from Branch and played the tin whistle at dances:

Strange Terrain

>   Dick claimed that one night as he was getting ready for bed some fairies entered the cabin. One of them took Dick's whistle from its place above the door and played a lively tune. Then the fairies departed. Dick took his tin whistle, tried the tune and found he could play it very well. From then onwards, Dick often played this tune, it was called "The Tune Dick Learned from the Fairies." This tune is played today by Mr. Patty Judge of Patrick's Cove and still bears the same title. (FSC80-315/*)

   For an Irish version of a piper who studies music with the fairies, see Evans Wentz (40).

3. Holinshed's *Chronicle of Scotland* describes Macbeth's and Banquo's encounter with the weird sisters:

   > ... when sodenly in the middes of a launde, there met them iii women in straunge & ferly apparell, resembling creatures of an elder world.... This was reputed at the first but some vayne fantasticall illusion by Makbeth and Banquo, in so much that Banquo woulde call Makbeth in jeste kyng of Scotland, and Makbeth againe would call him in sporte likewise, the father of many kings. But afterwards the common opinion was, that these women were eyther the weird sisters, that is as (ye would say) the Goddesses of destinie, or els some Nimphes or Feiries. (Briggs *Anatomy* 237)

   Minor White Latham comments on the passage:

   > ... in the original source of Holinshed, Hector Boece's *Scotorum Historiae a Prima Gentis Origine*, and in the immediate source of Holinshed's *Chronicle of Scotland*, *The History and Chronicles of Scotland* by Hector Boece, translated by John Bellenden, from which this account is taken, the term, "three women," is the only designation given the three beings who appeared. The explanation of these women as fairies was added by Holinshed. (71–72)

   According to Wright, "The 'white ladies' are mentioned in the *Life of Hereward* [the Saxon hero] ... in such a manner as to leave little doubt on our minds of their having been identical with the fairies of later times" (248–49). Walter Scott cites Schott's *Physica Curiosa* of 830 on "witte wiven" (white women) who stole people away to subterranean caverns, from which "cries of children, groans and lamentations of men, and sometimes imperfect words, and all kinds of musical sounds were heard to proceed" (*Minstrelsy* 2:315). Burchard of Worms inquired of his flock, "Has thou done as some women are wont to do at certain times of the year? That is, hast thou prepared the table in thy house and set on the table thy food and drink, with three knives, that if those three sisters whom past generations and old-time foolishness called the Fates should come they may take refreshment there?" (McNeill and Gamer 338).

The "fair ladies" of Hungarian folk tradition lead people astray, cause illness, and steal babies (Dömötör 92–94); they have been seen singing and dancing in the form of beautiful women in white (98–99), as have the Greek nereids (Blums *Dangerous Hour* 112–18).

4. An old cure: Cross reports one got rid of the nightmare in western North Carolina by "getting out of bed and turning shoes over," and that stockings turned inside out before retiring kept off witches (276). A correspondent of Robert Hunt's gave as a measure against night cramps, placing slippers with the toes turned inward at the foot of the bed (409). David Hufford has done a major study of the old hag in *The Terror That Comes in the Night*.

5. "This fellow from Coley's Point was down fishing off the Labrador one summer. He disappeared off his ship and after a week's search was found on one of the small coastal islands. The man said he felt he had only been gone for five minutes. He was in perfect health, even though he had been missing for a week. Those involved felt this man had been taken by the fairies" (68-19E/2). Katharine Briggs devotes the first chapter of *The Vanishing People* to "The Supernatural Passage of Time in Fairyland."

6. Tickle Harbour was abandoned when people moved to the "mainland" around the turn of the century. A short history of Bellevue (so named in 1896) is given in 84-370A/5-6, which states that settlers came from England

and Ireland, but that it has always been a completely Catholic community. The first census of 1836 showed forty-eight inhabitants; there are about four hundred today. The move inland was precipitated by a growing population and a storm that uprooted the trees on the Ridge.

7. After my interview, I found this Survey Card written by one of Mrs. Nolan's children:

> My mother once told me this story about her mother. One day Aunt Annie, as she was called, left to go picking berries several miles away. However, on her way she felt the urge to sit down and rest. Doing so she found herself dozing and apparently she must have fallen asleep. When she woke up she was outside of a community twenty miles away and it was dark when she woke. She always said that the fairies or "banshees," as she called them, had taken her away for the day. For it was not possible to get to the place without tremendous difficulty, and totally impossible if one were asleep.

One student mentions a fiddle tune known in Green Cove, "The Chase the Banshee" (*sic*).

8. "There is an old man in my community [Trepassey] who insists that he has been taken by the fairies many times and has been brought home at midnight by them. However, this man likes to drink and people say that this accounts for his trips" (FSC75-179/*).

9. Sexual suggestiveness is an old strain in fairy lore; a character in John Fletcher's *The Faithful Shepherdess* says:

> Yet I have heard (my mother told it me,
> And now I do believe it) if I keep
> My virgin flower uncropt, pure, chaste, and fair,
> No goblin, wood-god, fairy, elfe, or fiend,
> Satyr, or other power that haunts the groves,
> Shall hurt my body, or by vain illusion
> Draw me to wander after idle fires;

> Or voices calling me in dead of night,
> To make me follow, and so tole me on
> Through mire and standing pools, to find my ruin.
> (M. Latham 136)

The shepherdess's lines also provide an example of the use of "toled" in connection with fairies, as in a Green Cove text:

> Fairy's were a particular nuisance, in that they had the nasty habit of "tolling away" children, and mothers wouldn't let the youngsters outdoors without a piece of bread in their pockets with which to pacify the little buggers should they be encountered.

10. The late Michael Hayes of St. Thomas described a fatal motorcycle accident near his home, after which the victim's boots were found up in a tree. Mr. Tucker (of Chapter 6) told how he once clinched an argument with an insurance adjuster over a collision of his truck, which had turned the battery around. The adjuster wanted to know how a bump to the back of the truck could have reversed the battery, cables intact; Mr. Tucker pointed out that if he (the adjuster) was involved in fatality cases, he must know that a person's shoes could fly off, laces still tied, at the moment of impact. The analogy convinced the adjuster because he was indeed familiar with the phenomenon.

11. Maarti Haavio gives an extensive discussion of water-symbolism in folklore in "A Running Stream They Dare Na Cross."

12. The full range of priestly powers is illustrated in one student's paper on "powerful priests" in the Carbonear area, which includes narratives of curing, cursing, exorcism, and calling up spirits of the dead (73-61). The idea that they must do penance for exerting these powers is also well known. Some priests are prominent in supernatural legendry of various areas; Father Enright of St. Joseph's in St. Mary's Bay, for example (who died in 1968), figures in many narratives, and one student said that some people today pray to him as to a saint (75-250/33).

Strange Terrain

Chapter Five

1. Uncatalogued paper by Darlene Smith submitted to Martin Lovelace (Winter 1989). Several students have provided histories that, while they differ on various points, indicate that the majority of settlers came from the West Country in the 1700s. One said that the first fishermen to "overwinter" were Quilties from Ireland and Smiths from Devon, and that they settled about a mile away from one another, at what are now opposite ends of the community (80-322/6) (Mr. Smith says that the Quilties only arrived in the late 1800s). One student traces his family to Wales (70-25/5). Some say the community's name was changed on the visit of an Anglican bishop around 1850 (80-322/7), another that an influx of people named Bishop led to the change (74-218/2), and a third that "the first Bishops settled there" (70-25/57). According to one paper, the bitter religious rivalry of the 1800s (there were riots in St. John's and Harbour Grace) had driven the Catholics out of the area by this century (80-322/8), but another says that there were a dozen Catholic families until about 1945 (72-262/3); in any case, there was never a Catholic church built there. An Island Cove student provides a capsule history:

   > The town of Upper Island Cove was supposed to have begun around the year 1595 when a banking schooner from Mercer's Cove ran aground on what is now known as the Big Island. The five surviving members of the crew made their way ashore and because it was late in the year had to spend the winter in Island Cove. When the summer came the five men, who were a Mercer, Sharpe, Barrett, Young, and Crane, liked the area so much they moved their families there (FSC 91-233/*).

2. The text is restricted and I thank Gus Smith for permission to use it here.

3. Jack escaped on an eagle's back, and the brothers were "frightened to death when he come up." There seems to have been no hard feelings, however, for the narrator concludes that "they were livin' very happy when I leaved." (The tale — AT301A — is in Halpert and Widdowson's *Folktales of Newfoundland: The Resilience of the Oral Tradition*; Martin Lovelace's commentary from private communication.)

4. Type 503 in the international classification system (Aarne and Thompson *Types of the Folktale*). Other Newfoundland versions are in 73-103/24-26, FSC80-311/*, and 67-21D/20-21. On hearing the version above, Mr. Smith said he knows a version in which three brothers manage to transfer their humps to three formerly straight-backed brothers.

5. F321.1.2.2 in the *Motif-Index* (Thompson 3:62).

6. M. Latham 70. Medieval demons also perpetrated impostures, usually for the purpose of temptation or defamation: one exemplum tells of a girl carried off by "devils" who leave one of their number to replace her while she is taken to a monastery to tempt the brothers; another tells of a jealous husband tricked by devils into seeing his wife out gallivanting when she was really at home (Tubach 135, 213).

7. According to Ritson, Ariosto writes (in Harington's "Translation") that:

> (Either aunciant folke believ'd a lie,
> Or this is true) A fayrie cannot die ... (33)

"Fairies often appeared as animals such as dogs or cats which would steal food or attack children. They couldn't be caught or harmed. They weren't born and couldn't die, at least by mortal means" (72-181/7).

8. An old motif that appears in connection with the healer Valentine Greatrakes, who flourished in seventeenth-century Cork. He cured by stroking with his hands, and once operating thus on two patients, chased their pain about their bodies until it was driven out through the toes (Charles Smith 366–67).

9. Mr. Smith said he never heard the name "Denies," but that Will Lynch of Island Cove is still called "Will Fairy." "The mickadenies will get ya!" — a St. John's fairy threat (80-75/19), presumably combining two Irish allusions. Virginia Dillon, noting the Catholic propensity for ghost stories, quotes a Protestant friend coming upon a storytelling session, "At the ghost stories again. No trouble to know you're a crowd of Micks" (64-1A/7). "Denies" is

probably related to "donnies" or "dawnies": Frances Kavanagh told me that if a person was not quite awake and talking without sense, people used to say that they were "in the fairies," but now they would say they are "in the donnies." A Conche student wrote:

> I remember that if I kicked up a fuss about coming in for the night my mother would often say, "It's almost dark out now, there's no one but the dawnies on the go at this hour," or "You don't want the dawnies to get you, do you?" The "dawnies" were fairies or "the good people." (FSC74-132/*)

Croker cites the Irish usage of "dony" to mean tiny (1:75–76), and Joyce gives "donny" as meaning "weak, in poor health. Hence donnaun, a poor weakly creature, same root with the diminutive" (*English* 248). Singleton describes "lurigadauns," little men in red jackets ("Dairy Lore" 459).

In *The Sunday Telegram* for 18 February 1990, Tom Furlong writes in a review of a book on "the devil's triangle": "In Fox Harbour, Placentia Bay, years ago when someone disappeared without a trace it was said: 'the macadandies took him'" (22). Creighton notes the use of "mick-leleens" in a story about Ireland told in an Irish area of Nova Scotia (*Magic* 104).

10. Green is a pseudonym. Mr. Green's suspicion is not as far-fetched as it might sound, for several years after our interview in 1985, Steven Ratkai was convicted in St. John's of spying at the American naval base in Argentia.

11. Croker gives a narrative of a girl who is struck with a switch by a small child; then a strange old woman slashes her across the knees and feet with a whip. She — "or whatsomever thing we had in her place" — died five days later, saying she had seen a "whole heap of fairies" on horses with girls behind them, waiting for her (Croker 1834:50–52).

12. I have discussed the Irish and English history of "the blast" in a separate paper (Rieti "'The Blast'"). For other references, see Kittredge (453–56) and Honko's Krankheitsprojektile.

13. Aunt Rachel is described by another student as "a sort of community doctor" (80-322/15). Gus Smith refers tantalizingly to "the fairy that Aunt Sarah used to see every night," saying that the story is on his tape (72-262/10); unfortunately, that tape is unintelligible.

14. Personal communication via Martin Lovelace. He also told Martin about the time he and some friends met some women in Toronto and were invited to one of their apartments, where, instead of the hoped-for romantic activity, the women wanted to paint the number "666" on their foreheads. Interesting that, far from devil-infested Bishop's Cove, he should meet a Satanic coven.

15. The motif of a captured fairy is not very common elsewhere either, although there are a few stories in which they are kept almost like pets. Robert Hunt gives the story of a Cornish man who takes one home to his children to play with, until the fairy parents come fetch him; it seems to be related to captured leprechaun stories in that the fairy promises to show them where crocks of gold are hidden (450–51). Lady Gregory spoke to a couple who kept a fairy on their kitchen dresser for several weeks, feeding it bread and milk (*Visions* 220).

Chapter Six

1. The term "urban" is always relative in Newfoundland: St. John's proper has about a hundred thousand people, with fifty thousand more in Mt. Pearl and adjoining areas.

2. Once Broad Cove. The spelling varies; Seary gives both St. Philips and St. Phillips (90, 273), but local usage tends toward the latter, so I have used that here. St. Phillips is now suburban car-commuter country, and has always been commuter country, being one of the chief supply areas for wood and farm goods for St. John's.

3. A student report from St. Phillips may contain a variant of this story. Like Mr. Tucker, the informant does not mention "fairies," but offers the account in response to a question about them:

> Asked a Mr. Francis Wayland about fairies and he told me that something unusual happened to him. He said that one day when he was walking across a path in on Thorburn Road [on the watershed] where he grew up, and [which he] knew like the back of his hand, he just became totally confused and disoriented, almost as if he was under a spell. He said that he tried between five to seven times to find his way in this familiar territory but just couldn't, so he finally went home. (FSC74-6/23)

4. Unaccessioned tape submitted to Marie-Annick Desplanques, Folklore 2000, Summer 1989. My transcription.

5. A famous event in Bell Island folklore. Philip Hiscock gives what he can recall of it, which he figures is probably fairly close to the general version: It happened on an Easter Sunday, and American military specialists from Texas flew in within twenty-four hours. They refused to speak to the press, although they supposedly determined it was not the Russians sending electric rays (or something like that) to Cuba; Philip thinks that it was finally given out to have been some kind of "super lightning" that was attracted to a patch of iron ore in the ground.

6. Field notes March 1985. The invitation may be traditional: Pádraig Ó Tuathail gives a story of three men driving a cart who see a crowd of small people in red coats:

> It was a pass-word with the people at that time to say: "Let them all come!" So they said it, and with that they all climbed on to the wheels and up on the horse's back and on every part of the car where they could possibly sit. (88)

> An old man who was "a friend of the fairies" near Ferryland used to "wave at something in the woods that no one could see, and say he was

waving to his friends in the woods"; when his cart would suddenly drag as if under a great weight, he would explain that "his friends were sitting on the back riding with him" (70-6/20).

7. "Okay, Mother Geheine, you can have her for the night but I wants her tomorrow morning," Dr. Cron supposedly said. Another student describes the murder of a Mrs. Geehan, whose body was put in what is now called "Geehan's Pit" (72-116/22).

8. The briefcase is reminiscent of the Black Heart (or Art) Book in that no one but the owner is supposed to see its contents, which give the owner magic powers (Rieti "Black Heart").

9. The field was probably Martin's Meadow behind Lime Street and Carter's Hill; one collector's grandmother saw the fairies there, "little men dancing around playing ring-around-the-rosie" and beckoning to her (80-75:C5614/m.t.).

10. They may have been thinking of the unearthly Newfoundland dog said to guide travellers lost on the road that runs across the barrens from Victoria to Heart's Content (Q68-37/5).

11. It seems to be part of the folklore of the incident that the story was famous around the world; on 29 April 1936, a writer to the *Telegram* "wondered why the press of St. John's made so little of this remarkable case while the press of other countries was featuring it under striking headlines" (4). (The St. John's *Daily News*, perhaps conceding a *Telegram* scoop, had limited itself to a second-page item on April 13, which quoted Lucy, "I'm the little girl who is lost.") I could not locate these "striking headlines"; the Associated Press did pick up the story, which ran April 10 on an inner page of the *New York Times* as follows:

> An eight-year-old girl, lost in the forest for twelve days, recounted in Perlican Hospital today how she had lain down to sleep like the 'babes in the woods,' expecting never to waken. The child, Lucy Harris, endured hunger, rain, snow and frost while the whole

neighborhood hunted for her, but hospital authorities said she would survive. Her hands and feet were frozen and she will probably be maimed for life. "I wasn't lonely or afraid because the birds sang," she whispered in hospital. The searchers never expected to find her alive. Her feeble cry: "Hello, I'm the little girl that's lost," startled them on the twelfth day of the search. (16L)

In London *The Times* carried a notice on April 14 in its small-print "Telegrams in brief" column:

> Lucy Harris, a nine-year-old girl who did not come back from a trout-fishing expedition, has been found. After a search lasting twelve days, in which two hundred people of New Perlican, Newfoundland, took part, her uncle heard a voice saying, "Hello, I'm the little girl who is lost in the woods." (9)

It is possible that the story was featured more prominently in less mainstream newspapers.

12. "Folk-Life" 237. In "The Origins and Development of Belief in Fairies," Sayce discusses "Lilliputian" and "microptic" illusions and their possible physical causes (ocular problems, stress, cold, fatigue) as sources of fairy visions (105–09).

13. Not implausibly, for "Lucy Gray" was in the *Royal Readers*, the contents of which were forcibly memorized in many Newfoundland schoolrooms. Hilda Chaulk Murray points out that *Royal Reader* content did enter everyday talk, as in that of a woman who used to say of a stormy day, "It's as bad as the time Lucy Gray was lost!" (58). Lucy Harris may even have been thinking of the poem herself, when she spoke of herself in the third person, "I'm the little girl . . ." (One arresting parallel with "Lucy Gray" is that, as in the poem, searchers for Lucy Harris found tracks in the snow that ended abruptly.)

14. A woman from Flatrock did say that she carried bread when she went into the woods "and would place it on a nearby stone if she wanted a favour" (72-181/4).

15. The city-dweller's view is not restricted to Newfoundland; Anthony D. Buckley has observed that in Ulster, magical cures and fairy belief are "typically associated in the popular imagination" with rural areas, old people, and Catholics, a profile that "does not remotely fit the facts" (19).

16. Yeats mentions "a topsy-turveydom of seasons" in the Irish fairy world (Gregory *Visions* 317). When an Argentia man cutting wood in midwinter suddenly found himself in a green garden with a band of fairies, he had the presence of mind to pick some grass as proof of the adventure (FSC74-123/*).

Chapter Seven

1. Jones said that she liked it that way, so it was disheartening to find, in 1988, that she had to give up living on her own after being accosted in her bed one night by a man (from the community) who threatened to kill her if she didn't give him money. The experience "took all the good out of her," she said, and she had been to the doctor three times since it happened.

2. Field notes, 28 September 1984. The same incident was recorded by the woman's granddaughter, whose uncle told her that she "received a blast from the fairies," which "meant that she was in someone's way." From the finger emerged "all kinds of strange things, for example, twigs, leaves, fur, hair and moss" (81-314/21-22).

3. Field notes, 28 September 1984. They had given the story earlier to Kathy Kimiecik, who kindly loaned me her tape recording of it. The late Paddy Deagon had joined that discussion, saying that the woman didn't have "a stitch of clothing on her" when she got to the lighthouse; they also said (in that recording) that there was another woman with her who kept calling to her to come back, but "she took off mad over across there."

4. Unaccessioned tape by David Abbott submitted to Marie-Annick Desplanques for Folklore 2000, Summer 1989.

5. According to one story about Will Kane, "a woman came along to him and hit him in the side of the face, and the way his face was moved, that was the way it stayed. He said he had never seen the woman before and never saw her again" (FSC70-10/104).

6. In a MUNFLA version (from Marysvale), a man working in the woods finds a bundle of clothes and brings it home; he is followed by a bird, which tears up the house that night. The next morning he turns out the bird in God's name. At last an old man, bent and grey, appears and tells him he has until twelve the next day to put the clothes back: "if not there's going to be trouble for you" (72-95/31-44).

7. In 1990, Cynthia Boyd began working with Mr. Winter as the subject of her master's thesis on his grandfather's furniture-making; she has a half-hour tape of fairy stories from him, which she got when she was asking about carpentry (personal communication, Fall 1990).

8. "The Fairy Faith" aired on the Canadian Broadcasting Corporation's *Ideas* series, 29 June 1989.

9. I don't think it is a caution against drinking from streams in general, although the "water wolf," a creature that grows in the stomach from ingested eggs or larvae, is like the blast in its hideous internal growth and eventual expulsion. Mr. MacDonald gave a good example of how the "wolf" must be starved, then lured out through the person's mouth with a bowl of milk; he said there is a specimen in a jar somewhere in the General Hospital.

10. Additional versions of the second informant's story may be found in FSC71-46/38 and FSC70-34/83.

11. Another collector interviewed Mrs. Hayes on laying out the dead. A second informant (for the same paper) said that Mrs. Hayes's father "used to see seven fairies on the Beach Road, and even he was afraid to go there" (75-33/42).

12. Mr. Murrin's family included some of the more prosperous farmers in the area, able to sell vegetables in St. John's even in the Depression. (I did not learn this from Mr. Murrin himself, but indirectly through other people in the area.)

13. An interesting example of folk practice prefiguring official prescription. In the presently dawning recognition of the ubiquity of sexual abuse, parents are counselled to cultivate assertiveness in children, for as one counsellor puts it, the children most at risk are those "who have been taught to follow the rules, who have a great deal of trust" ("Frank discussion"). This is not to say that the encouragement of brashness Power cites was so motivated — presumably girls would have been similarly encouraged if that were the case — but that fairy tradition in this instance provides a model of a world beyond the parental pale in which it does not do to be too tractable.

Bibliography

This is a general bibliography for the study of fairy lore; references cited in this book are marked with an asterisk (*).

*Aarne, Antti, and Stith Thompson. *The Types of the Folktale: A Classification and Bibliography*, translated and revised by Stith Thompson. 2nd rev. FF Communications No. 184. Helsinki: Suomalainen Tiedeakatemia Academia Scientiarum Fennica, 1973.

Addy, Sidney O. *Household Tales with Other Traditional Remains: Collected in the Counties of York, Lincoln, Derby, and Nottingham*. 1895. Rpt. as *Folk Tales and Superstitions*, introduction by J.D.A. Widdowson. Wakefield: EP, 1973.

Alderson, E.S. "Green Fairies: Woolpit Green Children." *Notes and Queries* 9th ser. 5 (1900):155.

Allies, Jabez. *On the Ancient British, Roman, and Saxon Antiquities and Folk-lore of Worcestershire*. 2nd ed. 1852. New York: Arno, 1977. [1st pub. 1840]

Amery, P.F.S. "Pixies in North Devon." *Reports and Transactions of the Devonshire Association* 24 (1892):52–53.

*"Ancient Superstitions in Tiree." *Folk-Lore Journal* 1 (1883):167–68.

Andrews, Elizabeth. *Ulster Folklore*. London: Elliot Stock, 1913.

*Arensberg, Conrad. *The Irish Countryman*. 1937. New York: American Museum Science Books, 1968.

*Ashton, John. "The Lumbercamp Song Tradition in Newfoundland." *Newfoundland Studies* 2 (1986):213–31.

Atkinson, Rev. J.C. *Forty Years in a Moorland Parish: Reminiscences and Researches in Danby in Cleveland.* London: Macmillan, 1907. [1st pub. 1891]

*Aubrey, John. *Brief Lives.* Edited from the Original Manuscripts and with a Life of John Aubrey by Oliver Lawson Dick. Ann Arbor: University of Michigan Press, 1957.

*———. *The Natural History of Wiltshire (Written between 1656 and 1691): Edited, and Elucidated by Notes by John Britton.* 1847, introduction by K.G. Ponting. Newton Abbot, Devon: David and Charles, 1969.

*———. *Three Prose Works: Miscellanies; Remaines of Gentilisme and Judaisme; Observations,* edited with an introduction and notes by John Buchanan-Brown. Carbondale: Southern Illinois University Press, 1972.

B., G. "Fairy Superstition." *Ulster Journal of Archaeology* 7 (1859):73–74.

Bairéad, Ciarán. "Scéalta agus Seanchas ón Achréidh." *Béaloideas* 32 (1964):99–147. [English summary].

*Baldwin, Dean R. "Fairy Lore and the Meaning of 'Sir Orfeo.'" *Southern Folklore Quarterly* 40 (1977):129–42.

Ballard, Linda-May [see also Smith]. "The Position of the 'Danes' in Contemporary Ulster Oral Narrative." *Ulster Folklife* 25 (1979):103–12.

*———. "Ulster Oral Narrative: The Stress on Authenticity." *Ulster Folklife* 26 (1980):35–40.

Banks, M.M. "Fairies' Methods of Securing Good Stock." *Folk-Lore* 51 (1940):113–14.

Baring-Gould, S. "Devonshire Household Tales: The Cow and the Pixie." *Notes and Queries* 3rd ser. 8 (1865):282–83.

*Baughman, Ernest W. *Type and Motif-Index of the Folktales of England and North America.* Indiana University Folklore Series No. 20. The Hague: Mouton, 1966.

*Begg, E.J. "Cases of Witchcraft in Dorsetshire." *Folk-Lore* 52 (1941):70–72.

*———. "Folk Tales Collected in Strathspey, Scotland." *Folk-Lore* 50 (1939):75–81.

Bell, William. *Shakespeare's Puck, and his Folkslore [sic]: Illustrated from the Superstitions of All Nations, but More Especially from the Earliest Religion and Rites of Northern Europe and the Wends.* 3 vols. 1852–1864. New York: AMS, 1971.

*Bennett, Gillian. *Traditions of Belief: Women, Folklore and the Supernatural Today.* London: Penguin, 1987.

Bennett, Margaret. *The Last Stronghold: Scottish Gaelic Traditions in Newfoundland*. Canada's Atlantic Folklore and Folklife Series No. 13. St. John's: Breakwater, 1989.

Binnall, Peter B.G. "A Brownie Legend from Lincolnshire." *Folk-Lore* 51 (1940):219–22.

Black, G.F. *Examples of Printed Folk-Lore Concerning the Orkney and Shetland Islands. County Folk-Lore* Vol. 3, edited by Northcote W. Thomas. London: David Nutt, 1903.

Blum, Eva and Richard. *Health and Healing in Rural Greece: A Study of Three Communities*. Stanford, CA: Stanford UP, 1965.

*———. *The Dangerous Hour: The Lore of Crisis and Mystery in Rural Greece*. London: Chatto and Windus, 1970.

*Bottrell, William. *Traditions and Hearthside Stories of West Cornwall*. 1870. Newcastle upon Tyne: Frank Graham, 1970.

Bourne, Henry. *Antiquitates Vulgares; or, the Antiquities of the Common People*. 1725. New York: Arno, 1977.

Bovet, Richard. *Pandaemonium, or the Devil's Cloyster*. 1684. With an Intro, and Notes by Montague Summers. Aldington, Kent: Hand and Flower Press, 1951.

*Bowker, James. *Goblin Tales of Lancashire*. London: W. Swan Sonnenschein, n.d. [*c.* 1881].

*Briggs, Katharine M. *The Anatomy of Puck: An Examination of Fairy Beliefs among Shakespeare's Contemporaries and Successors*. London: Routledge and Kegan Paul, 1959.

*———. *A Dictionary of Fairies: Hobgoblins, Brownies, Bogies and Other Supernatural Creatures*. Harmondsworth: Penguin, 1977.

*———. *A Dictionary of British Folk-Tales*. 4 vols. London: Routledge and Kegan Paul, 1970, 1971.

———. *The Fairies in Tradition and Literature*. London: Routledge and Kegan Paul, 1967.

*———. *The Vanishing People: Fairy Lore and Legends*. New York: Pantheon, 1978.

Britten, James. "Changelings in Ireland." *Folk-Lore Journal* 2 (1884):91–92.

Brockie, William. *Legends and Superstitions of the County of Durham*. 1886. N.p.: Norwood, 1974.

Bruford, Alan, ed. *The Green Man of Knowledge and Other Scots Traditional Tales*. Aberdeen: Aberdeen UP, 1982.

*Brunvand, Jan Harold. *The Choking Doberman and Other "New" Urban Legends*. New York: W.W. Norton, 1984.

Buchan, David, ed. *Scottish Tradition: A Collection of Scottish Folk Literature*. London: Routledge and Kegan Paul, 1984.

*Buchan, David. "The Wit-Combat Ballads." *Narrative Folksong: New Directions* (W. Edson Richmond Festschrift), edited by C.L. Edwards and K.E.B. Manley. Boulder, CO: Westview, 1985, pp. 382–400.

*Buckley, Anthony D. "Unofficial Healing in Ulster." *Ulster Folklife* 26 (1980):15–34.

Burke, Martin. "Tipperary Tales." *Béaloideas* 4 (1933):277–91.

Buss, Reinhard J. *The Klabautermann of the Northern Seas: An Analysis of the Protective Spirit of Ships and Sailors in the Context of Popular Belief, Christian Legend, and Indo-European Mythology*. Folklore Studies 25. Berkeley: University of California Press, 1973.

Butler, Gary R. *Saying Isn't Believing: Conversation, Narrative and the Discourse of Belief in a French Newfoundland Community*. Social and Economic Studies No. 42. St. John's: Institute of Social and Economic Research, 1991.

*Byrnes, John Maclay. *The Paths to Yesterday: Memories of Old St. John's, Newfoundland*. Boston: Meador, 1931.

C., J.H. "Chaucer's 'Canterbury Tales.'" *Notes and Queries* 4th ser. 2 (1868): 196–97.

*Cambrensis, Giraldus. *The Historical Works of Giraldus Cambrensis*, translated by Thomas Forester and Sir Richard Colt Hoare; edited by Thomas Wright. London: George Bell, 1894.

*Campbell, Lord Archibald. *Craignish Tales and Others*. Waifs and Strays of Celtic Tradition, Argyllshire Series No. 1, 1889. New York: AMS, 1973.

Campbell, John F. *Popular Tales of the West Highlands: Orally Collected*. 4 vols. Paisley: Alexander Gardner, 1890–92. [1st pub. 1860]

Campbell, Rev. John Gregorson. *Clan Traditions and Popular Tales of the Western Highlands and Islands, Collected from Oral Sources*. Waifs and Strays of Celtic Tradition, Argyllshire Series No. 5, 1895. New York: AMS, 1973.

*———. *Superstitions of the Highlands and Islands of Scotland: Collected Entirely from Oral Sources*. Glasgow: James MacLehose, 1900.

Carmichael, Alexander. *Carmina Gadelica: Hymns and Incantations with Illustrative Notes on Words, Rites, and Customs, Dying and Obsolete: Orally Collected in the Highlands and Islands of Scotland*. 6 vols. Edinburgh: Oliver and Boyd, 1928–54.

*Casey, George J. "Traditions and Neighbourhoods: The Folklife of a Newfoundland Fishing Outport." MA thesis. Memorial University of Newfoundland, 1971.

*Cavanagh, John Eugene. "Irish Folk-Lore." *Notes and Queries* 4th ser. 1 (1868):262–63.

Chambers, Rosa. "Episode on an Irish Farm." *Folklore* 72 (1961):345–46.

*Chaucer, Geoffrey. *The Works of Geoffrey Chaucer*, edited by F.N. Robinson. 2nd ed. London: Oxford UP, 1968.

*Child, Francis James, ed. *The English and Scottish Popular Ballads*. 5 vols. 1882–98. New York: Dover, 1965.

*Christiansen, Reidar Th. "Some Notes on the Fairies and the Fairy Faith." *Hereditas: Essays and Studies Presented to Professor Séamus Ó Duilearga*, edited by Bo Almqvist et al. 1975. New York: Arno, 1980, pp. 95–111.

*———. *The Migratory Legends: A Proposed List of Types with a Systematic Catalogue of the Norwegian Variants*. FF Communications No. 175. Helsinki: Suomalainen Tiedeakatemia Academia Scientiarum Fennica, 1958.

———. *The Dead and the Living*. In *Studia Norvegica: Ethnologica and Folkloristica*, edited by Christiansen et al. No. 2 in Vol. 1 (1–4). Oslo: H. Aschehoug, 1946.

———, ed. *Folktales of Norway*, translsated by Pat Shaw Iverson. Folktales of the World. Chicago: University of Chicago Press, 1964.

Clark, M.S. "Pembrokeshire Notes." *Folk-Lore* 15 (1904):194–98.

Clayton, Owen. "The English Literary Fairies: From the Beginnings to the Renaissance." PhD diss., University of California at Berkeley, 1972.

*Cohn, Norman. *Europe's Inner Demons: An Enquiry Inspired by the Great Witch-Hunt*. New York: Basic Books, 1975.

Collison, F.W. "North Devonshire Folk Lore." *Notes and Queries* 3rd ser. 1 (1862):404–05.

Colum, Pádraic. "The Fairies and the Hunchback." *Béaloideas* 3 (1932):211.

*Cooke, J. "Notes on Irish Folklore from Connaught, Collected Chiefly in North Donegal." *Folk-Lore* 7 (1896):299–301.

Coote, Henry Charles. "The Neo-Latin Fay." *Folk-Lore Record* 2 (1879):1–18.
*Coulton, G.G. *Life in the Middle Ages*. New York: Macmillan; Cambridge: Cambridge University Press, 1935.
*Courtney, M.A. *Cornish Feasts and Folk-Lore*. 1890. N.p.: Folcroft, 1977.
*Cousins, John. "Horses in the Folklife of Western Prince Edward Island: Custom, Belief, and Oral Tradition." MA thesis, Memorial University of Newfoundland, 1991.
Coxhead, J.R.W. *The Devil in Devon: An Anthology of Folk-Tales*. Bracknell: West Country Handbooks, 1967.
——. *Legends of Devon*. N. Devon: Western Press, 1954.
Craigie, W.A. "A Fairy Dog's Tooth." *Folk-Lore* 11 (1900):450–52.
——. "Some Highland Folklore." *Folk-Lore* 9 (1898):372–79.
*Creighton, Helen. *Bluenose Ghosts*. Toronto: Ryerson, 1957.
*——. *Bluenose Magic: Popular Beliefs and Superstitions in Nova Scotia*. Toronto: McGraw-Hill Ryerson, 1968.
*Croker, T. Crofton. *Fairy Legends and Traditions of the South of Ireland*. London: John Murray, vol. 1, 2nd ed., 1826; vols. 2 and 3, 1828.
*——. *Fairy Legends and Traditions of the South of Ireland*, edited by Thomas Wright, and with a memoir of the author by his son, T.F. Dillon Croker. London: William Tegg, [1834].
——. *Researches in the South of Ireland, Illustrative of the Scenery, Architectural Remains, and the Manners and Superstitions of the Peasantry*. London: John Murray, 1824.
Cromek, R.H. *Remains of Nithsdale and Galloway Song: With Historical and Traditional Notices Relative to the Manners and Customs of the Peasantry*. 1810. Paisley: Alexander Gardner, 1880.
*Cross, Tom Peete. *Motif-Index of Early Irish Literature*. Indiana University Publications, Folklore Series No. 7. Bloomington: Indiana UP, n.d.
*——. *Witchcraft in North Carolina*. Studies in Philology 16. 1919. N.p.: Norwood, 1975.
*Crossing, William. *Tales of the Dartmoor Pixies: Glimpses of Elfin Haunts and Antics*. London: W.H. Hood, 1890.
*Curtin, Jeremiah. *Tales of the Fairies and of the Ghost World Collected from Oral Tradition in South-West Munster*. Boston: Little, Brown, 1895.

*D., J.D. "Hay Lifts." *Notes and Queries* 2nd ser. 4 (1857):164–65.

D., R. "The Significance of Three Knocks." *Journal of the Cork Historical and Archaeological Society* 2nd ser. 9 (1903):202–03.

Dalyell, John Graham. *The Darker Superstitions of Scotland.* [1835]. Norwood, PA: Norwood, 1973.

Danum. "Fairy Superstition of the Present Age." *Notes and Queries* 2nd ser. 7 (1859):313.

*Davies, Jonathan Ceredig. *Folk-Lore of West and Mid-Wales.* Aberystwyth: Welsh Gazette, 1911.

Deeney, Daniel. *Peasant Lore from Gaelic Ireland.* London: David Nutt, 1900.

De Garis, Marie. *Folklore of Guernsey.* St. Pierre du Bois, Guernsey: printed for the author by the Guernsey Press, 1975.

Dégh, Linda. *Folktales and Society: Story-telling in a Hungarian Peasant Community*, translated by Emily M. Schossberger. Bloomington: Indiana UP, 1969.

Delattre, Floris. *English Fairy Poetry from the Origins to the 17th Century.* 1912. Folcroft, PA: Folcroft, 1969.

Dempster, Miss. "The Folk-Lore of Sutherlandshire." *Folk-Lore Journal* 6 (1888):215–52.

Dendy, Mary. "Staffordshire Superstitions." *Folk-Lore* 7 (1896):398–99.

Denham, Michael Aislabie. *The Denham Tracts: A Collection of Folklore by M.A. Denham and Reprinted from the Original Tracts and Pamphlets Printed by Mr. Denham Between 1846 and 1859*, edited by James Hardy. 1891. Nendeln/Liechenstein: Kraus, 1967.

*Dickman, Ilka D. *Appointment to Newfoundland.* Manhattan, KS: Sunflower UP, 1981.

*Dinham, Paul S. *You Never Know What They Might Do: Mental Illness in Outport Newfoundland.* Newfoundland Social and Economic Studies No. 20. St. John's: Institute of Social and Economic Research, Memorial University of Newfoundland, 1977.

Doherty, Thomas. "Some Notes on the Physique, Customs, and Superstitions of the Peasantry of Innishowen, Co. Donegal." *Folk-Lore* 8 (1897):12–18.

*Dömötör, Tekla. *Hungarian Folk Beliefs,* translated by C.M. Hann. Bloomington: Indiana UP, 1981.

*Duffy, Patrick. "The Making of an Irish Mud Wall House." *Béaloideas* 4 (1934):91.

*Duley, Margaret. *Cold Pastoral.* Toronto: Griffin, 1977. [1st pub. *c.* 1939]

Duncan, Leland L. "Fairy Beliefs and Other Folklore Notes from County Leitrim." *Folk-Lore* 7 (1896):161–83.

*——. "Method of Starting a New House in the Olden Times." *Folk-Lore* 10 (1899):118–19.

——. "Staffordshire Superstitions." *Folk-Lore* 8 (1897):69.

*Dundes, Alan. "Wet and Dry, the Evil Eye: An Essay in Indo-European and Semitic Worldview." In *The Evil Eye: A Folklore Casebook*, edited by Alan Dundes. New York: Garland, 1981, pp. 257–312.

*Eberly, Susan Schoon. "Fairies and the Folklore of Disability: Changelings, Hybrids and the Solitary Fairy." *Folklore* 99 (1988):58–77.

*Edwards, Gillian. *Hobgoblin and Sweet Puck: Fairy Names and Nature.* London: Geoffrey Bles, 1974.

Evans, E. Estyn. *Irish Folk Ways.* London: Routledge and Kegan Paul, 1957.

*——. *Mourne Country: Landscape and Life in South Down.* Dundalk: Dundalgan (W. Tempest), 1967.

*——. "Peasant Beliefs in Nineteenth-Century Ireland." *Views of the Irish Peasantry: 1800–1916*, edited by Daniel J. Casey and Robert E. Rhodes. Hamden, CT: Anchor, 1977, pp. 37–56.

*Evans Wentz, W.Y. See Wentz.

"Extracts from Old Chapbooks &c." *Folk-Lore Record* 2 (1879):197–201.

Eyre, Margaret. "Folk-Lore of the Wye Valley." *Folk-Lore* 16 (1905):162–79.

Fairfax-Blakeborough, J. *Yorkshire Village Life, Humour and Characters.* London: A. Brown, n.d. [*c.* 1950s]

"Fairies under Trees." *Folk-Lore Journal* 1 (1883):90–91.

Faris, James C. *Cat Harbour: A Newfoundland Fishing Settlement.* Newfoundland Social and Economic Studies No. 3. St. John's: Institute of Social and Economic Research, Memorial University of Newfoundland, 1972.

*Farmer, Sarah Bridge. "Folk-Lore of Marblehead, Mass." *Journal of American Folklore* 7 (1894):252–53.

*Favret-Saada, Jeanne. *Deadly Words: Witchcraft in the Bocage,* translated by Catherine Cullen. Cambridge and Paris: Cambridge UP, Editions de la Maison des Science de l'Homme, 1980.

Fenwick, John George. "Curious Superstition." *Folk-Lore Record* 2 (1879):209.

*Fielden, Marjory B. "Pysgies on Dartmoor." *Report and Transactions of the Devonshire Association* 64 (1932):159.

*Firestone, Melvin M. *Brothers and Rivals: Patrilocality in Savage Cove*. Newfoundland Social and Economic Studies No. 5. St. John's: Institute of Social and Economic Research, Memorial University of Newfoundland, 1967.

*———. "Mummers and Strangers in Northern Newfoundland." In Halpert and Story, *Christmas Mumming in Newfoundland*, edited by Herbert Halpert and George M. Story. Toronto: University of Toronto Press, 1969, pp. 62–75.

*Flower, Robin. *The Western Island or the Great Blasket*. 1944. Oxford: Oxford UP, 1978.

"Folk-Lore of the Feroe Islands [from Landt's *Description*, 1810]." *Folk-Lore Journal* 6 (1888):129–33.

*Foster, Jeanne Cooper. *Ulster Folklore*. Belfast: H.R. Carter, 1951.

*Fowler, Raymond E. *The Watchers: The Secret Design behind UFO Abduction*. New York: Bantam, 1990.

*"Frank Parent–Child Discussion Best Prevents Sexual Abuse." *The Evening Telegram* [St. John's, Newfoundland], 26 March 1990:17.

G. "Green Fairies: Woolpit Green Children." *Notes and Queries* 9th ser. 5 (1900):155.

Gatty, Mrs. Alfred. "Tales of the Fairies from *A Holiday in Ireland in 1831*." *Béaloideas* 3 (1932):365–70.

Gibson, H.N. "The Human–Fairy Marriage." *Folk-Lore* 66 (1955):357–59.

———. "Status of the Offspring of the Human–Fairy Marriage." *Folk-Lore* 64 (1953):282–85.

Glanvil, Joseph. *Sadducismus Triumphatus: Or, A full and plain Evidence, concerning Witches and Apparitions*. 4th ed. London: A. Bettesworth and J. Batley, 1726.

Glassie, Henry, ed. *Irish Folktales*. New York: Pantheon, 1985.

*———. *Passing the Time in Ballymenone: Culture and History of an Ulster Community*. Publications of the American Folklore Society, New Series, Vol. 4. Philadelphia: University of Pennsylvania Press, 1982.

Gomme, George Laurence. *English Traditions and Foreign Customs: A Classified Collection of the Chief Contents of "The Gentleman's Magazine" from 1731–1868*. London: Elliot Stock, 1885.

———. *The Gentleman's Magazine Library: Being a Classified Collection of the Chief*

Contents of the Gentleman's Magazine from 1731 to 1868: Popular Superstitions. London: Elliot Stock, 1884.

Grambo, Ronald. "Guilt and Punishment in Norwegian Legends." *Fabula* 11 (1970):253–70.

———. "The Lord of the Forest and Mountain Game in the More Recent Folk Traditions of Norway." *Fabula* 7 (1964):33–52.

Grant, Anne MacVicar. *Essays on the Superstitions of the Highlanders of Scotland.* 2 vols. 1811. N.p.: Norwood, 1975.

Green, Roger Lancelyn. "Shakespeare and the Fairies." *Folklore* 73 (1962):89–103.

*Gregor, Rev. Walter. "Bread." *Folk-Lore Journal* 7 (1889):195–98.

———. *Notes on the Folk-Lore of the North-East of Scotland.* London: E. Stock, 1881.

———. "Stories of the Fairies from Scotland." *Folk-Lore Journal* 1 (1883):25–27, 55–58.

*Gregory, Lady [Isabella]. *Visions and Beliefs in the West of Ireland: With Two Essays and Notes by W.B. Yeats.* 1920. Gerrards Cross: Colin Smythe, 1979.

*———. *Poets and Dreamers: Studies and Translations from the Irish.* 1903. Port Washington, NY: Kennikat, 1967.

Grenfell, Wilfred Thomason. *A Labrador Doctor: The Autobiography of Wilfred Thomason Grenfell.* London: Hodder and Stoughton, 1919.

Grice, Frederick. *Folk Tales of the West Midlands.* London and Edinburgh: Thomas Nelson, 1952.

Grimm, Jacob. *Teutonic Mythology*, translated from the 4th ed. with notes and appendix by James Steven Stallybrass. 4 vols. 1883–87. New York: Dover, 1966.

Grimm, Jakob and Wilhelm. *The German Legends of the Brothers Grimm*, edited and translated by Donald Ward. 2 vols. Translations in Folklore Studies. Philadelphia: Institute for the Study of Human Issues, 1981.

Groome, F. Hindes. "The Influence of the Gypsies on the Superstitions of the English Folk." *The International Folk Lore Congress, 1891: Papers and Transactions*, edited by Joseph Jacobs and Alfred Nutt. London: D. Nutt, 1892, 292–308.

Grose, Francis. *A Provincial Glossary, with a Collection of Local Proverbs and Popular Superstitions.* 1787. Menston, England: Scolar, 1968.

Gutch, Mrs. *Examples of Printed Folk-Lore Concerning the North Riding of Yorkshire, York, and the Ainsty. County Folk-Lore* Vol. 2. London: David Nutt, 1901.

*Haavio, Martti. "A Running Stream They Dare Na Cross." *Studia Fennica* 8 (1959):125–42.

*Haddon, A. C. "A Batch of Irish Folk-Lore." *Folk-Lore* 4 (1893):349–64.

Haffter, Carl. "The Changeling: History and Psychodynamics of Attitude to Handicapped Children in European Folklore." *Journal of the Behavioral Sciences* 4 (1968):55–61.

Halliwell, James Orchard. *Illustrations of the Fairy Mythology of a Midsummer Night's Dream*. 1845. New York: AMS, 1970.

*Halpert, Herbert. "Legends of the Cursed Child." *New York Folklore Quarterly* 14 (1958):233–41.

*———. "Pennsylvania Fairylore and Folktales." *Journal of American Folklore* 58 (1945):130–34.

*——— and G.M. Story, eds. *Christmas Mumming in Newfoundland: Essays in Anthropology, Folklore, and History*. Toronto: University of Toronto Press, 1969.

*Hand, Wayland D. "European Fairy Lore in the New World." *Folklore* 92 (1981):141–48.

———, Anna Casetta, and Sondra B. Thiedermann. *Popular Beliefs and Superstitions: A Compendium of American Folklore from the Ohio Collection of Newbell Niles Puckett*. 3 vols. Boston: G.K. Hall, 1981.

Hardwick, Charles. *Traditions, Superstitions, and Folk-Lore, (Chiefly Lancashire and the North of England:) Their Affinity to Others in Widely-Distributed Localities; Their Eastern Origin and Mythical Significance*. Manchester: A. Ireland; London: Simpkin, Marshall, 1872.

*Harrington, Michael. "Lucy Harris: Babe in the Woods." *Evening Telegram* [St. John's, Newfoundland] 1 April 1985:8.

*———. *Offbeat Mystery of Newfoundland and Labrador*. St. John's: Harry Cuff, 1988.

*Hartland, E. Sidney, ed. *Walter Map's "De nugis curialium*, translated by Montague R. James; Historical Notes by John Edward Lloyd. Cymmrodorion Record Series No. 9. London: Honorable Society of Cymmrodorion, 1923.

*———. *The Science of Fairy Tales: An Inquiry into Fairy Mythology*. 2nd ed. London: Methuen, 1925. [1st pub. 1890]

Hazlitt, W. Carew. *Fairy Tales, Legends, and Romances Illustrating Shakespeare and Other Early English Writers*. 1875. Hildesheim and New York: Georg Olms Verlag, 1977. [Amalgamation of earlier works by Ritson (1831) and Halliwell (1845)]

———. *Faiths and Folklore: A Dictionary of National Beliefs, Superstitions and Popular Customs, Past and Current, with their Classical and Foreign Analogues, Described and Illustrated*. (Forming a New Ed. of *The Popular Antiquities of Great Britain* by Brand and Ellis). 2 vols. London: Reeves and Turner, 1905.

Henderson, W.A. "Changelings." *Notes and Queries* 8th ser. 8 (1895):94.

Henderson, William. *Notes on the Folk Lore of the Northern Counties of England and the Borders*. 1866. East Ardsley, Yorkshire: EP, 1973.

Henningsen, Gustav. "The Ladies from Outside: Fairies, Witches and Poverty in Early Modern Sicily." Unpub. Trans. courtesy of David Buchan.

Herbert, Gwen. "Pixies." *Report and Transactions of the Devonshire Association* 60 (1928):116–17.

*Herrick, Robert. *The Complete Poetry of Robert Herrick*, edited by J. Max Patrick. New York: New York UP, 1963.

Hibernia. "Chaucer's 'Canterbury Tales': Folk-Lore and the Belief in Fairies." *Notes and Queries* 4th ser. 2 (1868):366–67.

*Honko, Lauri. "Four Forms of Adaptation of Tradition." *Adaptation, Change, and Decline in Oral Literature*, edited by Honko and Vilmos Voigt. Studia Fennica 26. Helsinki: Suomalaisen Kirjallisuuden Seura, 1981, pp. 19–33.

———. *Geisterglaube in Ingermanland*. FF Communications No. 185. Helsinki: Suomalainen Tiedeakatemia Academia Scientiarum Fennica, 1962.

*———. *Krankheitsprojektile: Untersuchung* über *eineUrtümliche Krankheitserklärung*. FF Communications No. 178. Helsinki: Suomalainen Tiedeakatemia Academia Scientiarum Fennica, 1959.

*———. "Memorates and the Study of Folk Beliefs." *Journal of the Folklore Institute* 1 (1964):5–19.

Hooper, James. "Led Will." *Notes and Queries* 8th ser. 8 (1895):486–87.

Howells, W. *Cambrian Superstitions: Comprising Ghosts, Omens, Witchcraft, Traditions, &c.* 1831. N.p.: Norwood, 1972.

*Hufford, David J. "The Supernatural and the Sociology of Knowledge: Explaining Academic Belief." *New York Folklore* 9 (1983):21–29.

*———. *The Terror That Comes in the Night: An Experience-Centered Study of Supernatural Assault Traditions.* Philadelphia: University of Pennsylvania Press, 1982.

Hultkrantz, Ake. *The Supernatural Owners of Nature: Nordic Symposion [sic] on the Religious Conceptions of Ruling Spirits (Genii Loci, Genii Speciei) and Allied Concepts.* Acta Universitatis Stockholmiensis, Stockholm Studies in Comparative Religion. Stockholm: Almqvist & Wiksell, 1961.

Hunt, Harriet. "County Donegal, Ireland, Parish of Killymard." *Folk-Lore* 49 (1938):193–95.

*Hunt, Robert. *Popular Romances of the West of England, or the Drolls, Traditions, and Superstitions of Old Cornwall*, 3rd ed. 1881. New York: Benjamin Blom, 1968. [1st pub. 1865]

*"Irish Folk-Lore." *Folk-Lore Journal* 2 (1884):138–42; 5 (1887):331–35; 6 (1888):51–64.

*Jackson, Kenneth. "Scéalta on Mblascaod." *Béaloideas* 8 (1938):3–96. [English summary]

*Jahoda, Gustav. *The Psychology of Superstition.* Harmondsworth: Penguin, 1970.

Jenkins, D.E. *Bedd Gelert: Its Facts, Fairies, & Folk-Lore*, with an introduction by John Rhys. Portmadoc: Llewelyn Jenkins, 1899.

Jenkins, Richard P. "Witches and Fairies: Supernatural Aggression and Deviance among the Irish Peasantry." *Ulster Folklife* 23 (1977):33–56.

*Jones, Bryan H. "Irish Folklore from Cavan, Meath, Kerry, and Limerick." *Folk-Lore* 19 (1908):315–23.

*———. "Stories from Leitrim and Cavan." *Folk-Lore* 15 (1904):336–41.

———. "Traditions and Superstitions Collected at Kilcurry, County Louth, Ireland." *Folk-Lore* 10 (1899):119–23.

*Jones, Ernest. "The Symbolic Significance of Salt." 2:22–109 in his *Psychomyth, Psychohistory: Essays in Applied Psychoanalysis.* 2 vols. New York: Hillstone, 1974.

Jones, T. Gwynn. *Welsh Folklore and Folk-Custom.* 1930. N.p.: Folcroft, 1976.

*Joyce, P.W. *English as We Speak It in Ireland.* 1910, with an introduction by Terence Dolan. Portmarnock County Dublin: Wolfhound Press, 1979.

———. *The Origin and History of Irish Names of Places.* 4th ed. 1875. East Ardsley, Wakefield, Yorkshire: EP, 1972.

K. "Fairy Annals of Ulster." *Ulster Journal of Archaeology* 6 (1858):354–61; 7 (1859):131–43.

K., G.H. "Stray Donegal Folk-Lore." *Folk-Lore Journal* 5 (1887):66–68.

K., L.L. "Elf-Shot." *Notes and Queries* 12th ser. 11 (1922):347.

Kaftal, George. "An Apocryphal Legend Relating to the Birth of Several Saints." *Folk-Lore* 54 (1943):308–09.

Kavanagh, Tobias. "Kilkenny Folk Tales." *Béaloideas* 2 (1929):10–25.

*Keightley, Thomas. *The Fairy Mythology: Illustrative of the Romance and Superstition of Various Countries.* New ed. 1850. New York: Haskell House, 1968. [1st pub. 1828]

*Kelly, Catherine. "Irish Sayings and Irish Fairies." *New York Folklore Quarterly* 1 (1945):174–78.

*Kennedy, Patrick. *The Fireside Stories of Ireland.* Dublin: M'Glashan and Gill and Patrick Kennedy, 1870.

*———. *Legendary Fictions of the Irish Celts.* 2nd ed. London: Macmillan, 1891. [1st pub. 1866]

*Killip, Margaret. *The Folklore of the Isle of Man.* London: B.T. Batsford, 1975.

Kilvert, Francis. *Kilvert's Diary*, edited by William Plomer. 3 vols. London: Jonathan Cape, 1961. [1st pub. 1938]

Kinahan, Frank. *Yeats, Folklore, and Occultism: Contexts of the Early Work and Thought.* Boston: Unwin Hyman, 1988.

Kinehan, G.H. "Cutting Down of Trees." *Folk-Lore Record* 5 (1882):168–69.

*Kinsella, P.J. *Some Superstitions and Traditions of Newfoundland.* St. John's: privately printed, 1919.

*Kirk, Robert. *The Secret Common-Wealth & A Short Treatise of Charms and Spels.* [1691]. Ed. and Commentary by Stewart Sanderson. Mistletoe Series. Cambridge: D.S. Brewer; Totowa, N.J.: Rowman and Littlefield, 1976.

*Kittredge, George Lyman. *Witchcraft in Old and New England.* New York: Russell and Russell, 1929.

*Klein, Barbro Sklute. *Legends and Folk Beliefs in a Swedish American Community: A Study in Folklore and Acculturation.* 2 vols. New York: Arno, 1980.

*Kvideland, Reimund, and Henning K. Sehmsdorf, eds. *Scandinavian Folk Belief and Legend.* Minneapolis: University of Minnesota Press, 1988.

*"Lageniensis." [Rev. John O'Hanlon]. *Irish Folk Lore: Traditions and Superstitions of the Country; with Humorous Tales.* 1870. Darby, PA: Norwood, 1973.

Lake, E.F. Coote. "Folk Life and Traditions." *Folklore* 71 (1960):53.

Lakeman, Joy. *Them Days: From the Memories of Joan Bellan*. Padstow, Cornwall: Tabb, 1982.

Lang, A., Elizabeth Taylor, and William Martin. "Goblins." *Folk-Lore* 13 (1902):183–87.

*Latham, Charlotte. "Some West Sussex Superstitions Lingering in 1868." *Folk-Lore Record* 1 (1868):1–67.

*Latham, Minor White. *The Elizabethan Fairies: The Fairies of Folklore and the Fairies of Shakespeare*. 1930. New York: Octagon, 1972.

Lavater, Ludwig. *Of ghostes and spirites walking by nyght, and of Strange noyses, crackes, and sundry forewarnynges, which commonly happen before the death of menne, great slaughters, and alterations of kyngdomes*, translated by Robert Harrison. London: Henry Benneyman, 1572.

*Lea, Avon. "Fairies." *Notes and Queries* 2nd ser. 2 (1856):83–84.

*Leach, MacEdward. "Celtic Tales from Cape Breton." In *Studies in Folklore*, edited by W. Edson Richmond. Bloomington: Indiana UP, 1957, pp. 40–54.

———. "Superstitions of South Scotland from a Manuscript of Thomas Wilkie." *Folklore International: Essays in Traditional Literature, Belief, and Custom in Honor of Wayland Debs Hand*, edited by D.K. Wilgus. Hatboro, PA: Folklore Associates, 1967, pp. 109–30.

*Leather, Ella Mary. *The Folk-Lore of Herefordshire*. Hereford: Jakeman & Carver; London: Sidgwick & Jackson, 1912.

*Lindow, John. "Rites of Passage in Scandinavian Legends." *Fabula* 19 (1978):40–61.

*———. *Swedish Legends and Folktales*. Berkeley: University of California Press, 1978.

Logan, Patrick. *The Old Gods: The Facts about Irish Fairies*. Belfast: Appletree, 1981.

"A Longford Fairy Tale." *Béaloideas* 3 (1931–32):52.

*"Lost and Frightened . . . Lucy Stayed Where She Was." *Evening Telegram* [St. John's, Newfoundland], 21 December 1961:48.

*Lovelace, Martin. "Animals Kneeling at Christmas: A Belief Topic and Its Calendar Context in Newfoundland." In *Studies in Newfoundland Folklore: Community and Process*, edited by Gerald Thomas and J.D.A. Widdowson. St. John's: Breakwater Books for Memorial University Department of Folklore, 1991, pp. 41–52.

*Lyle, E.B. "The Ballad *Tam Lin* and Traditional Tales of Recovery from the Fairy Troop." *Studies in Scottish Literature* 6 (1969):175–85.

*———. "The Teind to Hell in *Tam Lin*." *Folklore* 81 (1970):177–81.

*Lysaght, Patricia. *The Banshee: The Irish Supernatural Death Messenger*. Dublin: Glendale, 1986.

M., G. "Fairies and Christening." *Notes and Queries* 180 (1941):85–86.

*MacAlister, R.A.S. "Boys in Petticoats." *Notes and Queries* 11th ser. 8 (1913):58.

MacCulloch, Sir Edgar. *Guernsey Folk Lore*, edited by Edith Carey. 1903. Norwood, PA: Norwood, 1973.

MacCulloch, J.A. "The Mingling of Fairy and Witch Beliefs in Sixteenth and Seventeenth Century Scotland." *Folk-Lore* 32 (1921):227–44.

———. "Were Fairies an Earlier Race of Men?" *Folk-Lore* 43 (1932):362–75.

MacCulloch, Mary Julia. "Folk-Lore of the Isle of Skye." *Folk-Lore* 33 (1922):201–14, 307–17.

MacDonald, Sheila. "Old-World Survivals in Ross-Shire." *Folk-Lore* 14 (1903):368–84.

MacDougall, Rev. James. *Folk Tales and Fairy Lore in Gaelic and English, Collected from Oral Tradition*, edited with an introduction by George Calder. 1910. New York: Arno, 1977.

*———. *Highland Fairy Legends: Collected from Oral Tradition*, edited by George Calder with an introductrion by Alan Bruford. 1910. Cambridge: D.S. Brewer; Totowa, N.J.: Rowman and Littlefield, 1978.

MacGregor, Alasdair Alpin. *The Haunted Isles: or, Life in the Hebrides*. London: Alexander MacLehose, 1933.

*———. *The Peat-Fire Flame: Folk-Tales and Traditions of the Highlands and Islands*. Edinburgh: Moray, 1937.

Macgregor, Rev. Alexander. *Highland Superstitions: Connected with the Druids, Fairies, Witchcraft, Second-Sight, Hallowe'en, Sacred Wells and Lochs, with Several Curious Instances of Highland Customs and Beliefs*, with a Foreword on Superstitions and Their Origin by Isabel Cameron. Stirling: Eneas Mackay, 1922. [1st pub. as articles 1891]

*MacGréine, Pádraig. "A Longford Miscellany." *Béaloideas* 2 (1930):261–73.

*———. "Comments on the Making of a Mud Wall House." *Béaloideas* 4 (1934):91–92.

Mackenzie, Compton. *Hunting the Fairies*. London: Chatto and Windus, 1949.

Maclagan, R.C. "Ghost Lights of the West Highlands." *Folk-Lore* 8 (1897):203–56.

———. "Sacred Fire." *Folk-Lore* 9 (1898):280–81.

Maclean, Calum I. "Fairy Stories from Lochaber." *Scottish Studies* 4 (1960):85–95.

———. "Traditional Beliefs in Scotland." *Scottish Studies* 3 (1959):189–200.

*Mac Manus, Diarmuid. *Irish Earth Folk*. New York: Devin-Adair, 1959.

———. *The Middle Kingdom: The Faerie World of Ireland*. London: Max Parrish, 1959.

MacPhail, Malcolm. "Folklore from the Hebrides." *Folk-Lore* 7 (1896):400–04; 8 (1897):380–86; 11 (1900):439–50.

MacPherson, John. *Tales of Barra Told by the Coddy (John MacPherson, Northbay, Barra, 1876–1955)*, with an introduction and notes by J.L. Campbell. Edinburgh: J.L. Campbell, 1961.

MacRitchie, David. *Fians, Fairies, and Picts*. 1893. N.p.: Norwood, 1974.

*———. *The Testimony of Tradition*. London: Kegan Paul, Trench, Trubner, 1890.

Mahon, Rev. Michael P. *Ireland's Fairy Lore*. Boston: Thomas J. Flynn, 1919.

Maloney, Beatrice. "How Mickey the Vag Taught the Fairy to Dance." *Ulster Folklife* 21 (1975):90–93.

*Maloney, Queen. "Trail Wanderings." *The Seniors' News* [St. John's, Newfoundland], October 1987.

*Mannion, John J. *Irish Settlements in Eastern Canada: A Study of Cultural Transfer and Adaptation*. University of Toronto, Department of Geography Research Publications. Toronto: University of Toronto Press, 1974.

*———. "A Transatlantic Merchant Fishery: Richard Welsh of New Ross and the Sweetmans of Newbawn in Newfoundland 1734–1862." In *Wexford: History and Society: Interdisciplinary Essays on the History of an Irish County*, edited by Kevin Whelan. Dublin: Geography Publications, 1987, pp. 373–421.

Martin, M. *A Description of the Western Islands of Scotland*. 2nd ed. 1716. In John Pinkerton. *A General Collection of the Best and Most Interesting Voyages and Travels in All Parts of the World*. 17 vols. London: Longman, 1809. V.3:572–699.

Mathews, F.W. *Tales of the Blackdown Borderland*. The Somerset Folk Series #13. London: Somerset Folk Press, 1923.

Maury, Alfred. *Les Fées du Moyen Âge*. 1843. 1896 ed. rpt. As *Croyances et Légendes du Moyen Age*. Geneva: Slatkine Reprints, 1974.

McAldowie, Alex. M. "Personal Experiences in Witchcraft." *Folk-Lore* 7 (1896):309–14.

McAnally, D.R., Jr. *Irish Wonders: The Ghosts, Giants, Pookas, Demons, Leprechawns,*

Banshees, Fairies, Witches, Widows, Old Maids, and Other Marvels of the Emerald Isle. Boston: Houghton, 1888.

McDermitt, Barbara. "The Belief System of a Scottish Traveller as Reflected in His Memorates, Legends, and Tales." *ARV: Nordic Yearbok of Folklore* 37 (1981):43–51.

McKay, J.G. "Scottish Gaelic Parallels to Tales and Motifs in *Béaloideas* Vols. 1 and 2." *Béaloideas* 3 (1932):139–48.

*McNeill, John T., and Helena M. Gamer. *Medieval Handbooks of Penance: A Translation of the Principal Libri Poenitentiales and Selections from Related Documents*. 1938. New York: Octagon, 1965.

*McPherson, J.M. *Primitive Beliefs in the North-East of Scotland*. London: Longmans, Green, 1929.

McPolin, Francis. "Fairy Lore in the Hilltown District, County Down." *Ulster Folklife* 9 (1963):80–88.

Menefee, S.P. "A Cake in the Furrow." *Folklore* 91 (1980):173–92.

—— and Lotte Motz. "A Further Note on A Cake in the Furrow." *Folklore* 93 (1982):220–22.

Messenger, John C. *Inis Beag: Isle of Ireland*. New York: Holt, Rinehart and Winston, 1969.

Moore, A.W. *The Folk-Lore of the Isle of Man: Being an Account of Its Myths, Legends, Superstitions, Customs, & Proverbs*. London: D. Nutt, 1891.

*Morris, Don. "Lucy Harris Recalls her Ordeal in the Woods." *The Sunday Express* [St. John's, Newfoundland], 10 April 1988:36.

Morris, Henry. "Features Common to Irish, Welsh, and Manx Folklore." *Béaloideas* 7 (1937):168–79.

Morrison, Sophia. *Manx Fairy Tales*. 2nd ed. Peel: L. Morrison, 1929. [1st pub. 1911]

*Moses, Louise von Blittersdorf. "Irish Fairies in Texas." *Publications of the Texas Folklore Society* 13 (1937):185–89.

Moule, Henry J. "Dorset Folk-Lore." *Folk-Lore Journal* 6 (1888):115–19.

*Murphy, Clara J. "The Use of Fairy Lore in Margaret Duley's Novel *Cold Pastoral*." *Culture & Tradition* 7 (1983):106–19.

Murphy, Michael J. *At Slieve Gullion's Foot*. Dundalk: W. Tempest, Dundalgan, 1945.

——. "Folktales and Traditions from County Cavan and South Armagh." *Ulster Folklife* 19 (1973):30–37.
——. *Ulster Folk of Field and Fireside*. Dundalk: Dundalgan, 1983.
*Murray, Hilda Chaulk. *More Than Fifty Percent: Woman's Life in a Newfoundland Outport 1900–1950*. Canada's Atlantic Folklore and Folklife Series No. 3. St. John's: Breakwater, 1979.
"Mysterious Serenades, or Music and Invisible Musicians." *Folk-Lore Journal* 5 (1887):156–57.
*Napier, James. *Folk Lore: or, Superstitious Beliefs in the West of Scotland within this Century*. Paisley: Alex. Gardner, 1879.
*Narváez, Peter. *The Good People: New Studies in Fairy Lore*. New York: Garland, 1991.
——. "Newfoundland Berry Pickers 'in the Fairies': The Maintenance of Spatial and Temporal Boundaries through Legendry." *Lore & Language* 6 (1987):15–49.
Newman, L.F., and E.M. Wilson. "Folklore Survivals in the Southern 'Lake Counties' and in Essex: A Comparison and Contrast." *Folk-Lore* 63 (1952):91–104.
Ni Bhrádaigh, Cáit. "Folklore from Co. Longford." *Béaloideas* 6 (1936):257–69.
Nicholson, John. *Folk Lore of East Yorkshire*. London:Simpkin, 1890.
Ni Shéaghdha, Nessa. "The Word 'áesán.'" *Éigse* 12 (1968):199–201.
*Northcote, Lady Rosalinde. "Devonshire Folklore, Collected among the People near Exeter within the Last Five or Six Years." *Folk-Lore* 11 (1900):212–17.
Nutt, Alfred. "The Fairy Mythology of English Literature: Its Origin and Nature." (Presidential Address). *Folk-Lore* 8 (1897):29–53.
Ó Broin, Tomás. "Scéalaí Tíre: Bailiúchán Seanchais Ó Ghaillimh." *Béaloideas* 24 (1955):1–133. [English summary].
Ó Casaide, Séamus. "Crofton Croker's *Irish Fairy Legends*." *Béaloideas* 10 (1940):289–91.
Ó Catháin, Séamus. "A Tale of Two Sittings: Context and Variation in a Fairy Legend from Tyrone." *Béaloideas* 48–49 (1980–81):135–47.
Ó Cianáin, S.F. "Folk Tales from Co. Sligo." *Béaloideas* 4 (1933):164–66.
Ó Conchubhair, Pádraig. "An Offaly Glossary." *Béaloideas* 20 (1950):188–91.
*Ó Danachair, Caoimhín. "The Luck of the House." *Ulster Folklife* 15/16 (1970):20–27.

Ó Dubhda, Seán. "Dha Eachtra ó Dhuibhneachaibh." *Béaloideas* 4 (1933):314–20. [English summary].

———. "Sgéalta Sidhe." *Béaloideas* 2 (1929):71–80. [English summary].

———. "Sgéilini Andeas." *Béaloideas* 1 (1928):264–69. [English summary].

Ó Duilearga, Séamus. "Editorial." *Béaloideas* 1 (1928):416–18.

———, ed. "Sidhe agús Pucai." *Béaloideas* 3 (1932):309–30. [English summary].

O'Faolain, Eileen. *Children of the Salmon and Other Irish Folktales*. Boston and Toronto: Little, 1965.

Ó Giolláin, Diarmuid. "The *Leipreachan* and Fairies, Dwarfs and the Household Familiar: A Comparative Study." *Béaloideas* 52 (1984):75–150.

*Ó hEochaidh, Seán. *Fairy Legends from Donegal*, translated by Máire Mac Neill. Dublin: Comhairle Bhéaloideas Éireann, 1977.

*———. "Seanchas Na Caorach." *Béaloideas* 37–38 (1969–70):131–209. [English summary].

———. "Seanchas Éanlaithe Iar-Uladh." *Béaloideas* 37–38 (1969–70):210–337. [English summary].

*Ó hÓgáin, Dáithí. "'An É AN tAM FOS É?' Staidéar ar fhinscéal Barbarossa (Móitíf D1960.2) in Éirinn." *Béaloideas* 42–44 (1974–76):213–308. [English summary and some texts].

*Oinas, Felix J. *Historical Reality and Russian Supernatural Beings*. Folklore Preprint Series 1:4. Bloomington: Indiana University Folklore Publications Group, 1973.

*Ó Muirgheasa, Énri. "A Co. Sligo Tradition." *Béaloideas* 2 (1929):138–39.

———. "Sean-Sgéalta ó Chúig Uladh." *Béaloideas* 1 (1927):123–33. [English summary].

*Ó Súilleabhain, Seán. *A Handbook of Irish Folklore*. 1942. Detroit: Singing Tree, 1970.

———. *Irish Folk Custom and Belief*. Dublin: Three Candles, n.d.

*O'Sullivan, Sean. *Legends from Ireland*. Totowa, NJ: Rowman and Littlefield, 1977.

O'Toole, Edward. "A Miscellany of North Carlow Folklore." *Béaloideas* 1 (1928):316–28.

Ó Tuathail, Éamonn. "Sgéal Chrófair na Cruite Ui Chear'lain [AT 503]." *Béaloideas* 1 (1927):64–65. [English summary].

*———. "Trí Sgéalta Ó Chloich Cheann Fhaolaidh." *Béaloideas* 1 (1927):158–66. [English summary].

*Ó Tuathail, Pádraig. "Folk-Tales from Carlow and West Wicklow." *Béaloideas* 7 (1937):46–94.

Owen, Elias. *Welsh Folk-Lore: A Collection of the Folk-tales and Legends of North Wales*. [1887]. Norwood, PA: Norwood, 1973.

*Parry-Jones, D. *Welsh Legends and Fairy Lore*. London: B.T. Batsford, 1953.

*Parsons, R.A. *Sea Room*. St. John's: Newfoundland Arts Centre, 1963.

*Paterson, T.G.F. *Country Cracks: Old Tales from the County of Armagh*. Dundalk: W. Tempest, Dundalgan, 1939.

Paton, C.I. *Manx Calendar Customs*. Publications of the Folk-Lore Society 110 [1939]. Nendeln/Liechenstein, Kraus, 1968.

Paton, Lucy Allen. *Studies in the Fairy Mythology of Arthurian Romance*. Second ed. enlarged by a Survey of Scholarship on the Fairy Mythology since 1903 and a Bibliography. Burt Franklin Bibliographical Series 18. New York: Burt Franklin, 1960.

Peacock, Mabel. "Staffordshire Superstitions." *Folk-Lore* 8 (1897):68.

*Piaschewski, Gisela. *Der Wechselbalg: Ein Beitrag zum Aberglauben der nordeuropäischen Völker*. Deutschkundliche Arbeiten 5. Breslau: Maruschte and Berendt Verlag, 1935.

Power, Thomas. "Belle Island Boyhood: A Memoir of Newfoundland in the Nineties, Part I," edited by David Buchan. *Newfoundland Quarterly* 85 (1989):20–28.

R., A. "Fairies." *Notes and Queries* 2nd ser. 2 (1856):119.

Rabuzzi, Daniel Allen. "In Pursuit of Norfolk's Hyter Sprites." *Folklore* 95 (1984):74–89.

*Redmond, Philip. "Some Wexford Folklore." *Folk-Lore* 10 (1899):362–64.

*Rhys, John. *Celtic Folklore: Welsh and Manx*. 2 vols. Oxford: Clarendon, 1901.

*Rieti, Barbara. "The Black Heart in Newfoundland: The Magic of the Book." *Culture & Tradition* 13 (1989):80–92.

*———. "'The Blast' in Newfoundland Fairy Tradition." In *The Good People: New Studies in Fairy Lore*, edited by Peter Narváez. New York: Garland, 1991.

*Rimbault, Edward F. "'Round about Our Coal Fire, or Christmas Entertainments': A Bibliographical Rarity." *Notes and Queries* 2nd ser. 8 (1859):481–83.

*Ritson, Joseph. *Fairy Tales: Legends and Romances Illustrating Shakespeare and other*

Early English Writers, to Which Are Prefixed Two Preliminary Dissertations, 1. On Pigmies 2. On Fairies. 1875. New York: AMS.

Rodenberg, Julius. *An Autumn in Wales (1856): Country and People, Tales and Songs.* 1858, translated and edited by William Linnard. Cowbridge: D. Brown, 1985.

*Roe, Helen M. "Tales, Customs and Beliefs from Laoghis." *Béaloideas* 9 (1939):21–35.

*Rogers, W. Stuart. "Irish Lore Collected in Schenectady." *New York Folklore Quarterly* 8 (1952):20–30.

Rose, H.J. ["Angels of Mons"]. *Folk-Lore* 54 (1943):368.

*Ross, Marvin. "Physiological Links to Autism Increase." *The Globe and Mail* [Toronto], 18 March 1989:D4.

*"The Royal Hibernian Tales," edited and notes by Séamus Ó Duilearga. *Béaloideas* 10 (1940):148–203.

*Ruehl, Franklin R. "UFO Experts Claim: Fairies thoughout History Were Really Space Aliens." *National Enquirer*, 20 December 1988.

Sanderson, Stewart F. "The Cottingley Fairy Photographs: A Re-Appraisal of the Evidence." *Folklore* 84 (1973):89–103.

———. "A Prospect of Fairyland." *Folklore* 75 (1964):1–18.

Saxby, Jessie M.E. *Shetland Traditional Lore.* Edinburgh: Grant and Murray, 1932.

*Sayce, R.U. "Folk-Life Studies in Britain and Abroad." *The Advancement of Science* [British Association for the Advancement of Science] 5 (1948):231–42.

*———. "The Origins and Development of the Belief in Fairies." *Folk-Lore* 45 (1934):99–143.

*Schloesser, Frank. "Motorists as Fairies." *Notes and Queries* 11th ser. 2 (1910):126.

*Schmitt, Jean-Claude. *The Holy Greyhound: Guinefort, Healer of Children since the Thirteenth Century*, translated by Martin Thom. Cambridge Studies in Oral and Literate Culture 6. Cambridge and Paris: Cambridge University Press and Editions de la Maison des Sciences de L'Homme, 1983.

Schreiber, Heinrich. *Die Feen in Europa: Eine historich-archaologische Monographie.* Frieburg: Universitäts-Buchdruckerie der Gebrüder Groos, 1842.

*Scot, Reginald. *The Discoverie of Witchcraft.* 1584, with an introduction by Montague Summers. London: J. Rodker, 1930.

Scott, Sir Walter. *Letters on Demonology and Witchcraft.* 1884, with an introduction and notes by Raymond Lamont Brown. New York: Citadel, 1970.

*———. *Minstrelsy of the Scottish Border*, revised and edited by T.F. Henderson. 4 vols. Edinburgh and London: Oliver and Boyd, 1932.

*"An Seabhac." "Cathalagus Fíothal." *Béaloideas* 1 (1927):157. [English summary].

*———. "Cnuasach ó Chorca Dhuibhne." *Béaloideas* 1 (1927):134–40. [English summary].

*———. "Scéalaidheacht Chorca Dhuibhne." *Béaloideas* 2 (1929):211–27. [English summary].

*Seary, E.R. *Place Names of the Avalon Peninsula of the Island of Newfoundland*. Memorial University Series No. 2. Toronto: University of Toronto Press, 1971.

*———, G.M. Story, and W.J. Kirwin. *The Avalon Peninsula of Newfoundland: An Ethno-linguistic Study*. Bulletin No. 219, Anthropological Series No. 81. Ottawa: National Museum of Canada, 1968.

*Sébillot, Paul-Yves. *Le Folklore de la Bretagne*. Folklore des Provinces de France 9. Paris: G.-P. Maisonneuve et Larose, 1968. Vol. 2.

*Shackleton, Sir Ernest. *South: The Story of Shackleton's Last Expedition 1914–1917*. London: William Heinemann, 1920.

Shirley, Ev. Ph. "Irish Folk-Lore." *Notes and Queries* 5th ser. 10 (1878):146.

Sikes, Wirt. *British Goblins: Welsh Folk-Lore, Fairy Mythology, Legends and Traditions*. Boston: James R. Osgood, 1881.

Simpkins, John Ewart. *Examples of Printed Folk-Lore Concerning Fife with Some Notes on Clackmannan and Kinross-Shires*, with an introduction by Robert Craig Maclagan and an appendix from the MS Collections by David Rorie. *County Folk-Lore* Vol. 7, Publications of the Folk-Lore Society 71. 1912. Nendeln/Liechtenstein: Kraus, 1967.

Simpson, Eve Blantyre. *Folk Lore in Lowland Scotland*. 1908. N.p.: Folcroft, 1976.

Simpson, Jacqueline. *The Folklore of the Welsh Border*. The Folklore of the British Isles. London: B.T. Batsford, 1976.

———. *Icelandic Folktales and Legends*. London: B.T. Batsford, 1972.

Simpson, W. Sparrow. "Suffolk Folk Lore." *Notes and Queries* 2nd ser. 9 (1860):259–60.

*Singleton, A.H. "Dairy Folklore, and Other Notes from Meath and Tipperary." *Folk-Lore* 15 (1904):457–62.

*Smith, Charles. *The Antient and Present State of the County and City of Waterford*. 1746. Cork: Mercier, 1969.

Smith, Charles C. "Fairies at Ilkley Wells." *Folk-Lore Record* 1 (1878):229–31.
*Smith, Linda-May [see also Ballard]. "Aspects of Contemporary Ulster Fairy Tradition." In *Folklore Studies in the Twentieth Century: Proceedings of the Centenary Conference of the Folklore Society*, edited by Venetia J. Newall. Totowa, NJ: Rowman and Littlefield; Cambridge: D.S. Brewer, 1978, pp. 398–404.
Smith, Peter Alderson. *W.B. Yeats and the Tribes of Danu: Three Views of Ireland's Fairies*. Gerrards Cross, Bucks: Colin Smythe; Totowa, NJ: Barnes and Noble, 1987.
*Smythe, Frank. *The Adventures of a Mountaineer*. London: J.M. Dent, 1940.
Spence, John. *Shetland Folk-Lore*. Lerwick: Johnson and Greig, 1889.
*Spence, Lewis. *British Fairy Origins*. London: Watts, 1946.
——. *The Fairy Tradition in Britain*. London: Rider, 1948.
——. "The Fairy Problem in Scotland." *Hibbert Journal* 36 (1938):246–55.
Spooner, Barbara C. "Traditions of Battles-piskey rings, etc." *Journal of the Royal Institution of Cornwall* 20 (1915):117–18.
St. Leger-Gordon, Ruth E. *Witchcraft and Folklore of Dartmoor*. New York: Bell, 1972. [1st pub. 1965]
Stephens, G. Arbour. "The Little People of Cwm Verman." *Folk-Lore* 50 (1939):385–86.
Stewart, W. Grant. *The Popular Superstitions and Festive Amusements of the Highlanders of Scotland*. Edinburgh: Archibald Constable, 1823.
*Story, G.M., W.J. Kirwin, and J.D.A. Widdowson, eds. *Dictionary of Newfoundland English*. Toronto: University of Toronto Press, 1982.
*Strieber, Whitley. *Communion: A True Story*. New York: Avon, 1987.
"Superstition in Ireland." *Folk-Lore Journal* 2 (1884):190–91.
T., H.G. "Pixies, or Piskie." *Report and Transactions of the Devonshire Association* 8 (1876):722–23.
Taillepied, Father Noel. *A Treatise of Ghosts: Being the Psichologie, or Treatise upon Apparitions and Spirits, of Disembodied Souls, Phantom Figures, Strange Prodigies, and of Other Miracles and Marvels, which often presage the Death of some Great Person, or signify some swift change in Public Affairs* [1588], translation and commentary by Montague Summers. N.d. Ann Arbor: Gryphon, 1971.
*Thomas, Aaron. *The Newfoundland Journal of Aaron Thomas: Able Seaman in H.M.S. Boston*, edited by Jean M. Murray. London: Longmans, 1968.

Thomas, Keith. *Religion and the Decline of Magic: Studies in Popular Beliefs in Sixteenth and Seventeenth Century England.* Harmondsworth: Penguin, 1971.

*Thomson, William A.R. *A Change of Air: Climate and Health.* London: Adam and Charles Black, 1979.

*Thompson, Stith. *Motif-Index of Folk-Literature.* 6 vols. Rev. ed. Bloomington: Indiana UP, [1955].

Tocher. "Away with the Fairies." 27 (1977):162–81.

———. "Duncan MacDonald (1882–1954)." 25 (1977):1–32.

———. "Fairies and Fairy Music." 26 (1977):102–19.

———. "A Host of Fairies." 28 (1978):193–226.

———. "Nan MacKinnon." 38 (1983):1–47.

———. "Trows and Trowshot." 34 (1980):275–76.

Tongue, Ruth L. "Odds and Ends of Somerset Folklore." *Folklore* 69 (1958):43–44.

*———. *Somerset Folklore*, edited by K.M. Briggs. London: The Folklore Society, 1965.

———. "Traces of Fairy Hounds in Somerset." *Folklore* 67 (1956):233–34.

"Traditions Regarding Earthworks." *Ulster Folklife* 4 (1958):55.

Tregarthen, Enys. *North Cornwall Fairies and Legends.* London: Wells Gardner, Darton, 1906.

———. *Piskey Folk: A Book of Cornish Legends.* Collected by Elizabeth Yates. New York: John Day, 1940.

Trevelyan, Marie. *Folk-Lore and Folk-Stories of Wales.* 1909. Darby, PA: Norwood, 1973.

———. *Glimpses of Welsh Life and Character.* London: John Hogg, 1893.

Trotter, R. De Bruce. *Galloway Gossip, or the Southern Albanich 80 Years Ago.* Dumphries: The Stewartry, 1901.

*Tubach, F.C. *Index Exemplorum: A Handbook of Medieval Religious Tales.* FF Communications No. 204. Helsinki: Suomalainen Tiedeakatemia Academia Scientiarum Fennica, 1969.

*Vallee, Jacques. *Passport to Magonia: From Folklore to Flying Saucers.* Chicago: Henry Regnery, 1969.

Vox. "Fairies." *Notes and Queries* 2nd ser. 2 (1856):338.

Walcott, Mackenzie. "Fairy." *Notes and Queries* 3rd ser. 12 (1867):411–12.

Walhouse, M.J. "Folklore Parallels and Coincidences." *Folk-Lore* 8 (1897):196–200.

Walters, Cuming, ed. *Bygone Somerset*. London: William Andrews, 1897.

Ward, Donald. "The Little Man Who Wasn't There: Encounters with the Supranormal." *Fabula* 18 (1977):212–25.

Weir, Gail. *The Miners of Wabana: The Story of the Iron Ore Miners of Bell Island*. Canada's Folklore and Folklife Series No. 15. St. John's: Breakwater, 1989.

*Wentz, W.Y. Evans. *The Fairy-Faith in Celtic Countries*. 1911, with a foreword by Kathleen Raine. Gerrards Cross, Buckinghamshire: Colin Smythe, 1988.

Westcott, Isabel M. *Seventeenth-Century Tales of the Supernatural*. No. 74 in *The Augustan Reprint Society: Publications Numbers 73–78*. 1958. New York: Klaus Reprint, 1967.

Westropp, Thomas Johnson. "A Study of Folklore on the Coasts of Connacht, Ireland." *Folk-Lore* 32 (1921):101–23.

Wherry, Beatrix A. "Miscellaneous Notes from Monmouthshire." *Folk-Lore* 16 (1905):63–67.

*Whistler, C.W. "Local Traditions of the Quantocks." *Folk-Lore* 19 (1908):31–51.

*Whitcombe, Mrs. Henry Pennell. *Bygone Days in Devonshire and Cornwall: with Notes of Existing Superstitions and Customs*. London: Richard Bentley, 1874.

*White, G.H. "Irish Superstition: Boys in Petticoats and Fairies." *Notes and Queries* 11th ser. 2 (1910):65.

*Widdowson, John. *If You Don't Be Good: Verbal Social Control in Newfoundland*. Social and Economic Studies No. 21. St. John's: Institute for Social and Economic Research, Memorial University of Newfoundland, 1977.

Wilde, Lady. *Ancient Cures. Charms, and Usages of Ireland: Contributions to Irish Lore*. London: Ward and Downey, 1890.

———. *Ancient Legends, Mystic Charms, and Superstitions of Ireland: With Sketches of the Irish Past*. London: Ward and Downey, 1888.

*Wilde, W.R. *Irish Popular Superstitions*. 1852. Shannon: Irish UP, 1972.

*Wildhaber, Robert. *Der Altersvers des Wechselbalges und die Ubrigen Altersverse*. FF Communications No. 235. Helsinki: Suomalainen Tiedeakatemia Academia Scientiarum Fennica, 1985.

Wilkinson, T.T. "Scarborough Folklore." *Notes and Queries* 4th ser. 4 (1869):132.

Williams, Noel. "The Semantics of the Word 'Fairy' in English between 1320 and 1820." PhD thesis. University of Sheffield, 1983.

Williamson, Duncan. *The Broonie, Silkies & Fairies: Travellers' Tales of the Other World*. New York: Harmony, 1987.

*Wilson, William. *Folk Lore and Genealogies of Uppermost Nithsdale*. Dumfries: Robert G. Mann, 1904.

*Wiltshire, Kathleen. *Ghosts and Legends of the Wiltshire Countryside*, edited by Patricia M.C. Carrott. Compton Chamberlayne, Salisbury, Wiltshire: Compton Russell, 1973.

*Wimberly, Lowry Charles. *Folklore in the English and Scottish Ballads*. Chicago: University of Chicago Press, 1928.

**The Witch of Inverness and the Fairies of Tomnahurich*. Inverness: John Noble, 1891.

Witcutt, W.P. "Notes on Staffordshire Folklore." *Folk-Lore* 52 (1941):236–37.

Witthoft, John, and Wendell S. Hadlock. "Cherokee-Iroquois Little People." *Journal of American Folklore* 59 (1946):413–22.

Wood, J. Maxwell. *Witchcraft and Superstitious Record in the South-Western District of Scotland*. 1911. [Wakefield: EP, *c.* 1973]

*Wood-Martin, W.G. *Traces of the Elder Faiths of Ireland: A Folklore Sketch: A Handbook of Irish Pre-Christian Traditions*. 2 vols. London: Longmans, Green, 1902.

*Woods, Barbara Allen. *The Devil in Dog Form: A Partial Type-Index of Devil Legends*. Folklore Studies 11. Berkeley: University of California Press, 1959.

*Wright, Thomas. *Essays on Subjects Connected with the Literature, Popular Superstitions, and History of England in the Middle Ages*. 2 vols. 1846. New York: Burt Franklin, 1969.

*Yeats, W.B. *The Celtic Twilight*. 1981. With an introduction by Kathleen Raine. Gerrards Cross, Buckinghamshire: Colin Smythe, 1987. [1st pub. 1893 and 1902]

*———. ed. *Folk and Fairy Tales of Ireland*. 1888 and 1892. Foreword by Kathleen Raine. Gerrards Cross, Buckinghamshire: Colin Smythe, 1973.

———. Notes to Jones, "Traditions." *Folk-Lore* 10 (1899):122–23.

———. "The Prisoners of the Gods." *The Nineteenth Century* 43 (1898):91–104.

Informant Index

This is a list of people to whom I have spoken myself, and does not include those quoted from MUNFLA documents. In closing, I would like to thank them all once again for their invaluable help.

Burke, Hubert and Ethel (Victoria) 214
Clarke, Arthur (Bell Island) 211
Costello, Dan (Avondale) Chapter 3 passim
Costello, Florence (Avondale) 86–87
Costello, Joe (Avondale) Chapter 3 passim
Deagon, Bertha (Bay Bulls) 245
Drover, Elsie (Upper Island Cove) 184
Ennis, Margaret (St. John's) 150–51
Eveleigh, Macpherson (Lewisporte) 78, 92
Flynn, Bernadine (Avondale) 100–01
Framton, Tuce (Bay Bulls) 79
Furlong, H. Miles (St. John's) 190–93
Harris, Lucy (New Melbourne) 214–25
Hayes, Alice and Michael (St. Thomas) 12, 46, 259–61
Hayes, Annie (Bay Bulls) 228–44, 253, 259, 263
Joy, Bill (Bay Bulls) 246
Kavanagh, Frances (Clarke's Beach) 83, 194, 249–54, 256–57, 261–63

Kelloway, Roy and Mildred (Perry's Cove) 109–20, 122–26, 129, 149–50, 152, 259, 269
Keough, Ellen (Marysvale) 16, 244–48, 263
Lewis, Julianne (Avondale) 67–68
Lynch, Jim and Katharine (Bellevue) 127–30, 132–38, 142, 149, 151–52, 170
MacDonald, Ed (Kingston) 201–05
Maher, Ron 102
Maloney, Queen (Bay Bulls) 120, 228–46, 263
Meaney, Marie (Riverhead) Chapter 2 passim, 116, 154, 162, 248, 262, 269
Mullaly, Elizabeth (Northern Bay) 265
Murrin, Richard (Shoe Cove) 12, 260–61
Nolan, Mary and David 138–49
Parsley, Bride and Jack (Avondale) 67–69, 79
Power, Elizabeth (Frenchman's Cove) 59, 262
Ryan, Mr. and Mrs. Joseph (Marysvale) 245–48
"Smith, John" (Bishop's Cove) 15, Chapter 5 passim, 199, 268–69
Tucker, William Clive (St. Phillips) 15, 194–99, 201–03, 205, 224, 269
Whelan, Melina (Pilleys Island) 84